FEAST

FEAST

FOOD THAT CELEBRATES LIFE

NIGELLA LAWSON

PHOTOGRAPHS BY JAMES MERRELL

HYPERION

NEW YORK

Copyright © Nigella Lawson 2004

Design and Art Direction: Caz Hildebrand
Cookery Assistant: Hettie Potter
Editorial Assistant: Zoe Wales
Layout/design: Julie Martin
Index: Vicki Robinson

ISBN 1-4013-0136-3

Hyperion books are available for special promotions and premiums. For details contact Hyperion Special Markets, 77 West 66th Street, 11th Floor, New York, New York 10023-6298, or call 212-456-0133.

FIRST EDITION

10 9 8 7 6 5 4 3 2

CONTENTS

FOR MIMI, PHOEBE AND BRUNO

INTRODUCTION

COOKING HAS many functions, and only one of them is about feeding people. When we go into a kitchen, indeed when we even just think about going into a kitchen, we are both creating and responding to an idea we hold about ourselves, about what kind of person we are or wish to be. How we eat and what we eat lies at the heart of who we are – as individuals, families, communities.

Not that feeding people – or, indeed, ourselves – is a minor part of the exercise. The thing about cooking is that although it can occupy the realm of metaphor, and is rich in meanings that have nothing to do with the culinary world, it is always a practical venture, and central to that is our basic need for sustenance to keep us alive. Anyone who has ever seen a newborn baby knows that the primal instinct is to feed, and that stays with us. For a baby, food and intimacy are inextricably linked and although this is demonstrated less baldly as we get older, that connection never goes away.

As cooking becomes less and less an everyday activity, there are those who tend to idealize it, and the cook is vaunted as the nurturer, the provider of good things and the person who gives an essential embrace. All that's true, but the shortcomings of the food-as-love brigade are not that too much emphasis is put on food, but not enough. Food isn't just love, food encompasses everything: it may be only a part of life but in an important way it underpins the whole of it. Basic to the whole thing of being human is that we use food to mark occasions that are important to us in life. *Feast* is not just about the way we cook and eat at the great religious festivals or big-deal special occasions, but about how food is the vital way we celebrate anything that matters – a birthday, a new job, an anniversary; it's how we mark the connections between us, how we celebrate life.

Different peoples eat different foods, and yet it is the desire to sit down at a table and eat with others – be they family or friends – that we share. And although food is nothing except fuel without the context in which it is eaten, you do not have to share the context to eat the food or to understand its meaning. You can borrow honestly. The rich curry banquet of Eid or the soothing but sprightly balm of the chicken soup for seder translate easily to those who celebrate neither. I'm not interested in theme-park cookery: there's no need to pretend to be a Venetian to cook recipes from the Venetian Feast; and though it can be absorbing and rewarding to wallow in the welcoming abundance of a full-on feast, part of cooking is about choosing what you want to eat, and piecing together recipes to make your own feasts. I've never seen my role as that of a kitchen dictator. I'm interested in the story of food; I leave the plot to you. It's your life, after all.

When I started writing about food, I stated that if the point of cooking was the end product, its meaning lay in the process. I think that still, perhaps even more forcefully. It means something that when you want to gather your friends around you, it tends to be around a meal, and the recipes you choose to cook are secondary to that. To be sure the recipes matter, and those that follow are ones that matter most to me, but it is what the food says that really counts.

BEFORE YOU USE THIS BOOK

• Roast meat is always better if you let it rest for a good, long time when it comes out of the oven.

• Remember that ovens vary. The cooking times I give are the ones that work with *my* oven. You need to get to know yours.

• Olive oil is not extra virgin unless specified.

• Captions are given for pictures only when a photo is not immediately opposite a recipe or when it might be difficult to identify.

THANKSGIVING & CHRISTMAS

As a brit, I am necessarily cautious about tackling Thanksgiving. It's not my party – though where there's food concerned, I'm always glad to be invited. But still, I do feel a certain hesitancy. It's not that the rules are hard to fathom: Thanksgiving, like Christmas, relies on the absolute acceptance of traditions, both general and within specific families, and as far as I'm concerned any menu that strays from the well-trodden path, doesn't understand what these meals are about. And now perhaps, we need the comfort of the traditional more than ever. The more sophisticated our tastes become, the more novelty-seeking our appetites and the more eclectic the ingredients available to us, the more grateful we must surely be (as cooks and as eaters) for such reassuring familiarity.

At their heart, Christmas and Thanksgiving share some central purpose: to bring the family together around food, to celebrate being together. In both feasts, the majestic, and much-maligned, turkey rules the roost. But Thanksgiving is different in one crucial, and for me exciting, respect. There is something magnificent in the idea of what the great French structuralists might have dubbed a meta-feast: that's to say, fancy epithets aside, an occasion when the very purpose of the feast is to celebrate the feasting. Thanksgiving really is about the food itself. Most crucially, it is about American food, a glorification of the luck of living in a world of plenty.

Now, modern (that's to say, post 1789) Thanksgiving is actually the conflation of two celebrations: one in October – more of a harvest festival – and one at the beginning of December, in memory of the Mayflower pilgrims' feast of Thanksgiving. When, in 1863, Lincoln gave the feast its legal status it was in an effort to unite members of the warring states at the end of the Civil War, and to urge them to accept and celebrate their shared status as Americans.

Unlike so many other feasts – Christmas, Easter, indeed any religious festival or those small local *fêtes* in France or *sagre* in Italy – Thanksgiving is not about segregation but unification, not about what marks you out, but about what you can share.

Of course, different groups bring their culinary traditions to bear. I've been into the Italian butcher on Sullivan Street in Manhattan – at the crossroads of Little Italy and SoHo – and seen turkey with a spinach-flecked stuffing studded with garlic; friends of mine in Chicago, whose parents originally came from Bombay, always make a stuffing for their Thanksgiving turkey that combines chilli, yogurt, ginger, cumin and cilantro with an out-and-out, all-American cornbread.

I'm an idealist here and take the view that Thanksgiving is the federal union in culinary form. It has within it the notion of uniformity as well as of individual difference. But only so much difference is tolerated. No Thanksgiving dinner is complete without the turkey (unless you're a vegetarian) or those marshmallow-topped sweet potatoes. In earlier days, the latter gave me, as a startled foreigner, much cause for alarm; now, grateful food-immigrant that I am, I cannot overstate my novitiate enthusiasm. Original recipes, which clearly predate the marshmallow innovation, mix sweet potatoes with maple syrup. Culinary historians have noted this significant mingling of an ingredient from the American South with one notably from the North. Perhaps after the war between the states this was a conscious effort to bring peace and harmony to the table. We all know what family gatherings are like in real life, but the idea is there and, against all odds, to be cherished.

Which brings us to Christmas. I have written before on the stresses of what is popularly known as the festive season, and to return to the gripes and moans now would not quite be in the spirit of the occasion. I always feel joyful about Christmas dinner, though. It's true that tackling it can be a nightmare, but like so much in life the key is in planning ahead. It's much easier then to face up to the seasonal demands and try to go with the flow. The great beacon of light as far as I'm concerned is what Christmas shares with Thanksgiving: the unfairly discredited turkey. People have covered reams decrying its irredeemable dryness: me, I love a turkey. I love the stuffing, too. And although it's unalloyed greed that makes me slaver most, I can't help enjoying the symbolic properties. That stuffed turkey, centrepiece of both feasts, tells us something: throughout folk history food has been stuffed to show the fabulous abundance of nature. It's a way of celebrating plenty (just as those medieval English banquets featured a swan stuffed with a peacock, stuffed with a pheasant, stuffed with a partridge) and showcasing the abundant fruits of the earth. Perhaps, most emotively, as Claudia Roden has pointed out in a quite different context, when writing about Sephardi cooking in her magnificent *Book of Jewish Food*, food is stuffed to show the fullness of life.

But this is where I should admit that I no longer actually stuff the bird itself, but fill a terrine with the stuffing and bake that alongside. It is, I do see, not quite the same thing, certainly as far as gorgeous symbolism is concerned, but there are practical and emotional advantages. A roasted slab of stuffing can be carved up to feed great numbers of people easily. You can never quite get enough stuffing in a bird to satisfy the amount of people the turkey itself feeds. I think it's probably true that there is a slight shortfall in meaty flavor when the stuffing's not baked within the turkey, but a good stuffing should have enough flavor of its own. Plus, you get that wonderful combination of crispy outside and melting stodginess within when the bready mixture is baked in a separate, open, container. But forget the concerns of the eater for once: let us concentrate on the burden placed on the cook. Much as I like a bit of gyno work in the kitchen and am perfectly happy with my arm up a goose (see page 21) as I ram it with compacted sauerkraut, or whatever the occasion demands, I find turkey-wrangling just one psycho-step too far. The bird is too heavy, the cavity too small, and the job just too tragi-comic to be managed alone and after all that Christmas wrapping, too. If there's someone in the kitchen to help – though without carping – I'm game. Secretly, I even quite enjoy it. But stuffing a turkey is easier to cope with when you're roasting one out of season, which I often do. Early Christmas morning, when there are brattish children to humor and sackloads of potatoes still to peel, does not find me in the best mood to stuff and truss a turkey.

Six Christmas dinners have come and gone since I first avowed my seasonal intent in *How to Eat*, and I still firmly believe that the menu is non-negotiable. Christmas without roast turkey and all the trimmings would just not be Christmas to me. I've fiddled a little with the particulars – what cook doesn't? – but the basic elements remain.

The Thanksgiving and Christmas feasts are so similarly driven that it makes sense to steer you to the recipes together. Besides, I rather like the idea of a little transatlantic exchange: some nutmeggy bread sauce dolloped on to the Thanksgiving turkey; a vivid whoosh of marshmallowed sweet potato on the Christmas dinner table. Supplementation rather than substitution is entirely in accordance with the tenets of festive eating.

Those who are roasting a turkey for Thanksgiving may well not feel inclined to have a rerun a month later. I have grown to accept that not everyone shares my appetite for turkey on a regular basis. Those less enthusiastic on this front than I am can either go the goose-route (see pages 18–23) or turn to page 218 and satisfy the seasonal need for abundance and excess by reading the recipe for roast rib of beef and maybe doubling it. I think it's not good enough just to have meat, even too much of it, on the table: it has to be a roast, it has to have commanding presence. This may be the primitive in me urging us towards some fleshly sacrifice, but as long as it's the turkey's and not mine (which it so often feels it could end up being), I must go with it.

MAIN COURSES

Obviously, I don't know how many people you are cooking for, but I have written these recipes with the idea that there could be anything from about 8 to 12 people and that they will not all be adults, and that, furthermore, since there will be a lot of noise and a lot of dishes, the actual quantities don't have to be that big. And I speak as someone who has never knowingly undercatered.

As for vegetarians, you will see that I have made no special suggestions for what to feed them. And there is no point in pretending that, with my tastes, they are anything other than "them." This is not because I have anything against vegetarianism or, indeed, vegetarians. I feel about it and them rather as I do about exercise: it's all fine so long as it's someone else doing it. But, the thing is, I don't see a vegetarian option as being necessary here. It seems to me that it's hard to beat a meal of roast potatoes, roast parsnips, lemony beans, buttery Brussels sprouts with chestnuts (obviously miss out the pancetta from the recipe below), cranberry and cornbread stuffing and cranberry and bread sauces. What on earth would you want to add?

Which brings us to:

THE TURKEY

The most important part of cooking your turkey is shopping for it. I'm not sure I always hold by the spendthrift's adage that you get what you pay for, but the chances are that a more expensive turkey is going to be a better one. Let's not be vulgar though: look at the breed not the price tag. What you're after, ideally, is a Bronze turkey (see Stockists); anyway, it's the one I always go for if I can. Its flesh is tender and, moreover, it has a taste. I know this is an extravagance – in terms of time as well as money – not open to everyone, but the best thing is to order your turkey from a butcher, not drag it from the supermarket bin. However, lots of supermarkets are beginning to stock superior birds, so all isn't lost if you have to buy the wherewithal for the whole meal in one frenzied swoop. Not that you should worry too much about this, or indeed any other factor here. Any big meal, especially when and where family is concerned, can be a grave source of stress, and there's no point in adding to it. Christmas, particularly, can be comparable to life in the first few days in a first-baby postpartum household: it's whatever gets you through… If your entire sense of worth and self-respect rests on the turkey you buy, then you may have to change rather more in your life than your butcher.

Now that I have dispensed with the actual stuffing of the bird, there is not much more to do here than remove the giblets (and you do this, should have done this – in fact – as soon as you get the bird home). Don't throw them away since you need them for the gravy, so take them out of whatever plastic they are wrapped in, rinse them under the cold tap and put them in a dish and cover with plastic wrap – or better still, if you have any with fitting lids, use an airtight container – and stick them in the fridge. Actually, I often make the gravy well in advance of cooking the turkey, indeed a couple of days in advance, so you might want to move straight to the gravy recipe or recipes now. But whatever, before putting the turkey in the fridge, wash the inside of the bird with cold running water. Drain well and blot dry with a few kitchen towels. The important thing is that you take the turkey out of the fridge a good hour before you want to start cooking it, so that it's at room temperature when you begin.

And come to the turkey-cooking itself without prejudice; that's to say, forget everything you've been told or might have thought up till now about the length of time it needs. People have been overcooking turkeys for generations, which explains why the dryness of the meat is so embedded in folk memory. Don't be alarmed by the shortness of the cooking times below. If you follow them, you will have a perfectly cooked moist-fleshed bird, provided you have not ignored the instructions to make sure it's at room temperature before you put it in the oven. If you've failed to comply, I cannot be held responsible.

note

See Stockists on page 460 for mail order turkeys of distinguished provenance.

Preheat the oven to 400°F. Rub the turkey breast with a little butter, or brush with goose fat if you've got any on hand. Put the turkey breast-down in the roasting tray: the only fat deposits in a turkey are in the back and this allows them to percolate through the breast meat as it cooks; this makes for the tenderest possible, succulent meat. It does mean you don't quite get that vision of the swelling-breasted bird at the table; the breast squishes down a bit, losing some of its proud splendor, but I have taken a policy decision not to let this trouble me, and advise you to do likewise.

Keep the oven at 400°F for the first 30 minutes, then turn it down to 350°F, and turn the bird the right way up for the last half hour of cooking to brown, basting well first. I tend to go for a bird of about 15lbs, which means that – startling though it might seem – the oven is occupied with it for under 3 hours, which makes all the potato and parsnip stuff, or whatever else you might need the oven for, very much easier to deal with. To see for yourself that the turkey is ready, poke a skewer or fork where the meat is thickest – behind the knee joint of the thigh – and if it is cooked, the juices will run clear.

I think it makes life very much easier if you have the turkey sitting somewhere to rest (not, sadly, an option for you) while you fiddle around with everything else, and there is always a lot of everything else. I tend to leave the turkey in its pan, only tented with aluminum foil. It doesn't bother me if it's left like that for a good hour; it won't get cold (as long as it's not near an open window or in a draft), and it'll be easier to carve. And while it sits, of course, it will be oozing lots of lovely juices which you can add to your gravy as you either finish it off or reheat it.

I've given weights in pounds here because I think of turkey in pounds, and I suspect I am not the only one.

TURKEY COOKING TIMES

Weight of bird	Cooking time
5lb	$1^1/_2$ hours
8lb	$1^3/_4$ hours
10lb	2 hours
12lb	$2^1/_2$ hours
15lb	$2^3/_4$ hours
17lb	3 hours
20lb	$3^1/_2$ hours
25lb	$4^1/_2$ hours

TRADITIONAL TURKEY GRAVY

When I say traditional, I mean this is the recipe I have customarily followed. I am aware, now I come to think about it, that Marsala could not be considered a traditional ingredient in anyone else's book. This gravy, which I wrote about in *How to Eat*, signifies a watershed in my life: the first time I ever managed to produce a gravy I didn't need to be ashamed of. Not everyone likes the idea of a gravy thickened with puréed liver, but I've never met someone who hasn't liked eating it. If you're squeamish, you can skip this stage (and, indeed, the allspice gravy on page 9 dispenses with it happily); the gravy will be less full-bodied and paler, but it will still taste good. Equally, I'm sure if you wanted, you could do without boiling up the giblets and just use some good store-bought, preferably organic, chicken stock instead. It is crucial, however, to have gravy: if you have a hot enough gravy you never need worry about how cold everything else has got – a very important factor when catering relatively large-scale.

Serves 8–10

giblets from the turkey
1 bouquet garni
4 black peppercorns
1 onion, peeled and halved
1 carrot, peeled and quartered
1 stick of celery, roughly chopped

bacon rinds if any left over from
  one of the stuffings,
  or 1–2 slices bacon
4 cups water
1 teaspoon salt
1 tablespoon all-purpose flour
1 tablespoon butter
1 tablespoon Marsala

Put all the giblets except for the liver in a pan (that's to say the heart, neck and gizzard), add the bouquet garni, the peppercorns, onion, carrot and celery and bacon, and cover with the water, sprinkling over 1 teaspoon salt. Bring to the boil, cover, lower the heat and simmer for a couple of hours. Strain into a measuring cup. Set it aside if you're doing this stage in advance, or else get on with the next stage, which takes place when the turkey's cooked and resting on its carving board.

Pour off most of the fat from the roasting pan, leaving behind about 2 tablespoons plus all the usual sticky and burned bits. Put it back on the burner at a low heat, and in a separate little bowl mix together the flour with, gradually, 3–4 tablespoons of the liquid from the pan. When you have a smooth, runny paste, stir it back into the pan. Cook for a couple of minutes, scraping up any bits from the bottom and incorporating them, but make sure the pan's not so hot it burns. Still stirring, gradually pour in 2 cups of the giblet stock, or more if it seems too thick, bearing in mind you may be adding the liver later.

While the gravy's cooking gently, leave it for a moment (though keep stirring every now and again) to fry the liver. Melt the butter in a small pan and toss the liver in it for 1–2 minutes, then remove liver to a board and chop finely.

Add the liver to the gravy. Add the Marsala, and stir well, cooking for another few minutes, before pouring into a couple of gravy boats.

note
Since first making this gravy I have bought a blender and would now add a little more of the giblet stock, say 600ml, and blend the gravy *after the* liver has been chopped and added.

ALLSPICE GRAVY

This is a relatively new addition to my life; and I present it here slightly out of sync. After coming up with the gingerbread stuffing (see page 14) for a plain roast turkey last year, I became somewhat obsessed with partnering that distinctively sober meat with the richer pull of aromatic spices. I'd known that the combination had worked with my spiced and super-juicy turkey (see page 10) of the year before and since I always seem to eat a version of Christmas lunch a good few times a year – certainly out of inclination, but sometimes in deference to magazine articles – I had time to practise. This is what I came up with, and have made – for chicken as well – several times since.

giblets from the turkey (not
  including the liver)
4 cups water
$^1/_2$ tablespoon allspice berries
$^1/_2$ teaspoon black peppercorns
3 bay leaves
$1^1/_2$ inch cinnamon stick
1 stick of celery, halved
2 carrots, peeled and halved

1 onion, halved not peeled
1 tablespoon sea salt/$^1/_2$
  tablespoon table salt
juice of 1 clementine or orange, to
  give approximately $^1/_4$ cup, plus
  pulp from the fruit scraped into
  the stock
2 tablespoons all-purpose flour
2 tablespoons honey

Serves 8–10

Put all of the above ingredients, except the flour and honey, into a saucepan and bring to a boil. Cover with a lid and then simmer gently for 2 hours.

Strain the gravy stock through a sieve into a large measuring cup. This should give you about 4 cups.

When you are ready to make the gravy, take the cooked turkey out of the roasting pan and let it rest on a carving board. In a small bowl, add a few tablespoons of the gravy stock to the flour and mix together. Then, with the roasting pan over a medium heat on the stove, add this paste to the juices in the pan.

Deglaze the roasting pan with the floury stock, getting all of the pan juices amalgamated with a whisk. Then slowly whisk in the stock and honey and let the gravy bubble away until it thickens and the floury taste disappears. Although the allspice is headily emphatic in this gravy it doesn't swamp it, or the turkey. And it is fabulous over the roast potatoes, especially if there's a dollop of mace-musky bread sauce quivering nearby: just makes them sing. Not that they ever really need help.

SPICED AND SUPER-JUICY ROAST TURKEY

The spiced and super-juiciness of this turkey, already given a brief mention, is not meant to suggest that the straightforward turkey above is deficient in either taste or texture, but nevertheless this is a very useful damage limitation exercise and the perfect recipe for those who have no confidence whatsoever in the quality of the turkey they're having to cook. What's more, the turkey it presents you with, once cooked, is, frankly, straight from central casting: the whole, bronze-burnished, bulging breasted deal. Just looking at this maple-glossy specimen of a bird on its carving tray makes me feel like Henry VIII after a particularly satisfying negotiation with his divorce lawyers. Bring on the serving wenches. Indeed, I am even happy to be one – which, I suppose, is just as well, all things considered.

What I'm requiring you to do sounds both more effortful and unpalatable than it is, for I'm going to say one word here, and it's not a pretty one: brine. I'll get to what that constitutes in a moment, but what you should know now is that it means you can cook a turkey of undistinguished provenance so that not only does it *not* dry out but it remains so gloriously juicy and oozing with seasonally-spiced flavor that even those dreary year-in, year-out, whining turkey-phobes will weep with greedy gratitude.

What brining actually involves is just filling up a huge pan, or whatever you can find that's big enough, with water to which you have added salt, sugar, maple syrup, honey, an onion, an orange, a cinnamon stick and assorted muskily scented spices (or any of your own choosing). You sit the turkey in this overnight or for a few days if it's cold and it makes life easier for you, then you just roast it, basting it occasionally with a mixture of maple syrup and melted butter (or goose fat). The great advantage here is that the brining's keeping everything moist enough as it is, so you don't need to roast the bird upside down for the first bit, thus you don't have to risk third-degree burns and a hernia as you fight to turn over this admirably monstrous bird.

The amount of water stipulated below, along with the flavorings, will make enough brining liquid for a turkey weighing up to about 12lbs. If the turkey is a bit bigger, just add more water; if a great deal bigger, augment other ingredients. I've kept to a smaller turkey than the regular roasted turkey because I more often do a brined turkey out of season when I'm less sure of getting a good bird (they're often frozen) and am cooking for a smaller crowd. Don't worry, though: a 12lb bird will still give you enough to feed eight with some to spare.

And above all, don't panic if you haven't got a pan big enough: just stick everything in a large plastic basin and cover with aluminum foil stuck down with masking tape. At this time of year, it's fine to leave this in a cold place. After all, who's got a fridge big enough?

It's an odd thing to say about a raw turkey covered in brine, but it looks beautiful as it steeps. I can never help lifting the lid for quick, blissfully reassuring peeks. And it smells so festive in its pot (and later on the plate) with all the heady spices and cinnamon-orangeness.

Serves 8–10

- 24 cups water, approx.
- 1 cup sea salt/$^1/_2$ cup table salt
- 3 tablespoons black peppercorns
- 1 bouquet garni
- 2 tablespoons white mustard seeds
- 1 cup superfine sugar
- 2 onions, peeled and quartered
- 1 x 2–3 inch piece of ginger, cut into 6 slices

1 cinnamon stick

1 tablespoon caraway seeds

4 cloves

2 tablespoons allspice berries

4 star anise

1 orange, quartered

$^1/_4$ cup/4 tablespoons maple syrup

$^1/_4$ cup honey

stalks from a medium bunch of
  parsley, optional

FOR THE BASTING

$^3/_4$ stick butter or goose fat

3 tablespoons maple syrup

Put the water into your largest cooking pot or bucket/plastic basin and add all the other brine ingredients, stirring to dissolve the salt, sugar, syrup and honey. (Squeeze the juice of the orange quarters into the brine before you chuck the pieces in.)

Untie and remove any string or trussing from the turkey, shake it free, remove the giblets and put in the fridge (and see gravy page 9), and add the bird to the liquid, topping up with more water if it is not completely submerged. Keep in a cold place, even outside, overnight or for up to a day or two before you cook it, remembering to take it out of its liquid and wipe dry with kitchen towel, a good 40 or 50 minutes before it has to go into the oven. Turkeys – indeed this is the case for all meat – should be at room temperature before being put in the preheated oven. If you're at all concerned – the cold water in the brine will really chill this bird – then just cook the turkey for longer than its actual weight requires. I think it's virtually impossible to dry this one out.

For the basting, melt the butter and syrup together slowly over a low heat. Paint the turkey with the glaze before roasting, and baste periodically throughout.

And as for the roasting time, just preheat the oven to 425°F and give the bird half an hour's roasting at this relatively high temperature, then turn the oven down to 350°F and continue cooking, turning the oven back up to 425°F for the last quarter of an hour if you want to give it a final, browning boost.

For a 10–12lb turkey, I'd reckon on about 2–2$^1/_2$ hours in total, but I've given a table on page 6, anyway, as a slightly more structured guide. But remember that ovens vary enormously, so just check by piercing the flesh between leg and body with a small sharp knife: when the juices run clear, the turkey's cooked.

Just as it's crucial to let the turkey come to room temperature before it goes in to the oven, so it's important to let it stand out of the oven for a good 20 minutes before you actually carve it (and see remarks concerning the regular roast turkey). Tent it with foil, and even longer won't hurt it.

I am clamoring to get on to other meats, but before I do there is the crucial element of stuffing. Quite how many types you make is entirely up to you. I would feel pitifully shortchanged if I had to go without the chestnut stuffing, but then again, I wouldn't want to be deprived of any of them. The gingerbread stuffing, with its medieval spicy depth and full-throated flavor, goes well with the hearty gunge of the chestnuts or the sprightly, sweet-edged sharpness of the cornbread one.

Above: Behind the brining turkey, the fully festive ham is being cooked.

CORNBREAD, CRANBERRY AND ORANGE STUFFING

OK, so the bad news is that first you have to make the cornbread. The good news is that this isn't hard.

Serves 8–10

FOR THE CORNBREAD

butter for greasing pan

1 cup cornmeal (or polenta: same difference really)

$^3/_4$ cup plus 2 tablespoons all purpose flour

$^1/_4$ cup superfine sugar

fat pinch of salt

1 tablespoon baking powder

1 cup milk

1 egg

3 tablespoons unsalted butter, melted and cooled

note

As a general rule, I think of this as a corn-yellow stuffing studded with the ruby of the cranberries. However, one year I did forget about the cranberries as they cooked in their pan and they turned to mush. If this happens to you, don't worry: all it means is that you miss something of the biting contrast between sweet bread and sour fruit, but not all; and by way of recompense, you end up with a slab of baked stuffing that is bizarrely but gratifyingly magenta.

Preheat the oven to 400°F then grease a square 9 inch pan (2 inches deep) with butter. Actually, since you'll be needing the cornbread to crumb, it scarcely matters what kind or size of pan you use.

Mix the cornmeal, flour, sugar, salt and baking powder in a large bowl. In a large measuring cup beat together the milk, the egg and cooled, melted butter. Then pour the wet ingredients into the dry, stirring with a wooden spoon until just combined. Don't worry in the slightest about the odd lump. Pour into the greased pan and bake for 15–20 minutes. When ready, the cornbread should be just pulling away from the sides.

You need most, sadly, of the cornbread for the stuffing, but the above makes just enough for you to eat one slice, still warm preferably, and maybe even spread with some soft butter to drip its melting way through it, first. Let the rest cool, and crumb it when needed. It might well suit to get started on the stuffing as the cornbread gets cool enough to crumb. You need, in full:

FOR THE STUFFING

1 large orange

12oz package fresh or frozen cranberries

$^1/_3$ cup honey, optional

1 stick plus 1 tablespoon butter

5 cups cornbread crumbs

2 eggs, beaten

1 teaspoon ground cinnamon

Zest and juice the orange. Put the cranberries into a heavy-based saucepan with the orange juice and zest. Bring to simmering point on a moderate to high flame, add the honey if you're going for that option (I like this vibrantly astringent and don't add it, but it is a matter of taste) then cover, turn down the heat slightly, and simmer for about 5 minutes. Add the butter in slices or spoonfuls and stir, off the heat, until it melts, then add the crumbled cornbread – and here's where you can leave it (for a day or so in a refrigerator) until you want to bake it. At which time, beat in the eggs and season with salt, pepper and cinnamon.

Now, if you do want to stuff the turkey with this, and it certainly benefits, since the stuffing absorbs the meatiness from the bird, remember to weigh the bird – as for any stuffing – before it goes in as you'll need to include the weight of the stuffing(s) in the total cooking time (and follow the stuffing method for Bohemian roast goose on page 21–22). Otherwise fill an ovenproof dish: I use a pan that's 8 inches square and $1^1/_2$ inches deep. I know that doesn't sound very big, but you'll get nine brownie-sized slabs out of it and I doubt any child present will be interested in eating any.

Should you have any stuffing left, here's what I suggest you do with one or two slabs. First, fry a slice or two of bacon in a drop of oil then, when it's crispy, remove it to a plate and quickly fry the leftover stuffing in the bacony fat. When done on both sides, let it join the bacon and eat them together, joyfully.

CHESTNUT STUFFING

This is a modest reworking of the stuffing, as made by Lidgate's of Holland Park, which appears in *How to Eat.* I've fiddled a little, but not much – it didn't need it – and this should make enough to fill a dish of just over 6 inches by 4 inches and about 3 inches deep, though I often use a foil container that is shallower and wider. Neither need more than 30 minutes' actual baking time.

This recipe doesn't make a huge amount, any more than the cornbread, cranberry and orange one does, so I occasionally double everything to make the big logs of stuffing you'll find for the gingerbread one (over page), which seems to go better with cold meat, which is why I start by making more.

For breadcrumbs, use stale real bread that you've crumbed yourself in a processor. If you need to (as I often do, since I try not to keep too much bread I'd actually want to eat in the house), just buy a loaf, slice it and leave it to stale overnight. It doesn't have to be dry as dust, just not squidgy. I often make breadcrumbs, anyway, as I go, and just stash them in the deep freeze. Quite often when I think I'm using breadcrumbs, I'm in fact using bagel crumbs (I always buy too many bagels on a Friday which then turn stale in the breadbin before the next week's begun) or indeed, from the opposite end of the spectrum, brioche crumbs, and neither seems to make much difference.

1 large or two small onions	5 cups breadcrumbs	Serves 8–10
4oz bacon	just under 2 cups unsweetened	
approx. $1^1/_2$ cups parsley leaves	chestnut purée	
$3/_4$ stick butter	2 eggs, beaten	
approx. 1 cup vacuum-packed	fresh nutmeg	
whole chestnuts		

Peel and roughly chop the onion or onions and stick the pieces in the processor with the bacon and parsley. Melt the butter in a largeish heavy-bottomed pan and, keeping the heat fairly low, cook the processed mixture until it softens, about 10 minutes. Remove to a bowl and, using your hands, crumble in the chestnuts so that they are broken up slightly then mix in the breadcrumbs and chestnut purée. This isn't so very hard to do by hand (a wooden spoon and brutal manner will do it), but I save myself and just use a free-standing mixer. If you want to make this in advance, then let it get cold now; otherwise, beat in the eggs, season with only a little salt (remember the bacon) and a good grating of fresh pepper and fresh nutmeg.

If you want to stuff the turkey with this, be my guest. If you don't want to stuff the turkey, butter a suitable receptacle and bake this, covered with aluminum foil, underneath the turkey for 30–35 minutes, taking the foil off for the last 10 minutes.

I don't deny there is, at least to look at, an almost cloacal quality here. No one's going to be presenting any aesthetic awards to this grainy, brown wodging, but what's pretty got to do with it? This is for me, one of the main lures of this time of year. And I need to scratch my seasonal itch.

GINGERBREAD STUFFING

I've always thought that it made sense to use one's obsessions to advantage, and this recipe is a case in point. I do see that normal people don't have eureka moments when the idea suddenly comes into an already food-saturated head to make a stuffing in which the breadcrumbs would be substituted by a crumbled gingerbread cake, but that's how my head works. (It gives me some anguish to reflect on what has been displaced to give room to such meanderings, but perhaps here is not the place to dwell on that.)

Serves 8–10

1lb (3 medium) onions, peeled
2 eating apples (11oz), peeled and cored
4 tablespoons butter
1 tablespoon oil
1$^1/_2$lbs bacon

zest of 2 clementines or 1 orange
1lb loaf good store-bought gingerbread, crumbled makes 5 cups
2 eggs, beaten
approx. $^1/_2$ teaspoon freshly ground pepper

Finely chop the onions and apples, using a food processor or by hand. Heat the butter and oil in a large wide saucepan and fry both until soft, about 10–15 minutes.

Now very finely chop the bacon in the processor, and add this to the softened onion and apple mixture. Cook everything, stirring frequently, for about 5 more minutes and then add the clementine or orange zest. If you're going to make the allspice gravy you'll need the juice from this fruit for that.

Take the pan off the heat and let it cool a little before mixing in the gingerbread crumbs. You can let this get properly cold now if you want and put it aside. Just before cooking the stuffing, add the beaten eggs and pepper, mix, and use it to stuff the main cavity of your turkey, or cook all of it (or what's left after stuffing your bird) in a buttered baking dish. Bake it in a hot oven with your turkey for about the last 45 minutes. If the stuffing's going into a very full oven – which it no doubt is as part of a festive meal – it might take longer to cook; alone, 35 minutes should do it.

Let the cooked stuffing sit in its terrine for a good 10 minutes before turning it out and slicing it.

note

This is also fabulous with roast pork. I don't think it would go alongside the pork with caraway and garlic on page 223 but I'd urge you to put together a different Sunday lunch one day by cooking the roast pork cinghiale on page 102, substituting for the lentils the "heaven and earth" from page 39 and making this gingerbread stuffing too.

It's also wonderful with the goose and sauerkraut on page 21; and I'm mad about both, together, cold and leftover, with some temple-searingly hot English mustard.

And as a still seasonal variation on the gingerbread, this stuffing, although it would taste significantly different and lighter, would be worth making with that Italian festive bread, panettone. If you have been given any for Christmas and it's lying about going stale, then crumb what's left, bag it up and freeze for later usage. And see the Easter turkey recipe on page 168.

FULLY FESTIVE HAM

My mother always cooked a ham at Christmas and so do I. Apart from anything else, it is a necessary part of my leftover table. (Who am I trying to kid? My leftover fridge. I rarely make it beyond the refrigerator door before eating.) I have nothing against a cold turkey, mayonnaise and mango chutney sandwich – indeed I absolutely insist upon one – but life really begins to pick up once you've slapped some turkey, ham and cranberry sauce between softly buttered slices of good white bread.

It's the cranberries that turn what is anyway spectacular into a seasonal affair. The ham is cooked in cranberry and apple juices (the apple counters the almost wince-inducing tang of the cranberry) and then, once cooked, the fat is scored, studded with cloves and given a rubied cranberry jelly glaze. I think if you're providing this with your turkey you really don't need to bother with the pancetta-wrapped sausages below. I feel a note of ration-controlling caution is creeping into my work now, and I think it's because I can't write about food without reliving some past eating of it, or planning some future one, and my tastebuds now alert me to the need for balance and pleasure rather than mere gustatory pile-up.

Serves 8–10

7$\frac{1}{2}$lbs ham
8 cups cranberry juice
8 cups apple juice

2 cinnamon sticks, halved
2 onions, halved but not peeled
1 tablespoon allspice berries

FOR THE CRANBERRY GLAZE
approx. 30 cloves to stud ham
$\frac{1}{4}$ cup cranberry jelly or
 6 tablespoons cranberry sauce
1 tablespoon honey

1 tablespoon English mustard
 powder
$\frac{1}{2}$ teaspoon ground cinnamon

Put the ham into a large saucepan and cover with cold water. Bring to a boil and then immediately drain and rinse the ham in a colander, which will get rid of any excess saltiness; the alternative is to leave it soaking in cold water overnight, but I've always preferred this method. It's up to you which you choose.

Rinse the saucepan and put the ham back in, and add all of the above ingredients (but not those for the glaze). If the fruit juices do not cover the ham then add some water; it really depends on how snugly your ham fits into the saucepan. Bring the pan to a boil and cook the ham at a fast simmer for about 3$\frac{1}{2}$–4 hours. Partially cover the ham with a lid if the liquid is boiling away and the top of the ham is getting dry.

Once the ham is cooked, remove it from the hot and now salty juice, and sit it on a board. If you want, you can cook this well ahead of schedule and let it get cold before glazing and roasting it. If that's the case, what I tend to do is cook it for about $\frac{1}{2}$ hour less and then let it get cold in the cooking liquid. I try to let it cool as fast as possible by sitting it near an open window, letting the wintry winds chill it in the old-fashioned way.

But if you're going ahead now, wait until the ham's bearable to the touch – easy to scald yourself on hot sugary fat – and then cut and peel the rind off the cooked ham, and make sure you take a thin layer of white fat off with it, or just use a knive to shave some fat off, so you're left with a thin coating. Meanwhile, preheat the oven to 425°F, though you can just make this work with whatever setting you need your oven to be. You could always give it a short go in a much lower oven and then whip out a blow-torch. I'm always keen. Score the now trimmed fat into a diamond pattern with a sharp knife, and stud the points of each diamond with a clove.

Heat the remaining glaze ingredients together in a saucepan until the jelly or sauce melts into the honey, mustard and cinnamon to make a smooth glaze. Well, it won't be that smooth if you're using sauce, but you can always leave the little burst berries in place or sieve the glaze. If you can get cranberry jelly, it just has a higher gloss, but it's not a big deal, or even that much of a difference. What matters though is that you let the glaze bubble into a syrupy sauce: it needs to be thick enough not to run off the ham completely as it blisters in the oven.

Sit the ham on a piece of aluminum foil in a roasting pan, which will make washing up easier later. Pour the glaze over the clove-studded ham so that all of the scored fat is covered. Put the Christmas ham, or whatever kind of festive ham it is for you, into the oven and cook for 15 minutes or until the fat is colored and burnished by the sugary glaze. If you've let the ham get completely cold before you glaze it, it'll need a good 40 minutes at 350°F and you might have to give a final blast of real heat at the end too. And this is based on its being at room temperature, not fridge cold, when it goes in.

note

If you wish, you could use the stock to cook some red cabbage, as per the Cherry Coke and ham stock-cooked cabbage in the note on page 206, only without adding the vinegar.

GOOSE

Goose is the opposite of turkey in one significant fact: it is easy to stuff but a nightmare to carve. It's perfect if you want a festive dinner for about six; any more than that and you've already moved into two-bird territory. But this is also why it is so good for a special holiday dinner for relatively few of you. It's a rarity, which makes it special, its flesh is rich and luscious, and wonderful cold too, turned into brown-bread sandwiches with some sour apple sauce. And its cavity is so capacious that, rarely for any bird, you can get enough stuffing inside for the amount of people the meat will stretch to.

Another drawback – or possible drawback – is linked to one positive advantage: a goose, to taste good, with melting flesh and crisp skin, takes a long time to cook; during which time the goose gives out the best fat that exists for roasting potatoes in the whole world. I love duck fat, too, but nothing beats goose for crunchy, sweet roast potatoes. (And see page 26.)

So, treating goose very differently from my turkey, I give recipes for two fully-stuffed birds. One recipe is a retread from *How to Eat*, but since it wasn't my recipe then, but rather picked up from Simon Hopkinson who'd picked it up from Peter Langan, who'd inherited it from his Irish grandmother, I don't feel I'm blowing my own trumpet by recycling it again. It's too good to leave out. The only change I've made is to use Marsala in place of Madeira, for no other reason than that is what I keep at home.

I'm not sure whether the recipe below is in Hopkinson's words or Langan's or his grandmother Callinan's; whichever, I've respected the prose in which this was first presented to me. This means that you are instructed to set about this in a more labor-intensive way than I would normally encourage. Indeed, you will see from my Bohemian goose (page 21) that I just take a bird and stuff it without any coathanger fandango, so I leave the degree of laziness or effort up to you.

GOOSE STUFFED WITH MASHED POTATO

Serves 6

note
Turn to Stockists on page 460 for a source of mail order geese.

1 goose, dressed weight about 9lb or so, with giblets
2 tablespoons vegetable oil
3lbs potatoes, peeled, cut into large chunks and rinsed
4 onions, chopped coarsely

FOR THE GRAVY
4 slices bacon, chopped
2 tablespoons goose fat
1 goose neck bone and gizzard, cleaned (ask your butcher) and chopped coarsely
2 sticks of celery, chopped
1 onion, peeled and chopped

4 tablespoons butter or goose fat (see below)
2 cloves garlic, peeled and chopped finely
1 tablespoon fresh sage, chopped
grated rind of 2 lemons

1 carrot, peeled and chopped
2 tablespoons Calvados
$^3/_4$ cup Marsala
$1^1/_4$ cups strong chicken stock
1 scant tablespoon redcurrant jelly
1 heaped teaspoon arrowroot

First prepare the goose, and render some lovely goose fat. Remove all the gobbets of pale fat that lie just inside the goose's cavity, attached to the skin. Put them in a pan with the oil, place on a very low heat and let melt. Render it all down, pour into a bowl or pan and add to this, later, the great glorious amounts of fat that drips off the goose into the pan as it roasts. The goose fat will be wonderful for roast potatoes on Christmas Day – or any day.

Now, get to work on the goose's skin, so that it crisps up in the oven like Chinese duck. Put the goose on a rack in a roasting pan, puncture the skin several times with the point of a thin skewer or very sharp knife, then pour boiling water over. Tip all the water out of the pan and let the goose dry. You can do this by placing it by an open window – at this time of year I think you can reckon on a fair breeze – and leave for hours, preferably overnight. Even better, direct an electric fan towards the bird for a few hours. Remember to turn it regularly so that all sides get dried. You are often advised to hang the bird up, but this is hard enough to do with a duck and a coathanger, and a duck is very much lighter than a goose. But if you've got a butcher's hook handy, and somewhere cool to hang it, why not give it a try?

Your goose is prepared: now preheat the oven to 425°F. Boil the potatoes in salted water until tender, drain well and mash coarsely; just use an old-fashioned masher or fork. Fry the onions in the recently rendered goose fat (or butter) until golden brown. Add the garlic and stir them both into the mashed potato, along with the sage, lemon rind and some pepper. Rub a generous amount of salt over the goose and put a good grinding of pepper inside the cavity. Then pack the mashed-potato mixture into the cavity and put the goose back on its wire rack over the largest possible roasting pan and place in the oven.

Roast for 30 minutes and then turn the temperature down to 350°F. Cook the goose for a further $2^1/_2$ hours or so. Don't baste: you want the fat to run off the goose, the more the better; but do remember to pour away fat regularly during the goose's cooking or you might have a messy and dangerous accident. Check around every hour.

Make the gravy while the goose is cooking. Fry the bacon in goose fat in a heavy-bottomed pan, until crisp and brown. Add the neck bone and gizzard, and cook until well colored, then do the same with the vegetables. Pour off any excess fat and add the Calvados and Marsala. Bring to the boil and reduce until syrupy. Pour in the chicken stock and redcurrant jelly and simmer for 30 minutes. Strain through a fine sieve into a clean pan. Allow to settle and, with some paper towels, lift off any fat that is floating on the surface. Stir the arrowroot in a little water, add, and bring the gravy back to a simmer until clear and slightly thickened. Make sure you don't let it boil or the arrowroot can break down and thin the gravy. Keep warm. Just putting the lid on a good saucepan should do this, or use a heat-diffuser and keep the flame low.

When your goose is cooked, remove it from the oven and let it rest for 15 minutes or so before carving.

note
Obviously, you don't need another stuffing here, but the fabulous sharpness of the cornbread and cranberry (page 12) with the oozing richness of the goose, makes me urge you to consider baking a batch if you've got room in the oven for another – small – pan.

Goose and red cabbage are natural partners, even though the sauerkraut stuffing in the next goose recipe rather overrides the need for it. But a plain roast goose with this red-wine-soused cabbage is pretty hard to beat. And it's very good with ham or pork, too; in fact, just what you need to complement sharp, salty flavor or rich, dense meat.

RED CABBAGE

There are many ways to cook red cabbage, and see the – admittedly specialized – approach on page 206. Nor is there anything to stop you using the hammy cranberry and apple juices in similar fashion as I've briefly noted a few pages back, but here is the way I now customarily make my red cabbage. It takes a long time, but I never mind that, as anything that can be cooked in advance seems to me to make life easier. And actually, to celebrate the advent of winter and the need for warming food, I make a huge batch of this and freeze in small portions so that I can make a mini but substantial feast out of an everyday supper. (It is a spectacular partner to some plain grilled or flash-fried salmon. It's not just the contrast of the wine-dark cabbage with the juicy coral flesh of the fish, which is pleasing, but that the two, surprisingly and emphatically, taste so good together. Once you eat salmon with red cabbage you realize how few vegetables can stand up to its robustness. And the sweet-sourness utterly offsets that sometimes troubling oiliness.)

Serves 6 depending on what else is going with it

note
This cabbage is also good with duck. I often get for supper two duck breasts and add them to a freezer bag with $1/3$ cup red wine, juice and zest of 1 small orange, 1 tablespoon Worcestershire sauce, 2 teaspoons vegetable oil and 1 (possibly) teaspoon sesame oil, 1 bruised garlic clove and 1 small onion, quartered. Leave for a day, grill or pancook the breasts, cut in thin slices to be served with a straggling claret-colored mountain of cabbage.

1 tablespoon olive oil
1 onion, halved and peeled
1 tablespoon sea salt/scant
  $1/2$ tablespoon table salt)
1 red cabbage (approx. 10 cups shredded)
3 tablespoons soft light brown sugar

$1^1/2$ cups red wine
juice of 1 orange ($1/2$ cup)
$1/4$ teaspoon mixed spice
2 eating apples

Heat the oil in a large heavy-bottomed saucepan or casserole. Finely slice the peeled and halved onion into thin half moons and add to the pan with the salt; this will stop it catching. Fry gently until the onion softens but doesn't become colored. Now, finely shred the cabbage – which you can do by hand or by pushing chunks through the slicing blade of the processor – and stir it into the onions in the pan.

Sprinkle over the sugar, and then add the wine, orange juice and mixed spice. Peel, quarter and core the apples, and then chop them into small pieces. Add these to the pan, and when everything has wilted down a little, carefully give the pan a stir. Cover with a lid and cook very gently at the lowest possible heat for about 2 hours. It really can't be overcooked and is anyway better reheated and eaten the next day or few days after. Check the seasoning when the cabbage is ready at the end, as the flavors only really come out once the vegetables have cooked down and softened.

BOHEMIAN ROAST GOOSE

In this recipe, Bohemia is the geographical entity rather than the lifestyle. This is a recipe that obeys rules and needs planning, though there isn't a scary amount of either involved.

The goose in question is stuffed with sauerkraut mixed with caraway and a little shredded apple, and roasted with some more apples, which circle it as it sits, crisped and bronzed, out of the oven. This is the sort of dish that looks like it's out of a banquet in a Disney fairytale (only it tastes better).

But what I like about this is how unfanciful it tastes: robust meat, sour, sharp stuffing and accompaniment. No one could accuse the food of Mitteleuropa of being light, but this really makes a meal out of a meal, without leaving you gasping for air.

| 1 goose, approx. 9¹/₂lbs | 8–10 eating apples, such as Royal Gala | Serves 6 |

FOR THE STUFFING

2 x Royal Gala or other sharp variety of apples
6 cups sauerkraut, drained

¹/₄ cup superfine sugar
1¹/₂ teaspoons caraway seeds

Preheat the oven to 425°F.

Un-truss, and pull the excess fat out of the cavity of the goose. Peel, core and roughly chop the apples for the stuffing. Put the chopped apples and all the other ingredients for the stuffing into a bowl and mix together.

Stuff the cavity of the goose with the sauerkraut and apple mixture and secure the neck opening with a skewer so that the stuffing doesn't escape during roasting.

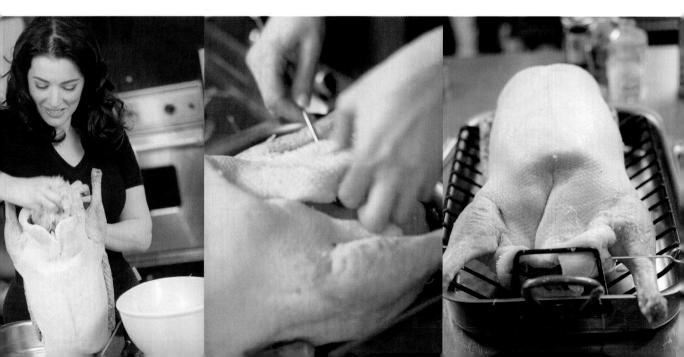

Sit the goose on a rack in a roasting pan and put in the oven for 30 minutes. Turn the oven down to 350°F and roast the goose for another $2^1/_2$ hours or so. If it doesn't look crisp enough, carry on for 3 hours in total. Don't baste it as you want the goose to lose as much fat as possible, and you will have to empty the fat that gathers in the roasting pan as the goose cooks, or it will become dangerously full.

When you are about 45 minutes away from the goose being cooked, score the eating apples around their circumference, as if drawing in the equator, and sit them in a roasting pan that has been lined with aluminum foil. Trim the bottoms of the apples if they do not sit firmly on their own. Put the pan on a rack below the roasting goose and cook the whole apples for about 45 minutes by which time they will be tender and cooked through but still holding their shape. If they need longer let them sit in the oven for another 15 minutes while the goose is standing, ready to be carved.

When the goose is cooked, remove it from the oven and let it rest for 15 minutes before carving, then arrange the whole apples around the resting goose. To be honest, six apples would be enough, since you're not really likely to want more than one per eater, but it just looks so beautiful on its carving board surrounded by apples. And it's not out of the question that some might want to come back for another apple…

Pull the skewer out that is securing the neck cavity and serve the stuffing and an apple with the goose as you carve.

ACCOMPANIMENTS

PANCETTA-WRAPPED SAUSAGES

This is scarcely a recipe, and in fact is dangerously near an accompaniment I was once happy to deride. But what's the point of a life in which your tastes don't change? Besides, the key point here is that the pancetta, or bacon, is good and so must the sausages be. By cocktail sausages, I don't mean those strange suppository-shaped compacted salami-cum-fake-frankfurter things. I mean real sausages in dinky mini-size, all the better to pop idly into an empty mouth, should one be available.

I make them to go alongside a roast turkey (given that I don't bother with a traditional sausagemeat stuffing) and I cook them in advance – only about an hour or two – and then cover them with aluminum foil (in the main to stop marauders) and reheat for 10 minutes or so in a very hot oven, such as the one the potatoes will be roasting in later, at the last minute.

Serves 8–10

50 cocktail sausages or chipolatas
50 very thin slices pancetta or
  25 thin slices bacon

approx. 3 tablespoons vegetable oil

Preheat the oven to 350°F.

Wrap each fine slice of pancetta around each cocktail sausage, or cut each slice of bacon in half across and use that instead. Spoon the oil into a roasting pan and arrange the sausages on top. Roast for 35–45 minutes until the bacon is crisp and the sausages within cooked. The only way to be sure is to make the ultimate sacrifice and taste one.

Take out of the oven and cover the pan with foil. If you've let the sausages burn a little, however, it may be better to remove them to a large piece of foil and wrap them in it; the sausages will continue to fry a little in the oil in the pan otherwise.

When you are about ready to eat, reheat the sausages just by posting the foil-wrapped pan, or parcel, in a hot oven for about 10 minutes. Naturally, you can just cook them 45 minutes before you need them, thus dispensing with the need to reheat, if you prefer.

MAPLE-ROAST PARSNIPS

I've always roasted honeyed parsnips alongside a turkey but as a marker of the culinary special relationship celebrated in this chapter, I've remodelled slightly, adding intensity of sweetness to the already sweet parsnips, not with honey but with maple syrup. And actually, this is more than a change, it's an improvement: there is more ambiguity about the maple syrup, it's sweetness less cloying.

2lbs parsnips
$^1/_2$ cup vegetable oil

$^1/_3$ cup maple syrup

Serves 8–10

It seems foolish to say "preheat the oven," when it's frankly going to be on anyway, but if you were cooking this to go alongside – say – some cold, leftover turkey, when it would be just as good as first time around, then you need a hottish oven, say 400°F, and the parsnips would need around 35 minutes in it. But if you've got the oven on very hot because of the roast potatoes, then you are better off parboiling the parsnips so that they need less time actually in the oven; 15 minutes should be enough to turn them chewy and maple-bronzed.

So, peel the parsnips and halve them crosswise, then halve or quarter each piece lengthwise, so that you have a bundle of spindly shards. Either blanch these fawn-colored twigs in salted boiling water for 3 or so minutes, or just put them straight into a roasting pan, pour over the oil, smoosh them about and then dribble over the maple syrup and roast until tender and stickily brown. Be careful as you taste to test: the sugar content of the parsnips, more even than the syrup, make these blisteringly hot.

PERFECT ROAST POTATOES

I have always, resolutely, been an anti-perfectionist, but in all honesty it is impossible to cook roast potatoes without needing them, tremulously, to be perfect. That means sweet and soft in the inside and with a thick golden-brown carapace of crunch without. And the strange thing is, no matter how many tricky things you can attempt and succeed at in cooking, no matter what elaborate techniques you might learn to master, nothing gives you that wholly happy yet unbrazen glow of pleasure in your achievement that cooking a good pan of roast potatoes does.

A good roast potato isn't about showing off or about striving desperately to impress. Nor is it a difficult thing to achieve, but I can't pretend it isn't a high pressure zone. You either get it right or you don't, and anything less than perfect is a disappointment. It's brutal but it's the truth.

However, unlike many things in cooking – and indeed life – it's relatively straightforward to achieve. That's to say, the crucial factor is the heat of the fat you roast the potatoes in. Get that right and the rest should follow. No reason why not.

And you can do things that help: cut the potatoes fairly small, so that the ratio of crunch to soft middle is high; use goose fat as your frying medium; parboil the potatoes (nothing new here), only before you roast them, sprinkle them and bash them about with semolina. These are not exactly tricks, but they are my most useful pointers.

There is nothing further to say: this recipe is most pleasing for its simplicity.

Serves 8–10

6lbs medium potatoes
2 tablespoons semolina

2 cups goose fat

Preheat the oven to the hottest possible temperature. I do this as soon as the turkey is out of the oven, which (for me) is very much later than the parboiling stage, but let's start with the oven since you may be cooking in different circumstances, or prefer different procedures.

Peel the potatoes, and cut each one into three by cutting off each end at a slant so that you are left with a wedge or triangle in the middle. See Fig. 1. (I've always wanted to say that.)

Put the potatoes into salted cold water in a saucepan, and bring to a boil, letting them cook for 4 minutes. Drain the potatoes into a colander and then tip back into the empty saucepan, sprinkling over the semolina. Shake the potatoes around to coat them well and, with the lid clamped on, give the pan a good rotation and the potatoes a proper bashing so that their edges disintegrate or fuzz and blur a little: this facilitates the crunch effect later.

Meanwhile, empty the goose fat into a large roasting pan and heat in the oven until seriously hot. (I often parboil the potatoes a few hours in advance, so the "meanwhile" doesn't always hold. And you can start heating up the fat in the oven that the turkey's in, turning it up to really hot once the bird comes out.) Then tip the semolina-

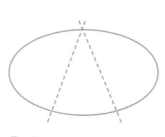

Fig. 1

coated potatoes carefully into the hot fat and roast in the oven for an hour or until they are darkly golden and crispy, turning them over halfway through cooking. If the oven's hot enough they probably won't need more than about 25 minutes a side; and it's better to let them sit in the oven (you can always pour off most of the fat and leave them in the pan) till the very last minute.

Boastfulness and vainglory are not attractive nor would I want to encourage them in you (or myself), but when you've cooked these and see them in all their golden glory on the table, I think you're allowed a quiet moment of silent pride.

SWEET POTATOES WITH MARSHMALLOWS

Sweet potatoes are so unlike regular ones that I see no reason to restrict yourself to one or the other. Indeed, they have far more in common with the parsnips (see page 25), but I still merrily feel that each and every one can be accommodated at the same meal. I think it is in the nature of the feast to have a groaning board; I want my plate to be overflowing with possible mouthfuls, different permutations. Although this array, in its familiarity, constitutes a kind of comfort food, it is the variation possible within each fresh forkful that makes it quite different from regular comfort food. What's comforting in the traditional feast is the tradition itself.

For many of us, this Thanksgiving stalwart is beyond untraditional. To a European reader, no doubt to any non-American reader, it is downright alienating. Although I've become an eater of sweet potatoes over the years, I've never quite taken the marshmallow element seriously, presuming it to be so obviously excessive, as unfathomable as a memory from someone else's childhood.

But it always pays to keep an open mind. I love these babies now, find myself strangely compelled by the luscious, syrupy purée, just tangy enough with lime to find a workable partnership with the white dots of marshmallow, tortoiseshelled by the heat of the oven.

I do add quite a bit of lime juice, although I don't think its inclusion is quite orthodox. But every person who cooks something has to make the recipe, the foodstuff, his or her own – not by effortful innovation but just by being true to your own taste.

All the same, I initially worried that I was making something that would taste all wrong to a native American eater, reared on proper – that's to say, non-British – Thanksgiving food, but James Merrell, my photographer here, took a Tupperware container of this back for his American ex-wife (isn't modern life complicated?) and she said it tasted immediately comforting and familiar. So I was as reassured as she, gratifyingly, was.

7lbs sweet potatoes
5–6 tablespoons vegetable oil
$^1/_4$ cup lime juice (1–2 limes)
2 teaspoons ground cinnamon

$^3/_4$ stick butter
1 tablespoon sea salt/$^1/_2$
tablespoon table salt
1 x 10oz package mini
marshmallows

Serves 8–10

note
If you want to roast the sweet potatoes very much in advance, it might make sense to make the purée and then heat it up in a saucepan before adding the marshmallows and blitzing it in the hot oven to brown.

Preheat the oven to 425°F.

Prick or puncture the sweet potatoes with a fork and put them each on a piece of aluminum foil large enough to wrap them in. I find these cook best in individual parcels, so just be prepared to make a lot of them: I find the weight above means you're dealing with 8 or 9 potatoes in one go.

Divide the oil between the foil sheets and then rub or turn the sweet potatoes in it and wrap into baggy but well sealed parcels. Put them on to a baking sheet or two and roast until the potatoes are soft and cooked through, approximately 1–1$^1/_2$ hours. This way of cooking the potatoes, apart from being very easy, means that you get maximum, un-watered-down flavor.

When the sweet potatoes are cool enough to handle, strip away the skin and fork or squeeze and pick the flesh into a large bowl. Pour in any syrupy juices from each of the foil parcels. Add all the other ingredients except for the marshmallows, and mix together to make the mash.

Spoon the sweet potato mash into an ovenproof dish: I use an old rectangular one of 13$^1/_2$ x 8 inches and about 2$^1/_2$ inches deep, but any you have around that size would be fine. Smooth the top of the mash and cover with the mini marshmallows.

Bake in the hot oven for 10–15 minutes by which time the marshmallows will have colored on top and melted together, like a rippled, bronzed duvet.

BRUSSELS SPROUTS WITH CHESTNUTS, PANCETTA AND PARSLEY

Just as I have never understood the sheer hostility that a turkey can induce in people, nor do I have much time for the antipathy displayed toward the Brussels sprout. Again, the cause for complaint stems from over-cooking. When a sprout is allowed to keep a bit of bite, it has a nutty freshness. It helps if the sprouts you're cooking are relatively small: once they've reached the large, blowsy unfurling stage they can be harder to deal with satisfactorily. But there are ways: should you want an alternative to the recipe that follows, you could shred them by pushing them through the fine slicing disc of a processer then briefly stir-fry them with either some bacon or ginger, or indeed, crumbled chestnuts; this snappily overcomes their overblownness.

The sprout recipe below is really only a slight detour from the traditional route. By all means, stick to the orthodox if you prefer by adding only buttery chestnuts to the Brussels sprouts, but what follows is now my own traditional way of cooking them. There is a lot of parsley, I know, but think of it as another vegetable ingredient rather than a garnish.

Serves 8–10

note

Obviously, if you can't get your hands on pancetta, it's fine to use bacon. Just scissor it up, and fry it in a little more oil than you need for the pancetta, before proceeding.

Much as I love these sprouts, I'd always hope for leftovers, not least because one of my favorite things in this book is the bubble and squeak on page 64. Otherwise, if you reheat with some vegetable or chicken stock (I prefer the latter, and the pancetta means you've already lost the vegetarian vote) and a handful of frozen peas, you can blitz or blend this into a sweet and comforting soup.

10 cups/2lbs Brussels sprouts
8oz pancetta, rind removed, cut into $^1/_2$ inch cubes (to give $1^1/_2$ cups)
1 tablespoon vegetable oil

2 tablespoons butter
$1^1/_2$ cups/8oz vacuum-packed chestnuts
$^1/_4$ cup Marsala
large bunch parsley, chopped to give about 1 cup

Trim the bottoms off each of the sprouts, cutting a cross into each as you go, or at least a slash. This may not be necessary, but I can't *not* do it. Then tip them into a large pan of salted boiling water and cook until tender but still retaining a bit of bite, about 5 minutes or so depending on size. Just spoon one out of the water and test (without burning your tongue and thus ruining the whole lunch for yourself) to be sure.

Meanwhile, in a pan large enough to take everything later (or just drain the sprouts and use their pan, once you've drained them), cook the pancetta cubes in the oil, with the rind for more salty fat rendering, until they're bronzed and crisp, but not cooked to the point of having dried out.

Add the butter and the chestnuts and, with a wooden spoon or spatula, press on the chestnuts to break them up a little. When they're warmed through, turn the heat up and throw in the Marsala, letting it bubble away, fusing with the pancetta fat and chest-nutty butter to form a glorious savory syrup. Add the drained sprouts and turn well, sprinkling in half the parsley as you do so. Give a good grinding of pepper; you shouldn't need salt, given the pancetta, but obviously taste to see. Decant to a warmed serving plate and sprinkle over the remaining chopped parsley.

GREEN BEAN AND LEMON CASSEROLE

Strictly speaking, I don't think of this as a casserole, but I know that this is the traditional nomenclature; and, besides, I do sometimes serve the beans in one so it seems silly to quibble.

This is another recipe I'd never have thought of adding to my Christmas till I started cooking for Thanksgiving, but I love its fresh, citrussy crunch. Actually, all I've done is bring on board an amplification of the way my mother always cooked green beans: just plenty of butter, plenty of pepper, and vicious amounts of lemon.

2lbs slender green beans	**1 lemon**	Serves 8–10
$^3/_4$ stick unsalted butter	**sea salt and fresh pepper**	
few drops olive oil		

Bring a big pot of water to the boil, while you top and tail (trim) the beans. Once the water has come to the boil, salt it and cook the beans until they have lost their rawness (about 6 minutes after the water comes back to the boil), but retain a bit of crunch.

Strain them, and put the pot back on the stove over a low heat with the butter and olive oil. While the butter melts, chop up the lemon. Put it on a chopping board, cut a slice off each end, just enough to remove skin and pith, and then cut downwards, turning the lemon as you go, to peel the fruit fully. Don't worry if in order to remove all the pith you cut into the fruit a bit: just take the pieces of fruity peel over to the pan and squeeze in any juice you can. Then cut the lemon up on the board: I just slice and let each slice tumble into bits on its own. Add the lemon pieces and all the juice that collects to the melted butter and stir well with a wooden spoon, adding the drained beans.

Swirl the pan vigorously and turn the beans in the lemony butter. Add salt to taste and lots of freshly ground pepper. I love white pepper (out of deference to my mother's taste and practice) or the much-abominated 1980s restaurant-style mixed pepper, but neither is crucial.

Remove to a warmed casserole making sure you don't leave any lemony, buttery juices behind.

You'd think all the above would be enough. But 33 pages into this chapter, and we still haven't finished dinner. No wonder everyone goes on a diet in the New Year.

BREAD SAUCE

I don't think it is decent to serve roast turkey without bread sauce or, indeed, cranberry sauce. When I was a child, bread sauce was always made from scratch and cranberry sauce came out of a jar. Now, who knows? But both these recipes are easy to make. I don't mind bottled cranberry, but never packaged bread sauce – please. All you need for the bread sauce is a little forethought: you need some good, that's to say, not plastic-sliced, bread in the house, and ideally you've let it stale slightly. If not, a quick go in a very low oven should do it.

I have returned to the way my mother always made her bread sauce, which is to say by tearing the slices of bread into rough crumbs and letting that cook to a creamy, nubbly porridge in the pot. I now feel using crumbed bread, which I have done, and can't really deny now, makes a too-uniform gruel.

There's something about the scent of a bread sauce in the air, the oniony milk, the bay and clove and mace, that is so immediately, warmingly festive to anyone brought up to a traditional British Christmas. And although it probably sounds as repellent to a non-Anglo eater as the marshmallow-sweet-potato thang does initially to a non-American, I don't think it would take more than a few mouthfuls (as long as they were alongside a properly mustard-smeared, gravy dampened slice of meat) to convince.

I always get this started well in advance. In fact, scenting the milk with the spices is pretty much the first thing I do after breakfast. My mother (who equally thought nothing of parboiling her potatoes the evening before she planned to roast them), prepared this completely, barring only a final melting in of the butter, a day earlier too. I see no reason to be quite so ahead of yourself, but bread-sauce making should be a pleasurably leisurely kind of activity.

Serves 8–10

1 day-old loaf unsliced white bread	2 teaspoons sea salt/
4 cups milk	1 teaspoon table salt
1 onion	2 tablespoons butter
4 cloves	2 tablespoons heavy cream,
2 bay leaves	optional
1 teaspoon white peppercorns	fresh nutmeg
Heaped 1/4 teaspoon ground mace	

Remove the crust from the bread, and tear at the denuded loaf with your bare hands to turn it into a mound of rough chunks or cubes. You should end up with about 3 cups cubes. If they are not slightly stale already, leave them out on a wire rack somewhere to dry out, or speed the process along by putting them in a very low oven – only don't forget they're there.

Pour the milk into a pan. Peel and quarter the onion, and stud each quarter with a clove as you drop it into the pan of milk. Add the bay leaves, peppercorns and sprinkle the ground mace over along with the salt and bring close to the boil, but do not actually let it boil.

Remove from the heat, cover the pan and let it foggily infuse. As I said above, I tend to do this first thing in the morning when I get up, but if you forget or can't cope with it then, then just make sure you get the infusion done about an hour before eating. Put the pan back on a very low heat, add the bread cubes and cook for about 15 minutes, by which time the sauce should be thick and warm and evocatively fragrant. I have to say I don't bother with removing any of the bits, the onions, the peppercorns and so on, but you can strain the milk before adding the bread if you want to. Just before serving, stir in the butter and, if you happen to have a carton open, the cream and some more salt if you think it needs it. Grate over quite a bit of nutmeg, adding more once you've decanted it into a warmed bowl or gravy boat.

REDDER THAN RED CRANBERRY SAUCE

There is always something ludicrous about the cartoon crimson of cranberries, but this just takes things a little further: a slug of cherry brandy is, on top of being an appropriately festive kind of déclassé tipple, a perfect sweetener for the tart berries and a glorious intensifier of their own beautiful color.

If you don't have any cherry brandy on hand, do not panic: just use some freshly squeezed orange juice (blood orange juice out of a carton, even, would keep you in the spirit of things) instead and be prepared to up the sugar slightly depending on how bitter or sweet the orange juice is. If you're squeezing the orange for juice, go that extra centimeter and zest it first over the cranberries in the pan.

12oz package cranberries	**¹/₄ cup cherry brandy**	Serves 8–10
1 cup superfine sugar	**¹/₃ cup water**	

What can I tell you? Put everything in a pan, bring to a boil and let it bubble away for about 15 minutes until you have cranberry sauce. The one thing you should bear in mind, though, is that the pectin-rich nature of the fruit means that it solidifies briskly as it cools, so take the pan off the heat to stop it cooking and reducing when you still think it's much too liquid. Once the berries have burst, which should be after about 10 minutes, it should be ready, but you will anyway have to remove a teaspoonful to taste whether it needs more sugar (if you find it too sweet, which is unlikely, just spritz in some lemon) so take two out to check the consistency of the second, cooled, teaspoon.

If you cook this way in advance it will chunk up a lot so just thrash it through with a fork before serving.

And I think that's it for lunch, but for one thing: I cannot countenance a roast turkey with all the trimmings without that searing, necessary ointment, English mustard. In 1988 I stayed with friends, who cooked everything so wonderfully, just as I'd want it, only there was no English mustard. That was a severe trauma for me. The fact that I can actually remember the date is the only thing that makes me feel I've bravely recovered from it. I've managed, bravely, not to repress the memory.

THE RUN-UP

It might seem logical to go on to dessert now, but just as I don't always feel able to tackle it after eating just about everything I've talked about above, nor do I want to broach the subject yet. By all means, if you feel differently, turn to page 67 and 68 for the pumpkin and apple crumble or pumpkin cheesecake (a hot and cold alternative respectively to pumpkin pie) or page 69 for a trad Christmas pudding, but first I'm going back in time.

One of the difficulties of an impending feast – panic, the weight of expectation and family tensions aside – is that everyone acts as if that is the only meal on the horizon. Now, on the run up to Thanksgiving or Christmas Day, it is only natural that a certain focus should be on the dinner itself, but other meals do exist. People need to be fed, and it's likely that family might be beginning to gather early on, especially if they need to travel cross country to see you. And they have to be given something. No one wants to eat too much, moreover no one wants to cook too much, but if you want to welcome and restore those who've spent the day travelling to come and see you, you have to provide more than a sandwich and a piece of fruit.

I have menus for both a Christmas Eve lunch and a Christmas Eve supper, both of which I have cooked, but never together in the same year. On the whole, I feel those with children are more likely to be doing a Christmas Eve lunch, whereas those who don't have to worry about the start of the second shift (the hell of the scrabble to get everything wrapped and all stockings stuffed before you go to bed) or the early wake-up call tomorrow morning will be happier to shop by day and feast by night.

COZY CHRISTMAS EVE OR HOLIDAY LUNCH FOR TEN

SAUSAGES WITH ONION AND CIDER GRAVY
"HEAVEN AND EARTH" MASH WITH PEAS
RHUBARB CRUMBLE AND CUSTARD
SATSUMA ORANGES, LYCHEES,
POMEGRANATES AND CHOCOLATES

This is the lunch I did for Christmas Eve last year, that's to say, 2003 and I'm ready to give an exact repeat performance this year, and indeed any year.

It's not just that it's easy and comforting, though both factors count for much, but it's a perfect menu for both adults and children, and I always seem to end up with a lot of the latter around this time of year, which is just how it should be I'm told.

beautiful

g cold tu

spring onio

125g sugar s

125g bean s

2 tsp groun

275g col

1 medi

125g c

SAUSAGES WITH ONION AND CIDER GRAVY

I know there are people with very fierce views as to how to cook a sausage correctly and I'm sure they're right. I would rather be wrong and give myself an easy life. I just put the sausages in a large pan with a little oil in a 400°F oven for about 45 minutes, turning them once or twice.

For some reason this offends people's sense of propriety, but much as I do appreciate the burnt-on black stickiness you get from frying the sausages in a pan, I don't want the kitchen filled with smoke and I don't have the patience. Or maybe I just lack the requisite skill, as I always end up with burned sausages that are raw in the middle.

Serves 10

3lbs (18-24) English or other breakfast sausages

1–2 tablespoons vegetable oil

FOR THE ONION AND CIDER GRAVY

8oz (2) onions

2 tablespoons olive oil

1 Cox's or other firm tart apple (6oz)

scant tablespoon light or dark brown sugar

1 teaspoon English mustard powder

1 scant tablespoon all-purpose flour

2 cups hot meat stock

$^2/_3$ cup cider

To cook the sausages, see the notes above. And you can cook the gravy while they're in the oven, or get started well in advance if you prefer.

Peel, halve and slice the onions into very thin half moons. Heat the oil in a wide saucepan, add the onions and cook slowly for about 10 minutes until they are very soft. Peel, core and finely chop the apple and add to the onion, stirring around for another 5 minutes. Turn up the heat and add the sugar, cooking over a high flame for 3 minutes. It doesn't really matter whether you choose light or dark brown sugar, certainly not in terms of taste, but I have a slight prejudice against pale gravies, so I go for the darker sugar if I've got some in the house.

Stir in the mustard powder and flour and stir while you let the flour cook a little. Take the pan off the heat briefly as, still stirring, you pour in the hot stock and cider, and then bring back to the boil, stirring all the time. As with the sugar, it doesn't really matter what type of meat stock you use, but I use beef stock (not homemade, but a good store-bought one) for its darker color.

Simmer the gravy gently for about 30 minutes; it will thicken and the apple should melt into the sauce.

This doesn't make a huge amount of gravy, but you don't need a huge amount, and much as I love leftovers I don't think you want to start to add to them *before* Christmas lunch.

"HEAVEN AND EARTH" MASH WITH PEAS

I can say, hand on heart, that it wasn't the name that lured me here, but the notion of the tastes: buttery mashed potatoes given a spritz by the addition of some puréed apple. But the name's good and especially at this time of year as we are enjoying the worldly and contemplating the divine. Still, I presume there is a more prosaic explanation which must simply be that the apples are plucked from the skies and the potatoes (as in *pommes de terre* or *Erdapfel*) dug out of the soil.

I came across a recipe for "heaven and earth" in a book I'm often to be found studying, mostly when I'm Atkinsing: Roy Finamore's *One Potato, Two Potato*. I've always had a soft spot for the obsessive focus of a single-subject cookbook and this is an admirable example of the genre. The recipe I thought, however, was far too labor intensive, involving little hanging baskets of thyme to be lowered into the potatoes as they cooked, so I just read the recipe, forgot about it and went about the business in my own lazy way.

As I wrote in *How to Eat*, my maternal grandmother always cooked sausages and apples together (the latter peeled, cored, cut into rings and fried in the sausage pan), so this gave me a special tug.

5 1/2–6lbs floury potatoes	1 stick plus 2 tablespoons butter	Serves 10
3 eating apples (I use Pink Lady)	3/4 cup heavy cream	
zest of 1 lemon	1 teaspoon freshly grated nutmeg	

Peel and halve (or quarter depending on size) the potatoes and cook them in salted boiling water for about 30 minutes. (If you're going to use a ricer to mash the potatoes, you don't strictly speaking need to peel them.) Add the peeled, cored and quartered apples and the lemon zest, and cook for another 20 minutes or until soft. Drain the potatoes and apples and then push through a ricer or mash back into the hot pan in which you have let the butter melt with the cream while you are draining. If you have a standing mixer, you can leave the bowl to stand filled with hot water while you cook the potatoes and apples, and then chuck the water away and mash everything using the flat paddle; in which case, warm the butter and cream in a small pan or the microwave before adding to the apples and potatoes in the mixer bowl.

Grate over the fresh nutmeg, and season with some salt, and then beat everything together. There are – and I thank Lindsey Bareham and her potato book for this – two distinct processes required to make perfect mash: the first is to purée the potatoes, the second is to aerate them. So even if you've mashed everything well, you do need to give everything a good beating with a wooden spoon before serving.

One absolute no-no, though: never, ever, under any circumstances, use a food processor. It does something vile to the potato starch and you end up with glue.

As for the peas on my menu, I use two to three jars of those sweet, grey-green French petit pois. Just heat through, removing slimy pieces of onion as you drain and season well. As well as English mustard, I feel you should have steak sauce.

note
I have to alert you to one thing, here. Young children tend to prefer their mash without apples in it. So, you can just do regular mash (and see also, given the seasonal burdens, lazy mash on page 334, only remember to augment quantities) or put some baking potatoes in the oven alongside the sausages, give them some grated cheese to go with and they can have sausages and cheesy jacket potatoes. If the children are under ten, I put a batch of cocktail sausages in for them.

RHUBARB CRUMBLE

You need to be lucky enough to find that puce-pink forced stuff – and it's not always possible to do so, before Christmas – but for the past two years I've found it in the shops by early December. This is the best crumble in the world, which possibly makes it the best dessert in the world.

This may seem a small amount for ten, but I've found that not everyone wants to eat dessert after all the sausages and mash and with lunch tomorrow looming: provide satsuma oranges, lychees maybe, some halved pomegranates definitely; besides, there is always, in the UK at any rate, the lure of seasonal candy. It's just got to be done, and now is a good place to start.

I think you do need custard with the crumble, but if it seems like one recipe too far, then heavy cream or, indeed, vanilla ice cream, will do just fine. I prefer the cold leftovers with Greek yogurt.

Serves 10

note

By vanilla sugar I mean superfine sugar which you've flavored with a vanilla bean or two. Obviously you don't just flavor such a small quantity but, rather, keep a jar of sugar somewhere with some beans stashed in it.

Although you can let the rhubarb stand in the pie dish, and the crumble mixture wait in its own container, you can't top the one with the other and let them hang around together, so don't cover the fruit with the crumble topping until you're ready to put it in the oven.

I don't think it ever matters how long the crumble sits after it's come out of the oven: there's no bad temperature at which to eat this; indeed, there is much to be said for a statutory 15-minute wait.

2lbs beautiful pink rhubarb, to give $1^1/_2$lbs when chopped into $^1/_2$ inch pieces ($7^1/_2$ cups)
$^1/_4$ cup superfine sugar

FOR THE CRUMBLE TOPPING
1 cup all purpose flour
1 teaspoon baking powder
1 stick unsalted butter, cold and diced

1 tablespoon butter
1 tablespoon best-quality pure vanilla extract
1 tablespoon cornstarch

3 tablespoons vanilla sugar or ordinary sugar
3 tablespoons brown sugar

Preheat the oven to 375°F, and put in a baking sheet (to sit the pie plate on and catch any drips later).

Toss the sliced rhubarb in a pan on the heat with the sugar, butter, vanilla and cornstarch for about 5 minutes, until the butter has melted and everything oozed together. You should end up with a glossy pan of pink gorgeousness.

Tip into a pie plate, approximately $8^1/_2$ inches in diameter and $1^1/_2$ inches deep. I often do this well in advance. This kind of job is good to get out of the way early, as is the making of the crumbs; in fact you can make these and stash them in the fridge, or indeed freezer, till needed. You don't need to thaw the crumble topping before covering the rhubarb with it.

Put the flour and baking powder into a bowl (or use self-raising flour), and rub in the cold, diced butter. It should resemble rough oatmeal.

Stir in the sugars with a fork and pour over the rhubarb-filled pie dish, taking care to cover the fruit well right to the edges of the dish so that it doesn't bubble up into the topping too much as it cooks. Bake for 35–45 minutes on the waiting sheet. Some pink juices will spill over though, despite efficient coverage, which is only desirable; and the top will be scorched brown in parts.

CUSTARD

To go with the rhubarb crumble, I like a very vanillary custard, so use an actual vanilla bean, split, with the little black seeds gritting up the yellow smoothness of the sauce, but a good vanilla extract would be a fine substitute.

It's probably easier for you to make the custard before you sit down to lunch; indeed while the sausages are cooking. If the crumble's hot, the custard doesn't need to be; indeed there are some schools of thought which hold that a cold custard's best with a piping hot pudding…

Serves 10

1 cup heavy cream
1 cup milk
1 vanilla bean

5 egg yolks
1 tablespoon superfine sugar

Pour the cream and milk into a saucepan. Split the vanilla bean in half lengthwise and scrape out some of the seeds with the tip of a sharp knife into the cream and milk in the pan. I often just hold the vanilla pod over the pan, cut it down the middle almost to the end, with a pair of kitchen scissors and then use the scissors to gouge out some of the seeds into the pan. Drop in the deseeded bean, too.

Bring the contents of the pan almost to the boil, then remove from the heat and let it infuse for about 20 minutes.

Whisk the yolks and sugar together and then pour the infused vanilla cream over them and stir. Wash out the pan (just water and a wipe with a kitchen towel's fine) and pour the uncooked custard back into it.

Meanwhile, fill the sink with cold water. I haven't the patience to cook custard for ages over a low flame, so I use a medium, even a relatively high flame, but keep a basin nearby filled with cold water so if the custard looks as if it might split, I can dash over and plunge my pan into the water, whisk like mad and avert catastrophe. And knowing the water's there makes you feel safer and therefore braver.

Put the custard on medium to low (or medium to high if you're like me), heat and stir until it thickens. As for how much it should thicken, well that rather depends on how you like your custard. When it's the consistency you like, stop. And if at any time while it's cooking – and I reckon it should take around 8 minutes, longer if you're timid – it starts to bubble, whip it off the stove and whisk with a little hand whisk, only plunging the pan into the cold water if you actually think it needs to stop cooking NOW or rather – A FEW SECONDS AGO.

Remove bean bits, pour into a pitcher and if, like me, you cannot abide a skin and shudder at the very mention of one, then take a piece of plastic wrap and press it down right against the surface of the custard, to cover and then drape it down over the pitcher.

SPRAUNCY CHRISTMAS EVE SUPPER FOR EIGHT

SEASONAL BREEZE
PINK PICANTE SHRIMP
TAGLIATA OF BEEF WITH ROSEMARY AND GARLIC POTATOES
SNOWFLECKED BROWNIES

This sounds like a lot to be eating on the eve of the great Christmas blow-out but there's no need to make vast quantities. I normally use one rump slice of beef (and you just need to ask your butcher or the butcher-counter at the supermarket, to slice across the whole rump to give you a steak about $1^1/4$ inches thick) for four people, thus ensuring sandwich-filling leftovers for later. But when I'm going in for the whole 3-course fandango, I provide the one steak (which needs to be marinated in advance, so start with that recipe) for 8. If you're eating shrimps first, then potatoes with and brownies (maybe with ice cream) later, believe me, a scant few strips of steak is just fine.

The thing to remember is that while a feel of welcoming abundance is wonderful, a seasonal sense of overstuffed bloat is not.

SEASONAL BREEZE

I'm not really one for cocktails and pitchers of funny drinks, but I came up with this a few years back and it was so good and the color so festive, I just had to go with it.

1 bottle Campari
3 cups chilled blood orange juice (from a carton)

3 cups chilled cranberry juice (also from a carton)

Mix the three components together, though you may find it easier to mix in smaller batches, making up more as you need it. Basically, it's just a third part Campari to a third part blood orange juice, to a third part cranberry juice.

PINK PICANTE SHRIMP

You can find raw shrimps ready shelled in the freezer compartment at the supermarket these days, so even though this is an extravagance to buy, it isn't difficult to cook. Think of this as the trade-off.

I have a real thing about pink peppercorns these days, proving that although you can take the girl out of the Eighties you can't take the Eighties out of the girl. I used to despise this sort of thing as naff restaurantishness: now that I've mellowed, I can't see what the problem is. These look beautiful and taste luscious. And if you can't bring yourself to use pink peppercorns, or can't find them, simply use white ones. Or, dispense with the crushed-pepper element (and the egg whites), use a little more hot smoked paprika and splash in some rosé wine as they cook, after they've been turned in the hot pan for a moment or so.

You should get about 36 shrimps out of 1¹/₂lbs, which is plenty for a starter for 8, with two courses coming after

1 tablespoon pink peppercorns, plus more to crush to decorate
1 tablespoon sea salt/¹/₂ tablespoon table salt
¹/₂ teaspoon cardamom seeds, or seeds from about 8 pods

1 teaspoon picante pimenton (hot smoked paprika)
2 egg whites
1¹/₂lbs peeled raw, medium shrimp
2 tablespoons oil for frying or as needed

note
You could chop some fresh parsley or cilantro and scatter it over. It was for reasons of vanity rather than out of gustatory concerns that I left this out: it was about the green bits in the teeth after. As long as you designate someone to be on teeth duty – signing to you when you need to go and defoliate – it'll be fine.

Crush the peppercorns, salt, cardamom seeds and picante pimenton in a mortar and pestle until you have an aromatic nubbly mixture, or you could grind the spices in a pepper or coffee mill. Turn out onto a large shallow bowl.

Hand-whisk the egg whites until they are foamy, but not stiff. Dip the shrimp into the egg white, and then toss them in the crushed spice mixture turning them so they are well coated.

Heat the oil in a large pan and stir-fry the spice-coated shrimp for 5–7 minutes or until they are cooked through. Remove to a serving dish and sprinkle with some more crushed pink peppercorns before taking them to the table.

You need provide no more than some good crusty French bread alongside: those baguettes must have been bought today, though.

TAGLIATA WITH ROSEMARY AND GARLIC POTATOES

FOR THE TAGLIATA

2 cloves garlic

1 tablespoon black peppercorns

1¼ inch thick steak, cut along
  the whole length of the rump,
  about 1½lbs in weight

1 small onion

¹/₃ cup plus 1 tablespoon olive oil

1 tablespoon good red wine vinegar

1 tablespoon Worcestershire sauce

sea salt to sprinkle

approx. 8 cups arugula

2 lemons

Squish down on the garlic cloves with the flat side of a knife to bruise them, and put them into a large plastic freezer bag. Add the peppercorns, pressing down on them, from outside the bag, with the end of a rolling pin or a soup can to bruise them too. Now add the steak, and quarter the onion (no need to peel it) and bung that in along with the olive oil, vinegar and Worcestershire sauce. Tie a knot or otherwise seal the bag and squoggle it about so the marinade ingredients mix and then put it in the fridge on a dish (in case of leakage) for 12 or so hours, or leave it out of the fridge for 2–3. Even half an hour would make a difference, so don't skip this step just because you haven't got a lot of time.

Let the steak get to room temperature before cooking on a griddle for about 6–7 minutes a side (or, after sealing it, cook in a very hot oven for about 15 minutes). It's hard to say how long it'll take: it so depends on how you like your meat. I like mine pretty well still quaking and trembling on the plate, so be prepared to cook it for longer if you want better-done meat. Test by prodding before you start poking knives in: if it's very very soft and bouncy, it's blue; springy, rare; springy but with resistance, medium-rare to medium depending on that resistance; hard, well, you know the answer to that.

Take the steak out and lay it on a large piece of foil, sprinkle with sea or other good rough salt, wrap it and then wrap the whole parcel in another piece of foil and let it stand for 10 minutes. Then carve thinly, crosswise, that's to say on the diagonal, and arrange on a plate lined with arugula leaves. Put a plate of lemon quarters on the table too.

FOR THE ROSEMARY AND GARLIC POTATOES

3lbs potatoes

½ cup garlic-infused oil

few sprigs fresh rosemary

sea salt to sprinkle

Preheat the oven to 400°F.

Wash and dry the potatoes, but don't bother to peel them, and cut them into about ³/₄ inch dice. Toss in a large oven tray and pour over the garlic-infused oil, smulching around with your hands to mix well. Tuck in some torn-up rosemary sprigs, and roast for about an hour, turning once or twice during that time, till they are wonderfully crispy and golden but still soft on the inside. When they're done, sprinkle with sea salt.

SNOW-FLECKED BROWNIES

These are dark, damp, melting-bellied brownies studded with miniature white chocolate buttons. Brownies start off by being one of the easiest things to cook and end up by being one of the best things you could ever eat. That's why I've made enough here for supper and then some…

To make them look more snowy, dust over some confectioners' sugar just before serving. Dusted or not, cut into squares, pile on a large plate, one on top of another, and stud several with a birthday-cake candle in a holder; then set them gloriously, seasonally alight.

Makes 20

note
Of course you could halve the quantities and make ten brownies in a smaller pan, but enough is not always as good as a feast: it's the pile up of lit brownies that is so beautiful. Anyway, you can always wrap remainders in aluminum foil and give them to your guests as take-home Christmas presents…

3 sticks plus 2 tablespoons unsalted butter
13oz best-quality semisweet or bittersweet chocolate
6 eggs
2 cups superfine sugar
1 tablespoon pure vanilla extract
1 1/2 cups plus 2 tablespoons all-purpose flour
1 teaspoon salt
9oz white chocolate buttons, preferably Montgomery Moore, or good white chocolate, chopped
approx. 2 teaspoons confectioners' sugar for dusting

Preheat the oven to 350°F. You can just turn the oven down the minute you take the potatoes out, or cook the potatoes in a lower oven for longer. Line the sides and base of a 13 x 9 x 2 inch baking pan with aluminum foil or baking parchment.

Melt the butter and dark chocolate together in a large heavy-based pan over a low heat.

In a bowl or large measuring cup, beat the eggs together with the superfine sugar and vanilla extract.

Allow the chocolate mixture to cool a little, then add the egg and sugar mixture and beat well. Fold in the flour and salt. Then stir in the white chocolate buttons or chopped white chocolate. Beat to combine then scrape and pour the brownie mixture into the prepared pan.

Bake for about 25 minutes. You can see when the brownies are ready because the top dries to a slightly paler brown speckle, while the middle remains dark, dense and gooey. Even with such a big batch you do need to keep checking on it: the difference between gungey brownies and dry ones is only a few minutes. Remember, too, that they will continue to cook as they cool.

To serve, cut into squares while still warm and pile up on a large plate, sprinkling with confectioners' sugar pushed with a teaspoon through a small sieve, and dotting with birthday candles, as you go. Set alight and enjoy the festive scene.

RUDOLPH PIE

If you want something simpler, in character rather than procedurally (the previous supper is not particularly demanding of your time or attention), then a seasonal take on a shepherd's pie is just right for gatherings of large numbers of people at this time of year. Because it can be cooked in advance, and is immediately comforting and bolstering, this is the ideal thing to have at home waiting after a Christmas party when you've got lots of people to feed but you haven't got it in you to start cooking from scratch. One of the demands on you, after all, at this time of year is that you end up having to feed more people at one sitting than you might regularly consider. I don't see that an ordinary shepherd's pie is anything to apologize for, but this one is subtly special. The base is made not with lamb, but ground venison – hence, I'm sorry, the name – and pork made boskily heady with porcini; the regular potato roofing is enriched with a nutmeggy, buttery mash of parsnips.

I know that you can get venison all the year round at the supermarket now, but there's something about game that cannot but feel richly seasonal. You do, however, need to balance the sweet intensity and densely grained leanness of the venison with the milder, gentler, juiciness of the pork. Besides, I take the view that one meat makes a meal but two meats make a feast.

Even if you want to stay trad and stick with lamb, don't leave out the porcini: these mushrooms permeate the pie with their woodsy resonance. Yes, using $1^3/_4$oz of them is extravagant, but feasting needs a certain luxurious lack of restraint. The important thing is that the food is cozy: you invite people round not to impress them but to welcome them. This is the best way of doing that.

Serves 14–16

note
There are really only two acceptable accompaniments to shepherd's pie: steak sauce and peas (frozen petits pois, sweet and buttered, or those French bottled ones, are fine).

If you suffer from occasional but necessary lapses in taste, as I do, then top, on serving, with a shiny red-nose glacé cherry.

For dessert, I suggest the ice cream with cranberry syrup (see page 81).

$1^3/_4$oz dried porcini
4 onions
4 carrots
4 cloves garlic
3–5 tablespoons olive oil
1lb button mushrooms, sliced or quartered
$2^1/_4$lbs ground venison
$2^1/_4$lbs ground pork
1 tablespoon sea salt/$^1/_2$ tablespoon table salt
2 tablespoons all-purpose flour

2 14oz cans tomatoes/ just under 4 cups
2 tablespoons tomato purée diluted in $^1/_2$ cup water
6 tablespoons Marsala
Worcestershire sauce to taste
9lbs potatoes
$3^1/_4$lbs parsnips
$^1/_2$ cup whole milk
1 stick butter, melted, plus extra to dot on the top
fresh nutmeg

This is one of those simple-hearted, down-home kind of dishes that in fact is rather fiddly. Nothing's difficult, but there are quite a few steps. But that can be the way with food that you can simply reheat when you need it: you have to put more hours in earlier. Often, especially at this time of year, it's worth it. I sometimes think that 1 hour's cooking alone, calmly and in advance, is preferable to 15 minutes' frenetic, last-minute activity when you're tired and have a roomful of people to entertain. I say this now, as a form of self-defense, but also to warn you, however encouragingly, of the labor to come.

So, to begin, pour 2 cups of near-boiling water over the dried porcini mushrooms and leave to steep while you get on with the rest of the cooking.

Peel the onions, carrots and garlic cloves and chop them; I use a food processor here, and do them in two batches of two each, but if you chop by hand, mince the garlic later over the onions and carrots after they've had time to cook a little.

Pour most of the oil into a very large, thick-bottomed pan and when it's warm add the chopped onions, carrots and garlic. Cook, stirring, for about 10 minutes, sprinkling in salt if the vegetables look as though they might burn.

Drain the porcini, reserving the soaking liquid, chop them coarsely and add them to the vegetable mixture along with the button mushrooms. After about 5 minutes, when the fresh mushrooms have cooked down a bit into the mixture, transfer the vegetables to a plate so that you can start cooking the meat. Add a little more oil to the pan then tip in the ground meats, breaking them up with a wooden fork or spatula. Stir for about 5 minutes until the rawness has left them a bit, add salt – about 1 tablespoon sea, half that of table salt – and then return the vegetable mixture to the pan. Stir in the flour and, still stirring, pour in the mushroom-soaking liquid, tomatoes, diluted purée, Marsala and a few drops of Worcestershire sauce. Stir well, cover partly with a lid and turn down the heat so that the mixture bubbles gently – some of the liquid evaporating and the flavors intensifying – for about an hour.

Once cooked, taste for seasoning then remove from the heat. If it helps, you can cook the base in advance (either freezing it or leaving it in the fridge for a few days) which means that when you want to serve the pie, you have only to bother with the topping. Some people are happy to make a shepherd's pie in its entirety and then leave it to be reheated, but I think that's only OK if you don't need to refrigerate it for days (it does something funny to the texture of the potatoes). An afternoon, even a longer stretch, in a cold wintry kitchen, though, is fine. An easier alternative might be to fridge up the cooked base and leave the mashed potatoes and parsnips in a bowl covered with plastic wrap in a cold place for up to a day or two, bringing them together just before they go into the oven. Given the amount of potatoes stipulated, I suggest you hand a peeler to anyone who asks if there's anything they can do. Or use a potato ricer, which means you don't need to peel them. Either way, boil the potatoes in a large pan of salted water until they are nearly ready and then add the parsnips which have been peeled and cut into chunks and cook for another 10 minutes or so. Bubble everything until the potatoes and parsnips are cooked to easily mashable tenderness, but not to the point of disintegration, then drain them and let them dry slightly in the colander while you warm the milk and melt the butter in the heat of the potato pan. Rice the potatoes and parsnips straight into this pan (or mash them) then grate in some fresh nutmeg and salt to taste.

Put the meat mixture into a large dish approx. $12^1/_2$ x $14^1/_2$ inches and approx. 3 inches deep. Then dollop the potato mash on top, spreading with a spatula, taking care to seal the edges to prevent the meat below from bubbling up in the oven. Fork lines over the top, then dot with butter and sprinkle with Worcestershire sauce. If you're cooking this right away, in other words while everything's still warm, about 10 minutes in a 425°F oven should be enough to make it piping hot and crispily golden on top. If cooking from cold, about an hour in a 375°F oven should do it.

LEFTOVERS

I don't feel a house is a home until there are leftovers in the fridge, and Christmas leftovers are my all-time favorite. To be honest, I'm happy simply knowing there's a Boxing Day – the day after Christmas – breakfast waiting for me, to be eaten with my fingers while standing in the open fridge door – of cold turkey, cold roast potatoes, cold bread sauce and a cardiac-red blob of cranberries. If there's bread in the house to turn this into a sandwich, so much the better, and at any time of the day.

But having spent much of my adult life declaring there was no better way to eat leftover Christmas turkey than slicing it and eating it as it is (a throwback to childhood when rehashed turkey meant throat-con-strictingly desiccated fricassee – though not at our house), I am now evangelical about twiddling, culinarily, with a turkey. The only rule (and I have, womanfully, tried a Thai green turkey curry with only limited suc-cess) is that with occasional exceptions you don't attempt to re-cook it.

Funnily, enough, my most successful turkey reworkings have been when I've taken it out of its nor-mal register. Drenched in a number of South-Asiany or Far-Easternish dressings, even uncovered and leftover breast meat plumps up and gains lusciously in taste and texture.

I think you have to take as your starting point, though, the unreconstructed bird – which in my book, means leaving it cold and just adding salad and chutneys to it – and a thick seasonally red soup before, or to offer as a replacement for those who, like my husband, inexplicably don't like cold meats. And for all that I've said not to re-cook the turkey, I offer you the two exceptions to this rule.

The first is my agent Ed Victor's celebrated turkey hash (which also appeared in *How to Eat* but like the turkey deserves rehashing) – when in truth the meat is not so much re-cooked as warmed through – and a turkey and ham pie. You always start a pie, at least I do, with cooked meat and it just warms up alongside some similarly leftover ham, in its white sauce as the crust bakes to a welcoming gold glaze.

RED SOUP

This soup is so damn Christmassy it's ridiculous. Given the holidays, I wanted as much redness under my belt as possible (a rather childish approach, but there it is) and since, customarily, in borscht the sweetness of the beets is countered by some cooking apple, it made perfect, festive sense to use sharp, seasonal cranberries instead. The juice and zest of the orange, along with the cloves, make it even more of an evocatively Christmas feast. You can eat it with a supper of cold turkey and salad, or as an altogether sprightlier alternative on its own. It's the sort of soup you might choose for a solitary dinner in front of the tv to make yourself happy and to feel virtuously rewarded.

Normally, beets take *hours* to cook, which is why I suggest you just bung them in the processor first. Actually, I loved the soup as it was when I tasted it in the pan, unpuréed, but truly this works best as a deep-toned, deep-flavored, velvety emulsion.

3 raw beets (weighing approx. 1¹/₄lbs)
1 large red onion
2 tablespoons olive oil (not extra virgin)
1¹/₃ cups cranberries, fresh or frozen

juice and zest of 1 orange
pinch ground cloves
4 cups vegetable stock
³/₄ cup sour cream, optional, for serving

Serves 4–6

note
If I cook this in advance, I leave it in its unpuréed state, whizz it cold then heat it up in a saucepan as and when I want to eat it.

Peel the beets and onion (wearing rubber gloves unless you want a touch of the Lady Macbeths) and chop them roughly. Put the chunks in a food processor and blitz till you've got a ruby-glowing pile of shreds; no need to be too fanatical, you just don't want large pieces evident. Spoon the oil into a large wide-based pan and tip in the onion and beets, and cook them over a gentle heat for 10 minutes or so. When they have begun to sweat down and soften, add the cranberries (no need to thaw frozen ones), the orange zest and juice and the ground cloves. Stir everything around for a couple of minutes and then pour in the stock. Bring to the boil, then cover the pan and simmer the soup for about 45 minutes to 1 hour. It should then be cooked enough to purée or liquidize to divine smoothness, though you may want to do this in a few batches to spare your kitchen walls.

Taste to see if you want salt or pepper, then pour into a warmed soup tureen and serve. If the idea appeals, pour over a swirl of sour cream into each person's bowl as you hand it out.

ED VICTOR'S TURKEY HASH

I thought of rewriting this in the conventional manner of a cookbook recipe, not that I have ever entirely grasped the convention myself, but in the end felt it would somehow take the character out of it. Nor would it be particularly helpful: a recipe that deals in leftovers can only be a guide: you add what you've got in whatever quantity remains, really.

But I do want to disagree – naturally – with two key propositions. The first is the notion that green peppers could ever be a good idea in any context (please, a red one). The second is his cheerfully rude sign-off. But what does he know? The man's an agent, after all.

Sauté chopped onions and green peppers in a mixture of butter and olive oil in a large pan. Add diced turkey (white and dark meat) plus any leftover stuffing to the cooked onion and peppers mixture, and cook till warmed through. You can season it at this stage with salt and pepper.

Then stir in pitted ripe black olives and toasted almonds. Finally drizzle over the top some beaten eggs mixed with heavy cream, and stir till set.

Optionally, you can finish the hash off with some grated Parmesan on top and brown it under the broiler.

Voilà! It's usually much, much better than the turkey itself. In fact, it's the only reason to eat turkey on Christmas Day!

TURKEY AND HAM PIE

Since I always cook a ham as well as a turkey round this time, here's what I make with some of what's left over. It's nursery food really, or the addition of corn kernels – essential for us – makes it seem, reassuringly, so. The amounts I give are not meant to be taken too literally, but they just happen to be the quantities that go to make up my usual pie. You could also look at the chicken pot pies on page 240 for guidance on amounts needed if you wanted to make some little individually portioned ones.

If you've cooked the ham in cranberry juice from page 16 – or indeed in Cherry Coke (page 205) – then I advise you against using ham stock for the pie here. If, however, you've cooked it in water or, an old favorite of mine from *How to Eat*, in cider, then go right ahead. To be honest, as often as not, I just add quite a bit of golden concentrated chicken bouillon to some milk to replace both stock and cream.

Serves around 6 depending on ages of eaters

FOR THE CRUST

$^3/_4$ stick cold unsalted butter, diced

1 cup all-purpose flour

1 egg yolk, beaten with a pinch of salt and 1 teaspoon iced water

milk to glaze

FOR THE FILLING

4 tablespoons butter

3 tablespoons all purpose flour

2²/₃ cups ham, chicken or turkey stock

1 cup heavy cream

3¹/₂ cups turkey, dark and white meat, in chunks

1³/₄ cups ham, in chunks

1 cup corn kernels

Make the pastry by first adding the cold diced butter to the flour in a tray or dish that fits in the freezer and freeze for 10 minutes. Then, either in the processor or in a free-standing mixer, rub the butter into the flour until you have something that looks like rubbly sand or oatmeal. Add the iced water, yolk and salt, mixing just till the pastry looks like it's about to come together in a ball, adding more iced water if needed. Form into a disc, wrap in plastic wrap and leave to rest in the fridge for 20 minutes while you get on with the sauce.

Preheat the oven to 375°F. Melt the butter in a decent-sized pan and stir in the flour. When your roux is formed and is smooth and nutty, take the pan off the heat and slowly whisk in the stock. I find my little whisk is what's needed here. When all's smoothly amalgamated, put back on the heat and cook, gently, until it starts thickening. Add the cream and carry on cooking until you've got a smooth, velvety sauce. Add the turkey, ham and corn kernels and then pour into your pie plate.

Roll the pastry out to a circle or oval, depending on the shape of what you're using (I use an 8 cup capacity oval dish measuring 10–11 inches at its longest point), a good inch or so larger in diameter than the dish. Cut out a strip, or strips from the pastry left on your work surface and, wetting the rim of the dish lightly, press this pastry strip down to provide a rim to which the pastry lid can adhere. Now lift the pastry lid to lie on top, cut off excess and pinch the edges to seal, or press down with an upturned fork, so that the tines press in, leaving little indented lines. This is easier to do than to explain, but see the pies on page 242 which I have forked round the edges as here. Make a few slashes in the pastry for steam to escape. Dip a pastry brush into some milk and paint to glaze lightly. Put in the oven for 20–30 minutes or until the pastry is a pale, welcoming gold.

I mooted earlier the inexplicably Asian influence in my dealings with the post-Thanksgiving/post-Christmas turkey. What follows, then, are three examples of this, my new-found genre. On top of that, in the spirit of global goodwill, I offer a turkey salad *all'Italiana* and one that is nothing if not essentially, toothsomely, North American.

BANG BANG TURKEY

One of the things that pleases me about this recipe is its name, so particularly resonant after a long and clamorous family Christmas lunch, but I love, most, its subtly fiery flavor. I know it's a bore having to get hold of Chinese vinegar and chilli-bean sauce but it's these ingredients that see off the glottally clotting gooeyness of the peanut butter. The sauce itself makes more than enough to coat the amount of turkey specified, but if you're making it you might as well make enough sauce for more than one outing: it's also very good dribbled over some hot-grilled chicken or pork chops or to dress an otherwise plain cucumber salad.

Serves 4–6

FOR THE BANG BANG SAUCE

2 teaspoons peanut oil

3 tablespoons smooth peanut butter

2 tablespoons Chinese chilli bean sauce

1 tablespoon superfine sugar

1 tablespoon soy sauce

$1^1/_2$ tablespoons Chinese black vinegar

2 tablespoons water

FOR THE SALAD

3 cups cold shredded turkey

1 medium head iceberg lettuce, 6 cups finely shredded

$^1/_2$ cup fresh cilantro, chopped

$^1/_2$ cup fresh mint, chopped

4oz cucumber

1 scallion

To make the sauce, heat the oil in a small saucepan, and let it cool. Pour it into a bowl, add the remaining ingredients and stir or whisk to make a smooth, thickly runny paste. That's it. And you can make it in advance and leave in a jam jar or bowl covered with plastic wrap for at least a week.

Arrange the shredded lettuce over the base of a large flat plate, then sprinkle the chopped cilantro and mint over the top. Drip 4–5 tablespoons of bang bang sauce over the lettuce and herbs and, in a smallish bowl, add 4 tablespoons to the turkey strips, turning them in the sauce until they are well coated.

Arrange the peanutty turkey strips in a rough line down the middle of the salad, and then just peel and deseed the cucumber and cut into fine strips. Halve the scallion and finely slice that too in long strips, then sprinkle both over the turkey. Dribble over a tablespoon or so more of sauce and your exertions are over.

VIETNAMESE TURKEY AND GLASS NOODLE SALAD

I am not going to make any false claims here: this salad is not actually from Vietnam, indeed I have no reason to believe they even eat turkey there, but it contains a mixture of Vietnamese elements. The first is the dressing, salty, sour, sweet and headily spiked with ginger, chilli and garlic, and then there are the noodles, eaten not hot but slippery-cool to form the basis of a light but still filling salad. I've specified glass noodles (sometimes known as cellophane or beanthread noodles) but you could easily substitute rice vermicelli.

I find a fine Microplane grater the best way of dealing with the garlic and ginger, but a mean hand with a sharp knife would no doubt do as well. Again, the dressing makes enough to be brought out for service later on in the week, too.

FOR THE DRESSING

2 cloves garlic, minced or crushed

2 fresh long red chillies, deseeded
  and finely diced

2 tablespoons finely minced
  ginger

4 tablespoons fish sauce (nam pla)

juice of 1 lime

4 tablespoons water

2 tablespoons superfine sugar

FOR THE SALAD

8oz cold turkey, cut into fine strips

6oz beanthread or glass noodles

4oz/$1^1/_2$ cups sugar-snap peas

4oz/2 cups bean sprouts

3 scallions, sliced into thin
  circles

2 teaspoons peanut oil

1 teaspoon sesame oil

$^1/_2$ cup fresh cilantro, finely
  chopped

Serves 4–6

note

This is highly addictive and you'd be well advised to keep the ingredients for it on hand at all times. (Certainly, I always have a small jam jar of the dressing in the fridge.) When not trying to use up seasonal remains, you could obviously replace the turkey with chicken, but I love this too, with shrimp.

To make the dressing simply mix all the ingredients together. This will keep very well in a tightly sealed jar in the fridge for at least a week.

To make the salad, marinate the turkey strips in $^1/_2$ cup of the Vietnamese dressing and while this is going on soak the noodles in freshly boiled water and once rehydrated (see package instructions) refresh them in cold water, then drain.

Put the sugar-snaps and bean sprouts into a colander and pour over them freshly boiled water from a kettle. Rinse them with cold water and drain well – just shaking the colander – so they're not actually wet.

In a large bowl, mix the marinated turkey strips, juicy with sauce and flecked with chilli, with the drained noodles, scallions, sugar-snaps and bean sprouts.

Dress with the oils and 2 tablespoons more of the Vietnamese dressing, though do taste to see if you want to add any more. It really depends on how astringent you want this. Sprinkle over the chopped cilantro and toss everything together well before arranging on a large plate.

RED SEASONAL SALAD

For someone who's never been to Vietnam, I am piling up quite a few recipes which are Vietnamese in inspiration if not origin. This is a festively toned take on what is sometimes referred to as "Vietnamese coleslaw," according to the great Nicole Routhier in her introduction to the *echt* version, *ga xe phay*. This one has the virtue of being pronounceable for those of us who are ill-travelled, and of celebrating the seasonal as well as seasonally evocative color: turkey takes the place of the more regular chicken and red cabbage stands in for the plain white one. Red onion and radishes are added (by me, too) for flavor and crunch and, yes, color.

2 red chillies	**black pepper**	Serves 8
1 clove garlic	**4 cups cold cooked turkey,**	
2 tablespoons superfine sugar	**shredded**	
3 teaspoons rice vinegar	**1¹/₂lbs red cabbage approx. 8 cups**	
juice of 1 lime, or 3 tablespoons	**when chopped**	
4 tablespoons fish sauce (nam pla)	**8oz radishes**	
3 tablespoons vegetable oil	**5 tablespoons chopped fresh cilantro**	
1 red onion		

Finely chop the chillies with or without seeds depending on how hot you like it, and drop them in a large bowl, in fact the largest bowl you have, then mince in the garlic. Add the sugar, vinegar, lime juice, fish sauce and vegetable oil. Peel and finely slice the red onion into half moons and add it to the mixture in the bowl, grind over some black pepper and leave to steep for 15 minutes, making sure everything's immersed in the astringent liquid.

Add the shredded turkey and leave to marinate for a further 15 minutes. Shred the red cabbage as finely as you can and add to the bowl. Cut the radishes into eight segments rather as you would open an orange (this way you get both more crunch and more red in each slice than if you'd cut the radishes in fine rounds).

Mix the cabbage and radishes into the bowl with the steeped turkey in its oniony dressing (which is why you needed to start with your biggest bowl) and toss together very well. Work through about half of the chopped cilantro and sprinkle the remaining half on top of the salad when you turn it out on to a plate or serving dish.

This is one of the salads, rather like the North American one on page 60, that is so crunchy and full of chew that you really feel you're getting a jaw and chin work-out as you eat it, which I find very satisfying, both psychologically and digestively.

NORTH AMERICAN SALAD

Since this salad was made up by me in my kitchen in London, there is an argument that says it isn't remotely American, North or otherwise. But it seemed to me that a salad comprising turkey, wild rice, cranberries and pecans couldn't really go under any other name.

Whatever it's called, it's fabulous.

Serves 6–8

note

By dried sliced cranberries, I mean the ones that are often sold in little tubs in the supermarket and which come ready chopped, but regular dried cranberries would do just fine; try and steer clear, though, of the ultra-sweet, almost candied cranberries.

I make this salad regularly without the turkey – or indeed any meat – component. It also happens to be strangely good, and very beautiful, as a side salad to serve with cold poached salmon.

3 cups wild rice
$^1/_2$ cup dried sliced cranberries
4 cups diced cold cooked turkey
2 tablespoons cranberry sauce or jelly

2 tablespoons lime juice
$^1/_4$ cup olive oil
$^1/_2$ cup halved pecans or pecan pieces
$^1/_2$ cup chopped flat-leaf parsley leaves

Cook the rice according to the package instructions, rinse and leave to cool.

Add the dried cranberries and turkey to the cold, cooked rice.

Make a dressing with the cranberry jelly, lime juice and oil by whisking everything together in a bowl.

Toss the dressing through the rice, cranberries and turkey. Snap the pecans in half (or if you're using pieces, just leave them as they are) and add to the salad with most of the parsley, turn out on to a plate or serving dish and sprinkle with the remaining parsley.

Opposite: top left, a pitcher of seasonal breeze; top right, insalata di tacchino; below, North American salad

INSALATA DI TACCHINO

The flounce into Italian is an innocent indication of exuberance, but it's also a nod to the origin of this turkey salad. I cobbled it together after remembering a really wonderful cold poached turkey, with Belgium endive and scattered with pomegranate seeds and pine nuts, I'd eaten while driving through northern Italy one November or December many winters ago. These days I cook rather more than I travel, but I'm happy with that.

All salads are provisional: that's to say, nothing needs to be exact, and both content and quantity depend to some extent on circumstance. So do feel free to change this according to how many people you need to feed and what you have in the way of greens or leftovers in the fridge. It's Christmassy by virtue of the turkey component, and is an excellent use for the meat left over from the Big Lunch, but it also works fabulously well with cold pheasant (the only good use for pheasant at all I can truly think of) or cold chicken. And the pomegranate, too, also makes it joyfully seasonal.

I've made this to be enough for about four people, but again, it's hard to be specific as it depends on what else you're serving with it.

Serves 4

note

If you're at all worried about the dryness of the turkey, then take a leaf out of the South-East Asiany salads above, and make up a salted lemony olive oil dressing and let the pieces of meat steep in it for a while before assembling the whole insalata and adding a squeeze of pomegranate juice when it's on the plate. Don't add the pink juice while the meat soaks, because it gives the meat an unappetizingly under-cooked look.

10oz leftover turkey meat, shredded, chunked or sliced
2 tablespoons pinenuts
1 head red radicchio
1 large or 2 small heads of Belgium endive
$2/3$ cup flat-leaf parsley
$1/2$–1 pomegranate, depending on size
2 tablespoons extra virgin olive oil
squeeze of lemon

Toast the pinenuts in a hot oil-less pan until they are scorched and remove to a cold plate while you assemble the salad. Tear off the radicchio and endive leaves and use to line a platter or serving dish. Add most, but not all of your parsley leaves, and then add the turkey bits. Scatter over pomegranate seeds (no need to measure, just use about two-thirds of the seeds from the fruit you have). In a cup mix the olive oil, some salt and pepper, and a squeeze of lemon and then squeeze the pomegranate half to extract a small amount of juice – just enough to give a hint of flavor, not so much as to tint the dressing too pink. Taste for seasoning or sharpness (adding more lemon or oil as you like) and pour lightly over the salad. Now, scatter over the toasted pinenuts, a few more pomegranate seeds and the remaining parsley.

Turkey isn't the only thing you're likely to have left over. In fact, if you didn't have any leftovers it would be a bad sign: from my point of view it wouldn't mean that lunch had been so delicious that not a morsel remained but, rather, that you hadn't provided enough to start with. Plenty is the very minimum you can think of producing. I think, though, this is a temperamental thing: some people fear extravagance, others meanness; in my own case, I just have a neurotic need for too much, too much everything.

STILTON RAREBIT WITH WALNUT AND BIBB LETTUCE SALAD

I'm not sure if, strictly speaking, this counts as leftover fare, but I include it because I always have a lot of cranberry sauce, some walnuts and quite a bit of Stilton hanging around at this time of year. This happens to be a favorite of mine regardless of time of year, too. I could have just suggested it as an ingredient-swap alternative for the Somerset "rabbit" on page 417, but I felt, on balance, that this shortchanged the seasonal offering here.

2 slices sourdough or rustic heavy
   brown bread
1 tablespoon butter
$1^1/_2$ tablespoons all-purpose flour
$1^1/_2$ tablespoons milk
$1^1/_2$ tablespoons white port
$^1/_2$ cup Stilton, rind off and
   crumbled

pepper
2 heads Bibb lettuces
$^1/_4$ cup walnut halves or pieces
1 teaspoon best-quality white wine
   vinegar
2 teaspoons walnut oil
2 tablespoons cranberry sauce

Serves 1 or 2, though halve
the salad requirement for one

note
If you don't have white port, I wouldn't give it another thought, just use vermouth or white wine.

If you don't have a really good white wine vinegar, *do* give it another thought. In fact, use lemon juice instead.

You don't need to use walnut oil, but I had some to hand, and it seemed appropriate: olive would be fine.

And finally, I just want to say that I often make a salad with these ingredients – give or take – to be eaten throughout the year: that's to say a Stilton (or other blue cheese), Bibb and walnut salad, as is inspiringly found on the menu of J. Sheekey, London.

Lightly toast the bread (I use the toaster here) and preheat the broiler to maximum.

Melt the butter in a small-to-medium heavy-based or non-stick saucepan, stir in the flour and cook for a few minutes. Off the heat, whisk in the milk then the white port and then, back on a low heat, stir in the crumbled Stilton. When all's amalgamated, grind in a lot of pepper and spread over the two slices of toast. Sit these on a Silpat or aluminum foil-lined pan and put under the broiler just till the green-blue cheese topping starts to brown and blister.

Remove to two plates. On each plate, alongside make up a quick salad out of one head of lettuce per person, outer leaves removed, and, for each, half the walnuts, $^1/_2$ teaspoon of white wine vinegar and a dribbled-over teaspoonful of oil. Sprinkle emphatically with salt.

Dollop some cranberry sauce next to the cheese on toast, and supper's ready.

CHRISTMAS BUBBLE AND SQUEAK

I think this is a true example of saving the best till last. God, how I love this. Part of the reason I love it so much, is that I always warm to an unplanned entity: I drive everyone mad on a photo shoot, but I am never so happy as when cooking off piste. So, we'd shot all the Thanksgiving and Christmas pictures for this book and the next morning I was just fiddling about in the kitchen, holding up the photographs we were meant to be taking and trying to use up leftovers from the day before for my breakfast; I was so excited with the result that I rushed up to show James, the photographer. He took its picture and we both ate it afterwards.

I am very specific about the ingredients below simply because I recorded exactly what I did and it worked so well, and fitted the pan so exactly. Don't feel obliged to be so painstakingly exact, though. A bubble and squeak is just a mish-mash of leftover potatoes and oniony veg and you should use whatever you want. This is good though: the saltiness of the pancetta; the sweetness of the parsnips and chestnuts; everything just works.

Serves 1–2

note

I've got some skillets that have removable handles and are therefore very useful for food that you want to sear and then bake or roast, but if you can't do that, then just preheat the broiler and cook the bubble and squeak slowly on the stove on one side, then finish it off under the broiler. You could otherwise just treat this like an omelette and fry it on both sides in your pan; just be patient, cooking it very slowly and turning it over very carefully.

10oz cold cooked roast potatoes
8oz cold cooked Brussels sprouts
  with pancetta (see page 30)
2oz cold cooked parsnips

2 scallions
1 egg
1 tablespoon olive oil
1 red chilli, chopped, optional

Preheat the oven to 325°F.

Put everything into a food processor except for the egg, oil and chilli, and process roughly, or chop everything by hand maniacally fine and mix together.

Add the egg and process again; it should resemble a knobbly purée. Heat the oil in a frying pan or sauté pan that can go in the oven, and tip the bubble and squeak into the hot oil in the pan. Fry for 3–5 minutes over a medium heat, leaving it whole like an omelette.

Put the pan in the oven and cook for about 20 minutes. Slide the bubble and squeak out of the pan on to a dish and – if you like a bit of fire, as I do – sprinkle with a Christmas confetti of red chopped chilli. To tell the truth, I'd have been perfectly happy just to dollop on a little chilli sauce, or maybe some drops of Tabasco, but as I was about to finish cooking my bubble and squeak I happened to see that my assistant, Hettie, was just finishing making a very neat pile of chopped chilli for the red seasonal salad, above, and I swooped down and swiped some. When such an opportunity presents itself…

THE SWEET STUFF

This time of year is quite simply unimaginable without the massive sugar-consumption. And I say that as someone who doesn't even have a particularly sweet tooth. Sweetness has always been an important part of festive eating. Within it is the notion of celebrating the sweetness of life, but I think it is significant too that sweet food is not a part of a staple diet, but is an indicator of excessive – and I mean this in a good way – intake. It's about adding what you don't need. Feasting, and on sugar particularly, is the very antithesis of the eat-to-live rule. It's about food as an expression of abundance, exuberance and gleeful luxury.

I haven't included a traditional pumpkin pie, preferring to offer either the warming ballast of the pumpkin and apple crumble below or the scented smoothness of the pumpkin cheesecake, and I felt that there should be some parity between the nations, so if I wasn't including a traditional Thanksgiving dessert, then it would only be fair to leave out a traditional Christmas pudding. Besides, I have given a relatively normal Christmas pudding recipe before (in *How to be a Domestic Goddess*) and I wanted to play a little here.

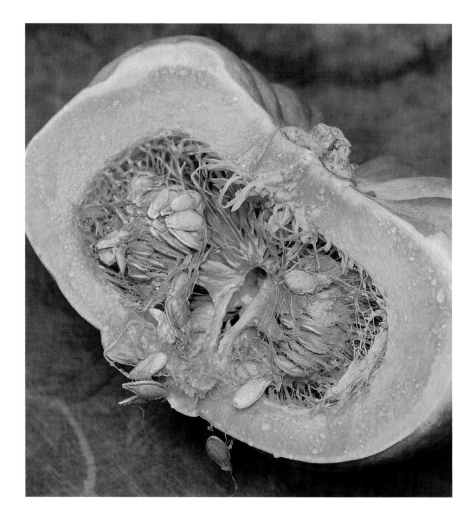

PUMPKIN AND APPLE CRUMBLE

Sweet, grainy cubes of pumpkin turned, with wincingly sour apples, in spiced butter and topped with a brown-sugar rubble of sandy crumble: this is the most cozy, warming dessert you could imagine. But it's its size that also makes it so festive. I cook it in a big round terracotta dish because I like to keep its rough-hewn edges, but you could certainly party it up if you wanted – perhaps steep the sultanas in some calvados or apple jack (as per the apple charlotte on page 427) before adding them to the pumpkin and apple and baking everything in some more chichi piece of oven to tableware.

I use golden sultanas, because I have a bit of a thing about them, but any old raisins would do fine.

3lbs pumpkin, to give 1lb 14oz
   when peeled and deseeded,
   cut into 2in pieces
2 tart cooking apples (2lbs)
1/2 stick butter
1/2 cup sugar

FOR THE TOPPING
2 cups all-purpose flour
1 teaspoon baking powder
1/4 teaspoon baking soda
1/2 cup plus 2 tablespoons cold
   butter

2 tablespoons lemon juice
1/4 teaspoon ground cloves
1 teaspoon ground ginger
1 teaspoon ground cinnamon
3/4 cup sultanas (golden raisins)
vanilla ice cream for serving

1/2 cup plus 2 tablespoons light
   brown sugar
2 tablespoons raw cane sugar or
   demerara sugar

Serves 8–12, depending how much has been eaten earlier

note
If you can't get cooking apples, replace with the sharpest eating apples you can – either Granny Smith or Braeburn probably. And really chop them small, as it's the sour fluff you get from cooking apples that's so good and eating apples don't mush down as much so need as much help as they can get.

Preheat the oven to 375°F.

Put the peeled and chunked pumpkin into a large pan, and peel and core the cooking apples. Cut them to a similar size to the pumpkin and add to the pan with the butter, sugar, lemon juice, spices and sultanas.

Cook over a medium heat for about 10–20 minutes, partially covering with a lid, until the pumpkin and apple have softened. Pumpkin can differ enormously in cooking times, hence the time bracket.

Tip the tender pumpkin and apple into a dish approximately 10in in diameter and 2in deep.

Put the flour, baking powder and baking soda into a bowl and rub in the cold butter to resemble rough oatmeal. Use fingers or a freestanding mixer for this. Fork in the light brown sugar, and then tip the crumble topping evenly over the pumpkin and apple in the dish. Finally sprinkle over the raw cane sugar. Cook for 45 minutes, turning the dish once in the oven to color evenly.

Let the crumble stand for about 20 minutes before serving, with some good vanilla ice cream preferably.

PUMPKIN CHEESECAKE

The pumpkin component here may come out of a can, but I don't see that's anything to be apologetic about. By all means, make your own purée if you prefer (making absolutely sure it is as drained as drained can be before adding it to the cheese) but that isn't the point of the exercise. This is the point: a delicate, rich, palest apricot dessert, fluffier and subtler than your regular cheesecake. And it is undoubtedly easier with a processor, if you have one.

Serves 8–12

note

This is fabulous, too, with the butterscotch sauce from the apple cheesecake on page 208 poured over it.

FOR THE CHEESECAKE BASE

2 cups graham cracker crumbs

1 stick butter, soft

FOR THE FILLING

1 15oz can unseasoned pumpkin purée

1 cup sugar

6 eggs

1$^{1}/_{2}$lbs cream cheese

juice of $^{1}/_{2}$ lemon

Place the graham cracker crumbs in a food processor and then add the butter, cut into pieces. Process until the crumb mixture starts to clump together like damp sand.

Press the crumb mixture into the bottom of a 9in springform pan to create an even layer. Put the pan in the fridge while you make the filling. Preheat the oven to 325°F.

Put the pumpkin purée and cream cheese into the processor and run the motor until the cheese blends into the pumpkin. Add the sugar and with the motor running, break the eggs one at a time down the tube of the processor. Scrape down and process again, adding the lemon juice and blitzing to make a smooth mixture.

Wrap the outside of the crumb-lined springform pan with plastic wrap. I give a good few layers to make sure everything is completely waterproof. Now sit this on a large piece of double-layered heavy-duty aluminum foil and bring it up around the edges of the pan to make a nest. Sit the foil-covered springform pan in a roasting pan.

Scrape the cheesecake filling into the springform pan, and then pour recently boiled water into the roasting pan to a level approximately halfway up the cake pan.

Bake for about 1$^{3}/_{4}$ hours, or until the filling has set with only a small amount of wobble left at its center; it is worth remembering that it will continue to cook as it cools down. Take the pan out of the water bath and sit it on a cooling rack, removing the foil as you do so. When it is cool enough, put the cheesecake in the refrigerator overnight, before removing the sides of the pan to slice.

NONCONFORMIST CHRISTMAS PUDDING

It is still perfectly possible to approach this in the traditional way: that's to say, have all the family in the kitchen with you as you make it, each one giving a stir in turn, the youngest first and the oldest last. In order to honor the three kings, you are meant to stir from east to west, but I don't have a compass and am not good enough at geography to work that one out. Stir-up Sunday, the day on which we are meant to make our puddings before they're left to mature in time for Christmas, falls towards the end of November, on the Sunday after Trinity, and is – as I've written before – a religious rather than a culinary injunction, as in "stir up, we beseech thee, O Lord, the wills of thy faithful people." But in life things are not always quite so clear cut. Some cooks make sure that thirteen ingredients only are used, to signify Jesus and his apostles, but then again, charms were early on included in the mix: a thimble which meant the person who found it in their portion would remain a spinster, a coin to indicate riches to come, a ring to signify a wedding in the offing and so on. Now that we're just interested in money evidently, it's only coins that are buried within the pudding. But there is still a whiff of the superstitious and pagan about the pud: each person is supposed to wish as they stir.

Historically, the Christmas pudding was seen as a religious affront. In 1664, Oliver Cromwell banned it as a "lewd custom," considering the rich pudding "unfit for God-fearing people," and the Quakers rather gloriously condemned it as "the invention of the scarlet whore of Babylon." I have to say I think the Quakers make Christmas pudding sound rather more exciting than it is but, wanting to rise to the occasion, I have tried to come up with a pudding that the scarlet whore of Babylon would be truly proud of.

The dried fruit remains. It has to: it's the basis of the pudding, after all. I've used blueberries and mission figs as well as currants, etc, simply because I had them in the house. It's true that I thought the blueberries gave a touch of luxurious unfamiliarity, and the figs brought with them an echo of the old "figgy pudding," but you don't have to comply. Simply keep the amounts and use whatever dried fruit you please. I have excluded mixed peel because I hate it. If you feel otherwise, do otherwise.

But I do want this to be more than the usual compacted-fruit pudding, much as I like it: I wanted something deep, dark and smoky and so soaked my fruits in coffee liqueur, and added cocoa to the flour and breadcrumbs. Ground almonds are to counteract the possibly drying effect of the cocoa, and butter is in place of the regular suet. The sour cream is above all to make this pudding tender, moist and melting.

2 cups dried mission figs
1 cup dried blueberries
1$^1/_2$ cups currants
$^3/_4$ cup coffee liqueur
1$^1/_2$ sticks unsalted butter
2 cups breadcrumbs
1 cup ground almonds
$^1/_2$ cup good-quality cocoa
$^2/_3$ cup all-purpose flour

1 teaspoon baking powder
$^1/_2$ teaspoon baking soda
1 cup, packed soft dark brown sugar
2 decent-sized eating apples
3 large eggs
$^1/_2$ cup sour cream
1 tablespoon pure vanilla extract

$^1/_2$ tablespoon apple pie spice
$^1/_2$ teaspoon ground nutmeg
1 teaspoon ground cinnamon
$^1/_4$ teaspoon ground cardamom (optional)
coins or charms, washed
1 sprig holly
$^1/_2$ cup vodka

Serves 10–12

note

The best way to clean coins is to soak them overnight in Coca-Cola. Frightening thought, isn't it? Makes them glisten as if newly minted.

If this suits, and if you're soaking the coins anyway, you could soak the dried fruits in coffee liqueur overnight instead of simmering them on the stove for 20 minutes. If so, melt the butter before adding it or just use it very soft, and process it along with the eggs, sour cream and spices.

To turn this back into a traditional pudding: forget the cocoa and just replace with more breadcrumbs; make the dried fruit up of mostly raisins, sultanas (golden raisins), currants and prunes, with slightly reduced quantities of glacé cherries and candied peel; and soak this fruit in rum or brandy; use suet in place of butter, and just stir it into the dry ingredients along with the zest of an orange and 2 teaspoons of pumpkin pie spice.

Butter a 10 or 12 cup heatproof plastic pudding basin, with lid, remembering to grease the lid, too.

Chop the figs in the processor and put in a saucepan with the blueberries and currants and add the coffee liqueur. Bring to a boil and let simmer for 10 minutes. Slice or spoon the butter on top of the simmering fruit and put a lid on, leaving it still to simmer, and the butter to melt, for another 10 minutes.

Measure the breadcrumbs, ground almonds, cocoa, flour, baking powder, baking soda and sugar into a large bowl.

Peel, quarter and core the apples and now bung them in the (not washed-out) processor and chop, or chop as fine as you can by hand; a mezzaluna works best. Add them to the bowl of dry ingredients, along with the dried fruit and butter.

Now, reassemble the processor (I do this to make sure all figgy or apple residue is collected up to go in the pudding but you can just beat the eggs and so forth by hand) and break in the eggs, adding the sour cream, vanilla and spices. Process to mix then pour into the pudding, scraping the sides with a spatula and making sure you've got everything. Finally, add your sparkling cleaned coins.

Mix well with a wooden spoon, either alone or in turn as folk-tradition decrees, and pour into the prepared pudding basin. Cover and steam for 4 hours. I do mine in the couscoussier (the large pan shown on the cover of the book) but you can use a regular steamer or simply stick the pudding basin in a saucepan of boiling water and clamp on a lid. If you can't get the pudding basin into the top part of the steamer and fit on the lid, or don't have a lid for the saucepan you're using, then just cover tightly with aluminum foil, twice: in other words, you have a double thickness and you are sealing the edges twice. Whatever method you're using, though, it's vital you check the water levels regularly so the pan doesn't dry out. I let that happen once and my pudding basin started melting and sticking to the saucepan. I still managed to eat some of the Christmas pudding, though it was beyond redemption as a servable entity.

Take the steamed pudding out of its pan carefully and leave to cool and set somewhere. If you can give it time to mellow and mature it will be better, which is why indeed it makes sense to fall in and take Stir-Up Sunday literally.

Tradition decrees that it will need another 3–4 hours steaming on the day you want to eat it, though without the suet I cannot see, from a logical-culinary perspective, why it should. I just gave it $1^1/_2$ hour's very gentle steaming before eating and it was just fine. What I would say, having tried this, is that I would give it longer if it doesn't make life harder: it certainly will go stickier and denser the longer it steams.

When you're ready to eat it, unmold, stick a sprig of holly on top and warm up the vodka for flambéing. It just isn't done not to flambé this, but it's not – quite – as frightening as that sounds. Traditionalists use brandy; I use vodka for its purer, more enduring flame. So, when the vodka's warm, strike a match, light it and pour it over the pudding. Then, in absolute discordance with all possible health and safety initiatives, bearing it aloft make a dash for the dining table so everyone can see this fabulous, flickering spectacle.

Serve with the rum butter, below. And since it is quite different in taste from a traditional Christmas pudding, you could take a very unorthodox route and provide coffee ice cream as an accompaniment. I would.

I think this is quite enough for ten, even twelve, adults; I've never met a child who likes Christmas pudding (only the coins in it) so I haven't pandered to juvenile taste here – it is very intense, very grown-up.

RUM BUTTER

I never, ever thought I would veer one little bit from my mother's brandy butter, but life's unpredictable. This is essentially the same, in that I've kept her addition of the ground almonds, for that marzipanny depth, but I have replaced the brandy with rum. The rum must be good – dark and mellow and not the cough-inducing stuff that could be used to strip paint.

I hate to say it, but this is better.

1¹/₂ cups confectioners' sugar
1 stick plus 2 tablespoons softened unsalted butter

¹/₂ cup ground almonds
3 tablespoons good dark rum, or to taste

Serves 10–12

The easiest way to make this is by using a processor, if you have one (but see note alongside if not). Quite simply, it means you don't need to sift the sugar. So, put the confectioners' sugar in the processor and process to get rid of any lumps. Add the soft butter and process again to mix well, and then scrape down the sides and add the ground almonds and process yet again. Now, with the motor running add the rum, tasting as you go, even though it gives you the onerous task of taking the lid off after each tablespoon. You may find one spoonful all you want; you may find that the suggested 3 is far from enough: it is a question of taste and what is lethally strong for one person seems insipid to another. You must please yourself since you can't please everyone.

note
If you're making this by hand, as my mother always did, or using a mixer, you will need to sift the sugar. Cream the butter until soft and then add the sifted confectioners' sugar and beat them together till pale and creamy. Mix in the ground almonds and when all is smooth add the rum a little at a time.

If you can get golden or unrefined confectioners' sugar, then do: it brings a glorious fudginess that is fabulous with the almonds and rum and, indeed, the pudding.

STAR-TOPPED MINCE PIES

I used to think that making your own mince pies was a ridiculous notion. Believe me, it isn't. There's nothing wrong in buying rather than baking and no one should embark on these out of a sense of grudging duty. There's no "should"; but I get pleasure out of these, both in the making and the eating. They are tiny things, one light, deceptively light I confess, mouthful each. The recipe is pretty well as it was in *How to be a Domestic Goddess*; I couldn't, in all immodest honesty, see how to improve upon it.

You can use good store-bought mincemeat, though making your own (see overleaf) is unnervingly straightforward.

Makes 36

$1^2/_3$ cups all-purpose flour
$^1/_4$ cup vegetable shortening
$^1/_2$ stick unsalted butter
juice of 1 orange
pinch salt
approx. $^1/_2$ cup mincemeat
1 large egg, mixed with a tablespoon
  water, to glaze, optional

confectioners' sugar for dusting
tray of miniature tart tins, each
  indent $2^3/_4$ inches in diameter
$2^1/_4$ inch fluted round cookie
  cutter
$1^3/_4$ inch star cutter

Measure the flour out into a shallow bowl or dish and, using a teaspoon, dollop in little mounds of vegetable shortening, add the butter, diced small, shake to cover and put in the deep freeze for 20 minutes. Mix the orange juice and salt and leave in the fridge to chill.

Empty out the flour and fat into the bowl of the food processor (or see note if you're doing it in a mixer or by hand) and blitz until you've got a pale pile of oatmeal-like crumbs. Add the salted juice down the funnel, pulsing till it looks as if the dough is about to cohere; you want to stop just before it does (even if some orange juice is left). If all your juice is used up and you need more liquid, add some iced water. Turn out of the processor and, in your hands, combine to a dough. Then form into three balls (since you're going to have to make these in three batches, unless you've got enough tart tins to make all 36 pies at once). Press each ball down into a fat disc and wrap each in plastic wrap and put in the fridge to rest for 20 minutes. Preheat the oven to 450°F.

Roll out the discs one at a time as thinly as you can without exaggerating; in other words, you want a light pastry crust, but one sturdy enough to support the dense mincemeat. This is very easy-going dough, so you don't have to pander to it: just get rolling and patch up as and when you need.

Out of each rolled-out disc in front of you cut out circles a little wider than the indentations in the trays. Press these circles gently into the molds and dollop in a scant teaspoon of mincemeat. Then cut out your stars – re-rolling the pastry as necessary – and place them lightly on top of the mincemeat.

note
If you prefer to use a standing mixer to make the pastry, put the bowl in the fridge to chill while the flour and fats are in the freezer for their 20 minutes. Use the flat paddle to cut in the fat and add liquid as above. I often, however, find the pastry uses more liquid in the mixer than the processor.

Right: mini apple pies and mincepies, palely unglazed, but dusted with confectioners' sugar

If you want to glaze the mince pies, then brush the stars with a pastry brush dipped into the egg and water mix. Sometimes I do, sometimes I don't: the difference really is one of appearance and only you can decide whether you want them pale and matt or gold and shiny.

Put in the oven and bake for 10–15 minutes: keep an eye on them as they really don't take long and ovens do vary. Remove from the oven, prising out the little pies right away and letting the empty tin cool down before you start putting in the pastry for the next batch. Carry on until they're all done. Dust over some confectioners' sugar by sifting it through a tea-strainer before serving them.

RHUBARB VANILLA MINCEMEAT

While I'm perfectly happy with the mincemeat recipes I've given before, I did want to do something different here. Not out of a desire for novelty in itself – this really isn't the time – but because last year, I came across some beautiful pink rhubarb early (which also explains the crumble for Christmas Eve, above) and suddenly felt it could provide the same, necessary, pectiny sourness for which cooking apples are normally used. Having decided on rhubarb, the idea of using vanilla seeds, deeply aromatic, black, wet and grainy, as a spice rather than vapid flavoring, was obvious: they form a ready partnership.

Mincemeat no longer contains meat, but it often has suet. This recipe doesn't: it is fatly, pleasurably mouthfilling all on its own.

Makes 5 cups

note

You will see from the mince pie recipe that only a teensy weensy bit of mince is needed for them, in which case you might feel that cooking up this amount of mincemeat is excessive. I don't see that as a problem in itself, but by all means halve the recipe if you prefer. However, arguments in favor of cooking the whole batch – other than the seasonally persuasive one of excess for its own festive sake – are that jars of mincemeat make very good presents. Also, I love mincemeat mixed with very sharp cooking apple in a crumble (you could follow the apple and pumpkin recipe on page 67 as a blueprint) or, indeed, used in various ways in cake and pastries. Basically, where you might add jam, you could substitute this mincemeat. My mother loved it spread on toast.

$2^1/_4$lbs rhubarb, trimmed and cut into $^1/_4$ inch slices to give 8 cups
2 cups dark brown sugar
2 vanilla beans
2 teaspoons ground mixed spice, such as apple pie spice

$1^1/_2$ cups raisins
$1^1/_2$ cups sultanas (golden raisins)
$1^1/_2$ cups currants
2 tablespoons brandy

Put the sliced rhubarb with the sugar into a large pan. Cut the vanilla pod into halves lengthways and scrape out the seeds, then cut each half into pieces, adding seeds and pod slices to the pan. Add the mixed spice and cook for about 5 minutes.

Add the dried fruits and simmer the pan for about 30 minutes. Stir in the brandy, and take off the heat. When its cool enough to handle, bottle in jars. How easy do you want me to make it?

MINI APPLE PIES

Mincemeat, however, isn't for everyone, so I have these tiny little spice-bronzed apple pies as an alternative. The pastry's the same, and the filling takes hardly any time to make. I have a special holly leaf cluster cutter which I use, in place of the stars, to make the lid, but feel free to cover the pies as you like: an apple cutter (and see the individual apple pies on page 347) would be good in a decidedly non-Christmassy way – perhaps for a harvest festival? – or you can simply cut out rounds and top the pies plainly, remembering to wet the rims to help them stick, pinching them to secure and then stabbing them once in the middle, with the fine point of a small sharp knife, to make an air vent.

mince pie pastry (see page 72)

1 large egg, mixed with a tablespoon
   water, to glaze, optional

Makes 36

FOR THE FILLING

2 Cox's or other firm tart apples
   (13oz total weight)

1 tablespoon superfine sugar

$1/_8$ teaspoon ground cloves

$1/_2$ teaspoon ground cinnamon

$1/_2$ teaspoon pure vanilla extract

zest of 1 orange, plus 1 tablespoon
   orange juice

1 teaspoon lemon juice

1 tablespoon butter

Peel, core and – relatively finely – chop the apples. Put them into a saucepan with all of the other filling ingredients and cook over a medium heat with the lid on for 5 minutes or until soft.

Transfer to a bowl and let the mixture cool.

Using the mince pie pastry on page 72, line the miniature tart tins in the same way and fill them with a scant teaspoon – it's probably nearer a heaped $1/_2$ teaspoon – of the apple mixture. Use whatever cutter you want to make lids, and paint or not with a glaze, as you like, baking in a 425°F oven for 10–15 minutes as for the mince pies.

IF IT'S CHRISTMAS IT MUST BE CRANBERRIES...

Just as this time of year invites the very making of desserts, so it makes a special case for the seasonal inclusion of cranberries. Since they come frozen, as well as dried, there's no real reason not to use them for the rest of the year, but somehow that doesn't seem quite right. Here and now is where they belong.

To be honest, since I grew up before fresh cranberries were much in evidence (in Britain, cranberries meant cranberry sauce, out of a jar), I've had to come to cooking with them gradually. Sometimes, their mouthpuckering sourness can be just too wince-makingly much. But the recipes that follow, together with the savory recipes that include them above, are all ones that make me feel Yule-spirited and jubilant and full of red-berried brightness.

CRANBERRY JAM

Most jams have to be carefully boiled with lemon or pectin along with the sugar to make the fruit set and turn from being a purée to a preserve: here the fruit does it all for you. Such is the pectin-intensity of the cranberry, that it pretty well sets to jam once the berries have burst. So if the idea of a jam recipe daunts, just relax in the knowledge that it means no more than putting fruit and sugar in a pan, cooking it relatively briefly then allowing to cool.

Makes 4 cups   **4 cups cranberries**   **1³/₄ cups superfine sugar**

Put a film of water in the bottom of a large saucepan and add the cranberries and sugar.

Stir patiently over a low heat to dissolve the sugar; this will take a little while. Turn up the heat and boil the pan rapidly until setting point is reached, approximately 7 minutes. (Alternatively it will have reached a jam like consistency.)

Pour the jam into a sterilized 1¹/₂ cup jar and seal immediately.

You have options here: you can use the cranberry jam just as it is, on warm, buttery croissants or bread, toast and so on, or you can use it as an alternative filling for the mince pies, on page 72.

I don't think you need an excuse to make it – it looks so ludicrously, festively red as it cooks, that that's impetus enough for me – but the cranberry Bakewell tart that follows really is the perfect seasonal pastry: a rich, sweet treat.

CRANBERRY BAKEWELL TART

In *How to Eat*, there's a fresh raspberry–cranberry tart, in which I did away with the sugar-iced top, replacing it with some plain, slivered almonds. Here, I've let the tart return to type. The sour edge to the sweet red cranberry jam, which lies between the buttery, crisp almond pastry and the even more buttery frangipane topping, allows for some unapologetic sweetness on top. But the real reason for it is that I'd found some beautiful gold sugar stars at the cake-making shop, and wanted an excuse to use them. If you can't find them, any gold sprinkles/nonpareils would be fine. As a further seasonal variation I make the icing up with clementine juice (the zest's gone fragrantly into the frangipane). Or forget the icing and sprinkle with slivered almonds as on the Bakewell slice on page 222.

Serves 8–10

note
I use instant royal icing because it's easy and makes for a denser firmer frosting, but you could just as easily use regular confectioners' sugar, in which case heat up the fruit juice before mixing. Or see the royal icing recipe on page 429.

FOR THE PASTRY
1¹/₄ cups all-purpose flour
¹/₃ cup ground almonds
¹/₃ cup confectioners' sugar
1 stick plus 1 tablespoon butter, cold and diced
1 egg, beaten
pinch salt
1–3 tablespoons iced water

Put the flour, almonds and confectioners' sugar into a food processor and pulse together. Add the diced butter and process again until the mixture resembles oatmeal. Or rub it by hand or mix in a standing mixer.

Beat together the beaten egg, salt and iced water, and tip down the funnel of the food processor as it is running to bind the pastry. Add more iced water if the pastry has not come together completely. The same goes for whatever method you're using. The almonds make this into a wonderfully pliable, Play-Doh of a pastry.

Form the pastry into a flat disc, wrap in plastic wrap and leave to rest in the fridge while you make the filling.

FOR THE FILLING
1 stick plus 1 tablespoon butter
¹/₂ cup plus 2 tablespoons superfine sugar
3 eggs
zest and juice of 1 clementine
1¹/₄ cups ground almonds
1 cup cranberry jam (see page 76)
8oz instant royal icing
few gold sugar stars or other decorations

Preheat the oven to 400°F.

Melt the butter, and leave it to cool slightly. Beat together the sugar, eggs and zest, and then add the melted butter. Stir in the ground almonds.

Roll out the disc of pastry to fit a 10 inch deep fluted tart pan, with a removable base, and prick the base with a fork. Spread the jam on to the base of the pastry and pour over the almond mixture, taking care to cover all of the jam.

Bake in the oven for 45 minutes. The filling will rise and look puffy in places but once it comes out of the oven it will fall back again to form an even surface. Leave the tart to cool completely on a wire rack.

When the tart has cooled, slip the base out from the sides and sit it on a plate. Make up the instant royal icing with the juice from the clementine and as much water as you need to make a thick but spreadable icing; the clementine juice (though of course orange would work as well) makes the icing a very pleasing pale peachy ivory. Work over the top of the tart and decorate as you wish.

CRANBERRY, ORANGE AND ALMOND PUDDING

Although I am evidently pleased with the cranberry jam, I wouldn't want it to dominate too much. One of the things about seeing all those bright bulging bags of cranberries around at this time of year, is that you want to think of different ways to cook them. The idea for this came to me when I read a very simple recipe, printed by that fantastic entity, the Pudding Club, which actually, I seem to remember, used apples. As you might imagine with anything of such a provenance, it is traditional, comforting, rib-sticking stuff. But that's just what you want at this time of year; a certain amount of seasonal indulgence is surely desirable. Don't fight it. Why can't you just do what everyone else does and promise yourself that you'll practise restraint come the New Year...

I call this a "pudding," but it has something of a soft-set pie about it: tender cake above and below, oozy fruit in the middle. Eat with custard preferably (and see the recipe on page 42, maybe substituting orange zest for the vanilla), but ice cream or softly whipped heavy cream are also fabulously good with it.

FOR THE FRUIT

Serves 4–6

$^1/_2$ stick unsalted butter
$4^1/_2$ cups cranberries

3 tablespoons superfine sugar

FOR THE BATTER

$1^1/_4$ cups all-purpose flour
2 teaspoons baking powder
$^1/_2$ teaspoon baking soda
$1^3/_4$ cups plus 2 tablespoons
  superfine sugar

2 eggs, beaten
1 stick unsalted butter, melted
few drops orange oil
$^1/_3$ cup slivered almonds
  raw brown sugar to sprinkle over

Preheat the oven to 325°F.

Melt the $^1/_2$ stick butter in a wide saucepan then add the cranberries and sugar. Cook over a fairly high heat until the fruit begins to pop. This will take hardly any time if the cranberries are fresh, and about 10 minutes if they're frozen. Remove the pan from the heat.

Combine the flour, baking powder, baking soda and superfine sugar in a large bowl and add the eggs, melted butter and orange oil. Mix to a smooth batter. Pour half the batter into a 2 pint round pie plate. Cover with the cranberries, then top with the remaining batter – don't worry if the cranberries are not covered completely.

Sprinkle slivered almonds and raw sugar over and cook in the oven for 45 minutes to an hour, until the top is golden brown and set.

ICE CREAM WITH CRANBERRY SYRUP

If the cranberry, orange and almond pudding is Aran-sweatered, thick-set comfort food, then this is very different: cool, satiny ice cream with a cranberry syrup so jewel-bright and shiny it could be made of molten lip gloss. My great aunt used to make an ice cream studded with raisins and candied peel that she called Australian Christmas Pudding; I loathed it. This, though, is my version, I suppose: something cold and sunny that is at the same time redolent of Christmas.

1 or 2 cartons good vanilla or white chocolate ice cream

Serves 8

FOR THE CRANBERRY SYRUP
1¹/₄ cups superfine sugar   **¹/₂ 12oz package cranberries**
1 cup water

note

To make the syrup, put the sugar and water in a pan and give a good stir, but do not stir thereafter: if you stir a syrup as it cooks it crystallizes and goes gritty; swirling the pan is permissible, however.

      Put the pan on the stove and dissolve the sugar in the water over low heat, then add the berries and bring to the boil, letting the pan boil until the syrup reddens and the berries pop; this will take anything between 5 and 10 minutes depending on the properties of the pan and whether the cranberries went in fresh or frozen. If you're watching the pan, it can seem to take longer.

      Remove to a pitcher, and serve warmish over cold, cold ice cream.

note
I can't help thinking of other possible uses for this syrup, but will try and confine myself to just two. Make a cheesecake along the lines of the apple cheesecake on page 207–8, only use rum in place of the apple schnapps. Make up half the cranberry syrup and use when cooled to dribble, like bumpy red patent leather in oozy liquid form, over the cheesecake instead of the butterscotch and apples. And if you're going for the baked Alaska, on page 86, using vanilla ice cream inside, then this would be wonderful poured over the doled-out bowls, hot, as each person eats.

CRANBERRY AND WHITE CHOCOLATE COOKIES

At this time of year, I think we all find it difficult to keep going between meals. This is the ideal, unnecessary but so gratifying filler, perfect with a cup of tea or, for those of under tea-drinking age, a glass of milk.

The oats make these wonderfully chewy and help convince yourself that they are actually very healthy and good for you. Nothing to feel guilty about at all.

Makes 30

1 cup all-purpose flour
$^1/_2$ teaspoon baking powder
$^1/_2$ teaspoon salt
1 cup rolled oats
1 stick plus 1 tablespoon soft
 unsalted butter
$^1/_2$ cup dark brown sugar

$^1/_2$ cup superfine sugar
1 egg
$^1/_2$ teaspoon pure vanilla extract
$^1/_2$ cup dried cranberries
$^1/_2$ cup pecans, roughly chopped
$^3/_4$ cup white chocolate chips

Preheat the oven to 350°F.

Measure out the flour, baking powder, salt and rolled oats into a bowl.

Put the butter and sugars into another bowl and beat together until creamy – this is obviously easier with an electric mixer of some kind, but you just need to put some muscle into it otherwise – then beat in the egg and vanilla.

Beat in the flour, baking powder, salt and oat mixture and then fold in the cranberries, chopped pecans and chocolate chips or white chocolate, chopped into small dice. Set the bowl of cookie dough in the fridge for 10–15 minutes.

Roll tablespoonfuls of dough into a ball with your hands, and then place them on a lined or greased baking sheet and squish the dough balls down with a fork. You may need two baking sheets or be prepared to make these in two batches.

Cook for 15 minutes; when ready, the cookies will be tinged a pale gold, but be too soft to lift immediately off the baking sheet, so leave the sheet on a cool surface and let them harden for about 5 minutes. Remove with a spatula or whatever to cool fully on a wire rack.

MASSACRE IN A SNOWSTORM

Few foods are more nostalgically Christmassy for me than pomegranates. I still remember trying to winkle out the seeds from the pomegranate my Christmas stocking always contained. This recipe is a seasonal take on Eton Mess, that summer pudding of berries, crumbled meringue and whipped cream. It is an instant, unimprovable pudding whenever you need one and yet don't have the time for any real cooking.

Readers of a more sensitive disposition might be reassured to know that this started off life on a tv "Christmas Special" I did a year or so back, as "pomegranate meringue mountain," but this is what we actually called it ourselves.

2 cups heavy or whipping cream   Serves 6
1 package 8 individual meringue nests (preferably some that are squidgy in the middle)
3 pomegranates

Whip the cream until thick. Roughly crumble in seven of the meringue nests – you need chunks for the texture. Halve the pomegranates and hold one half, cut side down, over the meringues and cream. Take a heavy wooden spoon and whack the pomegranate with it; after a few hits the glorious red beads will rain down into the mixture. Repeat with the remaining pomegranates, reserving one half for later. When you've got most of the seeds out, press the emptied halves together in your hands to squeeze out some of the juice. The seeds are the main thing, though: too much juice and the cream will be too liquid to hold its shape.

Fold the cream, fruit and juice together and turn the mixture on to a large plate in a rough mound. Scatter over the seeds from the remaining pomegranate half then sprinkle over the finely crumbled reserved meringue, allowing the seeds and meringue to spill over the plate and rim.

PIÈCES DE RÉSISTANCE

CHESTNUT CHEESECAKE

There is no doubt about it, anything with chestnuts in it, even if they come vacuum-packed or canned and are perennially available, is so right for this time of year. And I should alert you here, to the chocolate chestnut cake on page 297, which so shrieks Christmas. This hums the tune, but in a subtler key. The chestnuts are present, in the form of a gritty, grainy sweetened purée: some to add to the cookie base; some to fold through the plain cheesecake filling before baking; and yet more – well, it is Christmas – to drip in a thick syrup over the cake when served. And yet, you know, the chestnuttiness is not blaring: there is something undeniably festive about this, but not in a full-on, party hat kind of a way.

As with all cheesecakes, you need to bake this the day before you want to serve it.

Serves 8

FOR THE BASE

4oz/2 cups Graham cracker crumbs
1/2 stick butter
1 heaped tablespoon sweetened
   chestnut purée

FOR THE CHEESECAKE

2 cups cream cheese
3/4 cup superfine sugar
3 eggs
3 egg yolks
3/4 cup sour cream
1 teaspoon lime juice
1 teaspoon vanilla extract
1–2 tablespoons rum
1 cup sweetened chestnut purée

FOR THE SYRUP

1/3 cup water
1/4 cup rum
1 tablespoon sweetened chestnut
   purée
1/4 cup superfine sugar
1 tablespoon butter

Preheat the oven to 350°F, and put the kettle on to boil.

For the base, process the crackers, butter and heaped tablespoon chestnut purée until like fine crumbs. Press the mixture into the bottom of a 9 inch springform pan and place in the fridge while you make the filling.

Beat the cream cheese until smooth and add the sugar. Add the eggs and egg yolks, beating them in one by one until they are incorporated into the cream cheese and sugar. Pour in the sour cream, lime juice, vanilla extract and rum, and beat again until smooth and creamy. Finally fold in the sweetened chestnut purée. Don't worry about making a fully amalgamated mixture: smooth cream cheese with grainy streaks of chestnut is just fine.

Line the outside of the springform pan containing the crumb base with a good wrapping of plastic wrap, so that the whole of the bottom and sides are enveloped in plastic. Do the same with aluminum foil, covering the layer of plastic wrap to make a very watertight casing. Stand the springform, thus covered, in a roasting pan and pour in the chestnut filling. Once that's done, pour water from a recently boiled kettle into the roasting pan to come just over an inch up the side of the pan (the plastic wrap will make it bob up and down a bit) and place in the oven to cook for an hour.

When the cheesecake's ready it should be just set on top with a hint of wobble underneath; it certainly carries on cooking as it cools. Take the cheesecake out of the roasting pan, take off the foil and plastic wrap and let the cheesecake cool on a rack. Refrigerate overnight before unmolding and leaving it to get back to room temperature. If you need to unmold it long before you want to eat it (I often do just because I like to get all bothersome stuff out of the way before people arrive) then just sit it on its serving plate in the fridge until about 20–30 minutes before you want to eat it. I'd take it out as you sit down to dinner or lunch or whatever.

You can make the syrup in advance but do not pour over until the actual point of serving.

You just put all of the syrup ingredients into a saucepan and melt together. Let the syrup boil for 10 minutes, then cool to just warmish (or even room temperature) before criss-crossing the top of the cheesecake with it.

BAKED ALASKA

I had originally intended a recipe for baked Alaska to go into *Forever Summer*. Indeed, I went as far as creating one during the photo shoot. But the minute it was made, I looked at it and knew I wanted to save it for a snowy day. What's more, I knew it was crying out for a small plastic figure skiing downhill on it. Am I right or am I right? I still think it's a viable proposition for summer, too, but I feel it deserves a proper, Christmas unveiling.

It's not as hard as you might think to make; I take it for granted that the ice cream will be bought. If you can find good quality raspberry ripple ice cream, do use that. Otherwise, I think I'd probably just go for vanilla, but the choice is yours.

Serves 8–10

FOR THE BASE

1 stick butter	$^1/_4$ cup cornstarch
6 egg yolks	1 teaspoon baking powder
$^1/_2$ cup superfine sugar	1 teaspoon pure vanilla extract
$^2/_3$ cup all-purpose flour	finely grated zest 1 lemon

Preheat the oven to 400°F. Butter and line the bottom of a 10 inch springform pan with parchment paper or Silpat.

If using a food processor, put yolks (reserving whites for meringue, later), butter, sugar, flour, cornstarch, baking powder, lemon zest and vanilla in bowl and blitz to a thick, smooth yellow batter. Or beat by hand, creaming butter and sugar and then beating in egg yolks, then vanilla and zest and finally the dry ingredients.

Spread into the bottom of the prepared pan and bake for 12–15 minutes until a cake tester comes out clean. Let the shallow Alaska base cool for a little in the pan on a wire rack before unmolding, and let become completely cold before using as the edible platform for your meringue-snow-clad ice-cream mountain. As with all cakes, this is better eaten on the day it's made.

FOR THE MERINGUE AND ICE CREAM

6 egg whites	1 cup superfine sugar
$^1/_4$ teaspoon salt	$1^1/_2$ teaspoons pure vanilla extract
1 teaspoon cream of tartar	2 1 pint cartons ice cream

Preheat the oven to the hottest it will go and make sure you've got a shelf down low.

Whisk the whites until they are foamy, then add the salt and cream of tartar and continue whisking until soft peaks form. Gradually add the sugar, beating well after each addition by which time you should have a thick and glossy meringue mixture. Fold in the vanilla extract.

Allow the ice cream to soften enough to make round balls with an ice-cream scoop. Place the cake on to a lined baking sheet and using both pints make a mountain of ice cream in the middle of the cake (there should be a good edge of cake around the outside). Pile the meringue over the top of the ice cream and completely cover the cake top and sides, creating a mountainous swirly effect. Make sure that there is no ice cream showing through as it will melt in the oven if not protected by the meringue.

Put the as yet unbaked Alaska on its baking sheet into the oven for the barest 5 minutes; don't leave it unattended and do pluck it out of the oven when the meringue has turned a golden color.

I found a skiing person to wodge onto the side, but you may not have quite my weakness for kitsch. Few people have.

BÛCHE DE NOËL

I've never gone in for Yule logs or roulades but this is so pleasing, so wonderfully Christmassy to look at and gooily seductive to the melting bite, that I am happy to make a culinary volte face.

Don't be put off by the rolling you need to do: for one, this flourless mixture is beautifully pliable, and for another, the icing you make will cover any hole or blip.

Indeed, it isn't until you ice it that it looks even remotely like the Yule log you have intended it to be. Once you've sliced the ends off the rolled-up cake at an angle, fashioned a twig or two out of some cut-off pieces of cake, covered everything in chocolate icing and etched – with a skewer or anything on hand in the kitchen – some wood-markings, it suddenly and gratifyingly comes to life.

Children – who hate Christmas cake as a rule – love this. But then, so do adults; if you're feeding a lot of people, expect great enthusiasm for the bûche and consider making two cakes, rolling them, setting them end to end and then covering them with a double amount, accordingly, of icing.

Makes about 8 slices

FOR THE CAKE

6 eggs, separated

$^3/_4$ cup superfine sugar

2 teaspoons pure vanilla extract

$^1/_2$ cup unsweetened cocoa

FOR THE ICING

6oz semisweet or bittersweet chocolate

2 cups confectioners' sugar

2 sticks soft butter

1 tablespoon pure vanilla extract

3–5 teaspoons confectioners' sugar to decorate

Preheat the oven to 350°F. Line a jelly roll pan with parchment paper, leaving a generous overhang at the ends and sides, and folding the parchment into the corners to help the paper stay anchored.

In a large, clean bowl whisk the egg whites until foamy and thick, then add $^1/_4$ cup of the sugar and continue whisking until the whites are holding peaks but not dry.

In another bowl, whisk the egg yolks and remaining sugar until they are pale and thick. Add the vanilla extract and sift over the cocoa, then fold both in.

Lighten the yolk mixture with a couple of dollops of the whites, folding in gently, and then add the whites in thirds, mixing carefully to avoid losing the air.

Pour the cake mixture into the lined pan, and bake in the oven for 20 minutes. Let the cake cool a little before turning it out on to another piece of parchment paper.

To make the icing, melt the chocolate – either in a bowl suspended over a pan of simmering water or, my preference, in a microwave – and let it cool. Put the confectioners' sugar into a food processor and blitz to remove any lumps, add the butter and process until smooth. Add the cooled melted chocolate and vanilla and pulse again to make a smooth icing.

Trim the long edges of the cake, as well as the shortest edge which should be towards you. Spread some of the icing thinly over the cake, going right out to the edges. Roll up from the short side facing you taking care to get a tight roll from the beginning, and roll up to meet the other short end. Cut one or both ends slightly, at a gentle angle.

Use the cake trimmings to make branches as you wish, and then ice the Yule log with the remaining icing, covering the cut-off ends as well . Create wood-like texture by going along the length of the log with a skewer or somesuch, etching in knots and so on if you feel creative; my decorating implement of choice (and see also the custard cream hearts on page 142) is a small corn-on-the-cob holder. Remember to do wibbly circles, as in tree rings, on each end.

You don't have to dust with confectioners' sugar, but I love the freshly fallen snow effect, so push quite a bit through a small sieve, letting some settle in heaps on the plate or board on which the log sits.

CHRISTMAS TREE DECORATIONS

This isn't the first time out for this recipe, but I've fiddled slightly. This is the recipe I turn to each year in recognition that, yes, it is actually Christmas. Being the same, part of a repeated cycle, is its whole point.

To be honest, I'm not sure I'd bother if it weren't for the children, but if you do find yourself with children at this time of year, either your own or borrowed ones, this is a perfect recipe for entertaining them (without having to run about or go outdoors) for a few hours. You'll need Christmassy cutters.

Makes 35–40

note

Of course you can make the cut-out cookies on page 266 – snowflakes are especially good for this time of year – and they certainly make neater cookies and are more obviously to be eaten but they are not so good for keeping and hanging. These are best for the tree; the cut-out cookies for the table (and stomach). It's not, either, that you can't eat these, but I deliberately add quite a bit of pepper to act as a disincentive to children.

FOR THE COOKIES

2 cups all-purpose flour
pinch salt
1 teaspoon baking powder
1 teaspoon ground cinnamon
$1/4$ teaspoon ground cloves

1–2 teaspoons freshly ground pepper
1 stick unsalted butter
$2/3$ cup soft dark sugar
2 large eggs, beaten with 4
    tablespoons runny honey

2 baking sheets, lined or non-stick

FOR THE ICING AND TRIMMINGS

$2^1/_2$ cups confectioners' sugar,
    sifted

3 tablespoons boiling water
gold or silver balls or sprinkles

Combine the flour, salt, baking powder, cinnamon, cloves and pepper in the food processor. With the motor on, add the butter and sugar, then, slowly, the eggs and honey, though don't use all of this liquid if the pastry has come together before it's used up. Form two discs and put one, covered in plastic wrap or in a plastic freezer bag, into the fridge while you get started on the other. Preheat the oven to 325°F. Have ready two baking sheets, and line with parchment paper if not non-stick.

Dust a surface with flour, roll out the disc, also floured, and cut out your Christmas decorations. Re-roll and cut out some more, setting aside the residue from this first disc, well covered, while you get on with rolling out the second. When you've got both sets of leftover clumps of dough, roll out and cut out again and keep doing so till all the dough's used up. Now take a small icing nozzle and use the pointy end to cut out a hole just below the top of each cookie (through which ribbon can later be threaded to hang them).

Arrange on the baking sheets and cook for about 20 minutes: it's hard to see when they're cooked, but you can feel; if the underside is no longer doughy, they're ready. Transfer them to cool on a wire rack. Make up ordinary glacé icing by mixing approximately 3 tablespoons of boiling water with the sifted confectioners' sugar – sifting is such a vile job in its relentless tediousness, I'd make the children do it – and stir till you've got a thin, glossy glaze. Ice the cold decorations using a teaspoon (the tip for dripping, the back for smoothing) and scatter sparkles or sprinkles as you like. I like to let an elegant, restrained, minimalist aesthetic dominate; children, I've found, prefer the Versace approach. But this is not the time to try and keep their vulgarity in check. Let them get it out of their system: better too many shimmering sprinkles now than a diamond navel stud later. Save your energies for then. Besides, if you can't find room for sugar-fuelled kitsch at Christmas, you haven't truly got into the spirit of things.

GINGERBREAD MUFFINS

Talking of rituals, I have recently ousted my Christmas morning muffins from the culinary equivalent of the box of decorations to be brought out each year (which is really what seasonal cooking is about) and replaced them with these.

Gingerbread is a traditional Christmas offering and these are just an easy, time-strapped take on them. They are fabulously simple to make and as they bake they fill the house with seasonally spicy warmth.

$1^2/_3$ cups all-purpose flour
$1/_2$ teaspoon baking soda
1 teaspoon baking powder
$1^1/_2$ teaspoons ground ginger
1 teaspoon ground cinnamon
$1/_4$ teaspoon ground cloves
1 egg

$1/_3$ cup packed dark brown sugar
$1/_3$ cup packed light brown sugar
$3/_4$ cup whole milk
$1/_4$ teaspoon balsamic vinegar
6 tablespoons vegetable or corn oil
4 tablespoons dark corn syrup
4 tablespoons molasses

Makes 12

note
If you want to go into ultra-Christmas mode, brush a little edible gold leaf on top of them when you get them out of the oven: the heat coming off the muffins will make it stick.

Preheat the oven to 400°F. Line a 12-cup muffin tin with paper muffin cups.

Combine the flour, baking soda, baking powder and spices in a large bowl. Whisk the egg in a large measuring cup then add the sugars, breaking up any lumps. Add the milk and vinegar then measure in the oil with a tablespoon. Use the same oily spoon to add the syrup and treacle so they don't stick to it. Whisk the mixture to combine and add to the flour and spices.

Stir until mixed but still fairly lumpy – the mixture may be more runny than you expect for muffins – but you need the dense stickiness of gingerbread, rather than a cakey crumb.

Spoon or pour the mixture into the muffin cups and bake for about 20 minutes until the tops are dry; the muffins will still feel squidgy when you take them out of the tins to cool on a rack. Note that because the mixture is moist, these muffins will not have the hump-topped look of store-bought ones. But unlike other muffins, these still taste gloriously good a couple of days after baking.

THE CHRISTMAS CAKE

You certainly don't need to do a proper, traditional Christmas cake. The pomegranate jewel cake on page 365 would, for instance, be wonderful here. But if you want a cake that's dense and fruity and will last, then you've come to the right place.

EASY-ACTION CHRISTMAS CAKE

One year when I attempted a traditional Christmas cake, I did as required, at least to start off with. The requisite months before, I bought dried fruit, chopped and stirred and steeped the mixture in alcohol. When the time came to make the cake, I was so exhausted with seasonal demands I didn't have the energy left actually to make it. So now I have evolved an easier, process-leaner method. Well, when I say I have evolved it, this is no more than my take on an old boiled fruit cake.

I just throw everything into a pan, let the heat from the stove send buttery rum and citrus juices permeating into the currants, sultanas and raisins, add flour and eggs, a can of chestnut purée to give grainy, Christmassy depth, bung the lot into a cake pan and let this stand in a low oven to produce a cake that is as dense, aromatic and fruity as you could hope for. The input from you is mimimal. Even a complete klutz can manage to stick a few nuts and candied fruits on the top, and what you end up with is a gorgeous creation that makes you feel that you've produced something of worth and beauty – and you have. Culinary self-esteem – and Christmas spirit – never came at so low an emotional cost. But then, I always make someone else do the wrapping with brown paper (and see below). I know my limits. We all know how it is: from happy in one's work to complete nervous wreck is a terrifyingly short step.

6 cups best-quality mixed dried
    fruit
$1^1/_2$ sticks unsalted butter
$1^1/_2$ cups dark brown sugar
$^3/_4$ cup/$8^3/_4$oz can sweetened
    chestnut purée or spread
$^1/_2$ cup dark rum
juice and zest of 1 orange

zest of 1 lemon
3 large eggs, beaten
$1^2/_3$ cups all-purpose flour
$^1/_2$ teaspoon baking powder
$^1/_4$ teaspoon cinnamon
$^1/_4$ teaspoon ground cloves
$^1/_4$ teaspoon ground nutmeg

TO DECORATE
4 tablespoons smooth apricot jam

approx. 2 cups assorted glacé fruits,
    blanched almonds, pecans and
    marrons glacés

Preheat the oven to 300°F (though you might prefer to do this after the fruits and so forth have started bubbling in their pan). Line the sides and bottom of a deep 8 inch round cake pan with a double layer of wax paper. The wax paper should be higher than the sides of the pan. Wrap a double layer of brown paper (the kind used for parcels) around the outside of the pan, tying it with string. The paper should be double the height of the pan, and this gives an extra layer of insulation for the cake so that it cooks slowly. If you don't have any brown paper, it is not absolutely necessary, but it will keep the cake from becoming too dark around the sides and top.

Put the dried fruit, butter, sugar, chestnut purée or spread, rum and orange juice and zests into a large wide saucepan and bring to the boil gently, stirring as the butter melts. Simmer the mixture for 10 minutes, and then take it off the heat and leave to stand for 30 minutes, by which time the fruits will have been soused and the mixture cooled slightly. Now, add the beaten eggs, flour, baking powder and spices and stir to combine.

Pour the fruit cake mixture very carefully into the prepared cake pan.

Place in the oven and bake for $1^3/_4$–2 hours, by which time the top of the cake should be firm and dry and will have cracked a little. If you insert a cake tester into the middle of the cake it will still come out a little sticky.

Put the cake on a cooling rack and take off the brown paper from around the outside of the pan. It will hold its heat and take a long while to cool, but once it has cooled completely, unmold it from the pan and wrap the cake well in a layer of wax paper and then aluminum foil until you want to decorate it.

Spoon the apricot jam into a saucepan and add a tablespoon of water. Heat gently, stirring to make a sticky glaze and then take off the heat to cool.

Paint the top of the cake with the apricot glaze, and then decorate with the fruits and nuts of your choice. I find it easier to cut the glacé fruits into pieces and then fit everything together like a jigsaw puzzle.

When the top is completely covered in the glacé fruits and nuts, paint a second coat of apricot glaze over the top to give a glossy finish.

The cake will keep for a couple of months well wrapped and in a cool dark place.

If you want a more boozy offering you can feed the cake with 3 tablespoons more rum as soon as it gets out of the oven. That's to say, pierce the top of the cake several times with a fine skewer, spoon over the rum and let it sink in.

You can also play with the fruits and taste of the cake (and see the chocolate fruit cake on page 280); for instance, substitute apricot jam for the chestnut purée and halve the mixed dried fruit, making up the weight with chopped dried apricots, replace the rum with apricot brandy, add a drop of almond extract to the cake mixture and cover with slivered almonds as you bake it. Obviously, it will not need icing or any fruit topping. Or you can reduce the fruit mixture, throw in many natural colored glacé cherries, quartered to make up the weight and replace the rum with cherry brandy and when the cake's cool, glaze with sieved cherry jam and cover just with pecan halves and natural, dark, glacé cherries. Over to you.

JEWELED CUPCAKES

I'd always wanted to do some fruit cupcakes, and to be honest, they are no different from the cake above, except in the oven temperature and the length of time they need to cook.

You could probably stretch the amount, above, to make 24 cupcakes, 18 with ease, though I prefer to make 12 and then one small Christmas cake, about 6 inches in diameter. It must still be a deep pan, though.

Buy foil cupcake cups – gold or silver – which come up a little smaller than the regular white paper ones.

The cupcakes take 35–40 minutes in a 325°F oven; bear in mind that the foil of the cups makes them continue to cook for a while once they've come out.

The smaller cake takes about 1$^{1}/_{4}$ hours. If I've done the jeweled cupcakes, then I tend to ice the cake more traditionally. Buy a block of marzipan and a 2lb package of ready-to-roll white fondant icing and roll away, decorating as you wish, remembering to brush the cake with apricot jam so that the marzipan sticks well. Also, it helps to use confectioners' sugar when you roll out the marzipan and fondant, much as you would dust a surface with flour when you roll out pastry. The multicolor gleam of the cupcakes leaves me calmed and I want only crisp, unblemished white-on-white. But fun – of a sort – could be had with some ready-roll red and green icing and some holly leaf cutters. And I did go Wedgwood one year with some ivy leaf cutters and stamp.

TIME-HONOURED CHRISTMAS CAKE

If you want to pursue the utterly trad Christmas cake option, then this is the cake to make. I repeat it from *How to be a Domestic Goddess* because too many people, devotees of the cake (a recipe passed down to me from the mother-in-law of my assistant Hettie's sister, to be precise about the provenance), had been shocked at my suggestion that it be left out. Even if you want to ignore the recipe, the table for the differing cake pan sizes and so on, is helpful to have anyway.

sultanas (golden raisins)	2 cups plus 3 teaspoons	4^1/$_3$ cups	6 cups
raisins	^{3}/$_4$ cup	1^1/$_2$ cup	2^1/$_3$ cups
currants	^{1}/$_2$ cup	^{1}/$_2$ plus ^{1}/$_3$ cups	1^1/$_2$ cups
glacé cherries	^{1}/$_3$ cup	^{2}/$_3$ cup	1^1/$_4$ cups
mixed peel	^{1}/$_2$ cup	1 cup	1^3/$_4$ cups
brandy or sherry	^{1}/$_4$ cup	^{1}/$_2$ cup	^{3}/$_4$ cup
butter	1 stick	2 sticks	3^1/$_5$ sticks
brown sugar	^{1}/$_2$ cup	1 cup	1^3/$_4$ cups
orange zest, grated	^{1}/$_3$ teaspoon	1 teaspoon	1^1/$_2$ teaspoons
lemon zest, grated	^{1}/$_2$ teaspoon	1 teaspoon	1^1/$_2$ teaspoons
large eggs	2	4	6
marmalade	1 tablespoon	2 tablespoons	3 tablespoons
almond extract	^{1}/$_2$ teaspoon	1 teaspoon	1 teaspoon
all-purpose flour	1^3/$_4$ cups	2^1/$_3$ cups	3^1/$_2$ cups
mixed spice	^{1}/$_2$ teaspoon	1 teaspoon	1^1/$_2$ teaspoons
ground cinnamon	pinch	^{1}/$_4$ teaspoon	^{1}/$_4$ teaspoon
grated nutmeg	pinch	^{1}/$_4$ teaspoon	^{1}/$_4$ teaspoon
salt	pinch	pinch	^{1}/$_4$ teaspoon
pan: round or square	7 inch 6 inch	9 inch 8 inch	10 inch 9 inch
temperature	300°F	300°F	300°F, reduce to 275°F after 1 hour
cooking time	2–2^1/$_2$ hours	3–3^1/$_2$ hours	4–4^1/$_2$ hours

Place all of the fruit in a large bowl, and add the brandy or sherry. Cover and let the fruit soak overnight.

Preheat your oven to 300°F. Wrap the outside of your pan with a double thickness of brown paper, tying it with string, and line inside with parchment paper, both to come up a good 4 inches above the rim of the tin.

Cream the butter and sugar, then beat in the orange and lemon zest. Add the eggs one at a time, beating well after each addition, and then the marmalade and almond extract. Sift the dry ingredients together, then mix the fruit alternately with the dry ingredients into the creamed mixture, combining thoroughly.

Put the cake batter carefully into the prepared pan and bake following the table above, or until a cake-tester comes out clean.

When the cake is cooked, brush with a couple of tablespoons of liqueur. Wrap immediately, still in its pan – using a double-thickness of aluminum foil – as this will trap the heat and form steam, which in turn will keep the cake soft on top. When it's completely cold, remove the cake from the pan and re-wrap in foil, storing preferably in an airtight tin or Tupperware, for at least three weeks.

It's difficult to give a precise ingredient list, at least in terms of quantities, for the icing, because I don't know which sized cake you are making. The quantities below are for a 9 inch diameter cake

FOR THE ICING

$^3/_4$ cup marmalade

confectioners' sugar for sprinkling

1lb marzipan

2lbs ready-to-roll fondant icing

Heat the marmalade in a saucepan and when hot and runny strain into a bowl to remove the rind. Or start off with a rindless one, of course. With a pastry brush, paint all over the cake to make a tacky surface. Dust a work surface with confectioners' sugar, roll out the marzipan and drape over the cake. Then press against the cake and cut off the excess with a sharp knife. If you need to do this twice (with two lots of 8oz marzipan), that's fine, but make sure to smooth over any joins, so that the icing on top lies smoothly. Dust the work surface again with confectioners' sugar and plonk down your block of icing. Beat it a few times with the rolling pin, then dust the top with confectioners' sugar and roll out. Cover the cake with it, again cutting off the excess and sticking bits together to patch up as you need, sprinkling with cold water first. Transfer the cake to a cake stand or board.

As for decorating, it is entirely up to you of course, but see my suggestions on page 98, overleaf, and, indeed, the photograph above right.

THE NON CAKE-MAKER'S CHRISTMAS CAKE

This cake has everything going for it except for staying power. That's to say, it will stale much like an ordinary cake, which means you should make it to be eaten, not to decorate a sideboard, gathering dust, for the duration of the festive season. Luckily, it tastes wonderful, so that's no hardship.

And it is ludicrously easy to make. You need never have baked before and own a minute cupboard of a kitchen and it's still a complete breeze.

Naturally, I presume the mincemeat will be out of a store-bought jar.

note
You can substitute $^1/_2$ cup of flour with ground almonds, which will make the cake heavier (not a bad thing in the context of fruit cakes of course) and more moist.

1 stick plus 1 tablespoon soft butter
1$^1/_2$ cups dark brown sugar
2 cups all-purpose flour
2 teaspoons baking powder
$^1/_2$ teaspoon baking soda
zest of 1 lemon

zest of 1 orange
2 tablespoons brandy
2 eggs
3 cups mincemeat
confectioners' sugar to decorate (or see below)

Preheat the oven to 325°F. Line a 9 inch high-sided round pan with baking parchment, lining the bottom and sides well.

Put the butter and sugar into a food processor and blitz together. The dark sugar can be very lumpy so it's best to do this first. Add the flour, baking powder, baking soda, zests, brandy and eggs, and process again.

Finally add the mincemeat and pulse to incorporate, as you don't want the fruit to be too finely chopped. Spoon the cake mixture into the prepared pan and smooth the top. Bake in the oven for 1$^1/_2$ hours. Check the cake after an hour, as you don't want it to be overcooked.

Let the cake cool completely on a wire rack before unmolding and unwrapping it. I love it just as it is with a snowy dusting of confectioners' sugar. But if you ever felt the urge to buy a dinky plastic model of Santa and his sleigh, this is the cake to put it on. Make up a package of instant royal icing (see page 429 for recipe from scratch) and pile it over the cake, forking to leave a rough snowy cover; you won't need to cover with marzipan first as the cake won't be sitting around long enough for the brown of the fruit to ooze through. Otherwise go extremely out of context by using the sort of cream cheese icing you'd expect to find on a carrot cake, but that would actually look just right here (and see page 286).

NEW YEAR

THERE IS something about New Year's Eve, all that enforced jollity, that tense hopefulness, that induces an ineluctable melancholy in me. New Year's Day, however, seems for once a date that lives up to its significance on the calendar. I feel it's like starting anew; my optimism returns, give or take, of its own accord, rather than having to be stoked up in the name of sentimental cameraderie. I want to see people, to eat with them. Of course, this is partly a question of age, or more accurately the stage one's at in life: with small children the possibility of sleeping in and doing nothing is out of the question (and it's probably been impossible to get a babysitter and therefore go out the night before anyway), so one may as well do something.

And once you start inviting people for lunch, you can find it turns into a mopping-up exercise. Be prepared for large numbers. Not that you have to do anything fancy. You might want to – within reason – but it's not a bad idea to go for the comfort-food option: a tureen of soup, a bowl of something starchy, a dessert you can really dive into. Even though I'm not a committed drinker, I can't help thinking that the menu in question should be considered for its hangover salving properties. And that's where the champagne risotto and the yellow split pea and frankfurter soup at the end of this chapter really come into their own.

The difficulty is, that it's easy to start thinking one is up to much more in the way of social activity than turns out to be the case. The New Year does not make a new you, even though renewed hope and an optimistic belief in the perfectibility of the self induces a confidence that all will be well, and all manner of things will be well.

For every action, as I unaccountably remember from high school science class (you see, Mr. Clarke, I was listening), there is an equal and opposite reaction. Which, roughly translated to life right now, means that plunged into expansive, hospitable holiday mood I issue to each and every one of my friends a warm invitation to lunch – only to sit slumped, head in hands, as I wonder how I'm going to feed them and hold on to my sanity. This season is fraught with contradictions: it's a time when you feel friendly, want to see people, indeed want to sit eating and chatting with them, but what with having the children home from school needing to be entertained at all times and in the aftermath of frenzied, family-wrought Christmas activities, you do not always have the energy for the follow-through.

It would be a pity not to indulge the time-honoured need for seasonal feasting, but it's important that this desire to be extravagantly hospitable doesn't become a stress-producing means of self-persecution. After all, inviting friends over should be a warming, relaxing proposition. You may laugh grimly at this notion, but it's all a question of strategy. And by this I don't mean you should be planning some military-style campaign: neither checklist nor clipboard is required for the safe passage of this lunch or dinner party. For me, it's about choosing recipes that don't need excessive attention as they cook, nor last-minute high-level fiddling as they are brought to the table. I need to feel that I am providing a proper feast, but I have neither the time nor – perhaps most pertinently – the temperament for formal banquet work; I am never going to be someone who goes in for fancy table settings or the kind of cooking that requires it. I hesitate to say this, only because I say it so often, but if you wanted you really could roast some chicken as a glorious festive but cheaper alternative. However everyday and ordinary roast chicken is, it always looks like a feast – especially if there are lots of bulging bronze birds, and I'd do three medium-sized ones for ten – and anyone who wasn't happy to be given roast chicken, well I wouldn't want to invite them for dinner in the first place.

I've divided the two New Year's feasts, below, into lunch and dinner, but there is no need to keep to my timetable. A hefty loin of pork and lentils could be eaten at night, just as the more elegant caviar and potato pancakes followed by sea bass and saffron-tinted mash could be a perfect lunchtime menu. But instinctively, I'd be more likely to keep them as they are, not least because I'm presuming children would be around for lunch; you might have managed to pack them off to bed or the TV by dinnertime, and the caviar and sea bass option is definitely less kiddie-friendly (as am I by that time of day).

I'd like, though, to put a plea in here for the consideration of the pancake and caviar option as a solitary indulgence or New Year's dinner for two of you. Caviar is an indulgent luxury when eaten by one, or at a pinch two. There's something so much more of a treat, in a luxurious way, about eating those beautiful pewtery black beads alone or *à deux*; the key issue, though, is excess and that is so much less likely to be a possible option when there is a group of you. For what it's worth, anything salty is good with the potato pancakes; you could consider some crème fraîche, scissored smoked salmon (or, my favorite, some salted anchovies that have been soaked in milk and then drained) and a sprinkling of capers as a less extortionate but still pleasingly extravagant option.

There are two things to be said about the champagne risotto: the first is that it doesn't need to be made with actual champagne, though I did devise it as a way of fruitfully using up the dregs from opened but unfinished celebratory bottles from the night before; the second is that I wouldn't consider making it for a crowd. I think of it truly as a perfect meal for two when you're happy to be friendless.

I've left the soup till last, but I could as easily have started with it: it is the alpha and omega of soups, one that salves woes, soothes headaches, offers promise and tastes wonderful. I have something of an addiction for it. My record is four meals on the trot: that's to say, I had this for lunch and supper two days running, and not even because it was leftover. I made it afresh on the second day. And could have gone on and on. Have it for a starter before the fish if you want to butch dinner up, or have it yourself, or with a tableful of friends or family for lunch in itself. There is no better way to start the New Year.

NEW YEAR'S LUNCH FOR EIGHT

ROLLED LOIN OF PORK "CINGHIALE"

Let me explain: *cinghiale* simply means wild boar in Italian, and this recipe is my way of trying to recreate a dinner eaten in Umbria last year: gamey boar, pebbly lentils, bitter leaves. I think it's a pretty unbeatable combination: rich yet earthy. This seems a suitable way to mark the New Year – shows how you mean to go on.

I can't pretend it doesn't make a difference if you get a butcher to remove the rind and roll the loin for you. It means you get the wherewithal to make fabulous crackling, plus you'll get the bones that have been taken out. Roast these with the joint and the flavor will deepen, giving you meat with more taste and a gravy to boot. But I've made this with fatless, or pretty well fatless, ready-rolled boned loin of pork and it's still good. That's the marinade for you: not only does it bolster the relatively delicate flavor of the pork, giving it something of the tang and oomph of boar, it also overcomes one of the problems of supermarket meat – the leanness which when cooked turns into dryness – by tenderizing and, in a manner of speaking, moisturizing it.

Like all meat, this pork is best when left to sit for a while, well wrapped in foil. Which is just as well, as the separated rind will have time to blister and burn in the now hotter oven, turning, as it does, into the crackliest crackling imaginable. It helps if the rind is scored diagonally crossways, making shapes all over – or that was how my mother did it – so if you've got a butcher doing the boning and removing the rind anyway, you may as well ask for the harlequined scoring to be done at the same time.

Serves 8

1 tablespoon pink peppercorns
1 tablespoon juniper berries
1 tablespoon allspice berries
1 clove
4 cloves garlic, bruised
1 tablespoon molasses
$1/2$ cup extra virgin olive oil
2 tablespoons Worcestershire sauce

2 tablespoons dark brown sugar
$1/3$ cup Marsala
2–$2^1/_2$ cups red wine
$4^3/_4$ lb tied pork loin, weighed without bones and rind (bones and rind reserved, and see above)

It actually doesn't add to the work much, if at all, to double this. Bear in mind, though, that the more people there are, the less you need per head, so two pork joints thus cooked should be fine for a lunch for 20. To be honest, if you're a good carver, you'll probably be able to feed even more. You might have to beg another piece of rind out of the butcher, as the crackling rations are anyway not excessive. You'd be surprised at how many people bafflingly prefer to have their pork without crackling so it should be possible to scrounge some extra.

Crush the peppercorns, juniper and allspice berries in a pestle and mortar with the clove. Or if you haven't got a pestle and mortar, just put them in a freezer bag and bash with a can of something heavy. Turn into a bowl and add the bruised garlic cloves, molasses, oil, Worcestershire sauce and the sugar. Whisk together to disperse the molasses and sugar before adding the Marsala and wine.

Put the pork loin into a large freezer bag and pour in the marinade, seal the bag well and try to get as much of the pork in the liquid as possible. Put in the fridge in a dish to avert accidents with leakages. Leave overnight or ideally for a couple of days. Keep the bones in the fridge, too, and wrap the rind in parchment paper to keep it dry.

Let the meat, bones and rind come to room temperature before you cook them, and at the same time preheat the oven to 400°F. Line a roasting pan with aluminum foil or Silpat, as the sugar in the marinade will make the pan burn.

Lay the bones from the pork loin in the bottom of the lined roasting pan and take out the meat from its marinade and lay it on top. Pour 2 cups of the marinating liquid over the pork and put it in the oven, reserving any marinade left to help make the gravy later. Roast the pork for $1^3/_4$–2 hours, basting the joint every now and then. The only way to tell the pork's cooked is really by spearing it with a slim sharp knife. And be prepared for it to shrink enormously.

After the pork has had an hour, put the rind in a shallow roasting pan and put it on the rack under the pork. It won't actually cook that much underneath the joint, but it will render down slightly, getting ready for its blitzing later. So, when the meat comes out to rest, turn the oven up to the hottest it will go to let the crackling become everything it can become. After about 20 minutes, the pork will be perfect to carve and the crackling ready to be splintered into crisp amber shards.

Meanwhile, make your gravy. Remove the bones from the pan – this is the best bit, cook's treat – and pour whatever juices remain into a saucepan, tipping in the rest of the marinade and as much water as you need to dilute into a gravy. It's so hard to give accurate directions here as, for example, liquid evaporates more in an electric oven than a gas one (and is why I prefer to cook meat in a gas oven). I'd start by adding about a $^1/_4$ cup of water and add more as the gravy heats on the burner. Whisk well before pouring into a warmed gravy boat or pitcher and again before serving to help disperse the oil, tasting as you do to make sure it's as you want it.

If you want to cook some Italian sausages to serve with the lentils, in place of the pork or, rather excitingly, to add to it, then simply buy about 2lb of either sweet or hot sausages and heat 2 bruised cloves of garlic in a little olive oil. Now, brown the sausages on both sides, throw in $^1/_2$ cup red wine and $^1/_3$ cup water. Let this bubble up, then turn down the heat, cover the pan with foil or a lid and cook for 15–20 minutes. Remove the sausages (break one to check it's cooked), arrange on top of the lentils, and over a high heat, bubble up the winey juices, mashing the garlic into them. Taste to check it isn't too salty (if it is, add some water and whisk in some unsalted butter) and pour over the sausages and lentils.

MY GRANDMOTHER'S APPLE HORSERADISH SAUCE

My maternal grandmother always ate horseradish and apple sauce with pork and I've combined the two here as a grateful gesture of affectionate remembrance. And because she was right to do so: the combination of heat and sharpness is a great one for the robust, meaty pork. I add crème fraîche, but Greek or wholemilk yogurt or, indeed, sour cream, would work well too (and see page 220).

Naturally, this would be wonderful made with fresh apples and freshly grated horseradish, but I'm trying to be realistic here.

4 tablespoons crème fraîche
4 tablespoons unsweetened
  apple sauce or purée

2 tablespoons hot horseradish sauce

Combine the above ingredients in a bowl (or combine them in one and decant to another if you're sloppy like me) to serve with the thinly sliced pork.

LENTILS BRAISED IN RED WINE

I think life is made very much easier if you can get as much stuff as possible done in advance. So when you put your pork in its marinade, you can start making these and, once they're cooked, leave them in a cold place until you're ready to reheat. I don't even take them out of the pan. You need to add quite a bit of oil and some water when you reheat them, but as long as the flame's low, they shouldn't come to any harm.

I've used Beluga lentils here, partly because I love the name, but mostly because I am very keen on these tiny, black spheres which, when slicked with oil, look like caviar. But do use the paler grey-green Italian Castelluccio lentils if you can get them, or indeed the slate-blue Puy lentils from France. The crucial thing here is that lentils be served on New Year's Day. In Italy, sausages and lentils are a traditional New Year's Day feast, as the lentils are supposed to resemble coins and therefore signal a year of prosperity ahead.

1 carrot
2 cloves garlic
1 stick of celery
1 large onion
4oz bacon
3 tablespoons olive oil
2$^1/_3$ cups Beluga lentils

2 bay leaves
2 teaspoons Dijon mustard
1$^1/_4$ cups red wine
3 cups water
olive oil
fresh parsley, optional

Serves 8

Peel the carrot and garlic cloves and chop finely with the celery, onion and bacon, or process everything until finely chopped. Heat the oil in a large pan, and add the chopped or processed vegetables and bacon. Cook them over a gentle heat until soft, which will take up to about 10 minutes.

Tip the lentils into the pan and stir them around to get slicked with the oil, and then add the bay leaves and Dijon mustard.

Pour in the red wine and the water, or enough water so that the lentils are just covered in liquid. Bring to the boil and cover and simmer for about 30 minutes or until just tender. One of the good things about the Beluga lentils is they tend not to turn mushy, so there's less problem about overcooking.

When the lentils are cooked, check the seasoning and add salt if necessary and dress with a little olive oil as you serve them. If you are cooking the lentils in advance, simply take them off the heat, and put the pan in a cool place somewhere (say on a chilly stainless-steel surface or near a window out of the sun). Warm through the next day by adding a little water and olive oil and keeping them, covered, on a low heat until warm. Then, by all means, take the lid off and stir through with a wooden spatula to help them get hot throughout.

Transfer to a serving dish, tasting for seasoning and dressing with a little olive oil as you do so. If you want some freshly chopped parsley on top, scatter as desired. I rather like, however, their uninterrupted muddy blackness.

BITTER ENDIVE SALAD

I love the cool sharpness of the endive leaves against the earthiness of the lentils and rich meatiness of the pork (or indeed sausages). I think it's important, too, as a recognition at the beginning of a new year, that life has its sweet and bitter moments, but maybe that's because I've been reading a lot of history of Jewish customs where finger-wagging to warn against glorying only in the good is a recurring theme.

But as for the practicalities of the salad itself: it's scarcely a recipe really, just the way I make it, give or take a change of mood and fridge-content. Add any other bitter leaves you want.

I think this is all you need here. Certainly, because of the lentils, I wouldn't think of serving potatoes, but if you really want to, then bake some in the oven alongside the pork if there's room (or in another oven if you've got a double one), bearing in mind that they'll take a lot longer in a cluttered oven (and the liquid from the marinade will stop them getting crunchy-skinned). The appley horseradish cream would be lovely spooned into baking potatoes, maybe with some chopped chives thrown in, so if you're going all out for potatoes, make sure to increase quantities of sauce.

I'm going through a pink-peppercorn phase, at least at time of writing, and since I've included them in the pork marinade, I am presuming you might have some in the house to use over the pale jade, sword-leafed salad. If you do, lovely, but if you are using ordinary peppercorns, well, that's fine too.

3–4 heads Belgian endive

Serves 8

FOR THE DRESSING
1 teaspoon grainy mustard
few drops honey

3 tablespoons extra virgin olive oil
1 teaspoon sherry vinegar

Trim the rooty ends of the endive and pull off the leaves. Arrange these, strewn as they are, in a large flat dish (or cut them into rings if you want a more chopped salad). Mix the dressing ingredients together in a cup with some salt and pepper, check to see you're pleased with how it tastes and drizzle over the waiting leaves.

note

This is also very good when you replace the olive oil with 2 tablespoons vegetable oil and 1 tablespoon walnut oil. If you're not serving the endive salad as part of this meal, but as a course in itself, you could add some walnut pieces and even some crumbled soft goat's cheese.

EASY HOLIDAY TRIFLE

There is something about a trifle which signifies an Occasion. It never feels just like dessert. This one, though, is somewhat fraudulent. I suspect the trifle became the marker of specialness in most homes precisely because it is such a fiddly, process-heavy rigmarole, despite its name. I use slices of *pandoro*, the unfruited version of the Italian Christmas cake (you could use panettone in its place if you prefer). In between the layers of sweet, yeasted *pandoro*, the golden bread, I add dried apricots poached with cardamom, orange and lemon juice and sugar. You could, I'd have thought, substitute canned apricots, using the syrup in place of the reduced poaching liquid, but sticking some dried apricots in a pan, then cooking and cooling them isn't hard.

The cake and fruit arrangement you can deal with a good day or two in advance, then just before serving all you need to do is add a layer of heavy cream whipped with Greek yogurt, then on top, drizzle honey and scatter over pistachios and slivered almonds.

What I love particularly is the gold coin look of all the plumped-up, poached apricots which, like the lentils, are there to signify the wish for a prosperous year ahead.

This will stretch to more than eight people easily, but it is also the generous size of the trifle that makes it so festive. This is, besides, no time for holding back.

Serves 8 generously

note

If you want a plainer dessert, that's easy: buy some good vanilla ice cream and sprinkle with the gold dust on page 117.

$4^1/_2$ cups dried apricots
6 cups water
$^3/_4$ cup superfine sugar
juice of 1 lemon
juice of $^1/_2$ orange or 1 tangerine
6 cardamom pods
$^1/_2$ *pandoro* or a 1lb piece pandoro or panettone

1 cup heavy cream
1 cup Greek or whole milk yogurt
3 tablespoons honey
$^1/_4$ cup pistachios
$^1/_4$ cup slivered almonds

Put the dried apricots into a saucepan with the water, and add the sugar and juices from the lemon and tangerine or orange. Bruise the cardamom pods with the back of a knife to release the seeds, and add to the pan, giving a stir as you do so. Bring to the boil, then turn the heat down and simmer for 30 minutes. Or, if it makes life easier, you can just bring the pan to the boil, turn it off immediately and let the pan stand, cooling, overnight.

Drain the apricots (discarding the cardamom seeds and husks as much as possible) and put the cooking liquid back into the saucepan, then boil over a high heat for 15–20 minutes to reduce to a syrupy consistency. I stop when I've reduced the liquid to about $1^1/_2$ cups. Leave to cool slightly before you go on to the next stage.

Cut the *pandoro* into $^1/_2$ inch slices; this should give you about eight long stripy slices in total. Line a wide and not-too-deep glass bowl (see picture opposite) with four of the slices of *pandoro*, and then spread half of the warm apricots over the cake. Pour half of the syrupy liquid over the *pandoro* and apricot base.

Do the same thing with the other slices, except lay them the opposite way in

the bowl so that the dish is evenly covered in *pandoro*. Add the remaining half of apricots and then the syrup, and leave to one side to let the cake absorb the liquid. I like to leave this overnight or for a day, covered with plastic wrap in the fridge.

To make the trifle topping, whisk the heavy cream until soft peaks form – be careful not to overwhip it – and then add the yogurt and beat or stir together just to combine. It should be soft and light enough to spread easily over the top of the trifle in a not-too-thick layer.

Drizzle the honey over the top with a teaspoon, chop the pistachios into splinters and mix them with the slivered almonds, then scatter both over the top of the trifle.

NEW YEAR'S DAY DINNER FOR TEN

POTATO PANCAKES WITH CAVIAR OR SMOKED SALMON

I'm beginning to feel bad now about the caviar. I know how expensive it is. But I'm not suggesting you rush out and buy Beluga and, as I've said, the pancakes are very good dolloped with crème fraîche, and topped with anchovies or straggly strips of smoked salmon and capers instead.

I know there's a tedious amount of griddling of these pancakes, but I don't think you can make under 50 pancakes if there are ten of you eating. They go down mighty easily. I have a confession to make: half a batch is not excessive for a caviar feast for two. As for how much caviar – well, how long is a piece of string? The thing is to buy as much as you can afford: there's no such thing as too much. If substituting smoked salmon, get about 12oz. Once it's ripped into shreds it'll go further. You'll need far less in the way of anchovies: probably three fillets, halved per head. Just to be on the safe side, I'd buy two 8oz tubs of crème fraîche, even though you're unlikely to get through both and, for the smoked salmon or anchovy option, one jar of capers should be fine.

By potato pancakes, I don't mean anything as labor-intensive and gruelling as grating potatoes or boiling, mashing them and whisking in egg whites (rapturous though the latke version and the crêpes Parmentier can both be) but something much simpler and that can be cooked in advance and reheated in a low oven or microwave with ease. These are simply pancakes made with the addition of potato flour.

Makes 50

note
You may want to serve vodka with these; it's certainly a good way to toast the New Year. If so, remember to stick a bottle in the deep freeze well before dinner. Just put

$1/_2$ cup potato flour
1 cup all-purpose flour
1 teaspoon baking powder
$1/_2$ teaspoon baking soda

FOR THE TOPPING
as much caviar as possible, if you feel like going mad, or 12oz smoked salmon, or 15 salted anchovies, filleted

$1/_4$ teaspoon salt
$1^1/_3$ cups buttermilk
2 eggs
2 tablespoons melted butter

2 x 8oz tubs crème fraîche

Put the potato flour, all-purpose flour, baking powder, baking soda and salt into a bowl. Whisk together the buttermilk, eggs and melted butter in a measuring cup and then beat into the dry ingredients to make a smooth batter.

Spoon tablespoonfuls of the batter on to a hot smooth griddle or skillet; they should be about 2 inches in diameter. These dense little pancakes won't make a lot of bubbles, as normal ones do, as they cook, so after a couple of minutes when the bottom feels set, flip them over carefully and cook for a few minutes on the other side. Don't worry if you make a mistake. The Russians have a saying to the effect that the first pancake is always botched. Take comfort in its literal application here. Lay the pancakes on baking parchment as you cook them in batches. Or they can be left to get cool, stored in the fridge or indeed frozen. Reheat in a microwave, uncovered or in a low oven (300°F) covered with some foil. Working with these numbers I much prefer the regular oven method. If you've saved some in the deep freeze to eat alone at some time later, it's a different story.

platters of food on the table and let people, stretchingly, help themselves. A bit of DIY is always relaxing at the table.

SEA BASS WITH GOLDEN MASH

Sea bass is undeniably expensive, but I feel that this meal has already lost any chance of being thought a low-cost option, so why worry now?

I think it makes life simpler to cook two fish rather than a single giant one, even if such a megafish existed: this is not only for the oven-fitting consideration but it just makes dinner flow more comfortably if you can have two plates going, one at each end of the table.

I first cooked this for an Epiphany dinner some years back and understandably felt that some sage, tucked inside, was the only appropriate herb for a feast connected with the three wise men, and it tasted so good – the rasping strength of the sage complementing rather than overshadowing the delicate fish – that I've stuck to it. There is no culinary obligation: use what you like or have at hand; I often use thyme and its vibrant scent here demonstrates again how even plain white fish is, against many people's prejudices, best with robust flavors. Besides, what better herb to mark the New Year?

The mash is tinted gold with saffron: the gold because neither frankincense nor myrrh is so easily represented, and because saffron is the traditional feast-day spice, conjuring up celebratory extravagance and exotic aroma. But no one's going to mind if you have recourse to turmeric; there are many precedents. I've said to leave the head of the fish on, partly because they look so magnificent like that (and fillets, being better pan-fried, are too bothersome to cook for a lot of people) and partly inspired by the tradition I've been reading about for the Jewish New Year (but which I haven't incidentally included in the Rosh Hashanah chapter) which dictates that a fish's head be served to show that in the year to come you will lead rather than follow. I think that's the gist of it, and felt that it was at least a positive, confident way to mark the occasion here.

Serves 10

note

As the fish and mash both have that comfort-food softness, the vegetable I'd cook to go with them would be slender string beans, topped and tailed, cooked in well salted water, then tossed when drained in butter, a good squirt of lemon juice, sea salt, freshly ground pepper and some toasted slivered almonds. (Let's say 2lb beans, $1/2$ stick butter, juice of $1/2$ lemon and $1/4$ cup or 4 tablespoons slivered almonds that

3lb whole sea bass, cleaned and scaled
2 tablespoons extra virgin olive oil, plus more for pouring over later

FOR THE MASH
4lb all-purpose potatoes
$3/4$ cup plus a tablespoon light cream or milk

small bunch fresh sage or thyme (about 10 leaves)
4 scallions
sea salt

$3/4$ stick unsalted butter
1 teaspoon saffron threads
fresh nutmeg, optional

Preheat the oven to 400°F, though it makes sense to get the potatoes – divinely inspired by the wonderful Simon Hopkinson's famous saffron mash – on the go first. I don't peel them since I use a potato ricer, which is I why I suggest 4lb of potatoes so coolly. Otherwise, cursing me I'm sure, peel the potatoes, cut them into large chunks and put them in a pan of cold water. Bring to the boil, salt generously and cook for 40 minutes or so until tender and ready to be mashed, though not breaking up. While this is going on, put the cream or milk into a pan with the butter and saffron and bring to the boil, then cover and take off the heat to infuse.

When the potatoes are drained, put them back in the hot pan on the stovetop (though you don't need to turn the heat on) so that any excess liquid evaporates and then proceed to mash them as you usually do. If you're using the ricer, just rice them from the colander back into the pan. Beat in the warm, infused milk. Taste for seasoning (a little nutmeg could be good) and add more butter if you want or dare. Plonk a lid on. I am happy to do this before sitting down to dinner, that's to say, quite well in advance of eating it, in which case I often leave any butter papers I have over it. If you don't have one, just leave a bit of golden milk in its pan and dribble over the top after you've beaten most of it in and just before you clamp on the lid.

To cook the fish, tear off two large pieces of aluminum foil, big enough to make a roomy parcel for each of the fish. Use some of the oil to grease each sheet and lay the fish on top. Divide the sage leaves between the cavity of each fish, then cut each scallion into three and squish slightly with the flat of a heavy knife and add these to the sage. Bring up the edges of the foil to make a baggy but tightly closed parcel and put them on baking sheets in the oven. (If you want, leave them in their parcels out of the oven for an hour before you need to cook them.) Cook them for 30 minutes before unwrapping one and checking to see it's cooked through; you may find you need another 5 minutes or so. Either way, it may be helpful to know you can get the fish well underway before the first course: you can leave them out of the oven, in their foil, while you eat your pancakes and caviar, or whatever.

Unwrap your packages, gingerly peel off the skin and, using a fish slice, fillet and serve the beautiful white fish.

you need to brown by toasting in an oilless pan first.) And to be honest, if I could get French beans instead, that's to say, ready sliced, in little bags from the supermarket, I wouldn't hesitate. If mash is too much like hard work, make a golden gratin by following the recipe on page 228, only replacing the cloves, mace and bay leaves with 2 sachets of powdered saffron. This has the advantage that you can prepare it in advance.

CHOCOLATE CHESTNUT CAKE

After the rich gold and white of the fish course comes the deep, grainy darkness of the chocolate chestnut cake, the recipe for which is in the Chocolate Cake Hall of Fame (page 297), where indeed it should be.

AND ANOTHER THING...

YELLOW SPLIT PEA AND FRANKFURTER SOUP

The glorious golden yellowness of the soup makes it a suitable marker for the New Year, implying as it does, a hope for golden times ahead. I felt, too, the split peas themselves were a kind of northern European take on the Italian custom of serving lentils for their coin-like appearance.

But the value of this soup is so much more than symbolic, important though that is in festive eating particularly. The grainy liquid is hearty on its own, and the best way of soaking up any excess alcohol – or after-effects of same – lingering in the system. The frankfurters, again to be sliced in coins if you want to play further on this theme, or cut in thick slices otherwise, make this a real meal and a half.

Serves 6–8

note
As ever, when I signal stock, I don't mean you have to start boiling up chickens or whatever. I use some concentrated broth that comes in little bottles and mix it with water as indicated on the label.

1 onion
1 carrot
1 clove garlic
1 stick of celery
2–3 tablespoons vegetable oil

$^1/_2$ teaspoon ground mace
$2^1/_4$ cups yellow split peas
5–6 cups chicken or veg stock
2 bay leaves
approx. 8 frankfurters

Peel the onion, carrot and garlic and cut the onion and carrot into rough chunks. Put them all, along with the roughly cut up stick of celery into the bowl of a food processor. Blitz till all are finely chopped.

Spoon the oil into a heavy-based wide saucepan and put on medium heat. When warm, add the chopped vegetables from the processor and cook for 5–10 minutes, until soft but not colored.

Add the ground mace – this may be a small amount but it's crucial to the taste – give a good stir and then add the split peas and stir again till they're glossily mixed with the oil-slicked, cooked-down vegetables. Pour over 5 cups stock and add the bay leaves, then bring to the boil. Cover, turn down the heat and cook for about an hour until everything is tender and sludgy, adding more stock as needed. Sometimes the peas seem to thicken too much before they actually cook and need to be watered down. Taste for seasoning once everything's ready.

You can add the frankfurters as you wish. It's probably easiest just to cut them into slices – I tend to add them in chunks of about an inch each – and throw them into the soup to warm, but I just put them into the microwave (40 seconds on high is about right for one or two franks; fiddle about with times when there are more), then slice them hot and add them to each person's bowl as they come. Not an elegant soup, I'll admit, but a near-perfect one.

CHAMPAGNE RISOTTO FOR TWO

Please, whatever you do, don't open a bottle of champagne specifically for this. I mean, not unless you want to, and drink the other half of the bottle as you eat, as a wallowing-in-luxury way to welcome in the New Year, in bed preferably.

It's a great way to use up any dregs from last night, though. And any fizzy white wine would do; indeed I most often make it with Prosecco which I love inordinately for its soft bubble and mood-enhancing Venetian zing.

Serves 2

note
To be honest, the wine you use doesn't even have to be fizzy; but it does have to be good: not great, but happily drinkable; you really taste it here.

And in place of the leeks you could use four fat scallions.

1 small stick of celery, $^1/_4$ cup when chopped
2 leeks, 1 cup when white part is chopped
$^3/_4$ stick unsalted butter
$1^1/_2$ cups champagne

1 teaspoon olive oil
3 cups chicken (or vegetable) stock
$1^1/_3$ cups carnaroli or arborio rice
$^1/_4$ cup Parmesan, grated
ground white pepper

Chop the celery and the white part of the leeks very finely. Melt $^1/_2$ stick of the butter with the oil in a wide saucepan and cook them gently until softened. In another saucepan, pour in 1 cup of the champagne and all of the chicken stock, and keep on a very low simmer nearby to your risotto.

When the vegetables are soft, tip in the rice and turn in the oil until slicked and glossy. Turn up the heat, pour in the remaining $^1/_2$ cup champagne and, stirring all the time, let it be bubblingly absorbed.

Turn down the heat slightly but not too low, and keep adding ladles of champagney stock, letting one ladleful be absorbed before adding the next, stirring all the while.

Once the rice is cooked – 18–20 minutes should do it – stop, even if you've got some stock left over. Equally, if the rice has absorbed all the stock and yet needs further cooking – both happen – add a little more, or if it's just a very little more you think you need, boiling water will do.

Off the heat, beat in the remaining butter and the Parmesan. Season with a good grinding of white pepper if possible to keep it looking pure and unspeckled.

GOLD DUST

This is just praline by another name; nuts and caramel are left to harden and then broken into pieces and blitzed to a mound of gold filings in the blender or food processor. And what can you do with this precious rubble? Scatter it over vanilla ice cream: some of it stays hard and crunchy while some melts into an almost-sauce.

May the rest of the year be as perfect. As if.

1 cup superfine sugar

$^2/_3$ cup water

1$^1/_4$ cups blanched almonds

Pour the sugar and water into a saucepan and stir to dissolve. Then, over medium heat, bring to the boil without stirring until the liquid reaches a golden caramel color. This should take about 10 minutes. Meanwhile roughly chop the pale nuts. Add them to the pan and allow to bubble away for a further 2–3 minutes until the mixture becomes dark and sticky.

Pour the mixture on to, preferably, some of that glorious re-usable, utterly non-stick silicon parchment paper, Silpat, or otherwise some oiled baking foil, on a baking sheet and leave to cool and set.

The mixture should be completely cold before you break it up and turn it into gold dust. For the greatest amount of glintingness, cut with a large sharp knife into splin-tery chunks, and then into smaller shards. Or, if you prefer, whiz it in a food processor for a blonder, less sparkling, mix: both taste fabulous.

Store in an airtight tin or Tupperware container. I keep the amber disc of it whole in the tin and just cut off what I want when I want it.

note

If you're feeling more ener-getic, you can make glitzy pancakes. Make crêpes according to the recipe on page 255. Dollop ice cream in the center of each cooked crêpe, wrap, and arrange on a plate. Cover with the shining gold dust.

Forget the blitzing, though, and you have a wonderful, cof-fee-accompanying nut brittle.

GALETTE DES ROIS

I couldn't entirely miss out Epiphany. It's a childish thing really, but it just happens to be my birthday and so the date has always had a particular resonance for me anyway. Here, I see it as a final trumpet in the New Year's celebrations. And this is my new take on the traditional French cake made, in some form or another, for aeons to celebrate this date.

It's meant to be a cake of almond paste, studded with some sort of charm, encased in puff pastry; the one who finds the charm is given a gold paper crown and made king for the day. I've made it here with filo, and infused it with the Middle Eastern scent of cardamom and orange-flower water, which seems in a sense to be more fitting for a cake to celebrate the successful journey by the three wise men following that star in the east.

Serves 8–10

note

Don't feel constricted by the date on which this is traditionally eaten: it happens to be a perfect alternative dessert for either the New Year's Day Lunch or Dinner.

1 stick butter
3 cardamom pods, bruised
1lb fresh filo pastry (not frozen)
1 china charm of your choice

FOR THE FILLING
1 stick plus 1 tablespoon very soft
  butter
2 cups ground almonds
$^3/_4$ cup sugar

1 golden cardboard crown from a
  party shop, or keep a crown from
  a Christmas cracker

3 eggs
1 teaspoon orange-flower water
1 teaspoon baking powder

Preheat the oven to 350°F, and put a baking sheet in the oven to heat up at the same time.

Melt the butter with the bruised cardamom pods in a small saucepan, and then take off the heat to cool slightly.

Brush the bottom and sides of a 10 inch-springform pan with the melted butter. Halve the filo pastry, and wrap one half in plastic wrap and put it back in the fridge.

Layer the filo sheets in the springform pan, buttering each one as you go. Overlap about three sheets of filo across the bottom of the pan with excess filo hanging over the sides (you will need this overlap to fold in later). Turn the pan and layer the next three sheets across the other way so there is even coverage in the round springform. Continue with the half quantity of filo until it is all used up.

Process all of the filling ingredients to make a soft marzipan like mixture, and spread this into the bottom of the filo-lined pan. Ease the filling into the edges of the pan so that the base is evenly covered. Hide your charm carefully within the grainy golden mix.

Take the remaining half of filo out of the fridge and cover the top of the galette in the same way as before, buttering each layer of filo and working across the pan in layers of three before turning again to do another layer.

Once the pastry is all used up, fold in the edges so that you cover the top with a rough crinkly layer of filo, and butter it well. Bake the galette for 40–45 minutes on top of the heated baking sheet. The top should be golden brown and crispy.

Leave on a cooling rack to stand for about 20 minutes before removing the sides of the springform pan. The cake is now ready for its coronation.

The filling stays pretty runny until it's cool, which is when you should start slicing into it. Use a sharp knife as otherwise you'll crush the galette as you try and press through the beautiful, crinkly, filo topping.

MEATLESS FEASTS

IT'S HARD to banish that primitive part of me that insists that a feast needs meat; when I celebrate I do indeed feel I want to bring on the fatted calf. And I don't think the impulse is entirely that of bloodlust. The feast, any feast, implies extravagance, using food as a way of wallowing in the nourishing blessings of life. That has always meant providing food which would be scarce at other times of the year; throughout history, meat has been everyday fare only of the rich. Mass industrialization and intensive farming (neither of which has served the cause of better food) have pretty well put paid to that, but the fact remains that protein still costs more than anything else, and is still, generally, what we feel we must provide to signify an occasion has worth. We may not like to think we are making such materially bound value judgments, but we do.

But the truth is, even if meat is no longer the luxury it was, time is an ever scarcer commodity. The gift of a feast, then, lies in finding that time and choosing to fill it with the preparations necessary to provide dinner, regardless of its fleshly content. When sentimentalists say that the secret ingredient of all good cooking is love, they are not wrong, only embarrassing.

And I think it tends to be the case that vegetarian food takes more time, more effort than most meat-heavy feasts. It's even more a labor of love if what you want to do is make someone who doesn't eat meat feel comfortable at the table. This is always a difficult area for me. I wouldn't want to be rude, and the idea of inviting someone who doesn't eat meat for dinner and then having the table heaving with flesh, except for some specially wrought, individual portion of some veggie-pleaser, however delightful, does make me uncomfortable. I do understand that the squeamishness, moral and visceral, of those who abhor eating meat would be hard to overcome.

Indeed, I live in terror of being infected with it. There is a Graham Greene play, *The Potting Shed*, which tells the angst-ridden story of the impact on a devoutly atheistic family when one of their number has a religious vision, smartly followed by a stunned conversion, in the potting shed of the title. The fear and tension of the family whose scornful disbelief is so suddenly shot to pieces resounds particularly with me, for I have a concomitant fear. One day something similarly terrible, so ideologically unforeseen, could happen to me: one day I could wake up and find myself vegetarian.

This is no proudly anti-PC stance, nor do I assume that you have to be a vegetarian to enjoy vegetables. I love them, and couldn't bear a meal which wasn't heaped up with them. But just vegetables? For an eager eater, it would be the cruellest blow, like being a painter who suddenly finds several colors taken away from his palette. Now, there is a lot to be said for limitations. At times when I have felt particularly saddled with them, I can turn brave and chipper and like to convince myself that cooking is, when you come to think of it, not unlike the sonnet form: the art lies in the constraints. But the whole of the fleshly kingdom, banished from the kitchen? Even I chafe at such constraints.

The issue here is not taste, but texture. Whenever I want to make a real, three-courser of a dinner party with full and frank veggie appeal, no sop provided for carnivores, I can feel the menu skeetering off balance all too easily. True, there are more varieties of vegetable than there are of meat, but I still think to get as many permutations of taste and texture without meat as you can with it is well-nigh impossible. That's not a disaster, but if you strive for balance and harmony it can pose problems. Not, I'm glad to say, insurmountable ones; and the thought processes alone devoted to overcoming them can be pleasurable. In some respects, even though you can feel tangled up trying to sort it out, that's the easy part. But you do just have to work harder. And by work harder, I mean strive for lighter effect. It's very easy for a vegetarian menu to weigh eaters down with its eager agglomeration of carbohydrates. And it's not just out of fashionable faddishness that I feel this is to be avoided. I am all for providing plenty, but not that turgid, after-dinner bloat and consequent slump.

There are many meat-free recipes within this book, but the three meatless feasts below are specifically formed to provide meals that – irritating though the phrase must be to vegetarian readers – do not seem remotely lacking to even the most committed and bloodthirsty carnivores.

ITALIAN-INSPIRED SUPPER FOR SIX

You do not have to be a vegetarian to appreciate the pleasure to be gained from dipping raw vegetables into untraditionally lemony guacamole, followed by griddled slices of eggplant, wrapped around a minted, garlicky easy cheese filling and doused in sweet tomato sauce, and then for dessert, a sugar-dusted pyramid of ricotta fritters. Anyone who doesn't want to eat this, doesn't deserve dinner in the first place.

It's no coincidence that the supper has an Italianate flavor. They may have a relatively low number of vegetarians in Italy, but Italians have a way with veg that ensures their mainstream position without special pleading. Still, I admit my Italianified guacamole is stretching a point: I've never eaten an avocado in Italy, nor met an Italian who'd countenance one. But I wanted some balance with sharp and strong *involtini* to follow and wanted a softer, less pungent version of guacamole: so lemon replaces the lime, summer-scented basil the cilantro; the chilli is out altogether. I always use scallions rather than regular, digestion-searing onion and I can't endure the inclusion of tomato. This is all green, all good – and forget (though you don't have to) tortilla chips, but use sugar-snaps, quartered fennel, or swords of bitter-sweet endive to dunk in, or smear this jade clay on fabulous, toasted sourdough bread.

The *involtini* is such a favorite of mine that I've scarcely written a book without some version of it. You, in turn, can fiddle with the cheeses that stuff the eggplant bundles as you can with the herbs. This is a dish, both from the point of view of the cook and the happy eater, that's hard to go wrong with.

The *baci di ricotta* – the perfect kisses, hot, soft and melting – are a surprisingly easy dessert if there aren't too many of you eating. It's just a question of mixing ricotta, sugar, cinnamon, vanilla, eggs and flour in a bowl (by hand) and then frying rounded teaspoonsful in just under an inch of oil until you have some light, small, vaguely ball-shaped fritters (like doughnut holes in solid form, really) which need no more than a powdery dusting with confectioners' sugar. I love them, too, with a few sliced strawberries on the side, but you don't even have to treat them as a proper dessert, with plates and cutlery. Just put the mounded dish of them on the table with coffee and watch them go.

I am mindful of the dairy build-up – cheese in two courses – but the *baci* taste too ethereal and fragrant to feel like further clogging by casein.

ITALIANIFIED GUACAMOLE

Anything to do with avocados is necessarily a last-minute affair, but this is the easiest thing to make. You can just fork away distractedly as you blather to your friends in the kitchen. And since the *involtini*, below, can be pretty well entirely done (bar the final oven-blitz) in advance, you can accommodate a small amount of kitchen-counter futtskying when everyone's about. In fact, it's partly this that makes this menu pretty well the perfect supper for me: enough can be made in advance to eliminate the need for tension or panic, while allowing for some low-level last-minute assembly which lets your friends feel cared for and lets you feel that you're warmly caring for them.

1 large lemon	3 medium fully ripe avocados	Serves 6
1 fat clove garlic	3 scallions	
2 teaspoons sea salt/1 teaspoon table salt	large bunch basil	

TO SERVE

4 slices sourdough bread, halved and toasted	2 cups sugar-snap peas, topped and tailed
1–2 heads red endive, separated into leaves	1–2 bulbs of fennel, trimmed and cut in strips

Zest the lemon and keep the little pile of yellow dust to one side for a moment. Juice the bald lemon into a bowl, mince in the garlic and sprinkle in the salt, trying to break it up with your fingers as it goes in (if it's the better, coarse salt, that is). Fork everything together to dissolve.

Peel and pit the avocados, and mash the flesh in the bowl with your lemony fork. Finely slice the scallions and chop up most of the basil leaves, reserving some choice small whole leaves for the top. Sprinkle over the lemon zest and then mix everything together with the fork; the consistency should not be a purée, more of a knobbly dip.

Dollop on to a serving dish, sprinkle with the reserved basil and serve immediately, with toasted sourdough (the *bruschetta nuda* of my fancy), chicory leaves, sugar-snaps and sliced fennel – or indeed any crudités of your choice.

note
Or make one of my favorite salads – see page 121 for a picture – by tossing together 8–10 cups baby spinach, $1/2$ cup pumpkin seeds and the scooped flesh of 2 avocados. Make a dressing of 1 teaspoon pumpkin oil, 2 tablespoons ground nut oil, $1/2$ teaspoon salt, and the zest and juice of 1 lime.

INVOLTINI

"*Involtini*" just indicates that something is wrapped – turned – around something else. I always use eggplants as the casing rather than, say, zucchini, partly because you can get more in, and partly because I think it's the best possible use of an eggplant. Each slice provides a firm-enough wrapper, but the buff-colored flesh, when tiger-striped on the griddle, softens so that it merges cosily into the filling inside and the sauce that covers it. This delectable melting texture is best savored when the *involtini* are what can only be described as lukewarm. I think most food is best neither hot nor cold but at that flavor-intensifying temperature which hovers around blood heat, and *involtini* stand as the sovereign example of this rule.

The griddling of the eggplants is an oil-spluttering and not particularly entertaining process, though not hard, and I tend to do this stage a day or two in advance. You could certainly mix up the cheeses etc. for the filling in advance, too, though not quite so far in advance, adding the egg at the last minute. Though as long as everything's cold, you can assemble this, complete with tomato sauce covering and a scattering of chopped mozzarella, and then stick it in the fridge until you want to bake them.

It would be better to let the *involtini* get to room temperature before you put them in the oven, but their meatlessness makes this less crucial; only be sure to cook them for longer than indicated below, even if you do want to let them sit for 20 minutes' cooling down later.

Serves 6

2–3 large eggplants (approx. 1lb each), cut lengthways in slices at most $^1/_4$in thick, to give about 18 slices
approx. $^3/_4$ cup olive oil (not extra virgin)

$2^1/_2$ cups tomato pulp
2 balls mozzarella ($1^1/_2$ cups when chopped)

FOR THE STUFFING
$^1/_2$ cup crumbled feta cheese
1 ball mozzarella
$^1/_4$ cup Parmesan, grated
$^1/_2$ cup pinenuts
$^1/_3$ cup raisins, soaked in $^1/_4$ cup hot water for approx. 10 minutes until plump, then drained
4 tablespoons extra virgin olive oil

2 tablespoons breadcrumbs
1 garlic clove, crushed or minced
zest of 1 lemon
$1^1/_2$ teaspoons dried mint
2 tablespoons freshly chopped flat leaf parsley
1 egg, beaten

Heat a griddle and paint the eggplant slices with the oil on both sides before you put them on the hot griddle. I've specified slices of around $^1/_4$in, but I didn't mean to suggest you get a tape measure out. Just aim for thin slices but not so thin that as you cut you shave away in places. Eighteen slices gives everyone three bundles each, which is more than it sounds; you get a decent wedge of *involtini* out of this. But if you want to up the number of rolls, buy more eggplants and boost stuffing ingredients as you wish; a little more cheese, and a tad more breadcrumbs should do it, without having to add an extra egg.

Cook the eggplant slices, turning them over until they are soft and crisscrossed on both sides with griddle marks. Remove them to a dish as you go, as they will have to be done in batches. Resist the temptation to wrap them for any length of time in paper towel or you will spend the rest of the day picking out bits of paper. By all means lay them in a sheet, doubled, of paper towel while you cook each new batch, but then remove them and put between pieces of parchment paper.

Leave the eggplant slices to cool as you make the stuffing. Or do as I always do and cook the eggplant some time in advance.

As you make the stuffing – if you are going straight ahead with the cooking – preheat the oven to 375°F. Crumble the feta into a bowl and then chop up the ball of mozzarella for the filling finely and add that along with the grated Parmesan. Throw in the pinenuts, the soaked and squeezed-out raisins, the extra virgin olive oil, breadcrumbs, garlic, lemon zest, mint and parsley. Crack in the egg and fork everything.

Take out each cooked eggplant slice in turn and place it on a table or work surface in front of you and dollop on a small amount of filling; I'd say this is like a bulging tablespoonful, but I don't use a measure – I just pinch in with my fingers. Roll it up fairly tightly to secure the filling and put each one, as you go, into a lightly greased gratin dish into which they'll fit snugly. You're going to end up with 18 fat little rolls, so it's pretty easy to work out which of your dishes will be best. The dish I use most often for this measures about 8 x 10in.

Pour over the tomato passata. Chop up the two balls of mozzarella; I use my mezzaluna for this, which is a strange feeling, the sharp blade biting into the ludicrously soft, damp flesh of the cheese. Drizzle with olive oil, add salt and pepper and bake in the oven for 25–30 minutes. Once out, let the pan stand for at least 10 minutes before serving.

note

Depending on the time of year, or your mood you could either serve some crunchy green beans with this or a lemony green salad. If you want to add more substance, drain 2–3 cans of garbanzos – or, even though they are not remotely Italian, some beauteous black beans – and warm them through in a little garlic-infused oil, or olive oil in which you have minced a small clove of garlic. Throw in some finely chopped deseeded red chilli pepper if you want a little more warmth, and feather with chopped parsley once in the dish. I just make this in a terracotta dish that goes straight from stove to table. As I do for the saffroned and sultana'd garbanzos on page 363, which you could, if in sufficiently rich feasting mode, absolutely consider.

BACI DI RICOTTA

I don't deny that having to stand stoveside frying 30 teaspoons of ricotta at the end of dinner is a slight draw-back, but these are so good, I really do think it's worth it. Besides, there's no getting around it. Somehow, that makes things easier for me. I just accept what has to be done, and get on with it. I wouldn't want to have to get up in the middle of some formal dinner and start deep-frying (or maybe I would: escape can be appealing for both host and guest at those sorts of gathering), but when it's just a case of your friends sitting around a table, it's not such a big deal. Go easy on the drink over dinner, though.

There are plenty of other desserts that would be easier to make but I can't, right now, think of any better. After the photo (opposite) was taken, despite admirable restraint throughout the shoot, I hoovered them up and had to be forcibly removed from them, at my own request and for my own good.

Makes 30

1 cup ricotta
2 eggs
$^1/_2$ cup all-purpose flour
$1^1/_2$ teaspoons baking powder
pinch salt

$^1/_2$ teaspoon ground cinnamon
1 tablespoon sugar
$^1/_2$ teaspoon vanilla extract
vegetable or corn oil for frying
2 teaspoons confectioners' sugar to serve

Put the ricotta and eggs into a bowl and beat until smooth. Add the flour, baking powder, salt, cinnamon, sugar and vanilla extract. Beat the mixture to make a smooth batter.

Fill a wide, shallow pan with about $^3/_4$in of oil. Heat the pan of oil until a tiny blob of batter sizzles when dropped into the hot fat.

Drop rounded teaspoons of the ricotta batter into the pan, about five or six at a time; don't be tempted to make them bigger, boring though this is – they will puff up on cooking. You need to turn them over quite quickly so it's best to do a few at a time. You don't want to get too frantic around all that hot fat. As they turn a golden brown, flip them over and leave them for a minute or so on the other side.

As you lift them out of the pan, place the cooked *baci di ricotta* on some paper towel, just to remove the excess oil. Then pile the balls of heat-bronzed ricotta on to a plate in a rough-and-tumble pyramid shape, and push the confectioners' sugar through a small sieve evenly but thickly over them. Eat straightaway. As if…

COZY BUT ELEGANT DINNER FOR EIGHT

LEMON, MINT AND SPINACH SALAD
GRIDDLED ZUCCHINI
MUSHROOM STROGANOFF WITH BASMATI RICE
PUMPKIN SEED BRITTLE

I don't, on the whole, go in for three-course dinners anymore but, in a sense, the main course is so much less cluttered when you're doing without meat that there's less chance of overloading people, or indeed yourself, when you stretch dinner out a little, as I have in all three menus here. If it all looks as if I'm tottering into four-course territory, I'm not. The griddled zucchini are not to be eaten at a separate course from the salad, but neither are they conjoined. Think of them as entirely separate entities that go well together. Sometimes I think that having a couple of plates of food to pick at on the table just loosens everything, and makes for a less straight-backed, tense, dinner-party atmosphere. If you'd prefer to shunt the zucchini into the main-course arena, be my guest. I don't feel enormously strongly but am, as ever, letting my instinct – nothing more than that – be my guide to the logic and flow of a menu.

Meat eaters might think a beefless stroganoff a pointless venture, but I'm one and think nothing of the kind. The mushrooms, unconventionally sherried, familiarly spiced, swathed in sour cream and banked about with plain boiled rice just scented with cardamom go to make something that hits that perfect note between comforting and elegantly uplifting. All I would say is that without the meat juices to add depth and flavor to the sauce, you need to add much more paprika and nutmeg than you would think necessary. But eating this, you can see why the Japanese ascribe another, fifth, taste along with salty, sweet, sour and bitter (the four the western palate recognizes) which they call "*unami*," meaning meaty or savory and which they locate, particularly, in mushroom or other edible fungi.

I am not a chef, am nothing like a chef, do not want to be a chef (which is just as well) but never-theless I do go to restaurants sometimes and come back dying to reproduce back home something I've eaten out. The pumpkin seed brittle is a case in point. I had some at one of my favorite New York restaurants, Beppe, and it has the virtue – leaving aside the joy of its consumption for now – of being simple to make. I know boiling up sugar to make caramel isn't everyone's idea of simplicity, and it can certainly be fraught. But it's not hard so long as you don't walk away from the pan; it requires focus not dexterity or skill.

If you're not too dairied-out after the stroganoff, by all means serve this with ice cream, but I don't really like anything to cloud the brittle's pure and sweet nuttiness. I want mine with nothing but a cup of devil-black coffee.

LEMON, MINT AND SPINACH SALAD

If this recipe looks like there's nothing much to it, that's because it's true. You're cutting up a lemon, chopping up some mint, and tossing them together with a little oil and some baby spinach leaves which, if you're like me, you're just tumbling out of a package. Simplicity itself, but an end result that has satisfying complexity. I love the balance between the gently ferrous tang of the baby spinach, the sour juiciness of the lemon, and mint, that often underrated herb which gives both peppery warmth and a cool, cool hit at the same time.

1 largeish lemon
$^1/_3$ cup fresh mint leaves, plus
   extra for the top

$^1/_2$ tablespoon sea salt
8oz/10 cups baby spinach leaves
3 tablespoons extra virgin olive oil

Serves 8

Cut off the top and bottom of a lemon, stand it on a wooden board and, cutting down with a small sharp knife, slice off the skin and pith, rotating the fruit until you come full circle. Cut the lemon flesh into $^1/_4$in circles and then each circle into eighths, putting them – and all juice – into a bowl as you go. In other words, you want the lemon in small chunks.

     Cut the mint leaves, with scissors for ease, into thin strips over the lemon pieces, and sprinkle over the salt and some pepper. Add the spinach leaves and oil and toss everything together with your hands. Now decant on to a large round or oval plate – or whatever you want to serve this on – and drop a few whole mint leaves over the dressed salad.

GRIDDLED ZUCCHINI

If you wanted to make *involtini di zucchini*, this is how you would go about things. In other words, you're not doing anything different from what you did to the eggplant, in the menu above (see page 124). What makes life easier is that you don't proceed with stuffing and baking. Unsurprisingly, this is far less substantial but, eaten warm, a toothsome accompaniment to the cold, astringent salad.

1$^1/_2$oz or 5 medium zucchini
$^1/_4$ cup olive oil

juice of 1 lemon
Sea salt

Serves 8

note
You can griddle the zucchini ahead, adding the lemon juice and salt when you are ready to eat.

Trim the ends of the zucchini, and slice each one lengthways just under $^1/_4$in thick. You should get roughly five slices from each zucchini. Put the oil into a large shallow dish, and add the zucchini slices, coating each slice with oil as you place it in.

     Heat a large ridged griddle and cook the zucchini until soft and burnished with griddle marks, turning the slices frequently to get a good scorched criss-cross pattern. Lay the griddled slices on a plate and spritz them with the lemon juice, sprinkle with the salt and serve the zucchini either warm or at room temperature.

MUSHROOM STROGANOFF WITH BASMATI RICE

This may seem to require an awful lot of mushrooms, but you have to remember how much they cook down: what you find difficult to cram into a pan, turns out, when cooked, just to fill one serving platter.

This is a good recipe to do when you're expecting friends round for dinner midweek – indeed the whole menu is – as you can get most of it done the minute you get back from work, leaving yourself time for a quick bath with a drink before everyone arrives. Plus, it doesn't matter if they're late – as I'm sure they will be – as all you need to do is put a flame under the pan of cooked mushrooms and onion, reheat, adding the salt, sherry, spices and parsley as and when your friends are ready to eat.

Serves 8

note
If you'd prefer to use white wine in place of the sherry, go right ahead.

1 large onion
2 cloves garlic
¹/₄ cup olive oil
8oz/approx. 4¹/₂ cups shiitake
    mushrooms
10oz/approx. 4 cups button
    mushrooms
8oz/approx. 4¹/₂ cups cremini
    mushrooms
8oz/approx. 4¹/₂ cups field
    mushrooms

1 stick butter
1 tablespoon sea salt/
    1¹/₂ teaspoons table salt
¹/₄ cup Amontillado sherry
1 tablespoon paprika
¹/₂ tablespoon freshly grated
    nutmeg
1¹/₂ cups sour cream
¹/₃ cup chopped parsley

Peel and quarter the onion and process with the peeled garlic cloves until everything is finely chopped. Heat the oil in a large wide pan and cook the onion and garlic mush until softened, but not colored.

Remove the stalks from the shiitake and slice them; quarter the button mushrooms and slice them too. Slice the cremini mushrooms, and peel and quarter the inky field mushrooms, discarding the stalks first.

Add the butter to the pan and tumble in the mushrooms when it has all but melted. Try and turn the mushrooms in the pan, although this will be difficult, I know, as even a big pan will be extremely full. Put a lid on the pan and cook the mushrooms for about 15 minutes. Stop at this point if you're cooking ahead of time.

Take off the lid (reheat first if you've done the above bit earlier) and add the salt, sherry, paprika, nutmeg and sour cream. I don't think this needs pepper, but by all means add it if you want to. Stir this deep, creamy buff-colored and nubbly mixture on the heat for about 5 minutes, add most of the parsley, stir again, then put it on whatever dish you're serving it from and sprinkle over the rest of the parsley.

THE RICE

I'd use 2$\frac{1}{2}$ cups basmati rice here. Cook according to package instructions. I have to say I am a firm believer in electric rice cookers (and see page 243 for a full enthusiastic exegesis on the subject) but don't want to get into my salesman's patter here. Whichever way you're cooking the rice, lightly press on 3 cardamom pods with the side of a knife, just to crush them slightly first, and chuck them into the water along with the rice. I don't salt my rice, finding the richness and depth of the aromatic and creamy mushrooms flavor enough. The cardamom provides musky fragrance, which is all this rice – beautiful in its plainness – needs.

PUMPKIN SEED BRITTLE

I hope I'm making your life easier when I say you should make this well in advance of dinner. This is not just because you need the brittle to be completely cold before shattering it into shards to serve with coffee, but because making caramel with an audience, or even the prospect of one, can be a step too far. I always like any form of cooking which involves a possible element of danger, but even so, regard that as a private pleasure. I wouldn't want to have a tableful of people waiting as I did it. It would be as nervy-making as reversing into a parking spot with a crowd of passers-by grinding to a halt to watch and make those irritating would-be-helpful hand signals as you do so.

1$\frac{1}{4}$ cups sugar	$\frac{1}{4}$ teaspoon cream of tartar	Serves 8
$\frac{1}{2}$ cup water	1 cup green pumpkin seeds	

note
This is just not the same made with supermarket, dried out, bleached-out husks. Use organic, still oily green pumpkin seeds only.

Cover a baking sheet with a piece of Silpat or other re-usable parchment, or tear off some aluminum foil and lightly oil it. Dissolve the sugar, water and cream of tartar in a saucepan over a low heat. Turn the heat up and bring the mixture to a boil but do not stir. Let the syrup bubble over a fairly high heat for about 10 minutes until it turns a deep golden amber color. Don't be tempted to wander away, make a phone call or leave the pan unattended, as the syrup could caramelize sooner. There are various factors at play here, and I know nothing of the dimensions of your pans or what materials they're made of – and that's not the whole story either.

Quickly tip the pumpkin seeds into the amber-colored syrup, swirl the pan so that they become evenly coated and then take off the heat. Pour the syrup immediately on to the Bake-O-Glide or oiled-foil-lined tray, trying to spread the molten liquid in a thin layer. It is possible to spread the brittle with a palette knife if it has mounded too much, but move fast: you will have only a short time to do this before it begins to set.

Leave the brittle to cool and harden completely before breaking it into pieces. I rather like to leave it as it is, a wibbly-wobbly outlined disc of green-studded amber, and quite, quite beautiful, bashing it into sharp pieces at the table.

SUPPER ALLA ROMANA
FOR TEN

PENNE ALLA VODKA
RICOTTA AND PINENUT SALAD
ICE CREAM WITH BLONDE MOCHA SAUCE

There are times when however much – in theory – you enjoy chatting to friends over a little chopping or stirring, it just isn't going to play. For me, the stress levels rise exponentially with the amount of people you've invited or the level of activity otherwise required of an evening. If you've got more than eight people over, even if it's only a little over, then the hubbub can get too great and even the most casual, last-minute preparation can nudge you over the brink.

Not that I would even begin to suggest going into full party-planner mode with a banquet here. This is very much supper, not least because the main part of it is a big bowl of earthily welcoming pasta. And yes, that pasta itself has to be cooked very much at the last minute but the sauce can be cooked well in advance and then reheated. Penne alla vodka is the perfect recipe for easy entertaining: short pasta is easier to cook in quantity than long stringy strands and the sauce is amusingly retro – think 1960s Rome, where indeed the dish emanated – but seriously good. I first ate it about 20 years ago in a brick-room of a place, in Rome, called Taverna Flavia, which had proudly been the location of post-filming suppers for cast and crew during the making of *Cleopatra*. For all I know, they still have their shrine to Elizabeth Taylor – "il Liz room" – as they had on my visit years after the movie was shot. I hope they still have the penne alla vodka on the menu too. It sounds the unlikeliest of inventions, but it works strangely well: the vodka gives a grainy depth balanced by the acid fruitiness of the tomatoes (think Bloody Mary), both mellowed by cream and the butter.

The rest of the dinner is not essentially Roman, but I'm letting that pass. Certainly, I'm not being very Italian by suggesting you serve a salad after rather than before the pasta. My feeling is that the pasta is a great main course and you don't need a starter before. Besides, nothing is less relaxing than having to jump up and attend to boiling pans in the middle of supper. Just get the pasta going, assemble the salad and sit back.

In the spirit of this laid-back, unfussy supper, I encourage you openly to supply good store-bought ice cream for dessert, and with it I press upon you a simple sauce that you can make in advance, my blonde mocha, so called because although it is based on a traditional mix of coffee and chocolate, the chocolate here is white. And I assure you, even those who hate white chocolate love this.

PENNE ALLA VODKA

As with all dishes that find their way into a country's repertoire, even oddball ones like this, there are many versions of this recipe: some add red pepper flakes, some cubes of bacon: I prefer it with neither, just the tomatoes, a base of onion and the butter and cream stirred through later. The vodka itself – and you may have to steel yourself for this – is better added to the drained pasta and not, as all the recipes I've seen, stirred into the sauce, but feel free to play with it as you please. You could, indeed, consider using pepper vodka. And if I suggest garlic-infused oil, that's just because I always have it to hand, and find it a lazy way to get the garlic flavor without running the risk of the garlic burning and becoming bitter as you cook the onion. But obviously, you can use real garlic, either minced (in which case watch out while you cook) or just add a peeled whole clove to give a softer, sweeter hit of garlic to the sauce. An Italian would add the garlic clove and remove it once it's browned; I find that as long as it's cooked whole with the onion it won't brown so much that it turns bitter and I'm happy to have an errant clove left in the sauce.

I know that two packages of pasta doesn't sound like enough for ten, and normally I'd agree with you. That's to say, I'd worry enormously about not giving people enough to eat if I cooked just one package of pasta for five. But it's always the case that the more people there are, the less they eat. I suppose it's because there's more conversation and therefore people give themselves less chewing time. Or something like that. By all means add more pasta if you feel safer that way, but I promise this makes a vatful.

1 good-sized onion	2lbs penne rigate or other short, preferably ridged, pasta	Serves 10
2 tablespoons garlic-infused oil		
salt	$^1/_2$ cup vodka	note
2 14oz cans/3 cups chopped tomatoes	4 tablespoons unsalted butter	I don't know why, but this
	Parmesan for grating	pasta is especially good cold
2 tablespoons heavy cream		too.

If you are cooking this just before you eat, put the water for the penne on to boil before you start the sauce. You will need a big pan, enough to take the pasta and its sauce later.

Finely chop the onion, either by hand or in a processor. In a large pan, heat the garlic oil and add the finely chopped onion and a good sprinkling of salt. Cook the onion fairly gently for about 15 minutes without letting it catch and burn, which just means giving it a stir every now and again. It should be very soft and almost beginning to caramelize.

Tip in the cans of chopped tomatoes and continue cooking over a gentle heat, simmering for another 15–20 minutes. If you're cooking this ahead, and I always do, stop here.

Reheat the almost-finished tomatoes (or just continue as you were if you're making this in one unbroken fluid movement), stir in the heavy cream and take the pan off the heat. When the water for the pasta comes to the boil add a good measure of salt and tip in the penne. Set a timer for 3–4 minutes less than the package instructions for cooking it, as you want to make sure it's cooked al dente and will need to start tasting early.

Drain the cooked pasta, tip it back in the pan and pour over the vodka, and add the butter and some more salt. Turn the penne in the vodka and melting butter and then tip it into the tomato sauce unless it is easier to pour the tomato sauce over the pasta: it depends on the sizes of pans you are using.

Toss the pasta in the sauce until it is evenly coated and turn out into a large, warmed bowl. Put it on the table along with a block of Parmesan and a grater.

RICOTTA AND PINENUT SALAD

I don't deny it – and why should I – that this salad is at its gently sparkling best when you use fresh ricotta for it. So if you live near an Italian deli, then you should definitely make the effort to go and get the real thing. But this should not be the clincher: you should still make it if you have to rely on supermarket tubs of ricotta. And I make no bones about the fact that I pretty well always use those ready-mixed packs of designer salad leaves.

I love the soft bland milkiness of ricotta, and this quiet-voiced salad is just the thing after the boisterousness of the penne before.

$^3/_4$ cup pinenuts

2 cups fresh ricotta cheese

$^1/_3$ cup (or supermarket package) basil leaves, plus more to decorate

8–10 cups mixed salad leaves

12oz Belgian endive

2 tablespoons good-quality red wine vinegar

4 tablespoons extra virgin olive oil

$^1/_4$ teaspoon paprika

Serves 10

Toast the pinenuts in a large dry pan until darkly golden in color and tip on to a plate to cool.

Break up the ricotta with a fork in a bowl, and roughly tear the basil leaves into the cheese, reserving a few whole leaves to go on top of the salad later. Season with salt and pepper and leave to one side, just while you get on with everything else. You can't leave the torn-up basil leaves for long, though, as they soon begin to blacken.

Arrange the leaves on two large platters, and tear each endive into pieces, adding these in a ramshackle way to the salad leaves. Mix together the vinegar and oil and season with some salt and pepper. Sprinkle over each plate of salad, tossing to mix in the dressing. Spoon several mounds of the ricotta mixture on to the bed of salad leaves on each platter, so that as each person takes some salad they get a helping of ricotta too. Sprinkle the paprika over the tender little mounds of ricotta, and decorate with the reserved basil leaves.

BLONDE MOCHA SAUCE

I've touched on this above, but just let me remind you that even those in the anti-white-chocolate party go for this: all the white chocolate does is cut through the necessary bitterness of the coffee (effortlessly supplied in the form of instant espresso powder) and together, with the cream, they make for an almost butterscotch-cappuccino taste. The best way to cook this sauce is the night before you want to serve it, so there's plenty of time for it to chill down and firm up in the fridge. To be honest, 4–6 hours ahead is probably fine, but I sometimes find evening tinkering about in the kitchen easier than early-morning action. Once it's whisked, poured into a jug and left to cool in the fridge, the sauce thickens voluptuously. If you don't make this ahead, but use it from the pan, it's rather like pouring a fabulous latte over your ice cream. Frankly, there's nothing to complain about with either option: in both cases, we're talking about a rewarding finale to a dinner menu that allows you to invite a whole gaggle of friends over without ending up resenting them for accepting.

Serves 10

8oz white chocolate
2 cups heavy cream

3¹/₂ tablespoons instant espresso powder, just about enough to fill an espresso cup

note

Another way of approaching a coffee-ish sauce for ice cream is to make either the gorgeously dark sticky toffee sauce on page 235, adding, along with the sugar, 2 teaspoons of instant espresso powder. Or make *affogato* by giving everyone a small bowlful of vanilla ice cream together with a coffee cup of hot, strong espresso which they tip straightaway over the vanilla ice.

Break the chocolate into chunks and put into a heavy-based saucepan over the lowest heat possible with all the other ingredients. When the chocolate has melted, take the pan off the heat and whisk vigorously to thicken the sauce. I just use one of my little hand whisks for this.

Pour the blonde mocha sauce into a pitcher or glass measuring cup, cover the surface with a thin skin of plastic wrap and when cool, stick it into the fridge.

When you are ready to pour it over the ice cream, take it out of the fridge, give it a good stir and use it straight from the pitcher.

VALENTINE'S
DAY

THERE ARE just some people who come over all hearts and flowers and pink-foil balloons and Hallmark-card sentiment around St. Valentine's Day and others, like me, who so do not. I snarl. I sneer. I scorn. So what am I doing here?

Well might you ask. The thing is, sooner or later, you're browbeaten. To keep moaning on and droning against it is to be a party-pooper, like someone who complains so much at a game of charades that she draws unwelcome attention to her one feeble effort. It's a bit like the Borg really: Resistance is futile.

Now it is really a children's festival as much as anything else. And whereas I am unstinting in my cynicism for most of life, I try and protect my children from the full brunt of it for theirs. They want hearts: I give them hearts. Uncomplainingly, really, considering how dark my own one is.

Perhaps it's my fear of being willingly, if unashamedly, seduced by the naffness of it all that scares me and makes me so vocal in my disdain. Certainly, once I started acutting-out hearts and devising lovesome menus, I felt I could have gone on for ever. Especially with those hearts. It's surprising how gratifying that peculiar shape is. Noël Coward wrote that it was strange how potent cheap music can be; the same – in a different sphere – holds true in the kitchen. Sooner or later, you yield to the potency of the cute. I only wish it could have been later.

LOVE BUNS

In another time I'd have been satisfied with calling these Valentine's Day buns but, as the saying goes, if you're going to get wet, you may as well go swimming.

Makes 12

note
If you want to make a similar-style offering but without the hard work, simply make the love buns, let them cool then spread them with strawberry jam. Whisk some heavy cream until thick and mound and swirl this on the little cakes to achieve much the same effect as the Mr. Whippy icing in the picture on the previous page, and serve immediately with or without sprinkles.

FOR THE BUNS
1 stick plus 1 tablespoon soft butter
$^1/_2$ cup plus 1 tablespoon superfine sugar
2 eggs
$^3/_4$ cup all-purpose flour

$^1/_2$ teaspoon baking soda
2 teaspoons baking powder
2 teaspoons real vanilla extract
2–3 tablespoons milk

FOR THE TOPPING
2 egg whites
$^1/_2$ cup light corn syrup
$^1/_2$ cup superfine sugar
$^1/_4$ teaspoon salt

$^1/_4$ teaspoon cream of tartar
1 teaspoon pure vanilla extract
heart-shaped sprinkles to decorate

Take everything you need out of the fridge in time to bring to room temperature – this makes a huge difference to the lightness of the love buns later – and preheat the oven to 400°F.

Put all of the ingredients for the buns, except for the milk, into a food processor and blitz until smooth. Pulse while adding the milk down the funnel, to make a smooth dropping consistency.

Divide the mixture into a 12-bun muffin tin lined with muffin papers or heart-patterned cases, and bake in the oven for 15–20 minutes. They should have risen and be golden on top; you want a little peak if possible.

Let them cool a little in their tin on a rack, and then take them carefully out of the tin to cool in their papers, still on the wire rack.

Now for the topping. Here there is a slight dilemma, as you'll make more than you need for the 12 buns, but if you halve the quantities, you won't have quite enough. If you're making these for you and your one true love, then I presume you won't need all 12 of them, in which case you could freeze most of the buns to be iced and eaten at some later date, and halve the topping ingredients to decorate the few you want today.

This is a frosting that has a kind of meringue base, by which you whisk egg whites over heat until they're stiff and gleaming. So make a double-boiler with a heatproof bowl that will fit snugly over a saucepan of barely simmering water, and put all of the ingredients for the frosting, except for the vanilla and sprinkles, into the bowl. Whisk everything with an electric beater until the icing becomes thick and holds peaks like a meringue. This will take about 5 minutes, so be patient.

Take the bowl off the saucepan and on to a cool surface and keep whisking while you add the vanilla. Then keep whisking until the mixture cools a little. You want a proper peaked and whipped covering here, so spoon some frosting over each bun, and then dollop another spoonful over in a swirly fashion. Immediately shake over your choice of sprinkles, as the icing will set very quickly. Indeed, these look rather like stage prop buns or the fake ones that some bakeries used to keep in their windows, so plasticky and gleaming are they.

CHOCOLATE RASPBERRY HEART

I am embarrassed about how much I love this cake, and how eagerly I make it. But then, apart from the Frederick's of Hollywood appearance, it has a lot going for it: the chocolate base is tender and luscious; the cake can be made in advance, and assembled at the last minute; it's cute to look at but not cloying to taste.

On top of that, I have had some vicarious success giving out early editions of the recipe for those who wanted, last year, to wow and to woo.

FOR THE CAKE

$2/3$ cup milk

1 tablespoon butter

1 tablespoon pure vanilla extract

3 eggs

1 cup superfine sugar

$1^1/_4$ cups all-purpose flour

3 tablespoons best unsweetened
   cocoa

1 teaspoon baking soda

FOR THE FILLING

$1/_2$ cup heavy or whipping cream

1 cup raspberries (and see ganache
   icing, over page)

FOR THE GANACHE ICING

$^2/_3$ cup heavy cream

$5^1/_2$oz dark chocolate, minimum 70% cocoa solids

1 tablespoon corn syrup

1 cup raspberries

Preheat the oven to 325°F. Grease and line two shallowish 9 inch heart-shaped pans with cut-out hearts of parchment paper.

Pour the milk into a small pan with the butter and heat until warm and the butter has melted. Or you can just stick a glass measuring cup in the microwave. When hot, add the vanilla.

Whisk the eggs and sugar till thick, light and frothy, really frothy; I use the flat paddle of my KitchenAid mixer for this, but you could equally well use a hand-held electric whisk. Meanwhile, combine the flour, cocoa and baking soda. Buy the best cocoa you can find, as this is what determines the rich and glorious taste of the cake.

Still beating the eggs and sugar, or going back to beat the eggs and sugar, pour in the hot buttery, vanilla'd milk and when incorporated, slowly fold in the flour-baking soda-cocoa mixture, either with the flat paddle on slow or with a rubber spatula by hand. You will need a final scrape-down and fold with a rubber spatula in any event.

Divide this mixture between the two pans and bake for about 20 minutes. Remove to a wire rack and let cool in their pans for about 10 minutes before turning the cakes out, and then turning them over so that they are sitting on the wire rack, out of their pans, the right way up. (This is because they are such tender cakes that the wire racks will leave indentations.) Now, I know the cakes look very thin and flat at this point, but I promise you the finished cake has the requisite depth once it's filled and iced.

Leave the cakes until cool before icing. You can make them a day in advance, but they are sticky so you must wrap them in parchment paper before wrapping in foil.

To fill the heart, whip the cream until thick but not stiff. Add the raspberries and crush with a fork, though not too finely. The cream should turn wonderfully pink, in a rose-and-white mottled fashion. Sandwich the hearts with this raspberry cream.

To ice, put the cream, the chocolate cut up in small pieces, and syrup in a pan over low to medium heat and when the chocolate seems to have all but melted into the warm cream, take off the heat and start whisking – just with a little hand whisk – until you have a smooth, glossy mixture. Pour, and then spread, preferably with a palette knife, over the top of the cake to the edges of the heart (not worrying too much about drips).

Take out your raspberries and, about $^1/_2$ inch or slightly less in from the edges of the heart, stud the chocolate topping with the raspberries (hole side down) or however, indeed, you like.

You can see from the picture that all is not lost, or not quite, if you are heavy-handed and sadly lacking in the decorative arts. I had thought of pretending that my children had iced the cake here as a cover for my clumsiness and ineptitude, but then decided it was better to come clean.

CUSTARD CREAM HEARTS

I have what I like to think of as a Wildean thing about reproducing artifice by more natural means. Thus, in *How to Eat*, I gave a recipe for graham crackers, and now I find myself propelled towards the homely accomplishment of the custard cream, hitherto – at least in my lifetime – only known in its packaged form. It's probably a brand heresy to say it, but these are so much better homemade. I knew that no one would be bothered to go through the motions in the normal run of things, but thought if I fashioned them as hearts, and designated them as a special token, you might consider it. And please do: they are not hard to make and fabulous to eat, on top of their heavenly appearance. To achieve this you need one piece of specialist equipment as well as the heart-cutters: a corn on the cob holder. This is my patented tool for making the dotted perforations like quaint stitching around the edges of each heart. And very satisfying work it is, too.

Makes approx. 14 custard cream hearts

FOR THE COOKIES

1 $^1/_4$ cups all-purpose flour
3 tablespoons Bird's custard powder
1 teaspoon baking powder
$^1/_2$ stick unsalted butter

$^1/_2$ cup Crisco (or other vegetable shortening)
3 tablespoons superfine sugar
1 egg
1 tablespoon milk or more to bind

FOR THE CUSTARD CREAM

1 tablespoon Bird's custard powder
$^3/_4$ cup confectioners' sugar

$^1/_2$ stick soft unsalted butter
1 teaspoon boiling water

Preheat the oven to 350°F.

To make the cookies, put the flour, custard powder and baking powder into a processor and pulse to mix. Add the butter, cut into smallish cubes and the Crisco, in mounded teaspoonfuls, and pulse to cut into the flour to create a crumbly mixture.

Tip in the sugar and pulse again, and then beat the egg and tablespoon of milk together. Pour down the funnel of the processor with the engine running until it clumps together into a ball. Go cautiously: you may not need all of the egg and milk or you may need to add more milk to make it come together. Form the dough into a ball, press down into a fat disc, then wrap in plastic wrap, and let it rest in the fridge for 20 minutes.

Roll the dough out on a lightly floured surface to a thickness of $^1/_4$ inch. Dip a 2-inch heart-shaped cutter in flour and then cut out your shapes. You want an even number of hearts, as you will sandwich them together later. It is possible to get about 30 cookies out of the dough, but you can get more if you re-roll the pastry. I generally stop around 28 so that you end up with 14 cookies, which seems appropriate for the date. That's when you know you're going downhill: when you let yourself be tainted with both commercialism and numerology.

Prick the outside edge of each heart all the way around on one side with a corn on the cob holder, or other pointed implement of choice. Cook on a lined baking sheet for 15 minutes, and then let the cookies cool on a rack before sandwiching them.

To make the custard cream, put the custard powder and confectioners' sugar into the processor and pulse briefly to combine and delump. Add the butter, and blitz together until you get a smooth cream. Add the teaspoon of boiling water and pulse again.

Sandwich each biscuit with about 1 teaspoon of custard cream, by gently spreading a layer of the cream over the unpricked side of a biscuit and then wiggling a matching top on to it. This helps avoid crumbling and breakage, as the cookies are quite frangible.

COOKING FOR THE ONE YOU LOVE

THE PERFECT SINGLE SUPPER

POTATO AND ONION HASH

Please don't think of this as a sad entry, in either the original or now datedly newfangled sense of the word.

Serves 1

1 small onion

1 tablespoon olive oil

2 cups all-purpose potatoes, cut
  into $^1/_2$ inch dice with skin on

$^1/_4$ teaspoon cayenne pepper

1 egg

Peel and halve the onion and slice finely into half moons. Heat the oil in a frying pan, add the sliced onion and cook over a medium heat with a sprinkle of salt to stop it catching. Scrub but do not peel the potato, cut into $^1/_2$ inch dice and add to the onion in the pan, sprinkling over the cayenne pepper.

Turn the heat down to low and keep moving the onions and potatoes about every now and then as you want them to caramelize rather than darken in color. Cook them slowly like this for about 30 minutes or until the potato is tender. Turn the heat up and push the potato and onion hash to one side of the pan. Crack the egg into the other half of the pan, and when it is cooked spoon the onions and potatoes on to a plate and top with the fried egg.

Retire to the comfort of the sofa or your bed and eat in perfect solitude.

A VALENTINE DINNER FOR TWO

My first thought for the day was that the only thing you should be making for dinner is a reservation but then I thought again – do you really want to be in a restaurant on this night of all nights, full of couples who don't speak to each other for the rest of the year? I don't. But nor do I want one of those ludicrous, labored special meals, all dainty-do and mango coulis. Perhaps it's a bit late in the day for me to be warning against falling into the trap of the twee, but I think dinner, while it can be playful, should be substantial, in concept if not in heft.

Please regard the first course as optional (though of course, everything is optional: I don't plan spot-checks to ascertain what you're cooking and when) but it is easy to make, and is light with it, and helps to make dinner into more of a ceremony.

CRAB COCKTAIL

While I love a shrimp cocktail, this I think has a slight, elegant edge. The hot, green mustardy horseradish, the wasabi paste, is not so hard to find these days but you could always substitute a small dollop of Colman's English mustard in its place I suppose. Similarly, you could shred some little Boston lettuce should you have difficulty locating the Chinese leaves.

$1/_4$ cup mayonnaise	$1^1/_2$ cups white crab meat	Serves 2
$1/_4$ teaspoon soy sauce	enough Chinese leaf cabbage to line	
$1/_4$ teaspoon Worcestershire sauce	2 small plates when shredded	
few drops sesame oil	1 scallion	
$1/_2$ teaspoon wasabi paste	approx. 1 teaspoon pink	
$1/_4$ inch fresh ginger	peppercorns	
1 lime, halved		

In a bowl, combine the mayonnaise, soy sauce, Worcestershire sauce, sesame oil and wasabi. Peel and mince or grate the ginger into the bowl and add the zest of $^1/_2$ the lime. Squeeze $^1/_2$ teaspoon of lime juice into the bowl and mix everything together.

Toss the crab in the sauce, and then finely shred the Chinese leaf cabbage. Arrange a bed of shredded cabbage on two plates. Divide the crab between them, piling it into the center of each one. Finely chop the scallion and scatter over each plate and then bash some pink peppercorns either in a pestle and mortar – rich in lewd symbolism – or put them in a freezer bag, close it and hit with a rolling pin (more of a comedy moment) and sprinkle these, too, over the crab cocktails.

Cut the remaining lime half into wedges and put on the side of the plates for extra spritzing.

SCHMALZY CHICKEN

I'm not sure how many roast chicken recipes one person can offer, but just bear in mind that this sort of food is never really much of a recipe, more a suggestion. "Schmalz," for those who don't know it, is in fact the Yiddish word for chicken (or goose) fat. In other words, you're being schmalzy when you're simply dripping with unctuousness.

This bird, however, is crisp and gold-breasted and not remotely unctuous. But I do use the term "schmalzy" in its literal sense here because I take the nosset of fat that lies just inside the chicken's cavity, render it down in a small pan and then anoint the breast.

This makes the most wonderfully crisp-skinned chicken you can imagine, but you do need a good, organic, free-range bird or you'll find it sadly lacking in requisite fat. Should that be the lamentable case, then you'll just have to fry two slices of bacon in a drop of oil and use the fat they've rendered to smear on the bird's breast, popping the fried bacon into the cavity of the chicken as it roasts. It's about as ethnically far from schmalz as you could get, but it does the trick. Otherwise, though probably less handily, use goose fat.

Serves 2   **1 small chicken**   **1 teaspoon sea salt**

Preheat the oven to 425°F.

Tear the chicken fat out of the inside neck cavity of the chicken. Put it into a small pan and render it down into liquid fat over a medium heat. If you're interested, the little curled-up piece that remains is called *grieben*, and considered something of a delicacy. You could just bung it into the bird's cavity to add further flavor as it cooks if you don't want to try tasting it yourself.

Put the chicken into a roasting pan and pour or brush the melted fat over the breast, and sprinkle with salt. (Don't use the salt if you've used bacon fat.) Put into the oven for 1 hour, or until it is very crisp and puffy and the juices between the body and thigh joints run clear when pierced with a knife.

Let the chicken rest for about 15 minutes before you carve it or just hack at it, the two of you, at the table.

PETITS POIS À LA FRANÇAISE

I have always thought that the only green vegetables men eat willingly are peas. Now, I don't presume that all Valentine's dinners are cooked by women for men, but as a heterosexual woman who tends to be the cook rather than the cookee, I can't help but take off from where I stand. And anyway, this is the dinner I would want someone – male or female – to cook for me.

These peas, luscious and coated in their savory syrup are all you need alongside the chicken. This is probably the only time I'd go along with the notion that enough's as good as a feast, but here it is surely true. You don't want a meal so huge that you're both left in a torpor of post-prandial bloat.

Serves 2

$^1/_4$ cup finely sliced scallions
3 tablespoons unsalted butter
1 drop garlic-infused oil (or any oil really)
1 cup shredded little butter lettuce

2 cups or 1 10oz package frozen petits pois
$^1/_2$ cup hot chicken stock (concentrate or cube and hot water is fine)

Slice the scallions finely, and cook them in the butter and oil until soft. Shred the lettuce and stir into the scallion, and when it's wilted add the frozen peas and stock.

Cook at a robust simmer, uncovered, until everything is tender and the liquid flavorful and reduced.

QUIVERING WITH PASSION JELLIES

You can make this the day before, or at least the jellied part, which should make life easier. The only thing to remember is that they must come out of the fridge in good time to come to room temperature otherwise that voluptuous, inner-thigh wobble will be lost.

Serves 2

note
If you want to pare down all activities, you can make a passionfruit fool or syllabub – truly, it's somewhere in the middle – by dispensing with the jelly bit and augmenting the quanties of cream to 1 cup, passionfruit to 6, confec-

FOR THE JELLIES
$^3/_4$ cup white wine
1 cup passion fruit pulp and seeds (about 5 fruits)

$^1/_4$ cup superfine sugar
1 gelatin sheet

FOR THE SYLLABUB TOPPING
2 passionfruit
2 tablespoons confectioners' sugar

1 tablespoon white wine
$^1/_3$ cup heavy cream

Bring the wine and seeds and pulp of the passion fruit to a boil in a saucepan, then take off the heat and stir in the sugar. Pour through a sieve into a glass measuring cup to strain, discarding the seeds and pulp.

Soak the gelatin in cold water until soft – I just use a small oblong dish filled with about $1\,^1/_2$ inches cold water from the tap – then wring it out and whisk into the strained liquid. Pour the mixture into two glasses and put in the fridge to set. I don't bother with wine glasses or anything fancy-looking: in fact I rather prefer the jellies in the very plain glasses you see, and which are cleaned, empty jars minus their lids.

When the jellies have set, remove them from the fridge and start on the topping. You can either top them before dinner and let them get to room temperature in their entirety, or let them sit and have the chill taken off before you spoon over the syllabub-like mixture. Either way, scoop out the seeds and pulp of the 2 remaining passionfruit into a bowl with the confectioners' sugar and wine and stir to mix. Add the cream and gently whip until you have a soft and floaty aerated mass to dollop on top of each of the fragrant jellies.

tioners' sugar to $^1/_3$ cup and wine to 3 tablespoons, or better still, replace with Southern Comfort.

The method is much the same: mix passionfruit, sugar and liqueur in a bowl and then pour in cream and whisk until you have requisite floaty mass and divide between two glasses.

COME BACK TO MY CAVE...

If you don't want a proper table-set dinner, and would prefer something oozy and sticky to take up to bed with you, well, that's fine by me. I would suggest something along the lines of the spaghetti carbonara on page 411 certainly, but if you're afraid of carb-induced stupor you could go all out and tear the flesh from these sticky bones with your bare teeth instead. You'll just have to fight the bourgeois instinct to fret about your nice clean sheets.

FINGER-LICKIN' RIBS

Serves 2

note

In the normal run of things I would suggest a scattering of freshly chopped cilantro over them on the plate, but I think it's best to avoid getting green things caught in the teeth here.

8 pork spare ribs
1 small onion
1 star anise
1 small cinnamon stick, broken into
  barky shards
1 green chilli

1 inch piece fresh ginger
juice and zest of $^1/_2$ lime
2 tablespoons soy sauce
1 tablespoon peanut oil
1 tablespoon molasses
$^1/_4$ cup pineapple juice (from a
  carton)

Put the ribs into a large plastic bag. Peel the onion and cut it into eighths and add to the ribs along with the star anise and the crumbled cinnamon stick. Roughly chop the chilli, removing the seeds if you don't want the heat from them and peel and finely slice the ginger and throw all in, too. Zest and squeeze the lime into a glass measuring cup and add the soy sauce, oil, molasses and the pineapple juice and stir together before pouring into the bag. Tie a knot and squidge everything around well, then ideally leave in a fridge overnight, or for at least a couple of hours in a cool place somewhere in the kitchen.

Preheat the oven to 400°F. Let the marinated ribs come to room temperature, and pour the whole contents of the bag into a roasting pan and put in the oven for 1 hour. Turn the ribs over about halfway through cooking time to brown a bit on the other side. To serve, turn out on to a large flat plate and you're done.

All I'd suggest afterwards is a big bowl of strawberries. Strawberries have just been found to increase sex drive more than any other foodstuff, if you can believe such things. I'm not sure how you could measure it, but apparently the zinc in the seeds is a natural aphrodisiac and is found in exceptionally high quantities in strawberries. It's an interesting case of people often believing the right thing for the wrong reasons – that's to say, people have believed for years that strawberries aroused sexual appetite because the seeds were meant to represent fecundity and were profusely abundant in the berries. Whether any of this kind of stuff is credible, I would hope neither party actually needs the fruity boost.

EASTER

LIKE MANY of the Christian festivals, Easter has decidedly pagan roots. One of the wisdoms of Christianity lies in its judicious appropriation of already existing celebrations: thus Christmas dovetailed with Saturnalia, and Easter gladly incorporated celebrations to welcome the spring and the renewal of life. Easter as a religious feast is a festival of redemption and regeneration. The central meal itself – the Paschal lamb – is emphatically symbolic: just as the lamb is sacrificed at the table, so the Lamb of God was sacrificed for us. You could say, then, that like the Eucharist, Easter incorporates an act of symbolic cannibalism, a strange mixture between the primitive and the devotional.

But there are, of course, other resonances here. The word "Easter" is supposed to derive from "Eostre," the Norse Goddess of Spring and Rebirth but, not only as a mark in the calendar, it shares much with the Jewish Passover, from the Paschal lamb (though in the latter to signify the sacrifice offered *to* God rather than *by* God) to the name itself: the Hebrew for Passover is *Pesach*; Easter is *Pâques* in French, *Pasqua* in Italian.

In a way, it is the braiding of various customs that safeguards the endurance of ritual. And it isn't always possible to untangle the skein of practices. It is surely right to see in the egg motif of Easter an underlying pagan and pan-religious symbol of birth and the continuity of life: and it is also part of the Passover ritual. Today, it may have been taken over by an amount of Cadburyization, but the custom of painting eggs and using them lavishly as part of the Easter feast has undoubted medieval Christian connotations. That's to say, just as the tradition of Pancake Day stems from the need to clear out the larder of eggs and butter and milk before the Lenten fast (and see page 255 for a recipe for Shrove Tuesday pancakes), so the abundance of eggs over Easter is surely because no one told the hens that eating eggs was forbidden so they kept on laying.

For a British person, there is not much more to be expected of Easter, from a culinary point of view, than hot-cross buns, lamb, Simnel cake and chocolate eggs. I like to make Easter eggs just as one should do, out of hens' eggs. Although when I was a child I pierced each end of the egg with a pin and blew out the contents in a bowl (that day's supper of scrambled eggs), since then I fear I have run out of puff. What I do now is hard-boil the eggs very gently: I fill about six pans with water and in each pan I stick a couple of eggs or so and an alarming amount of food coloring paste, a good teaspoonful certainly, more if the pan's big. I bring the water to the boil, and then turn down the heat and let the eggs simmer for 2 minutes. I then turn the heat off and leave the eggs in their pans for 24 hours. When you take them out, they should be gently, beautifully tinted. It's better to start off with white eggs, but they are hard to find now, since too many of us seem to believe, wrongly, that eggs from a "real" farm should be brown. I've been told that if you let eggs steep overnight in a bowl of vinegared water, they'll take the dye better, but I like the pale, marbled effect as it is.

BLAKEAN FISH PIE

This is my idea of the perfect Good Friday supper, which is why I've allowed myself the luxury of borrowing it from *How to Eat*. I admit that the inclusion of saffron (a quintessentially costly spice and traditional marker of the grander gastronomic occasions), as well as cream makes it hard to justify in a meal that is supposed to be soberly restrained, but on my reckoning, since it's fish, that makes it OK. Anyway, apart from its excessive deliciousness, this doesn't make for an especially flamboyant supper.

The reference to Blake is only because of its coloring – flashing like one of his glorious golden sunburst paintings underneath the blanket of mashed potatoes.

Serves 2–4

1 carrot
$^1/_2$ cup white wine
1 bouquet garni
2lbs all-purpose potatoes
8 tablespoons/1 stick unsalted butter
8oz cod fillets
8oz haddock cutlets
8oz salmon fillets

1 cup light cream, or $^1/_2$ cup heavy cream and $^1/_2$ cup milk
$^1/_4$ cup all-purpose flour
pinch of ground mace
$^1/_2$ teaspoon powdered saffron
5oz cooked, peeled jumbo shrimp
fresh nutmeg

Peel the carrot, halve it lengthways and then cut each half into three or four and put the pieces in a skillet with $^1/_2$ cup water, the wine, a good pinch of salt and the bouquet garni. Bring to the boil, and then turn off the heat and let cool. Cook the potatoes in salted water and mash with about $^3/_4$ of a stick of the butter. The best instrument for this is a potato ricer: it costs little and you don't need to peel the potatoes; the skins stay behind as you push the potato through. Set aside until you've cooked the fish and sauce. Alternatively, if it suits better, you can cook the fish and sauce first and set them aside, and do the potatoes after.

Put the white fish in the carroty water and wine, bring to simmering point and poach for about 3 minutes. Remove to a plate, then add the salmon to the water and poach for about 3 minutes. Add this to the white fish. Strain the liquid (keeping the bouquet garni) into a measuring cup and make up to 2 cups with light cream.

Melt the remaining butter in a saucepan and stir in the flour and mace. Cook, stirring, for a few minutes then, off the heat, stir in the cream mixture slowly, beating all the time to prevent lumps; I like to use my little hand whisk for this. When it's all incorporated, put back on the heat and throw in the sodden bouquet garni. Keep cooking and stirring until thickened – about 5 minutes, but I am too impatient to keep the heat very low – then add the saffron and cook, stirring, for another 5 minutes. Set aside for 10 minutes (or, if you're doing this in advance, let it cool altogether).

Butter a 5 cup pie plate – I use a battered oval enamelled plate that I inherited from my mother – and put in the cooked fish and the shrimp. Pour over the saffron sauce (discarding the bouquet garni) and let it sink into the fish and spread it gently over with a rubber spatula.

Cover with the mashed potato, beating it first so that it is supple and light. Make sure the potato completely covers the pie dish so that no sauce can bubble up and spill over. Use a fork to scrape wavy lines up and down the top, or not, as you wish. Grate over some nutmeg and cook in an oven preheated to 375°F for 20–40 minutes depending on how cold the pie was when it went in.

I think all fish pies must be eaten with peas, which at Easter, if you've got the energy, could be fresh, but in my house are nearly always frozen.

KEDGEREE RISOTTO

This is just the thing for a light Saturday lunch if there are few of you. Although it's likely you might have friends over now and again during the Easter weekend, I don't think of it as an entertaining high point of the calendar.

This is a strange hybrid of a recipe (see next page): kedgeree cooked as if it were a risotto, that is to say Anglo-Indian influence, Italian method. I admit, however, that Italians may look askance at this recipe: after all, it calls on spices entirely alien to the Italian kitchen. But the cumin, coriander and turmeric are there to evoke that great dish of the Anglo-Indian empire, kedgeree, in which smoked fish, rice and spices are bound together. As a risotto, though, it is better: you get the sticky toothsomeness that comforts with every mouthful.

Poach the smoked fish in a little flavored water for just under 5 minutes then use the water to flavor the vegetable stock for the risotto. Some lemon zest at the beginning of the cooking time and a squirt of lemon juice at the end and you have a bright, golden, flavor-rich but not aggressively fishy risotto that makes the perfect cozy supper for two but more often I make it as a substantial starter, or light lunch, for four.

Just one bossy proviso: add no grated Parmesan to this risotto. Italians never grate cheese on fish pastas or fishy risottos and even if this dish is not strictly speaking Italian, their strictures still hold good.

The quail's egg was a fashion ingredient overused in the 1980s, but that's not altogether a good reason to ignore it now. Besides, I like the small but perfectly formed reference to an essential Easter symbol. At other times of the year, I may be less concerned to include them.

Serves 2–4

10oz smoked haddock fillet or any skinless firm smoked white fish fillet

pepper

1 bay leaf

1 blade mace (or add $^1/_4$ teaspoon ground mace with the other spices later)

1 sprig parsley

2 cups water

vegetable stock (a good stock cube, concentrate or powder is fine)

2 tablespoons butter, plus 1 teaspoon

$^1/_2$ teaspoon vegetable oil

1 leek (to make 1 cup finely sliced)

$1^1/_2$ cups arborio rice

$^1/_4$ teaspoon ground cumin

$^1/_4$ teaspoon ground coriander

$^1/_4$ teaspoon turmeric

zest of 1 lemon, plus 1 teaspoon juice

$^1/_3$ cup white wine

6 quail's eggs (optional)

2 tablespoons freshly chopped parsley

Cut the haddock into two or more pieces to fit into a frying pan (preferably one with a lid). Add some pepper, the bay leaf, blade of mace, if you have one, and sprig of parsley, and pour over the water. Cover the pan with a lid, or some tightly sealed aluminum foil, and bring to the boil. Turn down and simmer the haddock for 3–5 minutes so that the fish is cooked through but not falling apart. Remove with a slotted spatula and wrap the haddock in foil and reserve the liquid from the pan, straining it into a measuring cup. Make the liquid in the cup up to the 4-cup mark with boiling water and add the vegetable broth granules or cube or whatever you're using. Pour this liquid into a saucepan and put over a low heat.

On a nearby burner, in a fairly wide saucepan, heat 2 tablespoons of the butter and the oil. Trim the leek, and then finely slice it into circles, adding it to the oily pan. Cook gently for about 5 minutes until the leek softens. Add the rice to the pan and turn well in the buttery oil until slicked and glossy then stir in the spices and lemon zest. Turn up the heat and add the wine, stirring until it is bubblingly absorbed. Then add a ladleful of the reserved fish cooking liquid mixed with vegetable stock in its nearby saucepan, stirring until it too is absorbed then proceed ladleful by ladleful until the rice is cooked and sticky – about 20 minutes – and the liquid is used up or nearly all used up. You probably don't need me to remind you, but let me anyway: it is important that each ladleful is absorbed before you add the next one.

Meanwhile, put the quail's eggs in a pan of cold water and bring to the boil. Once the water's come to the boil, drain the eggs and put them in a bowl of cold water, running the tap for a while over them to make sure they stop cooking.

Once you have reached the right point with the risotto, and the rice is done, add the fish, minimally flaked with a fork or your fingers, to the rice along with the remaining butter and the lemon juice, beating well, off the heat, with your wooden spoon to make sure everything is creamy and well amalgamated. Spoon the risotto on to a large plate so that it is fairly flat, add the peeled and halved quail's eggs *au choix* and sprinkle with the parsley.

HOT CROSS BUNNY

It's true, and it would be pointless to deny that I came up with this feisty rabbit curry just so that I could give it this name, but I wouldn't have included it here unless I was, in turn, mad about the outcome.

If you're not a bunny-boiler, then be assured this curry can be made equally well with chicken; in which case, I'd advise skinned but not boned thigh joints, about 3lbs total weight.

This is a very soupy curry that needs to be eaten in bowls, always a good start so far as I am concerned. Potatoes and peas are already included, so you don't need to worry yourself about cooking anything to go with, though the bland, absorbent starch provided by a pan of white rice is always welcome.

Serves 4

1 cup buttermilk
3 tablespoons Thai red curry paste
1 rabbit, skinned and portioned
2$^1/_2$ tablespoons vegetable oil
1 large onion, cut into fine half moons
1 teaspoon ground turmeric
1 teaspoon ground coriander
4 cups chicken stock

2 tablespoons tamarind paste
1 15oz can cream of coconut (just under 2 cups)
1lb new potatoes, scrubbed and halved
3 cups frozen petits pois or indeed freshly shelled peas
few tablespoons freshly chopped cilantro for serving

In a large dish, mix the buttermilk and red curry paste and then turn the rabbit pieces in the marinade. Cover with plastic wrap and leave for two days in the fridge. Or mix up the simple, but effective, marinade in a freezer bag, add the rabbit pieces and give a good squelch before tying fast and refrigerating the bag (placed on a big plate).

When you're going to cook the curry, remember to bring the rabbit to room temperature before starting, but be advised too, that this tastes best if you are able to cook the curry in advance and reheat later to eat. It's the steeping that does it.

Put the oil into a large saucepan and heat with the onion half moons, and cook slowly and thoroughly until they're soft and beginning to color, even catch in some places, about 10 minutes, maybe a little more.

Stir in the turmeric and coriander, and having removed the rabbit pieces to a plate from the dish or freezer bag, scrape in every last bit of buttermilky marinade. Stir the pan well and add the stock, tamarind and cream of coconut. Put the rabbit pieces in, and the halved new potatoes and bring to the boil. Turn down to a gentle simmer, partially cover and leave to cook for 1$^1/_2$ hours, checking occasionally.

Leave to cool. The next day, or evening indeed, reheat, and when the bunny is warm and about 7 minutes from serving, add the peas.

Provide bowls, spoons, good napkins and the freshly chopped cilantro for everyone to sprinkle over as they eat.

HOT CROSS BUNS

I am not sure at which point during the weekend I'd ideally instruct you to try your hand at these, but I think it's wise to get in early. You're meant to eat them on Good Friday, but I don't think we have to be so tied by tradition. Still, there are so few true examples of seasonal eating left, it would be pity to leave these out altogether.

I know you'd think, indeed I'd have thought, that it would be pointless to make something at home when the bought versions can be so good, but I find it peculiarly satisfying to make these, and although they look slightly ramshackle and unprofessional, they do have the edge on any store-bought stuff.

I make my hot cross buns slightly smaller than is traditional. Don't know why, just like them that way, but you form them the size you want, please. Just one thing I must be strict about: you do need to use proper bread flour here, not the usual all-purpose. There's no point going to all this effort and ruining your chances of success over such a small but significant point.

By effort, I don't mean you need to be hugely active or expert to make these; you just need the patience to sit around while they rise and the faith to believe they will. Very appropriate.

FOR THE DOUGH

$2/3$ cup milk

$1/2$ stick butter

zest of 1 orange

1 clove

2 cardamom pods

3 cups bread flour

1 package active dry yeast ($1/4$ oz)

$3/4$ cup mixed dried fruit

1 teaspoon ground cinnamon

$1/2$ teaspoon ground nutmeg

$1/4$ teaspoon ground ginger

1 egg

Makes 16

note
You could ignore my instructions to leave the dough in the fridge to rise slowly overnight and instead leave the dough to rise for $1-1^{1}/_2$ hours in a warmish place in the kitchen, but I always find it easier to go the overnight route, plus I think it gives a better taste and texture.

FOR THE EGG WASH

1 egg, beaten with a little milk

FOR THE CROSSES ON THE BUNS

3 tablespoons all-purpose flour

$1/2$ tablespoon superfine sugar

2 tablespoons water

FOR THE SUGAR GLAZE

1 tablespoon superfine sugar

1 tablespoon boiling water

Heat the milk, butter, orange zest, clove and cardamom pods in a saucepan until the butter melts, then leave to infuse. I have gone rather cardamom-mad recently, but this short, aromatic infusion gives a heavenly scent to the little fruited buns later.

Measure the flour, yeast and dried fruit into a bowl and add the spices. When the infused milk has reached blood temperature take out the clove and cardamom pods, and beat in the egg. Pour this liquid into the bowl of dry ingredients.

Knead the dough either by hand or with a machine with a dough hook; if it is too dry add a little more warm milk or water. Keep kneading until you have silky, elastic dough, but bear in mind that the dried fruit will stop this from being exactly satin-smooth. Form into a ball and place in a buttered bowl covered with plastic wrap, and leave to rise overnight in the fridge.

Preheat the oven to 425°F. Take the dough out of the fridge and let it come to room temperature.

Punch the dough down, and knead it again until it is smooth and elastic. Divide into 16 balls and shape into smooth round buns. I wouldn't start worrying unduly about their size: just halve the dough, and keep halving it until it's in eight pieces, and use that piece of dough to make two buns. Or just keep the dough as it is, and pinch off pieces slightly larger than a ping-pong ball and hope you end up with 16 or thereabouts. Not that it matters.

Sit the buns on a parchment paper or Silpat-lined baking sheet. Make sure they are quite snug together but not touching. Using the back of an ordinary eating knife, score the tops of the buns with the imprint of a cross. Cover with a kitchen towel, and leave to prove again for about 45 minutes – they should have risen and almost joined up.

Brush the buns with the egg wash, and then mix the flour, sugar and water into a smooth, thick, paste. Using a teaspoon, dribble two lines over the buns in the indent of the cross, and then bake in the oven for 15–20 minutes.

When the hot cross buns come out of the oven, mix the sugar and boiling water together for the glaze, and brush each hot bun to make them sweet and shiny.

SIMNEL CAKE

Originally, this cake was made for Mother's Day, but it has for a long, long time been an essential Easter confection, the marzipan balls on top representing the apostles: eleven in total as, for understandable reasons, Judas is persona non grata.

I make this a very light fruit cake, totally different in taste and texture from the damp, dark offerings of Christmas.

Makes at least 11 slices

$^1/_2$ cup glacé cherries
$3^1/_2$ cups mixed dried fruit
$1^1/_2$ cups plus 2 tablespoons soft unsalted butter
$^3/_4$ cup superfine sugar
zest of 1 lemon
$1^1/_2$ cups plus 2 tablespoons all-purpose flour
1 teaspoon baking powder
$^1/_2$ teaspoon ground cinnamon

$^1/_4$ teaspoon ground ginger
$^1/_4$ cup ground almonds
3 eggs
2 tablespoons milk
$2^1/_2$ lbs yellow marzipan to decorate
confectioners' sugar for rolling
1 tablespoon apricot jam, melted
1 egg white

Take everything you need out of the fridge so it can get to room temperature. Preheat the oven to 325°F. Butter and line the bottom and sides of an 8 inch springform pan with a double layer of parchment paper. Detailed directions for this are given on page 92–3. Chop the cherries very finely and add them to the rest of the fruit.

Cream the butter and sugar until very soft and light, and add the lemon zest. You could do this by hand, just with bowl and wooden spoon, but I own up to using my standing mixer here. But it's not crucial, not least because the intention with fruit cakes is not to whip air into them. Measure the flour, baking powder, cinnamon, ginger and ground almonds into a bowl and stir to combine.

Add 1 of the eggs to the creamed butter and sugar with 2 tablespoons of the dry flour-and-spice ingredients, then beat in the remaining eggs in the same way. Beat in the rest of the dry ingredients, and then the milk. Finally fold in the fruit.

Dust a surface with a little confectioners' sugar and then roll out about 14oz of the marzipan. Cut it into an 8 inch circle which will fit in the middle of the cake later. Spoon half of the fruit cake mixture into the springform pan, smoothing it down with a rubber spatula, and then lay the marzipan circle on top of it. Spoon the rest of the mixture into the pan on top of the marzipan circle and smooth the top again. Bake for half an hour and then turn the oven down to 300°F for another $1^1/_2$ hours or until the cake has risen and is firm on top. Let it cool completely on a rack before you spring it open.

Unspring the cooled fruit cake, and unwrap the lining from the cake. Roll out another 14oz circle of marzipan, paint the top of the cake with the melted apricot jam, and then stick it on.

Make 11 apostle balls out of the remaining marzipan, roughly 2 inches in size. Beat the egg white – just till it's a bit frothy and loosened up a little, no more – and use that as glue to stick the apostles around the edge of the cake.

Now for the bit I love, but you can ignore altogether. Paint the whole of the cake with egg white, and then blow-torch the marzipan so that it scorches slightly, giving a beauteously burnished look.

THE PASCHAL LAMB

Neither of the lamb recipes that follow have weights beside the joints specified. This is for a reason: you can only find the size of lamb that's available. So there's no point requiring you to cook a 5lb leg of lamb, if the lambs that are gambolling about, or have until recently been gambolling about, are not of sufficient stature to have legs that weigh more than 4 lbs each.

Anyway, I think that generally, unless you are feeding six people or under, you would probably have to cook two legs anyway. I know there'll be leftovers, but there is nothing worse than carving and desperately worrying, after you've handed out the plates to four of your friends or family, that you won't have enough to feed the next four. In most good-sized roasting pans you can squeeze in two legs, fitted like shoes in a box, the narrow end up on one and down on the other. Bear in mind, however, that the more crowded the oven, the longer the meat will take to cook. Or that's how it is with my oven, but then I abominate a fan.

SLOW-COOKED LAMB WITH BEANS

If Easter's early, and the wind still chill, then this is the sort of lamb you'll want for your Easter lunch: homey, warming, comforting. Oh, and very good. I like this kind of old-fashioned food; how the French cooked before "la crise," when the tradition of cooking local produce, *la cuisine du terroir*, started going belly-up.

If you want to use leg in place of shoulder here, you can but just remember (as with the braised lamb that follows) you don't end up with restaurant rareness, but soft strands of dark, melting meat.

This doesn't take quite as long as the slow-cooked lamb salad with mint and pomegranate of one of my earlier books, but you do stash it out of sight in the oven for quite a long time. I find that makes my life easier: the less I do when I've got people hovering about, the more I enjoy both the cooking and the people.

Serves 6–8: at the top end, there's not a lot of meat for each person, but that doesn't really seem to matter

6 cups dried white beans	1 tablespoon vegetable oil
4 onions (about 1 1/2 lbs), quartered	1 cup white wine
6 cloves garlic, peeled	3 large sprigs rosemary
1 carrot, peeled and cut into chunks	sea salt
1 shoulder of lamb	3 tablespoons chopped parsley

Put the beans into a large bowl of cold water, and soak them overnight.

You need to pre-cook the beans, for all that they linger in the oven for hours and hours later, so put them in a large saucepan and cover them generously with cold water, bring to the boil and cook them for 20 minutes. Then drain but reserve the liquid.

Preheat the oven to 325°F. Either finely chop the onions, garlic and carrot or bung them all in a processor and blitz. Sear the lamb in a deep roasting pan, fat-and-skin-side down, over a fairly high heat on top of the stove until it takes on some color, and then remove.

Add the onion mush to the roasting pan, adding only a spoonful of oil as the lamb should have rendered some fat, and turn down the heat to fry gently, stirring every now and again, for about 5 minutes. Add the beans, stirring them in well, and then pour in the wine and 4 cups of the reserved bean liquid. Tuck the rosemary sprigs into the pan, then place the lamb back on top of the beans (right way up this time), season with plenty of sea salt (about $1\,^1/_2$ tablespoons or half that of table salt if you must) and bring it to the boil. When it begins to bubble, cover the pan with foil, baggily but with tightly sealed edges, and place in the oven for 4 hours. Or turn down to 275°F after 3 hours and leave for up to 8 hours; it'll be fine to eat after 3.

Remove the tented pan from the oven and let sit for 10 minutes, then remove the foil, and transfer the lamb – momentarily – to a board. Stir the beans well in the roasting tin and taste for seasoning. Spoon them on to a large dish and then carve the lamb into shreds and chunks and arrange on top. Sprinkle a little more salt over, if you think the lamb needs it, scatter over the chopped parsley and let people dig in. I wouldn't claim this to be elegant, but it is wonderful.

note

There are so many beans in this that I really wouldn't bother with any other vegetables. Though I might suggest a plain tomato salad, not to be eaten alongside, but after, with maybe a little Dijon mustard dressing.

In fact, contrary to culinary dictates, I love mustard with lamb. My stepfather used to taunt me with the old English saying "Mustard with mutton, sign of a glutton." And?

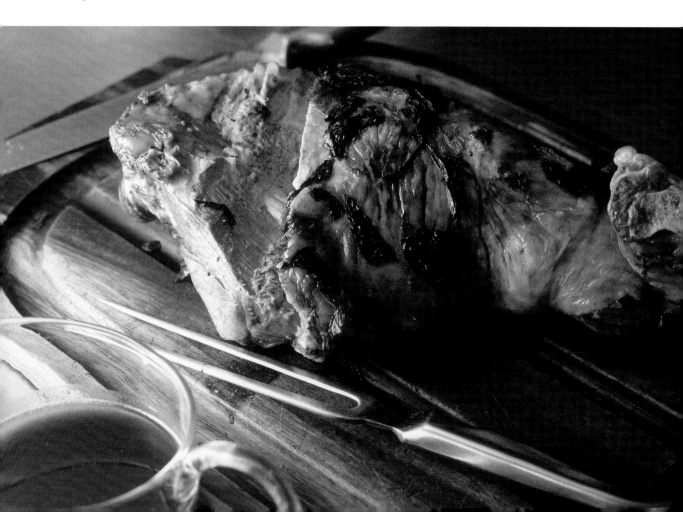

SAFFRON ROAST LAMB WITH STICKY GARLIC POTATOES

Although the saffron makes its appearance just at the end of the cooking time, as you deglaze the roasting pan, its taste is so pronounced that it defines the dish, enhancing the intense lemoniness that infuses this sweetest of meats.

And mint and lamb, for all that the French ridicule us, are born to be together; I wouldn't be above serving some sweet mint jelly alongside either.

Serves 6

note

Read the sticky garlic potato recipe now so that you can co-ordinate your movements. And, to go with, I'd want no more than a bowl of green, green peas, turned in some butter with some blanched snow peas.

I sometimes cook lamb escalopes this way. That's to say, if there are only four of us or so and not at Easter, I get the butcher to cut me some – say six – thin steaks off the leg joint, marinate then flash-fry them, and deglaze the pan with 1/2 teaspoon redcurrant jelly and 1/4 teaspoon saffron threads steeped in 3 table-spoons hot water. I stick absolutely and cohesively to the sticky garlic potatoes below.

1 leg of lamb
1/3 cup olive oil
3 cloves garlic, bruised
6 scallions
2 bay leaves
juice of 1 lemon

small bunch mint, 1 1/2 oz including stalks, torn roughly makes 1 cup
1/2 teaspoon saffron threads, soaked in 1 cup water from recently boiled kettle
1 teaspoon redcurrant jelly, optional

Put the lamb in a large freezer bag, pour over the olive oil and then throw in the garlic, trimmed scallions and bay leaves, squeeze in the lemon juice and throw in the squeezed-out lemon halves too, then add the torn-up bunch of mint. Seal the bag and marinate in the fridge overnight.

Bring the lamb to room temperature before you even think of putting it in the oven, and preheat that to 425°F when you take the lamb out of the fridge.

Pour the entire contents of the freezer bag into a roasting tin and roast for about 15 minutes a pound, or until the lamb is cooked a perfect, *à point* pink; you will just have to pierce it with a knife to see. Just before the lamb is due to come out of the oven, put the saffron strands in a measuring cup and pour over the hot water – from a recent-ly boiled kettle – so that it can get on with steeping.

Remove the lamb to a wooden carving board to rest. Pick out the scallions and the lemon rinds, and then put the roasting pan on the stove over medium heat, and stir until it starts bubbling. I think most gravies are better with a little redcurrant jelly in them, but I don't necessarily expect you to share that view. But if you want to go with me, stir in the jelly, and then the saffron in its water and add more water – tasting for seasoning as you go – as needed to let this bubble into a small amount of ungloopy gravy. I would more accurately call it a *jus* if I wouldn't hate myself for it.

Carve the lamb on to a large warmed plate and strain the saffrony juices, stir-ring in any liquid first from the carving board, over the pink meat.

STICKY GARLIC POTATOES

I suppose this is my take on those Italian roast potatoes, the ones that are roughly cubed and thrown into a pan of olive oil strewn with the odd sprig of rosemary. Only, these are rougher-hewn and much more intense: the potatoes are boiled, drained and roughly bashed in the pan, splitting and squashing some, and then tumbled with the garlic until it's time to cook the whole lot in some hot oil. The potatoes are somewhere between mashed and roasted, though nearer the latter, and the garlic caramelizes stickily in the heat.

$1^1/_2$ lbs little new potatoes
8 cloves garlic (more if you like)

$^1/_2$ cup olive or other vegetable oil

Serves 6

Bring a saucepan of water to the boil and add some salt, add the potatoes and cook for 30 minutes. Drain, and put back into the dry pan.

Peel the garlic cloves by squishing with the flat of a knife so that they bruise slightly and the skins slip off. Put them in the dry pan with the potatoes, and then bash potatoes and garlic with the end of a rolling pin so they are cracked and split. You can do this ahead and leave them in the pan – though with the lid off, so that they don't get watery – until you want to roast them.

Preheat the oven to 425°F (or, if you're cooking this with the lamb above, you will already have it on) and slip a roasting pan in to heat up at the same time. Once the oven's hot, pour in the oil and let it, in turn, heat up for 10 minutes.

Carefully tip the potatoes and garlic into the hot oil and cook for 15 minutes. Turn the potatoes over and then give them another 15 minutes. You will thank me. Or you will if there's any justice in the world.

THE EASTER TURKEY

Maybe not the obvious alternative to the Paschal lamb, but well worth considering if you've got a huge tableful of people for lunch. Follow either of the turkey recipes in the Thanksgiving and Christmas chapter, but make one seasonal adjustment for the stuffing. Follow the recipe for gingerbread stuffing, only in place of the gingerbread, use slightly stale hot cross buns, and turn them into crumbs in the processor. I certainly wouldn't make my own for this, but buy enough to make 5 cups of crumbs (probably about six or seven buns) and leave them around for a day before crumbing.

And to the onions in the pan, once they've been slightly softened, add 2 very finely sliced or chopped sticks of celery and $1/2$ cup chopped parsley to fill half a teacup. Or just stick the celery and unchopped parsley into the processor with the onions before you begin.

I certainly wouldn't consider the traditional winter-holiday accompaniments to the turkey, though: go for the sticky garlic potatoes (previous page), quantities augmented as needed, which you can roast in a turned-up oven while the turkey rests, with a bowl of buttery spring greens and another of sugar-snap peas.

EASTER EGG NEST CAKE

This has been my Easter stalwart for the past few years and I don't see that changing – ever. Make this just once, and you will be similarly convinced. Even if I wanted to stop making this, I wouldn't be allowed to.

FOR THE CAKE

8oz semisweet chocolate, chopped
1 stick unsalted softened butter
1 teaspoon pure vanilla extract
6 eggs: 2 whole; 4 separated

$^1/_3$ cup plus $^1/_2$ cup superfine
    sugar: $^1/_3$ cup for the yolk
    mixture; $^1/_2$ cup for the whites

It serves 8–10, but I make it if there are just 4 of us, frankly.

FOR THE TOPPING

4oz semisweet chocolate, chopped
1 cup heavy cream
1 teaspoon pure vanilla extract

1 cup of robin's eggs or other small
    sugar-coated pretty little Easter
    eggs

Preheat the oven to 350°F. Line the bottom of an 8-inch springform pan with parchment paper or, better still, Silpat but do not grease the sides of the pan.

Melt the 8oz chocolate with the butter in either a double boiler or a microwave and then set aside to cool slightly.

Whisk the 4 egg whites until firm, then gradually add the $^1/_2$ cup of sugar and whisk until the whites are holding their shape and peak gleamingly – but not stiff.

Remove this bowl (if you're using a standing mixer, as I do, though a hand-held job would do fine) and set aside while you whisk, in another bowl, the 2 whole eggs and 4 egg yolks with the $^1/_3$ cup of sugar and the vanilla extract, and then gently fold in the chocolate mixture. Lighten the mixture with some of the egg whites – just dollop a large spoonful in and stir briskly – and then fold in the rest of the whisked whites gently, in about three goes.

Pour into the prepared pan and bake for 35–40 minutes or until the cake is risen and cracked and the center is no longer wobbly on the surface. Cool the cake in its pan on a wire rack; the middle will sink as it cools and the sides splinter. You want this to look like a cake with a crater in it, so do not panic at the vision of imperfection in front of you. That's one of the reasons this cake is so unstressful to make.

To finish the cake, carefully remove it from the pan and place it on a plate or cake-stand, not worrying if bits fall off here and there. Put them back in a loose fashion.

Melt the chocolate for the topping and leave it to cool a little. Whip the cream until it is firming up and aerated but still soft, and then add the vanilla and fold in the melted chocolate. Fill the crater of the cake with the chocolatey cream, easing it out gently towards the edges of the cake with a rubber spatula, and then arrange the little sugar Easter eggs on top.

LEMON MERINGUE CAKE

In all honesty, the origin of this cake is simply that I cannot make a go of a lemon meringue pie. I've tried, and I've tried, and it's not that I've utterly failed, but I haven't completely delighted myself. There's enough of that kind of falling short in the rest of life, without having to usher in disappointment and self-loathing in the kitchen. This, then, is the easy option. After the effortless success – no credit to me, it's just a simple recipe – of the strawberry meringue layer cake in *Forever Summer*, it seemed obvious to make a few marginal changes to turn it into this. And the funny thing is, the layers of cake, with their crisp-carapaced squashy-bellied meringue topping are sandwiched with tart lemon curd and softly whipped cream, so much better than a lemon meringue pie could ever be. I include it here because it seems to sing with springtime and Easter hopefulness, but I wouldn't push it away at any time of the year.

Makes 8 slices

note

After I'd made this a couple of times, it occurred to me, that if I were to fill the cakes with passionfruit curd, in place of lemon curd (which I buy, but it must be a good one) it would be particularly appropriate for Eastertime. Hence the recipe on page 172. Or stir the pulp of 2 passionfruit into some good bought lemon curd.

If you want to make your own lemon curd, then more or less follow the recipe for passionfruit curd, overleaf, but in place of the passionfruit, use the finely grated zest and the juice of 2, preferably unwaxed, lemons.

1 stick plus 1 tablespoon very soft unsalted butter
4 eggs, separated
1$^{1}/_{2}$ cups plus 1 teaspoon superfine sugar
$^{3}/_{4}$ cup all-purpose flour
2 tablespoons cornstarch
1 teaspoon baking powder
$^{1}/_{2}$ teaspoon baking soda
zest of 1 lemon
4 teaspoons lemon juice
2 teaspoons milk
$^{1}/_{2}$ teaspoon cream of tartar
$^{2}/_{3}$ cup heavy or whipping cream
$^{1}/_{2}$ cup plus 2 tablespoons good quality lemon curd

Preheat the oven to 400°F. Line and butter two 8-inch cake pans.

Mix the egg yolks, $^{1}/_{2}$ cup of the sugar, the butter, flour, cornstarch, baking powder, baking soda, and lemon zest in a processor. Add the lemon juice and milk and process again.

Divide the mixture between the prepared pans. You will think you don't even have enough to cover the bottom of the pans, but don't panic. Spread calmly with a rubber spatula until smooth.

Whisk the egg whites and cream of tartar until peaks form and then slowly whisk in the cup of sugar. Divide the whisked whites between the two pans, pouring or, more accurately, spreading the meringue straight on top of the cake batter. Smooth one flat with a metal spatula, and with the back of a spoon, peak the other and sprinkle 1 teaspoon sugar over the peaks. Put the pans into the oven for 20–25 minutes.

With a cake-tester, pierce the cake that has the flat meringue topping to check it's cooked all through. (It will have risen now but will fall back flattish later.) No sponge mixture should stick to the tester. Remove both cakes to a wire rack and let cool completely in the pans.

Unmold the flat-topped one onto a cake stand or plate, meringue side down. Whisk the heavy cream until thick but not stiff and set aside. Spread the flat sponge surface of the first, waiting, cake with the lemon curd and then spatula over the cream and top with the remaining cake, bronze-peaked meringue uppermost.

PASSIONFRUIT CURD

This recipe comes from *How to Be a Domestic Goddess*, and it's not hard work, though a bit fiddly. But this is the way to go if you want to make a cake that symbolically marks the Passion.

And what you don't use up in a cake, you can slather over a thick slab of white bread for an Easter morning breakfast.

Makes 1$^1/_3$ cups

11 passionfruit
2 large eggs
2 large egg yolks

$^3/_4$ cup superfine sugar
1 stick unsalted butter

Put the seeded pulp of 10 of the passionfruit into the processor and blitz just to loosen the seeds (so only do this insofar as it could be helpful to you). Strain into a glass measuring cup or bowl.

Beat the eggs, egg yolks and sugar together.

Melt the butter over a low heat in a heavy-based pan, and when melted stir in the sugar-egg mixture and the passionfruit juice, and keep cooking gently, stirring constantly, until thickened.

Off the heat, whisk in the pulp – seeds and all – of the sole remaining passionfruit, let cool slightly, then pour into a clean jar. Use what you need for the cake, keeping the rest in the sealed jar in the fridge.

PASSOVER

PASSOVER WAS my introduction to the full richness of ritualized, festive eating. This is a strange thing to say, considering I've celebrated Christmas forever but gave my first Seder Night dinner – the feast that marks Passover – barely ten years ago. And that also happened to be the first Seder Night I'd ever been to. But it showed me what these rituals mean, and what they could give.

When my first husband was diagnosed with cancer, just as that year's Passover was about to begin, he suddenly felt – out of the blue, it seemed to me – that he wanted to mark this occasion, much as he had as a child. That's understandable, though at the time it didn't seem so to me. In fact, it felt vaguely threatening, as if some alien force were making itself felt in my home. True, no religious adherence was expected of me; his was never really a religiously motivated decision. But nothing can seem stranger than the rituals of others, and because of my upbringing, the Jewish rituals, for all that I am of the blood pure, were not my rituals.

So, while I could see the point of Passover, it still seemed weird to me, and didn't, at that stage, evoke anything symbolically meaningful. I felt faintly fraudulent and – if I'm to be completely honest – a bit squeamish. But I went along with it then, as I did for a few years, and although I wouldn't go so far as to say I saw the light, I did catch a glimmer of what it all meant.

For one thing, it helps that the Passover text is a great story, the story of the end of the Jews' captivity in Egypt, the Exodus. And it's a political story above all else, the story of liberation and the right to self-determination; it's about the vileness of slavery and refusal to be persecuted. And it is for this reason that many Jews in concentration camps needed to perform some version of the Seder Night service themselves, in whatever way they could.

But what made the biggest difference to me, and what turned me around, was the cooking. Not the food, exactly, but the cooking. It has nothing to do with the way you'd get a dinner party together, and nothing to do with contemporary fashions or clever fiddling with ingredients. The first part of the meal anyway is the ritual part: matzoh – or unleavened bread – to symbolize the Jews having to flee Egypt without waiting for the bread to rise; a lamb shank to represent the Paschal sacrifice in the Temple; *haroset*, a sludge of long-cooked dried fruit and nuts, to symbolize the mortar used by the Jews as they built for the Egyptians; bitter leaves or stinging horseradish to represent the suffering of the Jews; a scorched hard-boiled egg for birth, renewal, beginnings – I never quite understood the meaning of the scorch marks, but presume they are to represent the burning of the Temple; and finally, fresh leaves – parsley or lettuce – again, for renewal and to celebrate spring and the refreshing of the cycle of life; but the leaves are dipped in salt water – as ever, presumably, to represent the tears shed by us suffering Jews.

The foodstuffs alone, traditionally arranged on a segmented, circular plate, say something so basic and yet conclusive about what it is to be Jewish. At its most primitive, the Jewish need to remind themselves and others of the tragic possibilities of life is perhaps a superstitious warding off of the evil eye. At the more analytical end, you could argue that it is a measured response to life, a real understanding that living includes misery and happiness, and it would be wrong to deny the existence of one or the other. For the same reason, I like the symbolism of the glass that's broken underfoot at a Jewish wedding. The message seems to be that joyous celebration is all well and good, in its place, but don't forget for one moment that life is full of darkness and hardship and trouble. As if. But of course, it also reminds that "what is shattered cannot be put back together"; in other words, marriage isn't all about Happy Ever After. Of course, being a Freudian, I feel it's really about the rupturing of the hymen; but that doesn't mean the other readings don't hold as well.

Passover is also, and fundamentally, about connectivity. You'd expect any festival marked by a particular culture to be about this, but I felt this most in the kitchen, not at the table later. There is something about the preparation, the long cooking of the *haroset*, the patient stirring and waiting until the dried fruits turn a deep brick red and so gungily thick it's hard to stir any more, that makes one feel connected with past generations in a way that ceremony alone never could. And this in a way is the great Jewish trick: to use food to make sense of it all, to make sense of anything.

It's common to point to the Jewish dietary laws and think those are the important things; that they keep a people's sense of particularity, of belonging. But I'm talking about something other. (I think you really do have to be religious to keep kosher, and that's where I part company.) I made the dinner with friends, and there we were, cooking food that one would normally think too strenuous, or just too much. We made chicken stock, and from that chicken soup – with lemon and turmeric (the yellow to represent happiness), mint, fava beans, zucchini and chicken meatballs. For those, we minced the flesh and pounded it with matzoh, mint, allspice, almonds. We cooked lamb; we stirred spinach. To end with, keeping to the injunction not to use leaven, we made two flourless cakes, and a plate of macaroons.

As you could imagine, this took the best part of a day and a half. You'd think one would feel exhausted by the activity, relieved it was over. But rather, it felt restorative. And this, surely, is the point.

SEDER NIGHT SUPPER FOR TEN TO TWELVE

HAROSET FROM THE VENETIAN GHETTO

I suppose it's as well to start with the premise that there is no such thing as Jewish food. This of course begets the wider political assertion that there is no such thing as a Jewish race. Faith is not the decider, and culturally, geographically, physically, Jews are too dispersed and just too different to be contained within any one definition. But perhaps it's simpler to stick with the eating: depending on descent, the food any one group of Jews eats will be radically different from another. The supper here has a decidedly Sephardic slant, that's to say the recipes will be more familiar to those who have either Spanish or Middle-Eastern origins. And, actually, even the dietary restrictions differ: Sephardi Jews eat rice and legumes at Passover; Ashkenazi Jews are forbidden. I've tried to formulate recipes suitable for either.

This *haroset* comes via Venice; in Britain and the United States, and for most of the world, in fact, you'd be more likely to come across a plainer version, made with apples, walnuts, cinnamon, red wine and some sugar or honey. This one is rich and sumptuous, and I relish it for much more than its symbolic properties. I don't want it as just the ritual precursor of the meal, but daubed on the lamb, or indeed whatever I'm eating, as a sort of multi-fruited and chestnutty *confit*.

Makes 2 cups

$3/4$ cup vacuum-packed chestnuts
$1/2$ cup sultanas (golden raisins)
$1/3$ cup dried figs
$1/2$ cup dried dates
$1/4$ cup dried apricots
1 eating apple
$1/2$ cup pinenuts

juice and zest of $1/2$ orange
$2^1/2$ tablespoons honey
2 cloves
1 cinnamon stick, crumbled
$1/4$ teaspoon ground ginger
$1/3$ cup sweet wine

Crumble the chestnuts into a pan, and add the sultanas. Then chop, or cut up roughly using scissors, letting them drop into the pan as you go, the dried figs, dates and apricots. Quarter, core and then roughly chop the apple (I don't bother to peel it), and add along with the rest of the ingredients. These look beautiful before they merge in the heat, as you can see to the right. Stir well, bring to the boil and then lower the heat, partially cover, and cook for $1–1\frac{1}{2}$ hours, until everything coheres in a dense sticky mass.

Pack into a jar or jars.

SPECIAL CHICKEN SOUP

This is the soup I cooked alongside an Egyptian friend all those years ago, or at least this is how I remember it. It often includes potatoes but I didn't want to murk up the broth, nor did I want to fill everyone up early on in the dinner. Neither did I want to follow the traditional way of serving it by which the clear soup would be ladled out first, with the meatballs and vegetables to be eaten as a main course after.

This makes a soup that doesn't stop anyone enjoying the roast meat later, and saves you having to cook huge quantities. It takes a long time, admittedly, and I'm sure it's perfectly possible to find good "fresh" stock in tubs in the shops that could replace the slow boiling up of bones, but I wouldn't want to do that. I like the gradual build-up, as well as the feeling that I've made it all, and it's not as if it is actually difficult.

Chicken wings are one of the best (and least expensive) ways of making chicken soup. The roasting birds that you buy even in good butchers just don't provide as much flavor, or anywhere near, pound for pound.

The meatballs are what turn this soup into a truly festive offering but the fava beans are a significant addition, too, if an almost equally fiddly one: it's not just that they represent spring, which they do, but also that they are known to have been eaten by the Hebrew slaves in Egypt.

FOR THE SOUP BASE

Serves 10–12

$4\frac{1}{2}$ lbs chicken wings
2 leeks, roughly chopped
2 carrots, roughly chopped
1 onion, halved
2 sticks of celery, roughly chopped
zest and juice of 2 lemons
handful parsley
2 tablespoons sea salt/1
  tablespoon table salt

2 bay leaves
1 teaspoon turmeric
1 tablespoon dried mint
1 teaspoon ground coriander
1 teaspoon cumin seeds
1 tablespoon black peppercorns
16 cups water

note

Just line a large sieve with
some muslin which you can
buy from anywhere that sells
babycare products if you
haven't a good cookware
shop that stocks it.

I often keep some of these
meatballs in the freezer for a
quick midweek supper, to be
eaten with plain rice, wet with
a little chicken stock, and
sprinkled with chopped
parsley and toasted pinenuts.

Put everything into a large saucepan, a very large saucepan, and bring to the boil. Then turn down the heat – skimming off any scum as you do so – and simmer gently for about 4 hours, partially covered.

When it has cooled, strain the soup through muslin to make about 10 cups. When the soup's cold, put it in the fridge overnight; the next day it will be easy to scrape off all the fat which will have risen to the top and solidified.

FOR THE MEATBALLS

1 matzoh sheet, soaked in 1 cup water for 10 minutes, then wrung out	1 tablespoon sea salt/$1^1/_2$ teaspoons table salt
14oz (2) skinless chicken breasts	zest of 1 lemon
2 scallions, finely chopped	$^1/_4$ cup ground almonds
$^1/_4$ cup parsley leaves	1 garlic clove, minced
2 teaspoons dried mint	black pepper
	1 egg

Put everything except the wrung-out matzoh sheet into a food processor and pulse until chopped. Add the matzoh sheet and pulse again until you have a finely chopped ground mixture. Tip into a bowl and leave in the fridge for 20 minutes.

Now, this is when you do feel a bit like someone from the old days, spending hours hunched over as you roll meatball after meatball.

Line a baking sheet with plastic wrap and have a bowl of cold water to hand. Take the ground meatball mixture out of the fridge and with wet hands form teaspoonfuls into tiny meatballs. You should get about 50 meatballs out of this mixture.

When you reheat the soup base you can add the meatballs and cook in the gently bubbling liquid for 7 minutes, or you can make the meatballs ahead and freeze them; drop them, unthawed, into the soup and cook them for 10 minutes.

FOR ADDING TO THE SOUP

2 cups shelled fava beans, fresh or frozen	bunch mint, chopped
4 zucchini (4 cups diced)	bunch parsley, chopped

Unless the fava beans are really young, you do need to remove their skins too. If they're fresh, shell them then blanch the beans in boiling water for a brief minute before plunging them into a bowl of icy cold water. The skins should slip off pretty easily. If you're using frozen beans, just let them thaw and then press gently on each bean so that the inner vivid green pair of kidney-shaped beans pops out of the casing.

Have the beans ready and finely dice the zucchini. Once the soup is hot again and the meatballs are cooked in it, add both vegetables to the soup. Sprinkle some mint and parsley over the full tureen, with a little more of both on each bowl of soup as you pass it round.

ROAST VEAL WITH ROSEMARY AND GARLIC

If you want to make this feed a whole tableful of people, you will need to double everything, which doesn't complicate matters since two roasts fit easily in one large roasting pan. I give the veal here in smaller quantities (even though for each of the lamb recipes that follow I've suggested two legs), since for one thing, it stretches to feed more than you'd think (certainly 8 people) and for another, I am wary of presuming that you're going to be able to offer veal without making allowances – in the form of an alternative – for those not happy to eat it.

I love this traditionally Italian Passover roast, the *taglio bianco*. It's a very simple recipe, as Italian food gracefully tends to be, but the depth of flavor you get in the juices from the roast, and the sweet tenderness of the meat are, together, exceptional.

Veal is a very densely woven meat, and takes much longer to cook than you might presume from its weight. Moreover, it benefits enormously from a long post-oven resting period. That's true of all meat, but particularly with veal, I've found. And it does mean, too, that you will be able to carve much thinner slices – it gets more compact as it sits – which also means it will go further.

All this makes sense anyway in the context of a big dinner. The one thing you don't want to have to do is get up after the soup and start fiddling with pans in the oven. With the veal, I take the meat out of the oven about 1 hour before I want to start carving it; with the lamb, I'd just take it out as I sit down.

---

3 fat cloves garlic
1 tablespoon sea salt
2 tablespoons very finely chopped rosemary
1 teaspoon fennel seeds

2 tablespoons olive oil
3lb 8oz veal loin, boned and rolled, and tied (keep the bones)
$1^1/_2$ cups white wine

Serves 6–8

note
You can make this simpler by dispensing with the paste-making bit, and using lemon juice in place of the fennel seeds. Put the joint in a freezer bag with the garlic cloves, just bruised, a sprig of rosemary, some wine and the juice of a lemon, chucking the squeezed out rinds in too.

And if you do have some of the gravy left over, keep it and heat it up the next day, for a beautiful lone supper, stirred into some plain steamed or boiled rice along with copious amounts of chopped parsley and some toasted pinenuts.

Peel the garlic and put it into a pestle and mortar with the salt and crush to a paste. Add the chopped rosemary and fennel seeds bashing them into the paste until you have a pretty cohesive mixture. Whisk in the olive oil.

Stab the loin at $^3/_4$–$1^1/_4$ inch intervals across the top of the loin, and dig in some of the paste. Smear the remaining paste over the top of the loin and put into a large freezer bag to marinate, swilling out the pestle and mortar with 1 cup of the white wine and adding to the bag with the loin. Leave in the fridge overnight or for two days to marinate.

Preheat the oven to 400°F; take the meat out of the fridge to bring to room temperature. Put the loin into a roasting pan with the marinade and bones. Cook for an hour, then add a cup water, and cook for a further 45 minutes.

Take the meat out of the oven, not panicking at how much it has shrunk, and cover with aluminum foil. Let the covered veal sit in the pan for about an hour to rest.

When you are ready to carve the meat, take it out and sit it on a carving board. Put the pan on a gentle heat and add a cup water and the remaining $^1/_2$ cup white wine. Deglaze the roasting pan and let the juices, water and wine bubble together for about 5–6 minutes to make a scant gravy or sauce to pour over the carved meat.

SPINACH WITH PINENUTS AND SULTANAS

If you're making baked potatoes to go with the meat, or indeed some boiled new potatoes, tossed in a little pepper, salt and olive oil at the end, and served warm (in other words, have them resting in the oil in the pan as you sit down to soup), then the amount of spinach below will do just fine. Otherwise, I'd double it. That's not as hard as you'd think as long as you wilt the spinach in batches; indeed I'd be tempted to do so anyway. That's to say, wash the spinach and then sit it in a large pan just with the water that clings to the leaves after you've drained it, and put the pan on the heat, stirring frequently. I tend to buy spinach in 8–10oz bags, and find the easiest way to go is to wilt two bags at a time. Remove each batch to a large sieve and proceed to the next batch. Push down on the wilted spinach to remove any excess liquid then put all that you're using into a bowl, and proceed as below.

Serves 6–8

1/4 cup sultanas (golden raisins)
1 onion
2 tablespoons olive oil
1/3 cup pinenuts

2 1/4 lbs baby spinach, about 32 cups!
2 tablespoons white wine

Put the sultanas into a small bowl, pour over some freshly boiled water, and leave them to plump up. Peel the onion and cut into fine half moons. Heat the oil in a large pan that can cope with all the raw spinach later (or wilt first as above), and cook the onion until golden and soft. Toast the pinenuts in a dry pan until they are colored and tip into a bowl to cool.

Rinse and drain the spinach if you haven't wilted it already. Add the wine to the golden onions and stir well, then tumble in the spinach, pressing it down in the heat of the pan. Keep stirring to cook the spinach evenly. Let the spinach cook down, so that the water evaporates from the pan as much as possible.

Drain the sultanas well, and add to the pan along with the toasted pinenuts. Season with salt and pepper and add a little more olive oil if necessary.

You can do all this in advance of sitting down, then just put a little heat under it while you're clearing the plates.

SEPHARDI ROAST LAMB

As I said above, Sephardi Jews eat rice during Passover, which is why the stuffing of this leg of lamb includes it. You do need a butcher, or at least I do, to carve out the bone neatly, leaving you a small tunnel to fill with this aromatic mixture. But if you wanted to make life simpler, I suppose you could double the amount of rice stuffing and use it to stuff four chickens.

There is some debate over whether lamb is suitable food for seder. Some authorities decree that it is an indispensable part of the menu; others forbid lamb to be cooked without liquid. That is why, although the lamb is in effect roasted, I have added the braising-element of some legitimizing liquid to the pan as it goes into the oven.

2 legs of lamb, bone removed; not butterflied, just tunneled out
$^1/_2$ cup white wine
$^1/_2$ cup water
1 tablespoon sea salt/$1^1/_2$ teaspoons table salt

2 tablespoons olive oil
4 cloves garlic, unpeeled
2 bay leaves
1 small cinnamon stick

Serves 10–12

FOR THE STUFFING

1 cup chopped onion
2 tablespoons olive oil
1 fat clove garlic, minced
$^1/_3$ cup basmati rice
$^1/_2$ teaspoon turmeric
pinch ground cloves
$^1/_2$ teaspoon ground coriander
$^1/_4$ teaspoon ground ginger

1 teaspoon cumin seeds
juice of 1 lemon
$^2/_3$ cup water
$^1/_2$ cup fresh dates (weighed with pits)
$^1/_4$ cup pinenuts
$^1/_3$ cup dried sour cherries

For the stuffing, peel and chop the onion and fry gently in the oil in a saucepan that has a lid. Add the minced or grated garlic and a pinch of salt and cook for about 10 minutes.

Tip in the rice and stir around to slick with the oil, then add the spices, stirring again to coat the rice, and finally pour in the lemon juice and water. Bring to the boil and then clamp on the lid and cook on the lowest heat possible for 10 minutes. Then take the pan off the heat, put a kitchen towel under the lid and let the rice sit while you prepare the other stuffing ingredients.

Pit and roughly chop the dates, and add them to the cooked rice with the pinenuts, and cherries, working everything together with a fork. Stuff the tunneled-out-bone section of the lamb legs with this mixture sealing the ends with skewers as firmly as you can (like a stitch). If you've let the stuffing mixture get cold before you put it into the lamb, you can let it sit like that until you're ready to cook it. If, however, it's still warm, you must put the meat in the oven immediately after you've stuffed them.

Preheat the oven to 400°F.

In a large roasting pan, heat the wine, water, salt, oil, garlic cloves, bay leaves and cinnamon stick. Bring to a gentle boil on the stove top, and then lay in the lamb legs, sprinkling them with salt and pepper. Cover loosely with a tent of aluminum foil and cook for 2 hours. Lamb like this is not intended to be eaten pink; and you do want to be sure that the stuffing is warmed through, too.

Let the lamb rest while you eat the soup, and then remove to a carving board to slice it. Don't try and carve too thinly, as the stuffing will just fall out. Well, it tends to do that a bit anyway, but you can easily scoop the fallen grains on to each plate with a small spoon as you serve.

THE ASHKENAZI ALTERNATIVE

The procedure is much the same as for the Sephardi roast lamb immediately above.

2 boned legs of lamb (*not* butterflied, just the bone tunneled out)
1 cup water
juice and husks of the zested lemon, below

FOR THE STUFFING
1 onion
2 cloves garlic
1 stick of celery
1 sprig rosemary
1lb button mushrooms
$1/4$ cup olive oil
1 tablespoon sea salt/$1^1/2$ teaspoons table salt

3 bay leaves
2 sprigs rosemary
1 tablespoon garlic-infused oil

1 teaspoon ground ginger
$1/4$ teaspoon grated nutmeg
8oz spinach leaves
$1/3$ cup sultanas (golden raisins)
black pepper
zest of 1 lemon
$1/3$ cup matzoh meal

Serves 10–12

note
I think the best accompaniment to either of the lambs would be some green beans, about 2lbs, cooked, drained, beans then dressed in a little olive oil and ground pepper.

Preheat the oven to 400°F. Put the water for the braising liquid into a roasting pan and add all the remaining braising ingredients except the lamb to the pan as well. Put on the stove top and let it come to a gentle boil.

For the lamb stuffing, process the peeled onion, peeled garlic, celery, rosemary needles and mushrooms until you have a fine if unattractive mush. Heat the oil in a wide pan and cook the processed vegetables for about 7 minutes or until soft. Add the salt and spices, and then stir in the spinach and sultanas.

Turn up the heat and cook until the moisture from the spinach has evaporated, then add a good grinding of pepper and the lemon zest and cook for about 12 minutes.

Take the pan off the heat, add the matzoh meal, stir and turn the stuffing into a bowl to cool.

Stuff the boned legs of lamb with the cooled spinach mixture. You will get about half the stuffing into each tunneled leg cavity depending on the size of the lamb leg. Secure the ends with skewers making a stitch to stop the filling from falling out. (It always bursts out a bit during cooking so don't think you've done anything wrong.)

Lay the stuffed legs in the hot roasting pan and cover loosely with aluminumfoil. Cook for 2 hours, and let the lamb rest as on facing page, carving likewise.

Opposite: Sephardi roast lamb

DAMP APPLE AND ALMOND CAKE

If you've eaten the veal as a main course, then I think I'd go on to the flourless chocolate orange cake on page 274. Cook that in a 9 inch rather than an 8 inch pan and omit the leaveners. And you can make it go even further by serving, alongside a bowl of raspberries over which you have finely grated the zest of an orange and dusted with confectioners' sugar.

This, however, is a huge cake, and needs no augmentation. Indeed, it really needs nothing further at all. It's astonishing how buttery it tastes, given that there is not – obviously – an ounce of butter in it. As with the chocolate orange cake, the flour is replaced with ground almonds – and cooked, cooled, puréed fruit provides moistness and flavor.

Makes 12 slices

note

If you'd like, by all means, mix in a pinch or so of ground cinnamon with the confectioners' sugar before you sift it on to the cake at the end.

And for another Passover cake, see the version of the pomegranate jewel cake in the note on page 365.

FOR THE APPLE PUREE
3 tart eating apples, such as Braeburns

1 tablespoon lemon juice
2 teaspoons sugar

FOR THE CAKE
almond oil/flavorless vegetable oil to grease pan
8 eggs
$3^1/_4$ cups ground almonds

$1^3/_4$ cups superfine sugar
1 tablespoon lemon juice
$^1/_2$ cup slivered almonds

TO DECORATE
1 teaspoon confectioners' sugar

Peel, core and chop the apples roughly. Put them in a saucepan with the lemon juice and sugar, and bring the pan to a gentle boil over a medium heat. Cover the pan and cook over a low heat for about 10 minutes or until you can mash the apple to a rough purée with a wooden spoon or fork. (You should have about 1 heaped cup of purée.) Leave to cool.

Preheat the oven to 350°F; oil a 10 inch springform pan with almond oil or a flavorless vegetable oil and line the bottom with parchment paper.

Put the cooled purée in the processor with the eggs, ground almonds, superfine sugar and 1 tablespoonful – or generous squeeze – of lemon juice and blitz to a purée. Pour and scrape, with a rubber spatula for ease, into the prepared pan, sprinkle the almonds on top and bake for about 45 minutes. It's worth checking after 35 minutes, as ovens do vary, and you might well find it's cooked earlier – or indeed you may need to give it a few minutes longer.

Put on a wire rack to cool slightly, then remove the sides of the pan. This cake is best served slightly warm, though still good cold. As you bring it to the table, push a teaspoon of confectioners' sugar through a fine sieve to give a light dusting.

Opposite: top, damp apple and almond cake; below, chewy macaroons

BREAKFAST

I THINK I should state straightaway that just because I've got a breakfast chapter in a book called *Feast* doesn't mean that I think you should be sitting down in the mornings, like some portly Regency gentleman, to a spread of deviled kidneys and legs of mutton, washed down with port. Breakfast is, quite literally, a feast in that it is a meal that breaks a fast, much as – traditionally – Easter is. And even if we don't turn off the alarm every morning joyfully greeting the new dawn, there is a sense in which that first meal of the day emphatically celebrates being alive. And I don't say that just because I have found empirically that those who don't eat breakfast tend to be grouchy all morning, or else are those studiedly saturnine types, who never quite shook off the feeling that a snatched cup of black coffee on the run was an act of cool, edgy rebellion.

Of course, there is a practical issue here, too, rather than just a psychological block: most days, few of us have the time to linger about, Waltons-style, flipping pancakes and baking muffins. Sometimes we really don't have time to eat breakfast let alone make it. But there are such things as weekends and, anyway, days when you don't have to rush off to work or get children to school are pretty rare. Why act as if the whole of life is a question of getting as much done as possible in as little time as possible? On days when you can sit around, do so.

Now, it's true that sitting around is a likelier option for those eating breakfast than those making it, but I don't suggest vast early morning banquets here. I absolutely have to eat breakfast – though not first thing if I can avoid it: I need a slow mug of tea to bring me round – but not too much of it. The only thing worse than the panicked tetchiness that only an empty stomach can induce is that lethargic feeling of starting the day off with a bloat, when all you want to do is go back to bed, hide under the covers and hate yourself.

MY FAVORITE BREAKFAST – BOILED EGG, MALDON SALT AND BUTTERED *PAIN POILÂNE* FINGERS

And no, I'm not going to give a recipe for a boiled egg, but I do feel it's worth reminding you that if the egg is fridge-cold it should go into the pan along with cold water when you put it on the stove, but if it's at room temperature – which is better – you should lower it into the water once it's started boiling. How long you want to cook it for is obviously up to you, but the beautiful, oozingly golden yolked egg on the previous page had 4 minutes, as indeed mine does every morning. I also throw in a matchstick – rather than the teaspoon of vinegar or salt that some people swear by – just because my great-aunt always did and told me that it stopped the white cloudily flowing out should the egg crack while cooking. I think it does work, but I do it because I've always done it, not because I have scientific proof that it's effective.

And that's the thing about breakfast: there is a strong ritualistic element; that, too, brings it in line with feasting in general. I have the same breakfast every day. Early mornings are bad enough without the specter of choice to haunt you too. First thing in the morning, I'd rather make breakfast than a decision and so I only ever swerve from this out of whim or, occasionally, dietary restraint.

And like everyone with a weak need to be bound by habitual behavior, I am irritatingly fussy. I want my egg to be Italian (free-range, organic and imported from Bologna, if you please: seeing it, you understand why Italians refer to the yolks as *i rossi* – "the reds" of the egg), I want my salt to be Maldon (sea salt) and

I want my sourdough bread to come from the Poilâne bakery down the road. As ever, my butter has to be pale and unsalted and not fridge-cold, but not all sloppy-soft and oily either. I don't mind having a different breakfast, but I don't want a lesser version of the same one. Maybe it's my age.

I know it is the convention to offer various savory delights for the breakfast table but in all honesty I can't oblige here. My feeling is simply this: apart from the iconic ideal of the boiled egg and soldiers, what could be better than fried eggs and bacon, poached eggs on toast, scrambled egg with sausages? Yes, as Lord Lambton memorably said when found with two hookers, one black, one white, we all want variety, but I don't see fiddling about with the basic components of a traditional breakfast to make strange and wonderful cheesey-bacony-eggy-bready concoctions ultimately that satisfying.

Having said that, I do want to suggest you look at the tomato and bacon hash in the Midnight Feasts section: I certainly wouldn't turn it away first thing in the morning. And on Saturdays, I have been known to have a soft-boiled egg, peeled and plonked on some salty slabs of halloumi cheese (page 412) which is really a kind of eggs and bacon for vegetarians, or semi-vegetarians. Otherwise my idea of making a treat for breakfast tends to fall into one of the categories below: something sugary perhaps, but never temple-achingly so, to usher in a day of corresponding sweetness.

BANANA BUTTERMILK PANCAKES

Whenever I'm trying to be Nice Mummy, rather than normal Bad-tempered Impatient Mummy, I make pancakes. Unfortunately, it can often be counter-productive, but the sad truth about parenting is that it's virtually impossible to learn from your mistakes. The whole business is a Dantesque punishment: you're trapped in the cycle, knowing what you're doing, but seemingly unable to stop.

There's no absolute need to veer from the regular breakfast pancakes ($2/3$ cup flour, $1 1/2$ teaspoons baking powder, $1/2$ teaspoon sugar, $3/4$ cup milk, 1 tablespoonful of melted butter, method as below, to make about twelve) but I always seem to have over-ripe bananas hanging about (and see also, banana breakfast ring, on page 200) and cannot bring myself to throw them away. And here's the thing: these pancakes do not taste remotely bananary. In fact, I'm not sure you would immediately notice anything about them other than that they are celestially light and tender. Some wonderful chemical reaction between the banana and buttermilk is responsible for their dream-texture; you need do nothing more taxing than tip the ingredients into a blender.

1 very ripe banana	**1 egg**	Makes about 20
1 cup all-purpose flour	**1 cup buttermilk**	
1 teaspoon baking powder	**1 teaspoon sugar**	note
$1/2$ teaspoon baking soda	**1oz butter, melted**	Although it's true the butter-milk makes these springy and sprightly, you can make them with ordinary milk, and before

Put all the ingredients except for the melted butter into a blender and liquidize to a smooth batter. Alternatively, you can put the flour, baking powder and baking soda into a you do anything to the pancake mix, drop $1/2$ teaspoon of good vinegar into the milk and let it stand, souring, for 5 minutes before proceeding.

I haven't specified what size or weight the banana should be. How ridiculous would that be? Small or big, you'll just make fewer or more of the pancakes depending.

bowl and whisk the egg, buttermilk and sugar in a bowl or glass measuring cup. Pour the wet ingredients over the dry, and now mash the banana and fold that in.

Whichever method you've used, pour the batter into a glass measuring cup and leave till you want to use it. Stir in the melted butter just before you set about frying the pancakes.

On a heated smooth griddle or non-stick skillet, or if you're strong enough cast-iron, skillet, dollop tablespoons of batter to form around 3 inch cakes, flipping them over once the underside is set, a minute if that, by which time it will also have turned a deep golden brown. Half a minute or so on the other side should do it, and transfer as you go to a warmed waiting plate or plates. I eat these sprinkled with pumpkin seeds and drenched with honey, as below.

CHEESECAKELETS

These are more or less what they sound like – though I suppose they could be anything – which is to say, old-fashioned cheesecake-flavored pancakes. And by old-fashioned, I mean that they remind me of a cheesecake my paternal grandmother used to make, using not cream cheese but cottage cheese, as indeed these pancakes do.

While a pancake made out of cottage cheese may not sound immediately appealing, I have to tell you that I find these addictive. There's something about that eggy-vanilla note underscoring the light sourness that is irresistible.

You could use syrup here, but I don't, preferring instead to eat them with luminescently red and juicy strawberries. It's the balsamic vinegar and sugar that gives them that slicked shine and stained-glass-window hue, and they are just what you want with the rich but light enticing cheesecakelets.

3 eggs
2 tablespoons superfine sugar
1 cup cottage cheese

$^1/_3$ cup all-purpose flour
1 teaspoon best quality vanilla
    extract

Makes 15

note
These are also very good just
with raspberries, no syrup, no
squishing, just tumbled out on
to the little cheesecake pancakes as they are.

TO EAT WITH
approx. 2 cups strawberries
$^1/_2$ teaspoon balsamic vinegar

$^1/_2$–1 teaspoon superfine sugar

Start with the fruit, just so that it can macerate while you make the pancakes. Depending on their size, chop the strawberries into quarters or eighths, sprinkle over the balsamic vinegar and sugar (you'll need more or less depending on how sweet and ripe the berries you have are) and swirl the bowl about a bit so the strawberries are coated before covering with plastic wrap and leaving to steep while you set about making your cheesecakelets.

Separate the eggs. Mix the yolks with the sugar, beating well. Add the cottage cheese, flour and vanilla. Then, in another bowl, whisk the whites till frothy (with a hand whisk only: you're not even approaching making meringue or anything) and fold the white spuma into the cottage-cheese mixture.

Heat a smooth griddle or non-stick skillet and dollop tablespoons of the curd-thick batter on to it to make cakelets of about $3^1/_4$ inch in diameter. Each cheesecakelet will take a minute or so to firm up underneath, when you should flip it and cook the other side. Remove to a warmed plate as and when ready.

Turn the strawberries in the ruby syrup they've made and squish some pieces with a fork at the same time. Decant them into a bowl, with a spoon for serving, and bring your cheesecakelets to the table at the same time.

MAPLE PECAN MUFFINS

This is another easy-assemble job (providing you have the ingredients, of course) but then it would be hard to find a difficult muffin recipe.

There's something about the smoky austerity of that pecan maple mix that makes these particularly good for breakfast. They bear no relation to something you might eat for dessert, though having said that, they would be excellent with sharp, strong cheese.

Makes 12

1 cup shelled pecans	$^1/_2$ cup milk
2 cups all-purpose flour	$^1/_2$ cup maple syrup
4 teaspoons baking powder	$^1/_2$ cup corn oil
$^1/_2$ cup wheatgerm	1 egg
pinch salt	1 tablespoon dark brown sugar

Preheat the oven to 400°F. Fill a 12-cup muffin tin with paper muffin cups.

Chop the pecans roughly, reserving about $^1/_4$ cup of them to use later to strew on top. Combine the rest of them with the flour, baking powder, wheatgerm and salt in a large bowl. In a measuring cup or, indeed, in another bowl, whisk together the milk, maple syrup, corn oil and egg. Pour into the dry ingredients and mix to combine but don't worry if the mixture is still lumpy as – to reiterate – it will make a better muffin. Spoon the batter into the prepared muffin tin.

Chop the reserved nuts a tiny bit finer and mix with the brown sugar and then sprinkle a little on to the top of each muffin. Bake for 20 minutes, by which time the muffins will have risen, although you mustn't expect them to turn very golden. Apart from their sugary nut topping, they are distinctly pale beauties.

Remove the muffins from their tins onto a cooling rack, and eat while they are still warm, either as they are, or split and spread with a little unsalted butter, and perhaps some more – please – maple syrup drizzled over.

GRANOLA MUFFINS

It might seem slightly odd to give a recipe for granola muffins quite a bit in advance of the recipe for granola itself (page 199), but then I scarcely intend you to go to all that effort making your own granola – and it is magnificent – just to lose so much of it to a batch of muffins. The thing is, as long as you buy good granola, you are fine here. What am I saying? More than fine: these, with their buttermilk-lightened crumb and dried fruit and nut filling, are just what you want your morning muffin to be.

As with all muffins, they are not much good cold, so eat as many as you can when they get out of the oven. On day two they will have staled a bit, but a quick burst in the microwave should bring them slightly back to warm life, but after that, forget it.

If you want to make your life really easy at breakfast, you can mix up the dry ingredients in a bowl and leave it covered in plastic wrap on the counter and mix the liquid ingredients in a measuring cup, also covered in plastic wrap, but this time stashed in the fridge overnight. Then all you have to do the next morning is preheat the oven, get out the muffin tin and papers and do a little casual stirring.

1 $^1/_2$ cups all-purpose flour	1 egg	**Makes 12**
1 teaspoon baking soda	$^3/_4$ cup light brown sugar	
$^1/_4$ teaspoon salt	$^1/_3$ cup vegetable oil	note
1 cup buttermilk	2 cups granola	To make muesli muffins, just use good-quality (ie large-textured, not that sawdusty stuff) muesli in place of the granola.

Preheat the oven to 400°F. Line a 12-cup muffin tin with paper muffin cups.

Combine the flour, baking soda and salt in a large bowl. In a wide-necked pitcher, whisk together the buttermilk, egg, sugar and oil. Pour this into the dry ingredients and mix lightly to combine. Fold in the granola and then divide the muffin mixture between the 12 paper cups. Bake for 25 minutes, by which time they should have risen and become golden brown.

Take the tin out of the oven, lift the muffins in their papers carefully out of the tin and let them cool, just a little though, on a wire rack.

RHUBARB MUFFINS

These muffins are a product of a couple of passions of mine, the first being for rhubarb; the second for those newspaper readers' recipe columns. I found, give or take, this recipe for rhubarb muffins in London's *Daily Telegraph* Readers' Recipes column, one of my favorites (and I'm glad to see all the recipes have since been compiled in a book, *It's Raining Plums*). Recipes that people do themselves all the time at home are always the best, and this one comes via Bev Laing from Edmonton, Canada.

    I think this may have deviated a little from the original printed version by now, as I've fiddled slightly, but I couldn't be happier with the crunchy topped sour-fruited sweet little muffins. For some reason, and it can't have been a good one (the desire to cut out or color in is always a bad sign, psychologically speaking), I got it into my head that I wanted to make some brown paper wrappers for these muffins. They do look beautiful, in their very homemade way, but I should own up that they take much longer than the muffins to make. Sticking to the bought paper cups, while less quaint, is probably a safer bet.

Makes 12

1 1/4 cup light brown sugar
1/3 cup vegetable oil or corn oil
1 egg
2 teaspoons pure vanilla extract
1 cup buttermilk
6oz rhubarb, cut into 1/2 in dice
  (1 1/2 cups when diced)

1/2 cup shelled walnuts, roughly
  chopped
2 cups plus 3 tablespoons all-purpose
  flour
2 teaspoons baking powder
1 teaspoon baking soda
1/2 cup wheatgerm

FOR THE TOPPING
2 tablespoons light brown sugar mixed
  with 1 teaspoon ground cinnamon

Preheat the oven to 400°F. Get out a 12-cup muffin tin and a roll of brown baking parchment. Cut out 12 x 6 inch square pieces of parchment and push them down into each cup-opening. They will sit on the surface now, I know, but once you squidge the mixture in they will sink down to form a kind of paper-tulip liner.

    In a large bowl, mix the sugar, oil, egg, vanilla extract and buttermilk. Stir in the chopped rhubarb and nuts. Sprinkle over the flour, baking powder and baking soda and add the wheatgerm. Fold together quickly until just blended but still rather lumpy.

    Spoon into a 12-cup muffin tin lined with papers either as above or bought, and sprinkle liberally with the sugar and cinnamon mixture.

    Bake for 20–25 minutes, by which time the sugar topping will be glistening and the muffins beneath a pale but definite gold. Eat warm and give thanks.

RHUBARB COMPOTE

The muffin issue can be put to rest, but I certainly haven't finished with rhubarb. This must be that gorgeously pink rhubarb that, on being roasted, turns a vivid, rock-candy puce. My feeling is that this is best, for breakfast, eaten cold, so just stick it in the oven in the evening, remembering to take it out before you go to bed. Leave it on the kitchen counter, decanted into a fresh bowl (it will carry on cooking too much in its original dish) with any excess juice left behind, but not thrown away, to be eaten the next morning. An excellent use for the leftover juice is as follows: boil it down a bit so it's reduced into a syrup. Cool, then chill, and eat over vanilla ice cream or again, Greek yogurt with, in the latter case, perhaps a sprinkling of shelled sliced pistachios, as ludicrously green as the rhubarb is pink. I wouldn't be above serving the rhubarb compote with the thick yogurt and sliced pistachios for a dinner-party dessert either.

1 1/2 lbs rhubarb to make about 6 cups, sliced

1 cup plus two tablespoons superfine sugar
finely grated zest of 1 orange

Serves approx. 8

note
When rhubarb is dessert, I want it warm and with custard, or cold and with cream. For breakfast or quickly grabbed fridge-raiding snacks at night, I must have it chilled and with Greek yogurt.

Preheat the oven to 375°F. Cut the rhubarb into 1 inch pieces and place in an ovenproof dish. Sprinkle over the sugar, add the orange zest, mix with your hands, and cover with foil. Bake in the oven for 45 minutes to an hour, by which time the fruit should be soft but still holding its shape and its glorious pink color.

Remove the foil and decant into another dish to cool.

RASPBERRY AND OATMEAL SWIRLS

I agree it might sound odd to start off a wonderful fresh-sounding fruit recipe by suggesting frozen berries, but I do this just because it means you can have the wherewithal to make this at a moment's notice. Plus I like the sorbet effect of the still icy blended fruit against the smooth creaminess of the yogurt and the sweet sandiness of the cookie crumbs.

I have given specific amounts as you can see, but be prepared to add fewer or more crumbs, fruit or yogurt as you go, depending on the dimensions of the glasses you are using.

Makes 6 smallish glasses

2 cups frozen raspberries
4 teaspoons confectioners' sugar

2 heaped cups Greek or wholemilk yogurt
$^1/_2$ cup oatmeal cookie crumbs

Put the frozen raspberries into a blender with the sugar, and purée until they make a vibrant super-pink sauce. You may have to be patient as they will be difficult to blitz at first since they are extremely hard when frozen.

Gather together six glasses of about $^3/_4$ cup capacity, and spoon 1–2 teaspoons of the raspberry purée into each one. (I wouldn't dream of sieving.) Then dollop in each glass about a couple of tablespoons of the yogurt, and then sprinkle a layer of cookie crumbs on top of that. To get the cookie crumbs, just put a few cookies in a bag and bash with a rolling pin, but if you wanted you could use a processor, though it scarcely seems worth the effort. Why give yourself another whole batch of stuff to wash up?

Cover the crumbs with one more layer of yogurt, then raspberry and finally cookie crumbs again.

Strange though it sounds, you can make these the night before, in which case don't sprinkle on the final layer of crumbs until you are ready to eat the swirls but leave the glasses, yogurt on top, covered with plastic wrap.

I prefer them made – and you can see that it's hardly heavy labor – *à la minute*, but I have many takers for the thickened, mellowed, fridge-softened version. These things, as with food generally, are a matter of taste, which of course is how it should be.

ARABIAN MORNINGS

This is not so much a recipe, more an enthusiastic suggestion: a scented, simple salad with which to greet a turquoise-skied summer's day.

2lbs watermelon (weighed with skin; about $^1/_2$ medium watermelon) to make approx. 8 cups when cut up

$^1/_2$ cup mint leaves
1 tablespoon rosewater

Serves 6

note
It's not quite in that dreamy Scheherazade register, but this is also very good as a morning freshener-upper with a box or two of ultra ripe strawberries, hulled, halved or quartered and tumbled in when you toss through the rosewater.

Cut the watermelon off the rind, pry out as many seeds as you can with the sharp pointy end of the knife and cut the melon flesh into just under 2 inch triangles; you're building beautiful glassy-red pyramids here. Put these in a large shallowish bowl. Chop up most of the mint and scatter over the watermelon, spoon over the rosewater and turn the fruit well, so both mint and rosewater are evenly allocated.

Sprinkle with a few remaining whole mint leaves and bring fragrantly to the breakfast table.

MUESLI

There is something about muesli, real muesli, that makes me feel I am some intellectual, beautiful free spirit, throwing pots and writing poetry or political diatribes in 1960s Hampstead. And it's a feeling I quite like.

$1^1/_2$ cups mixed nuts
2 cups organic rolled oats
$^1/_2$ cup sunflower seeds

1 cup sultanas (golden raisins)
1 tablespoon brown sugar

Makes 4 cups

Preheat the oven to 375°F.

Put the mixed nuts into a food processor and pulse so that some are finely chopped to blend with the oats and others are bigger to give texture.

Spread the oats, mixed chopped nuts and sunflower seeds on to a baking sheet and toast for 20 minutes. After 10, take the sheet out, give it a good shake so that everything toasts evenly, and put the baking sheet back in the oven.

Then, when it's had its full time, take the baking sheet out again, give the contents a stir around, and then leave on the baking sheet to cool completely.

Once cool stir through the sultanas and brown sugar and store in an airtight container.

ANDY'S FAIRFIELD GRANOLA

This is an extraordinary bonus from my last book, in the sense that while I was on tour in the States to promote *Forever Summer*, I did a signing in a Borders bookstore in Fairfield, Connecticut, and just behind the bookshop was a deli called The Pantry. Well, I can never just buy *enough*, don't even know what that would mean: I always leave any foodshop with about five shopping bags, even when I know I'm going on a transatlantic flight the next day. So I schlepped home with bags of good things to eat, including (and probably, illegally, I'm afraid) several tons of their granola. I got so anxious about the prospect of finishing even that copious supply that I phoned for the recipe – it happens to be only the best granola you'll ever taste in your life – and Andy Rolleri supplied it, for which I am enormously grateful. Every time I've given this to people, they've asked for the recipe and have gone on to make it at home. That can only be a good sign.

You may think making your own breakfast cereal is a strange way to go about life, and certainly I'd never have thought I'd be the kind of person who does this, but the only big deal here is the shopping – the actual making is incredibly easy – and even there, don't be daunted by the length of the ingredients list. It means one big sortie to a health food shop and then you've got the goods to make this again and again. I love having a big jar of it in the kitchen, to eat with milk for breakfast, over yogurt and drizzled with honey late at night, or as it is, by the grasped handful, any time I pass by the jar.

4¹/₂ cups rolled oats
1 cup/4oz sunflower seeds
³/₄ cup/4oz white sesame seeds
³/₄ cup/6oz apple compote or apple sauce
2 teaspoons ground cinnamon
1 teaspoon ground ginger
¹/₃ cup brown rice syrup or rice malt syrup, or failing that, golden syrup

¹/₄ cup clover honey or other honey
³/₄ cup light brown sugar
2 cups/8oz whole natural almonds
1 teaspoon sea salt
2 tablespoons sunflower oil
2 cups raisins

makes approx. 10 cups

note
I make a chocolate and peanut version of this, using 2 cups raw peanuts in place of the almonds, and adding ¹/₄ cup best-quality cocoa powder along with the oats, sunflower seeds and sesame seeds, giving everything a good raking over with my hands, so that the cocoa is evenly dispersed before I add the remaining ingredients. And I sometimes leave the raisins out of Andy's granola, but I absolutely *never* include them in this version. You could, however, tinker with the idea of some dried cherries.

Mix everything except the raisins together very well in a large mixing bowl. I use a couple of curved, rigid spatulas; normally, I'd be happy to use my hands, but here it just leaves you covered with everything.

Spread this mixture out on two baking sheets (the sort that come with ovens, and are about the width of a rack) and bake in a 300–325°F oven, turning over about halfway through baking and re-distributing the granola evenly during the baking process. The object is to get it evenly golden without toasting too much in any one place. This should take anywhere from about 40 minutes. I use a gas oven, which doesn't brown as fast as an electric one, so often leave it in for up to an hour.

Once it's baked, allow to cool and mix together with the raisins. Store airtight.

BANANA BREAKFAST RING

Almost all you need for this is a bowl, a fork and some nearly gone-off bananas.

There's just something about this gently fragrant, very plain pale cake that makes it the perfect breakfast slice. Eat still warm, with maybe some maple syrup drizzled over or smeared with Nutella if you must, but there's no need to add anything other than a mug of tea or coffee or, indeed, glass of milk.

Makes 8–10 slices

1lb (3 medium) bananas, mashed
  gives 1 cup
$1/4$ cup corn oil or other oil
3 eggs
zest and juice of $1/2$ lemon

1 teaspoon pure vanilla extract
1 cup sugar
$2^1/4$ cups all-purpose flour
1 teaspoon baking powder
$1/2$ teaspoon baking soda

Preheat the oven to 350°F and oil a $9^1/2$ inch/6 cup ring mold.

Mash the bananas, and add the oil, eggs, lemon juice and zest, vanilla and sugar. Whisk everything together and then fold in the flour, baking powder and baking soda.

Pour into the oiled pan and bake for 40 minutes. Let the ring sit for about 5-10 minutes before turning it out.

BREAKFAST BISCUITS

These are biscuits in the American sense of the word: not crunchy cookies but light little scone-like discs. The fabulous thing about them is this: you make the dough, cut out the biscuits then lay them on a small baking sheet wrapped in plastic wrap and stick them in the freezer; once they're frozen you put them in a freezer-bag and you have them there ready to bake, as they are, so all you need to do is put them in the oven, bake them, split them, spread them with good unsalted butter and jam and a perfect breakfast awaits you in return for scant early-morning effort.

The recipe is adapted from *The King Arthur Flour Baker's Companion*, whose Baker's Catalogue (and see Stockists page 461) I am dreadfully addicted to.

Makes 9–10

note
Both butter and jam are
what's needed on these celestially light little biscuits. For
me, that has to be unsalted
butter and for preference plum
jam.

$1^3/4$ cups all-purpose flour
1 teaspoon salt
1 tablespoon sugar
$2^1/2$ teaspoons baking powder
$1/2$ stick cold butter

$1/4$ cup Crisco (or other vegetable
  shortening)
$1/4$ cup milk
1 egg

Put the flour, salt, sugar and baking powder into a bowl. Add the butter cut into $1/4$ inch cubes and vegetable shortening in $1/2$ teaspoon lumps and rub them into the flour to give you an oatmeal-like consistency.

Whisk together the milk and egg, and then add as much as you need to the buttery flour to give you a rollable dough.

Flour your surface and roll out the dough to $^3/_4$ inch in thickness. Cut out $2^1/_2$ inch circles, re-rolling as you go; I tend to use a crinkled cutter, and do remember to dip it into some flour as you go. Try to make the dough as smooth as possible since any cracks while rolling will show in the finished biscuits, not that this is life or death.

Put the cut-out biscuits on to a baking sheet and freeze them for a minimum of 30 minutes before you cook them. Ideally make them in advance and keep in an airtight freezer bag, so you have a stock for breakfast ready in the freezer.

At breakfast time, preheat the oven to 400°F, and cook the biscuits straight from frozen for about 18 minutes.

BREAKFAST BISCOTTI

If you really don't want much more for breakfast than a cup of black coffee, then this is the more you might just want: hard-baked, Italian dunking cookies studded with dark chocolate.

Makes 20

1 egg
$^1/_2$ cup superfine sugar
$^1/_2$ teaspoon pure vanilla extract
few drops almond extract
$^3/_4$ cup plus 2 tablespoons
  all-purpose flour

$^1/_2$ teaspoon baking powder
$^1/_4$ teaspoon salt
$^1/_3$ cup natural shelled almonds
$^1/_3$ cup semisweet chocolate chips

Preheat the oven to 350°F.

Whisk the egg and sugar until pale and moussily thick; I use an electric mixer here, as you want the mixture whipped enough so that when you lift the whisk attachment out of it, you are left with a trail of ribbons. Beat in the vanilla and almond extracts, and then slowly fold in the flour, baking powder and salt.

When the batter's all combined, fold in the whole almonds and chocolate pieces, and then form the dough into a loaf-like log of about 10 x 2 inches, slightly tapering the ends.

Lay the biscotti log on to a piece of baking parchment on a baking sheet and cook for 25 minutes: it will be a pale brown color. Leave for 5 minutes to harden slightly, and then cut diagonal slants of about $^1/_2$ in thickness along the length of the loaf to give finger-like pieces.

Put these back on to the parchment paper covered baking sheet and cook again for another 10 minutes, turn the biscotti over and then cook for another 5 minutes. Let the golden brown biscotti cool on a rack and then store them in an airtight container ready to be plucked and dunked at a moment's anticipatory notice.

KITCHEN FEASTS

PEOPLE GO slightly mad when they house-hunt, and tend to think a prospective home is better if it has a dining room. But there's no point spending money on a room that hardly ever gets used – except, in my experience, as a dumping ground for stuff you can't find a home for elsewhere – when the reality is the room you eat in every day is the kitchen. I feel the same way about cooking. It's not the special events and the calendar-starred occasions that should be your major concern, important though they are, but the dinners or lunches you make to share with your friends and family, as part of an everyday celebration of life.

Perhaps that "everyday" is over-optimistic. Most days, I admit, none of us has the time to shop and cook or even, sometimes, to sit down long enough to have a proper meal. That's why it matters so much when we can and do. I pointedly avoid the term "dinner party": I hate the formal connotations and the whole socially fraught scene.

I don't think this is just my problem, for I've noticed that something strange comes over people the minute they invite even their oldest, coziest friends to this notional dinner party. Suddenly, their necks tense, their shoulders rise: they feel they need to follow some old-style, entertaining formula: course after course of exhaustingly cooked food, the full ambassadorial feast. And if you start feeling that you have to impress your friends, of all people, then you start not wanting to see them at all – and what would be the point? Certainly, you would truly have nothing to celebrate.

When I invite people over to supper, I take radically simplifying steps. This stops both me and the people I'm feeding getting into a twitch. I stick the cutlery and plates straight on the table, not even laid out, but plonked there so that everyone can take their own. Immediately, everything is less formal. Moreover, I ditch the starter. A first course makes everything too complicated: there's the clearing away of the plates, the having to go back and forth from table to stove as you fuss to get the timing right for the main course; and there is, too, the important consideration that everyone works long hours these days, and a three-course dinner can make the evening too late. Maybe I'm just trying to find excuses for my own laziness. For it's not that I mind having food for people to pick at over drinks; I don't want to rush them to the table the minute they're through the door. I want only to remove the constraining formality of the one-two-three procession of courses.

For some reason, I tend to invite people over to supper on a Friday. In the middle of the week, I'm too harried and I always presume it's difficult for people to get babysitters on a Saturday. Besides, I really do think in all of us there resides some basic impulse to celebrate throwing off the shackles and cares of the working week. And I say that as someone who not only doesn't have a strict working week as such, and moreover, in common with most parents, am not entirely clear as to the relaxing benefits of the weekend. Indeed I have even thought of going into production with some TGIM buttons: I'm sure there'd be a market for them, if the faces of my fellow mothers at the school doors come Monday morning are anything to go by. On the other hand, it's because of the familial obligations – and I don't mean that as grudgingly as it might sound – of the weekend, that it's such a good time to invite people over to lunch. And I still love a proper Sunday lunch. This doesn't have to mean roast beef, roast potatoes, Yorkshire pudding and all the works, though it can do (and see page 217) but an expansive few hours for people to get together, relax and talk, over a table of welcoming food.

A SIMPLE CELEBRATORY SUPPER FOR EIGHT

HAM IN CHERRY COKE
CREAMED SPINACH AND BAKED POTATOES
APPLE CHEESECAKE WITH BUTTERSCOTCH SAUCE

HAM IN CHERRY COKE

Ever since my ham in Coca-Cola I'd been desperate to try cooking in Cherry Coke, and all I can say is that it is a triumph.

I usually don't soak ham, but do what my mother always did and immerse it in a pan of cold water, bring it to the boil, then chuck the water away. Then I rinse the ham under the tap, put the roast back in the pan and pour over the Cherry Coke and proceed. If you're pressed for time, you may find it easier to leave it in a basin of cold water overnight, as then you cut down on actual cooking time.

This is time-consuming, though very easy to make, and obviously the smaller the ham, the less time it will take to cook. I always reckon on 25 minutes a pound, but the bigger the ham, the more chance you have of leftovers. This cold ham makes fabulous sandwiches, for one thing, and I also use it for the pasta with ham and peas (page 244) for the children on Saturday. And there are other gratifying ways of using it up too: the point is that out of one feast, come many.

5–6lb boneless mild cure ham	**1 onion**	Serves 8
approx. 6 12oz cans Cherry Coke		

FOR THE GLAZE
approx. 16 whole cloves
3–4 tablespoons cherry jam

1 teaspoon *pimentón dulce* **or**
smoked paprika
$^1/_2$ teaspoon red wine vinegar

note
This tends to be what I cook if I'm giving a dinner to celebrate a friend's birthday. I might add the birthday custard cake (page 260) or some brownies (page 46) with candles stuck into them to the apple cheesecake, or just prong the cheesecake with candles instead.

Put the ham snugly into a large saucepan (you really need the tightest fit you can, so that you don't have to use lots and lots of Coke to cover it later) and fill with cold water. Put the pan on the heat and bring to the boil, then drain the ham into a colander, wash the ham under the tap and rinse the saucepan before putting the ham back in. This will get rid of some of the saltiness. Or just soak overnight, as above.

I hate throwing anything away, but felt the stock would be too sweet to make soup; so I tried cooking red cabbage in it, and it was wonderful. If you're cooking the ham in advance (give it slightly less time to cook, let it cool in the liquid and leave in the fridge overnight before stripping the rind and proceeding with the glaze, for approx. 40 minutes at 400°F), you could eat the red cabbage with it.

Otherwise use later. Bring the ham stock back to the boil, add 2 tablespoons red wine vinegar and 1 head red cabbage, shredded. Cook for approx. 1–1$^1/_4$ hours at a steady simmer, covering the pan if losing too much liquid.

Add the Cherry Coke and the onion, halved, to the ham and if the liquid doesn't cover it then add some water. Put back on the heat and bring to the boil, then turn down to a simmer and partially cover the pan. Cook for approx. 2–2$^1/_4$ hours.

When you are ready to glaze the ham, preheat the oven to 450°F. Remove the ham from the liquid, reserving it for later, and sit the ham on a board. Strip off the rind, and a little of the fat layer if it's very thick, and cut a diamond pattern into the remaining fat with a knife in lines about $^3/_4$ inch apart. Stud each diamond with a clove.

Put the jam, *pimentón dulce* and red wine vinegar into a saucepan and whisk together over a high heat, bringing it to the boil. Let the pan bubble away so that the glaze reduces to a syrupy consistency that will coat the fat on the ham.

Sit the ham in a roasting pan on a layer of aluminum foil, as the sugar in the glaze will burn in the oven as it drips off. Pour the glaze over the diamond-studded ham and then put it in the oven for about 15 minutes, or until the glazed fat has caught and burnished. Take the ham out of the oven and return it to the carving board to rest before you carve it.

CREAMED SPINACH

This is my favorite vegetable of all time and I'd eat it every day if I could, and sometimes do. I've tried it with frozen spinach and, although it works, it just isn't as good: it gets too watery no matter how often you remove the uncreamed spinach to a sieve and press to squeeze out excess liquid. Because such huge amounts of spinach cook down so much, you need to wilt the spinach in batches. There's no such thing as a pan big enough to take all of the raw spinach at once.

But this has its advantages: you can wilt all the spinach and leave it in a colander dripping, then just reheat, adding the cream and so forth, just before eating.

2lb 12oz (too many cups to count!) spinach	**3 tablespoons cornstarch**	Serves 8–10
1 stick unsalted butter	**1 cup heavy cream**	
2 tablespoons garlic-infused oil	**1 teaspoon ground nutmeg**	
	2 tablespoons grated Parmesan	

Rinse the spinach under the tap and then put it in batches, with no more water than is clinging to the shaken-out leaves, in a large pan, tamp down with a wooden spoon, and stir a little over medium to high heat until the spinach wilts and shrinks. Remove to a colander and continue till all the spinach is done.

Heat the butter – using less if this amount frightens you – in the pan with the garlic-infused oil and when melted, stir in the spinach and cook for a few minutes. Sprinkle in the cornstarch and stir into the spinach for another minute or so, then pour in the cream and stir well. Leave to cook for a couple of minutes, then give another stir. If it's too watery, keep bubbling away, otherwise taste to check the spinach is tender enough, and then stir in the nutmeg and Parmesan and season to taste.

You will find a little pale green puddle collects around the spinach as it sits in the serving bowl, but there's no way of avoiding it. Besides, it is not a problem: that oozing jade cream tastes heavenly.

note

Just because it makes your cooking-life much easier, and because they're cozy and homey, I'd bake some potatoes to go with this, to be eaten with butter or sour cream flecked with chives. But bear in mind that a potato gratin (see pages 228 and 426), though adding to the work load, is a fabulous partner, too. And if you are not a spinach-eater, then don't fret but cook some peas or sugarsnaps, or a buttery mixture of both, to go alongside.

APPLE CHEESECAKE WITH BUTTERSCOTCH SAUCE

When I originally made this cheesecake, I peeled and sliced some apples, sautéed them in butter and a spritz of lemon juice, then toppled them, when cooled, on the also cold cheesecake, before dripping over the warm butterscotch sauce. Feel free to do that, too, but I now find the appliness of the liqueur in the cheesecake and sauce is enough for me. And besides, it's the combo of cool, smooth cheesecake with the warm fudgy sauce that is the clincher here. The fact that you make this a day ahead means you can relax more on the night.

And if you're buying a bottle of apple schnapps to make this, it makes sense to plonk it with some shot glasses, alongside.

Serves 8–10

FOR THE CHEESECAKE

2 cups oatmeal cookie crumbs

$^3/_4$ stick soft unsalted butter

$1^1/_2$lbs cream cheese

$^1/_2$ cup superfine sugar

4 eggs

1 egg yolk

$^1/_2$ cup heavy cream

2 tablespoons cornstarch

1 teaspoon pure vanilla extract

$^1/_4$ cup apple schnapps

FOR THE BUTTERSCOTCH SAUCE

$^1/_2$ stick unsalted butter

3 tablespoons light brown sugar

2 tablespoons white sugar

$^1/_2$ cup corn syrup, light or dark
  as you wish

$^1/_2$ cup heavy cream

2 teaspoons, or to taste, apple
  schnapps

Put the cookies into a processor and blitz till crumbed. Now add the butter and pulse till it clumps together. Press the sandy mixture into the bottom of a 9 inch springform pan to create an even layer. Put the pan in the fridge while you make the filling. Preheat the oven to 325°F.

Put the cream cheese, sugar, whole eggs and extra egg yolk, heavy cream, cornstarch and vanilla into the – cleaned out – processor and run the motor until you have a smooth liquidy mixture. Scrape down and process again, and with the motor running add the schnapps.

Wrap the outside of the crumb-lined springform pan with plastic wrap. I give a good few layers to make sure everything is completely waterproof. Now sit this on a large piece of double-layered heavy-duty aluminum foil and bring it up around the edges of the pan to make a nest. Sit the foil-covered springform pan in a roasting pan.

Scrape and pour the cheesecake filling into the springform pan, and then pour recently boiled water into the roasting pan to a level approximately halfway up the cake pan.

Bake for approx. $1^1/_4$ hours, or until the filling has set with only a small amount of wobble left at its center; it is worth remembering that it will continue to cook as it cools down. I'd check at an hour to see how it's doing.

Take the pan out of the water bath and sit it on a cooling rack, removing the aluminum foil and plastic wrap as you do so. When it is cool enough, put the cheesecake in the refrigerator overnight, before unspringing it from the pan on its serving plate.

Make the butterscotch sauce simply by putting the butter, both sugars and syrup in a small pan, bring to the boil and let simmer for a few minutes, then add the cream and schnapps, stir and give another minute's bubbling. Remove from the heat and let cool down a little: you want this warm but not boiling as you pour over the cheese-cake.

Dribble a little sauce over the unclipped cheesecake on its plate or stand, and put the rest in a pitcher for lucky people to pour over as they eat.

A NURSERY SUPPER FOR EIGHT

DOUBLE HADDOCK FISHCAKES WITH GHERKINS, PEAS AND CAPERY SALAD
ORANGE-SCENTED BRIOCHE PUDDING

DOUBLE HADDOCK FISHCAKES

Even people who don't like fish much love fishcakes, which may be a negative way in to this, but I thought it needed pointing out up front. It always sounds hideously immodest to present a recipe I've done and then expound on its brilliance, but I am pleased with this, not least because I've only ever come across fishcakes that you need to fry, which I find too hellish with a load of people floating about the kitchen. These ones here I make up and form ahead, dip into crumbs – Ritz cracker crumbs at that – then bake in the oven at dinner time. So easy; so good.

3lb 4oz all-purpose potatoes
2lb 4oz skinless haddock fillet
1lb 10oz smoked haddock fillet,
  skinned if possible
2 cups milk
parsley stalks
5 tablespoons very finely chopped
  parsley

2 hard-boiled eggs
4 teaspoons prepared English mustard
zest of 2 lemons
1 tablespoon lemon juice
7oz (1 package) Ritz crackers, about
  2¹/₄ cups crumbs

Serves 8–10

note
You could easily substitute equal quantities of other white fish, but these are best as a mixture of plain and smoked.

You do need big fat gherkins to eat with these, and I heat some jars of French peas to go with, as well as the salad on page 239. But you could forgo the salad, buy some watercress and sit a tangled pile under each fishcake as you serve. Also very good with those ready sliced green beans in bags, tossed in melted butter and toasted slivered almonds.

Peel and roughly chop the potatoes, put them into a pan of salted water and bring to the boil. Cook until tender and then mash into a bowl.

Put the fish, with the smoked fish underneath, into a large skillet with the milk, parsley stalks and a good grinding of pepper. Bring the pan to a simmer and cook for about 5–8 minutes, turning if necessary.

Take the cooked fish out of the pan, flake it into a bowl and add the chopped parsley. Finely chop the hard-boiled eggs and add them with the mustard, lemon zest and juice.

Turn the flaked fish mixture into the mashed potato and mix very thoroughly. If you're making these ahead, wait till contents of both bowls are cold before combining. Check the seasoning, adding salt and pepper as needed.

Crush the Ritz crackers which is very satisfying: put them in a freezer bag, bashing and rolling them with a rolling pin until they are crumbs. Line the bottom of a tray or shallow roasting pan with these crumbs.

Shape the fish and potato mixture into 10 fishcakes, each weighing approximately 10oz (4 inches across by an inch thick). As you make each fat patty, press them into the Ritz cracker crumbs on both sides to get a good coating and leave them in the tray or pan. I think they're better not refrigerated but if you are making them a lot in advance, it would, of course, be better to sit them in the fridge.

When you are ready to cook them, preheat the oven to 400°F. Put the fishcakes on to a baking sheet, shaking off the excess Ritz crumbs but leaving a visible coating around each fishcake. Cook them for about 20 minutes or until they are heated through. If they are in the oven for too much longer they will crack a little, but no other harm comes to them, so don't worry too much if people take a long time to make it to the table to eat.

Makes 10 fishcakes: these are so large no one is likely to need seconds, but it's good to know you can provide more if required.

ORANGE-SCENTED BRIOCHE PUDDING

This is really an old-fashioned bread and butter pudding with a fragrant flourish. You can get ready-sliced long brioche loaves, which makes life simpler, but if you need to get out a bread knife yourself, just try to slice thinly.

butter for greasing
$^1/_2$ cup sultanas (golden raisins)
3 tablespoons Grand Marnier
16 slices slightly stale brioche
8 teaspoons very fine cut or
   shredless marmalade

2 tablespoons sugar
2 eggs
3 egg yolks
2 cups heavy cream
1 cup milk
2 teaspoons brown sugar

Serves 8

note
I use Tiptree "crystal" orange marmalade for this, but any good unchunky marmalade would do.

I think this is better warm rather than hot straight from the oven, so if you haven't got a double oven, you will have to cook this, then turn up the oven for the fishcakes.

Preheat the oven to 325°F. Butter an 8 cup pudding dish.

Put the sultanas and Grand Marnier into a small saucepan, bring to the boil and simmer for a minute or so, then turn off the heat and leave the fruit to plump up in the orange-scented liquor.

Make marmalade sandwiches with the brioche slices, using about a teaspoon in each. Because brioche is so buttery, don't spread any butter in the sandwiches or the pudding will be greasy. Cut each sandwich into a triangle and put these triangles, one point side up, the next one pointy bit down and so on, in the buttered dish. You will probably have two sandwiches left after the dish is full from oval-tip to oval-tip, so squish these two in, one either side of the line of sandwiches. Sprinkle over the sultanas along with any remaining liquor in the pan.

In a bowl whisk together the sugar, whole eggs, yolks, cream and milk. Pour over the brioche sandwiches and leave to stand for 15 minutes.

Before the pudding goes in the oven, sprinkle over the brown sugar, then bake for 45 minutes, by which time the rich custard should be at the very point of setting.

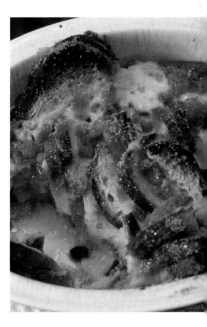

SCANDI-SUPPER FOR SIX

VODKA-MARINATED STEAK WITH DILL-FEATHERED BOILED POTATOES
MERINGUES WITH BERRIES

VODKA-MARINATED STEAK

I have always loved Scandinavian food, which I suppose comes from childhood summers spent in Norway, and this recipe is adapted from one by a Norwegian writer, Andreas Viestad, from his book *Kitchen of Light*. I know there doesn't seem to be much meat, but I cook the steak, then when it's rested, carve it thinly in diagonal slices, so it goes further than if you were handing around great chunks. But, by all means, provide more meat if you feel safer. There's nothing wrong with having cold beef in the fridge.

Serves 6

a slice of beef cut from the top of the rump, about an inch thick, weighing approx. 1lb 8oz

note

I think this has to be served with plain boiled potatoes. For six people, I'd cook about 3lb 12oz potatoes, peeled and cut into chunks. Toss in a very little butter, and sprinkle with some fresh dill.

I wouldn't bother cooking any other vegetables, but would make a tomato salad, with or without onions as you prefer, and a plain green salad.

FOR THE MARINADE

1 tablespoon sea salt/$^1/_2$ teaspoon table salt

2 tablespoons black peppercorns, crushed

3 tablespoons finely chopped parsley

2 tablespoons finely chopped thyme

3 cloves garlic, crushed

$^1/_3$ cup vodka

$^1/_4$ cup olive oil

TO COOK

2 tablespoons vegetable oil for frying

approx. $^3/_4$ cup plus 1 tablespoon beef stock

1 tablespoon butter

Combine all of the marinade ingredients and put into a freezer bag with the rump slice. Smear the contents around to get the beef evenly coated in the salt, pepper and herbs. Leave for two or three days in the fridge. This makes a really big difference, but if you can't find the time, then leave the steak to marinate for a good 3 hours at room temperature.

Bring the beef in its marinade to room temperature. Take the steak out of the marinade, but reserve the marinade itself. Heat the vegetable oil in a large skillet, and sear the beef on both sides over a high flame until it colors. Turn the heat down to low and cover the pan with aluminum foil as a lid. Cook for approx. $3^1/_2$ minutes on each side (or

longer if you don't like your beef rare) and then wrap in a layer of foil to rest while you make the sauce. I like the meat to rest, wrapped, for a good 15 minutes.

Strain the marinade into a measuring cup and then make the liquid contents up to $^2/_3$ cup with beef stock. Pour into the frying pan and deglaze, adding any resting juices that the beef has made. When the sauce is sizzling, whisk in the butter.

Carve the meat into thin diagonal slices, arrange on a plate, and pour over the sauce.

MERINGUES WITH BERRIES

Serves 6

Follow the meringue recipe on page 430, only use 4 egg whites and $1^1/_4$ cups superfine sugar. You should get 6 large meringues out of this, or make 7 and have 1 extra for someone who just has to have a second. Whip $1^1/_2$ cups heavy or whipping cream till softly peaking, and put this in a bowl with a spoon and serve a plate of mixed berries just dusted with confectioners' sugar.

TUNISIAN FRIDAY NIGHT SUPPER FOR EIGHT TO TEN

MEATBALLS AND COUSCOUS
HONEYED ALMOND AND ORANGE CAKE WITH FIGS

MEATBALLS AND COUSCOUS

The fact that Tunisian Jews customarily eat meatballs, couscous and honeyed and orange-scented nutcake to celebrate the Sabbath, doesn't mean you have to be Tunisian or Jewish to enjoy it; nor, indeed, do you need to save it up for a Friday night. I could eat this sweet, root vegetable stew with or without the meatballs, but definitely the couscous, any night of the week.

Both the meatballs and the stew can be cooked ahead (though I would not combine the two until the reheating stage) and the couscous takes a few minutes and no work. Follow the recipe for lamb meatballs on page 441, then get on with the sweet, soused stew. As for the couscous, because I have got a couscoussier (and you can admire it on the front cover) I use that, soaking the couscous in cold water for 10 minutes then pouring it into the top part of the pan and steaming it over the hot stew for 15 minutes, but you can just as easily follow the package instructions on the couscous or see my alternative method below. If you can't find the rose harissa – though I got mine from the supermarket – then use regular harissa, that fierce chilli and spice paste, and add a drop of rosewater, though only a drop, mind.

FOR THE VEGETABLE STEW

2 onions	1 teaspoon ground turmeric	Serves 8–10
2 sticks of celery	$1/2$ teaspoon ground ginger	
4 carrots	$1/2$ cup dried apricots	
3 cloves garlic	$3^3/_4$ cups tomato pulp or 2 14oz	
$1/2$ cup vegetable oil	cans chopped tomatoes	
1 red onion	3 cups chicken stock	
1lb rutabaga	2 teaspoons rose harissa	
1 parsnip		

FOR THE COUSCOUS

$4^1/_2$ cups couscous	2 teaspoons table salt
$1/2$ teaspoon ground cumin	7 cups boiling water
$1/2$ teaspoon ground coriander	

TO SERVE

1 pomegranate, optional	3 tablespoons chopped cilantro

Begin by making the vegetable stew. Peel and roughly chop the regular onions, and roughly chop the celery. Add them to a food processor with half the carrots, peeled and roughly chopped, and the peeled garlic. Process to a fine mush, or chop it all very finely by hand. Heat the oil in a large pan before tipping in the finely chopped vegetables to soften.

Peel and halve the red onion, cutting into half moons, and add to the pan of softened vegetables, stirring around for a few minutes. Peel and roughly chop the remaining carrots and the rutabaga and parsnip. Add them to the pan and let all of the vegetables soften in the oil, sprinkling over the spices and stirring to coat everything. Snip each of the dried apricots with scissors into four and let them drop into the vegetable stew. Stir in the chopped tomatoes.

Add the chicken stock and rose harissa, stirring again, and bring to the boil before putting on the lid and cooking at a gentle simmer for an hour.

To cook the couscous without a couscoussier, put all of the ingredients except for the water into a bowl and stir to combine. Boil a kettle, and add the water giving it a stir and then cover the bowl with plastic wrap and leave to stand for 15 minutes.

Heat the meatballs in the stew, and then fluff the couscous into a bowl with a fork and serve with the vegetable stew. If there are any pomegranates around, scatter the top with the seeds and sprinkle over some freshly chopped cilantro at the same time.

HONEYED ALMOND AND ORANGE CAKE WITH FIGS

note

I also love the baklava on page 446 after the couscous, though tend to make it here with a mixture of walnuts and pistachios, leaving out the cardamom. (It is thus no longer the Iraqi version.) The butter that coats the filo pastry makes it dietetically incorrect, should you be thinking of a Friday Night supper in its devotional sense, but for all other purposes it is glowingly appropriate.

For the honeyed almond and orange cake, follow the chocolate orange cake recipe on page 274 but in place of $1/2$ cup of unsweetened cocoa just add another $1/2$ cup ground almonds. Bake in a 9 inch springform pan and start checking it after 40 minutes. If they're in season, serve with fresh figs, quartered and spritzed with a little orange juice or orange-flower water and dribble some amber honey over each slice of damp cake as you serve; otherwise make the beautifully squishy honeyed figs on page 447, drizzling some of their aromatic juice, instead, over the cake.

SUNDAY LUNCH

THE ULTIMATE ENGLISH SUNDAY LUNCH FOR EIGHT TO TEN

ROAST RIB OF BEEF WITH ROAST POTATOES AND YORKSHIRE PUDDING
SAVOY CABBAGE, CAULIFLOWER CHEESE AND HORSERADISH SAUCE
BAKEWELL SLICE

I hope I don't harbor a foolish sentimental affection for the institution of Sunday lunch. I am fully aware that family meals can be far from the idyll of multi-generational togetherness – indeed some friends of mine, independently scarred by the ghastly memory of family meals when they were children, vowed when they had a child never ever to instigate the heinous process themselves – but as long as you bolster numbers by enough outsiders, by which I mean friends not total strangers, bad behavior should be kept in check.

Two of the recipes you need here are given in full elsewhere: see page 26 for perfect roast potatoes; now turn to page 38, where you will see a recipe for a cider gravy. Make that up, only cook the onions in butter and dispense with the apple; in place of the 2 cups beef stock and $^2/_3$ cup cider, use $2^1/_2$ cups beef stock and 2 tablespoons Marsala and, once it's cooked, purée it in a blender (or food processor if you don't have a blender), pour it back in the saucepan and add, on reheating, any gorgeous red juices from the beef.

I think you need to go for a 10lb roast here. A roast rib has to look resplendent and, besides, leftovers are part of the point.

I do nothing to mine, save put it in the fridge the night before. Then rub it well with salt and pepper and stick it in a pan with a little dripping if I've got it, and failing that a smear of oil.

THE RIB

You have choices about the temperature at which you roast. For rare meat you can either cook the beef at the highest possible temperature for 15 minutes and then turn it down to 350°F and cook for 15 minutes per lb (I still find it easier to calculate the cooking time of meat per lb) or at 425°F throughout for 15 minutes per lb, which is what I tend to do. Think of 15 minutes per lb as about 33 minutes for every 2lbs. I usually do 15 minutes per lb and then add on an extra 5 minutes so that those who don't like rare meat have a bit of slightly more cooked beef from the ends. Those who don't like blood don't have to get it: the rest of us gratifyingly do. If you want it medium rare, I should reckon on 20 minutes per pound or 44 minutes for every 2lbs.

However you cook it, the thing that really matters is that you let the meat rest properly. Cover it loosely with aluminum foil and leave it for at least 15 minutes and up to 35 minutes on its board. Not that I mind even longer, actually. And do see the quick-cook, long-rested fillet in the note on page 342.

YORKSHIRE PUDDING

I always used to cook the pudding in one big pan – and you can, too, in one measuring 12 x 7^1/$_2$ in and 3 in deep, or a round one of approx. 10 inches across – but have since graduated into a 12-cup muffin pan. It means everyone gets an equal measure of squidgy eggy interior and bronze edge, puffed up and crisp.

1^1/$_3$ cups 2% milk
4 eggs
^{1}/$_2$ teaspoon salt
1^2/$_3$ cups all-purpose flour

1 tablespoon (and see below)
beef dripping or vegetable
shortening

Whisk the milk, eggs and salt well and let stand for 15 minutes, then whisk in the flour and let stand again until you need it.

The important thing with Yorkshire pudding is that it's cooked at the highest temperature possible. But if you're cooking this with the beef, I'll presume it's at 425°F. So put the muffin tin in the oven to heat up for a good 10–15 minutes, with a ^{1}/$_4$ teaspoon dripping or vegetable shortening in each muffin compartment.

When the pan and the fat have been heated, pour in the Yorkshire pudding batter and cook for 15–20 minutes or until they have puffed up gloriously.

This leaves us with the veg and the horseradish. To start with the latter…

HORSERADISH SAUCE

I used to think that making fresh horseradish sauce was, frankly, unnecessary. I was wrong: and you should either keep a fresh horseradish root in the fridge (they keep for ages) or grate some and freeze it. And see also page 105 for apple horseradish sauce.

If it's tradition you're after, you could easily ignore the chives here, though I think they are an addition that deserves inclusion.

While we're on sauces, I need to make it clear that English mustard on the table is non-negotiable. It could ruin someone's Sunday lunch were you to forget it.

Serves 8–10

note

I just as often use 2 cups crème fraîche in place of both the yogurt and heavy cream. And be prepared to add more or less horseradish depending on how strong you want this.

1 cup Greek yogurt
$^2/_3$ cup heavy cream
$^1/_2$ teaspoon sea salt or good pinch table salt
4 tablespoons grated fresh horseradish

1 teaspoon Dijon mustard
2 teaspoons best-quality white wine vinegar
8 tablespoons chopped chives

Beat together the yogurt, cream, salt, horseradish, mustard and vinegar in a bowl. I do this early on, finely chopping and adding the chives just as I serve – in a clean bowl or pair of smaller bowls (for ease and to make for less passing up and down the table).

SAVOY CABBAGE THE BEST WAY

Cooking cabbage like this is miles away from just plonking it in a pan of boiling water. Plus you can get it started well in advance if that helps.

Serves 8–10

note

If you've got some cabbage left over, it reheats well with some extra butter. If you want a more pronounced lemon taste, you can spritz with lemon juice, too; or if you don't want the lemon, you can

2 Savoy cabbages
$^1/_2$ stick butter
1 tablespoon vegetable oil

zest of 1 lemon, optional
1 cup vegetable stock

Discard the outer leaves from the cabbages and shred the cabbages as finely as you can, discarding the core. I'm lazy and tend to do this by pushing wedges through the slicer of the food processor.

Heat the butter and oil in a large pan, and grate in the lemon zest if you're using it, and then add the shredded cabbage and over a medium heat let it wilt and become glossy. Pour in the stock and turn the cabbage in the pan, cover with a lid and let it cook for 3–5 minutes: it should still be a vibrant green. At this point you can take it off the heat and remove the lid, and leave the cabbage to reheat later.

If you are preparing the Savoy cabbage to eat straightaway then continue to cook it with the lid on for about 5–10 minutes longer. You want the cabbage to be cooked through but not soggy, and still have some bite. Check the seasoning before you serve it, adding salt and pepper as necessary.

replace it altogether with 1 teaspoon caraway seeds. I use caraway seeds if I'm cooking the cabbage to go with sausage or pork (though not the pork on page 223 since it already has the seeds in with the meat).

CAULIFLOWER CHEESE

Nothing beats roast beef with cauliflower cheese: I just love the way the blood oozes into the savory sauce on the plate.

You could easily double this, using two heads of cauliflower, but with so much else going on you will probably find that no one takes that much of any one thing.

This method of cooking the cauliflower, that's to say, barely cooking at all, makes the sauce much less runny and oddly granular later. The tip comes via Nick Jones of Soho House in London.

1 large head cauliflower	$^1/_3$ cup all-purpose flour
2 bay leaves	2 cups milk
1 stick butter	3 cups strong Cheddar, grated, plus
2 teaspoons English mustard	$^1/_2$ cup for sprinkling on the top

Serves 8–10

Cut the cauliflower into small florets, put into a saucepan with the bay leaves and cover with cold water. Add a sprinkling of salt and bring to the boil, then drain and refresh with cold water. Let the cauliflower drain again in a colander, pluck out the bay leaves and discard. When the cauliflower is completely drained, put into an ovenproof dish in an even layer. You can cover the dish with plastic wrap at this point and leave it to finish later.

Preheat your oven to 425°F. To make the cheese sauce, melt the butter in a heavy-bottomed saucepan, then whisk in the mustard and flour, and cook over a gentle heat for about 5 minutes. Whisk in the milk off the heat, and then put it back on the heat and keep stirring until it becomes really thick and begins to bubble.

Sprinkle in the 3 cups grated cheese and stir it over the heat until it has melted into the sauce. Check the seasoning, then pour it over the cauliflower in the dish, and scatter the remaining cheese over the top. Cook for 20 minutes at the temperature above, or whatever your oven is at for the roast lunch, or until the cauliflower is hot, the sauce is bubbling and the cheesy top is slightly browned.

BAKEWELL SLICE

There are a number of suitable desserts to have after roast rib of beef – see the crumble on page 40, the apple charlotte on page 427 and the chocolate cherry trifle on page 406 inter alia – but I'm not sure that after the meat, the potatoes, the cauliflower cheese and the Yorkshire pudding, anyone's really going to be able to negotiate anything else. So, two suggestions: either ditch the Yorkshire pudding as a savory adjunct and serve it afterwards with whipped cream or ice cream and maple syrup (see the picture on page 217); or postpone the sweet course and make something gorgeous to have with a cup of tea later. You think you're not ever going to be able to eat another thing, but alas, you will find yourself feeling strangely peckish around teatime. The more you eat, the more you want. That's the way it goes.

This is a very easy take on Bakewell pudding, that traditional English tart of jam and frangipane. The ease lies in the fact that you don't have to do any rolling of pastry but, rather, make a shortbread base in the processor that you squidge in with your fingers. I use a disposable aluminum foil pan to cook this in: it makes the base absurdly crisp and melting, the slices are easy to remove and there's no washing up. Up till now I've always gone for the raspberry jam option (tumbling in some fresh raspberries too) but after reading Tom Norrington-Davies's *Just Like Mother Used to Make*, I felt compelled to try this with plum jam. Now I keep *jars* of plum jam, just in case the urge comes upon me.

Serves 8–10

note

You can eat this with cream or ice cream, but I love it eaten just in the fingers, as is. It's at its peak with the breath of the oven still on it, but cold leftovers are not to be scorned.

FOR THE BASE
$1^1/_2$ cups plus 1 tablespoon
   all-purpose flour
$^1/_3$ cup confectioners' sugar

pinch salt
2 sticks butter

FOR THE FRANGIPANE FILLING
$1^1/_3$ sticks butter
4 eggs
$^3/_4$ cup superfine sugar

$1^1/_2$ cups ground almonds
$^2/_3$ cup slivered almonds
1 heaping cup jam

Preheat the oven to 350°F, and put in a metal baking sheet to heat up with the oven. Put the flour, confectioners' sugar and salt into a food processor and blitz to remove lumps. Add the butter and process again to a crumbly mixture that's beginning to come together. Tumble into an aluminum foil pan – about $9^1/_4$ x $11^3/_4$ x $2^1/_4$ in. Push and press patiently into the base of the pan: you will feel you don't have enough, but I promise you will. Cook in the oven for 20 minutes.

For the topping, melt the butter and set aside. Put the eggs, sugar and ground almonds into the processor. Blitz the mixture together, and then toast the slivered almonds in a dry pan. I like these really golden, and they don't brown as nicely in the oven but you can skip this step. When the base is cooked, take out and let sit for about 3 minutes before spreading it evenly with the jam. With the processor motor running, pour the slightly cooled melted butter down the funnel into the other frangipane ingredients and then pour this golden mixture over the jam-covered base. Top with the toasted slivered almonds and bake for 35 minutes. Cool before cutting into 16 slabs.

COMFORTING LUNCH FOR SIX

ROAST LOIN OF PORK WITH CARAWAY, LEMON AND GARLIC
SPRING GREENS AND BAKED POTATOES
LOKSHEN PUDDING

ROAST LOIN OF PORK WITH CARAWAY, LEMON AND GARLIC

For some reason, roast pork doesn't get the respect it deserves. I often cook a boned loin, but then I do think you need a marinade (and see pages 102–4) since pork is bred so lean these days it can be fibrous and indigestible just plain roasted.

Here, you have the bone to infuse the meat with flavor, and a spice rub to keep the meat moist under its golden layer of crackling. What you must do is ask the butcher to score the rind – to make the crackling really crisp – and crack the bones, so that you can cut the chops off easily.

If you can't get a roast thus described, then get a boned loin, put it in a freezer bag, and marinate overnight in the rub ingredients, adding an extra 2 tablespoons of olive oil and 1 more of lemon juice.

These quantities give everyone just 1 slab of pork chop each, but that should be enough – especially with the vast pudding that follows.

6-chop loin of pork on the bone, approx. 5^1/$_2$lb, prepared as outlined above
2 cloves garlic
1 teaspoon sea salt
^{1}/$_8$ teaspoon ground cloves
^{1}/$_2$ teaspoon caraway seeds
1 tablespoon lemon juice

pepper
1 teaspoon chilli oil
2 bay leaves
1 onion
1 tablespoon olive oil
6 small eating apples, each approx. 4oz

Serves 6

note
If you haven't got chilli oil, use any vegetable oil and a small sprinkle of dried chilli flakes.

Preheat the oven to 425°F. Take the pork out of the fridge to bring to room temperature. Peel and crush the garlic cloves in a pestle and mortar with 1 teaspoon sea salt. The garlic should become like a paste with the salt. (Or you could just grate or mince the garlic into the spices in a little bowl.) Add the cloves and caraway seeds, lemon juice, some pepper and the chilli oil and crumble in the bay leaves. Bash well then stir the spiced

Make some spring greens following the Savoy cabbage
method on page 220: that's to
say, shred about 2 heads of
greens, approx. 1lb each, and
wilt them in a little oil in a big
pan and then add 1 cup vegetable stock. Season to taste
and stir in a little butter when
cooked.

I'd serve some baked potatoes alongside, too, and consider putting sour cream and
chives on the table as well as
butter for people to dollop in
to the hot, white flesh.

paste about and then spoon into the cracked section of the chops where they join on to the bone at the base; there should be a cavity running along the length of the roast. Rub any extra paste around the pork, leaving the rind dry.

Peel the onion and then slice it into about six discs. Rub the bottom of a roasting pan with the tablespoon of olive oil and then overlap the onion circles in a line down the length of the pan. Sit the loin of pork on the bed of onions and sprinkle a little salt over the pork rind. Roast in the oven for $1^{1}/_{2}$ hours. If the pork was still fridge-cold before going into the oven, it might need longer. It's wise to check that the meat is cooked through anyway.

45 minutes before the pork is due to come out of the oven, score the apples around the circumference of each one, as if drawing the line of the equator with the point of a sharp knife. If the apples do not sit upright without wobbling, trim the bottom of each one so that it is flat. Arrange the apples around the pork in its roasting pan and cook everything together for another 45 minutes. Let the pork rest for about 10 minutes on a board, keeping the apples warm. Slice the loin of pork into individual chops and serve each one with an apple.

LOKSHEN PUDDING

I know I risk offending some people by suggesting the quintessentially Jewish lokshen pudding (aka kugel) after the roast pork – and if so, I suppose it's a bit late to apologize. Those who don't know what I'm talking about might not be convinced by the idea of a pasta pudding: but just remember how fabulously comforting rice pudding is and try not to be alarmed. In any event, you must try it. There's no one I've made it for so far who hasn't loved it – and that includes Italians and good old-fashioned English yeomanry.

The recipe comes from Ellen Fishman in San Francisco – I demanded it – and is her Grandma Judy's. In keeping with the spirit of things, I have kept the vast quantities. Besides, I love it cold and so do my children, wrapped up to take to school for their break. But I know in my heart that even half-quantities make more than enough – and I mean more than enough – for six. Either way, this is the ultimate carb-feast. If you do want to go for the relatively streamlined approach, halve the ingredients and cook in a 10 in square pan about 2 in deep, and check after 45–50 minutes.

Since you want this warm rather than hot, it probably makes sense – whether or not you have two ovens – to cook it first, turning the oven up for the pork.

Serves 6–8

1lb fine noodles, vermicelli or
   angel's hair
a little less $^{1}/_{2}$lb (1 cup when
   melted) unsalted butter
8 large eggs

2 cups superfine sugar
1 teaspoon pure vanilla extract
pinch salt

4 cups cottage cheese

Preheat the oven to 325°F.

Cook the noodles and set aside. I try and get the proper lokshen for this, which are shorter strands of very, very fine noodles. Melt the butter and let it cool slightly. Beat the eggs.

Combine the warm or cooled, but not hot, melted butter with the sugar, vanilla, eggs, salt and cottage cheese. Add the noodles and mix well. Put in a pan of approx. 9 x 13 in (14 cup capacity) and bake for 1 hour to 1 hour and 10 minutes until the top is just golden where the buttery threads of pasta have caught in the heat.

EASY LUNCH FOR SIX

ONE-PAN SAGE-AND-ONION CHICKEN AND SAUSAGE

I took it into my head one day that I wanted to marinate and cook some chicken with the flavors of a tradi-tional sage-and-onion stuffing. So onion, mustard, sage and lemon infuse the cut-up bird, and sausages are cooked alongside the pieces in one big pan. I started off with English butcher's sausages but this works just as well with Italian sausages (no bread, so good for carb-avoiders) and also, though taking on a different char-acter, with spicy Spanish chorizo.

As you can imagine, it is hardly any work, and if you haven't got time to give a proper night's mar-inating in the fridge, then leave everything, bar the sausages, to steep in the roasting pan for a couple of hours or so at room temperature. And even if you leave the sausages in, it won't matter.

Serves 6

note
You can easily substitute the cut-up chicken with 10 thigh pieces, bone in and skin on.

1 large onion or 2 small onions	1 lemon
$1/_2$ cup olive oil (not extra virgin)	1 tablespoon Worcestershire sauce
2 teaspoons English mustard	4lb chicken, cut into 10 pieces
1 tablespoon dried sage	12 sausages
ground pepper	2 tablespoons chopped sage leaves

Peel and cut the onion into eighths, and put into a freezer bag with the oil, mustard, dried sage, a good grinding of pepper, the lemon juice, the squeezed-out rinds cut into eighths, and the Worcestershire sauce. Squidge everything around to mix (the mustard needs help to combine) and then add the chicken pieces. Leave to marinate in the fridge overnight, or for up to two days.

Preheat the oven to 425°F. Allow the chicken to come to room temperature in its marinade.

Arrange the chicken pieces in a roasting pan, skin-side up, with the marinade, including all the bits and pieces, and tuck the sausages around them. Sprinkle the fresh sage leaves over the chicken and sausages and then put the pan into the oven to cook for 1 hour and 15 minutes. Turn the sausages over halfway through to color them evenly.

Arrange the chicken and sausages on a large platter.

BREAD-SAUCE-FLAVORED POTATO GRATIN

After the sage-and-onion stuffing flavored chicken, the idea of infusing a potato gratin with the scent of a bread sauce seemed only appropriate. A gratin might not seem like the most straightforward way of cooking potatoes, but I include them under the banner of an easy lunch, as so much of the work can be done in advance that it simplifies everything. Besides, the only other accompaniment I suggest are some peas, and those the French ones out of a jar: soft and sweet and oniony.

Serves 6

note

This makes an awful lot of gratin, but that's surely a good thing. I love it the next day, reheated with lots of freshly ground pepper and freshly chopped parsley all over it.

If you want to make it ahead and leave it in the pan to sit for a while, then be prepared to cook it for about 30 minutes. Either way you need to see the creamy sauce bubbling and the top beginning to blister.

2 cups whole milk
2 cups heavy cream
1 onion
2 cloves
$1/_2$ teaspoon ground mace

3–4 bay leaves
1 tablespoon sea salt/$^1/_2$
  tablespoon table salt
$4^1/_2$lbs all-purpose potatoes
butter for greasing

Preheat the oven to 425°F.

Put the milk and cream into a large saucepan. Peel the onion, cutting it in half, then stick each half with a clove, adding the studded pieces to the pan. Add the mace, bay leaves and salt to the pan, then bring nearly to boiling point. Turn off the heat, and put the lid on to infuse the milk.

Meanwhile, peel the potatoes and cut them into $^1/_2$ inch slices. Put them into the saucepan of infused milk and cream, and bring the pan back to a boil with the lid on. It doesn't look as if there is enough liquid for all those potatoes, but there is.

Lower the heat to a simmer, and take off the lid (this will lower the temperature further) if the pan is spluttering too much and erupting down the sides. Cook the potatoes until they are tender but not dissolving into mush.

Fish out the onion and bay leaves, and then grease a large roasting pan (of approx. 15 x 12 in) with butter. Pour in the potato mixture from the pan and cook in the oven for about 15 minutes or until the potato is bubbling and browned on top. Let it stand out of the oven for about 10 minutes before you serve it with the sage-and-onion chicken and sausages.

CHILLI-CINNAMON CHOCOLATE PUDDING

This is a miracle of low-effort, high-reward cooking. You have a bowl of dry ingredients and another of wet ones and you just stir the two together. Admittedly, it looks alarming when you make it – it's hard to believe that sprinkling sugar and cocoa on top of a cake batter and then pouring hot water over it will end up edible, but it truly does. I won't lie: it isn't the most beauteous creation (there is a touch of the cowpat about its appearance) but looks are not everything. This is a luscious, homey dessert, one of those self-saucing puddings which turn themselves as they bake into a layer of gooey molten chocolate sauce topped with tender cake.

By all means dispense with the chilli and indeed the rum (though make up the liquid quantity with more water) if you want to appeal to junior diners, but know that the chilli isn't frightening: it supplies depth rather than heat. Think Aztec flavor rather than odd combination of ingredients.

butter for greasing	$1/2$ cup best-quality unsweetened cocoa	Serves 6
1 cup all-purpose flour	$1/2$ cup milk	
2 teaspoons baking powder	1 teaspoon pure vanilla extract	
$1/2$ teaspoon baking soda	$1/4$ cup corn oil	
1 teaspoon ground cinnamon	$1/2$ cup dark brown sugar	
$1/4$ teaspoon chilli powder	$3/4$ cup boiling water	
1 cup superfine sugar	$1/4$ cup dark rum	

Preheat the oven to 350°F, and butter an approximately 8 cup capacity/9 in round baking dish.

In a large bowl, combine the flour, baking powder, baking soda, a pinch of salt, cinnamon, chilli, sugar and half the cocoa. Beat the milk, vanilla and corn oil together in a glass measuring cup, and pour this into the dry ingredients. Mix it with a wooden spoon to make a thick smooth batter, then spoon it into the buttered baking dish.

Combine the remaining $1/4$ cup cocoa and the dark brown sugar in another bowl, making sure there are no lumps. Sprinkle this over the top of the cake batter in the dish. Measure out $3/4$ cup freshly boiled water and pour it over the cocoa and sugar-topped batter. Tip over the dark rum and put the pudding in the oven. Cook for 30 minutes, by which time the top of the cake should have set to a bubbly chocolatey cake but the underneath will be wobbly and liquid. Spoon out helpings, taking care to give each one some of the cakey top and gooey chocolate sauce from underneath. And serve some vanilla ice cream alongside for cooling contrast.

DÉJEUNER SUR L'HERBE FOR EIGHT

BROAD BEAN BRUSCHETTA
ROAST CHICKEN SALAD
PASTA SALAD PRIMAVERA
PEACH MELBA

BROAD BEAN BRUSCHETTA

This is the lazy person's version of the bruschetta of the same name in the second *River Café Cook Book*. By that, I just mean you don't have to use a pestle and mortar, though it is better if you do. I often start by intending to use mine, but then move on to the processor. You need fava beans (also called broad beans) that are young and tender, but this is one instance when you cannot substitute frozen. So you do have to be sufficiently un-lazy to shell the beans, or find children who will gladly do it for you.

Serves 8

note

If you like the idea of this sort of starter, but can't face the shelling or can't find tender enough beans, then smear some cooled toasted rustic bread, as used here, with the avocado, lemon and basil mixture – the Italianified guacamole – on page 123.

3lb 4oz young fava beans in the pod; 11oz shelled weight or 2^1/$_3$ cups
1 clove garlic
^{1}/$_4$ cup fresh mint
1 teaspoon sea salt/^{1}/$_2$ teaspoon table salt

^{1}/$_4$ cup grated pecorino (or Parmesan)
zest and juice of 1 lemon
2 tablespoons extra virgin olive oil
12 slices rustic bread

Put the shelled beans in the processor, mince or grate in the garlic, chuck in the mint and the salt and then blitz to a rubble. Now add the grated pecorino, the zest and juice of the lemon and a good grinding of pepper and blitz again. Stop the machine, open the lid, scrape down with a rubber spatula and then put the lid back on and, with the motor running, add the olive oil.

Toast the bread, and when still warm but not hot smear with this nubbly green paste.

ROAST CHICKEN SALAD

There is nothing better in the height of summer than a plate of roast chicken salad. You can just roast a chicken and tear it apart with your bare hands once it's cooled a little, rather in the style of the chicken from the Venetian ghetto in *How to Eat*, tumbling it over some lettuce leaves rather than pasta, but this is easier and the marinade not only keeps the chicken tender but also serves as a base for the dressing.

For once, you find me suggesting chicken breast portions – the white meat works best here – but they must still have their skin.

4 whole boneless chicken breasts with skin	**$^1/_4$ cup pinenuts, toasted**	Serves 8
$^1/_4$ cup Marsala	**$^1/_4$ cup sultanas (golden raisins), soaked in warm water**	
$^1/_4$ cup garlic-infused oil	**2 teaspoons good-quality white wine vinegar, sherry vinegar or Muscat vinegar, or to taste, and see method below**	
1 teaspoon sea salt/$^1/_2$ teaspoon table salt		
1 Romaine lettuce heart	**handful parsley leaves**	
1 small head red endive or radicchio		

Marinate the chicken breasts in the Marsala, garlic oil, salt and some pepper for no longer than one hour at room temperature or overnight in the fridge.

Preheat the oven to 400°F. Tip the chicken and marinade into a roasting pan and when at room temperature roast in the oven for 30 minutes, by which time the meat should be cooked through and the skin bronze.

Put the roasting pan aside somewhere to let the chicken breasts cool down a little. Get out a large plate and arrange the salad leaves on it.

Chunk up the chicken and place on the salad, scattering with toasted pinenuts and soaked and squeezed out sultanas as you go. If the marinade has largely evaporated – this happens when I use my electric oven but not when I use gas – stir in 2 teaspoons good-quality white wine vinegar or other vinegar, another tablespoon of Marsala and 2 of olive oil, otherwise just stir in the vinegar. Taste to see if there's anything else you might want to tinker with, and then pour over the salad. Sprinkle with parsley.

PASTA SALAD PRIMAVERA

I'm not sure I need anything other than the chicken salad if I've had the bruschetta bean-feast first, and want to hold a little something back for the peach melba later. But I am never quite happy if even the *possibility* of undercatering shimmers on the horizon. And I wouldn't be happy leaving out this recipe. It does involve a lot of fiddly preparation, but what it creates is addictive; every mouthful repays the effort a hundredfold. What's more, you can stash it in a Tupperware or similar container and leave it in the fridge for easy pickings for a good few days after your lunch. This salad is eating proof that you can't have too much of a good thing.

Serves 8

note

This lends itself perfectly to a moveable feast. Could even make a picnic bearable.

1 lb package orzo or puntarelle pasta
2 tablespoons extra virgin olive oil
1 lb bunch slender asparagus
$^3/_4$ cup shelled fava beans

1 lb fresh peas in the pod; 2 cups shelled peas
1 cup snow peas
1 cup slender green beans
1 tablespoon garlic-infused olive oil
juice and zest of 1 lemon
$^1/_3$ cup chopped chives

Cook the pasta according to the package instructions, and after draining the cooked orzo (or puntarelle as this barley- or rice-like shape is called in the De Cecco range), rinse under cold water and leave to drain again.

Tip the drained pasta into a large mixing bowl and stir through the olive oil to prevent it from clumping together.

Bring a large pan of water to the boil, and add some salt. Meanwhile snap the woody ends off the asparagus and then cut each stalk into inch long pieces on a diagonal. Shell the fava beans and shell the peas. Get the snow peas out and trim the green beans, cutting them in half.

Cook each vegetable in the boiling water until almost cooked through but still with bite. You have to taste as you go to get the timing right. I find it easier to cook each one in turn, placing in a sieve, and refreshing under a cold tap. Then it's easy to squeeze the cooked fava beans to remove the casing, leaving you just the vibrant inner pods. All this might seem a lot of fiddly work, but, actually, I get into the slow rhythmed pace of it, and find it strangely relaxing after a while.

Tip the cooked, refreshed and drained vegetables into the pasta and dress with the garlic oil, salt and pepper, lemon juice and zest, and $^1/_4$ cup of chopped chives. Mix together – the salad in the picture has yet to be combined – and check the seasoning, then decant into a bowl. Sprinkle with the remaining chopped chives to serve.

PEACH MELBA

This is it – summer on a plate. Most days I take the view that cooking fruit rather loses the point of its delectable freshness, but this somehow intensifies it. Besides, most peaches are disappointingly hard or lacking in luscious peachiness, so poaching the fruit gives even lackluster peaches the boost they need, restoring them to their rightful glory.

FOR THE PEACHES   Serves 8

3 cups water   1 vanilla bean, split lengthways
3¹/₂ cups superfine sugar   8 peaches
juice of ¹/₂ lemon

FOR THE RASPBERRY SAUCE

3 cups raspberries   juice of ¹/₂ lemon
¹/₄ cup confectioners' sugar

TO SERVE

1 large carton vanilla ice cream

Put the water, sugar, lemon juice and vanilla bean into a wide saucepan and heat gently to dissolve the sugar. Bring the pan to the boil and let it bubble away for about 5 minutes, then turn the pan down to a fast simmer.

Cut the peaches in half, and, if the pits come out easily remove them, if not, then you can get them out later. Poach the peach halves in the sugar syrup for about 2–3 minutes on each side, depending on the ripeness of the fruit. Test the cut side with the sharp point of a knife to see if they are soft, and then remove to a plate with a slotted spoon.

When all the peaches are poached, peel off their skins and let them cool (and remove any remaining pits). If you are making them a day in advance, let the poaching syrup cool and then pour into a dish with the peaches. Otherwise just bag up the syrup and freeze it for the next time you poach peaches.

To make the raspberry sauce, purée the raspberries, confectioners' sugar and lemon juice in a blender or else a processor. Sieve to remove the seeds and pour this fantastically hued purée into a jug.

To assemble the peach melba, allow two peach halves per person and sit them on each plate alongside a scoop or two of ice cream. Spoon the raspberry sauce over each one, and put the remaining puce-tinted red sauce in a pitcher for people to add themselves at the table.

SUNDAY LUNCH AFTER THE SATURDAY NIGHT BEFORE

KEEMA

STICKY TOFFEE PANCAKES WITH ICE CREAM

This is not the sort of Sunday lunch for a calm gathering of friends and family, but rather what you need when a small group of you might be nursing a hangover or otherwise be in need of the bolstering that only the bite of chilli and the comfort of sugar can provide.

note

I haven't specified numbers here, as, although there's enough for four, I wouldn't change quantities if there were only two of you. I'd just have twice as much of the keema, forgo the pancakes and make the sticky toffee sauce to eat with ice cream.

KEEMA

Keema just means ground meat but the recipe here is for that fabulous sharp and spiky Indian dish of ground lamb with peas that makes a reviving feast in a bowl. I've come across versions of this all over the place but the recipe that prompted me, finally, to try it – even though what I do differs somewhat – comes from Vicky Bhogal's wonderful book, *Cooking Like Mummyji*.

Serves 4

2 tablespoons vegetable oil
1 onion, finely chopped
1 clove garlic, minced, grated or finely chopped
$1^3/_4$ cups canned chopped tomatoes or 1 x 14oz can chopped tomatoes
1 inch root ginger, finely grated or chopped

1 birds-eye red chilli, finely chopped with seeds, or other small hot chilli
$1^1/_2$ teaspoons salt
1 teaspoon garam masala
$2/_3$ cup chopped cilantro
$1^1/_2$ lb ground lamb
2 cups frozen peas
1 cup boiling water
juice of $1/_2$ lime, or to taste

Heat the oil in a wide saucepan – big enough to take everything comfortably later – and add the onion and garlic. Cook on a high heat until golden brown. Turn the heat down, and add the can of tomatoes, ginger, chilli, salt, garam masala and a $1/_3$ cup chopped cilantro. Stir until the mixture becomes shiny, and then add the ground meat, breaking it up with a fork in the sauce.

Add the frozen peas, stirring everything together for a few minutes, and then add the boiling water. Bring the pan to the boil and then turn it down to a very gentle simmer. Cook for about 20–30 minutes, by which time most of the water should have evaporated and the lamb will be tender and the peas cooked through. Squeeze in some lime juice to taste and sprinkle the remaining chopped cilantro over the finished dish, or into individual bowls as you serve.

I love warmed thick flat breads with this – and most supermarkets sell naans or rotis now – but even without the added carb, just spooned straight into my mouth, this keema does the trick.

STICKY TOFFEE PANCAKES

This is another one of the recipes I got, give or take, from a *Daily Telegraph* reader. But I lost the torn-out bit of newspaper in between reading it and making these, and I can see – now I have since found the ur-text again – that my version differs quite a bit. Still, I love these the way they are and am grateful for the inspiration. I couldn't ask for more. And I thank one Jossie Parker for it.

FOR THE SAUCE
$^3/_4$ cup plus 1 tablespoon dark brown sugar
2 tablespoons dark corn syrup

$^3/_4$ stick unsalted butter
$^2/_3$ cup heavy cream

FOR THE PANCAKES
1 cup dried chopped pitted dates
2 cups boiling water
$^1/_2$ teaspoon baking soda
2 tablespoons butter
2 eggs
$1^1/_3$ cups plus 1 tablespoon flour

$^1/_4$ cup dark brown sugar
pinch of salt
1 teaspoon baking powder
$^1/_2$ teaspoon baking soda
1 cup Greek or whole milk yogurt
$^2/_3$ cup milk

Serves 4–6 (makes approx. 20)

note
These also make the ideal hungover breakfast, though more helpfully so if the person making them is not also suffering. But for first thing, I'd ditch the ice cream and substitute some slices of potassium-boosting banana.

To make the sauce, put the sugar, syrup and butter in a pan and slowly – so the butter melts and the sugar dissolves – bring to the boil and let bubble away for a couple of minutes before adding the cream. Cook for another 2–3 minutes or until the sauce is thick and sticky and glossy.

Now get on with the pancakes, and you can do this before you sit down to lunch, keeping them warm – once cooked – in a 300°F oven, wrapped in aluminum foil. Soak the dried dates in the boiling water and $^1/_2$ teaspoon baking soda while you potter around with everything else. Melt the butter and set aside. Separate the eggs, whisking the whites until firm, but not too dry or stiff.

Measure out the flour, sugar, pinch of salt, baking powder and baking soda into a large bowl. Beat the egg yolks with the yogurt and milk and then pour this wet mixture into the bowl of dry ingredients and mix till smooth; this is a pretty thick batter, especially by this stage. Drain the soaked dates, squeezing out excess liquid and chop them up; I use a mezzaluna for this which gets them good and squidgy. Fold these into the batter-so-far.

Heat up a smooth griddle – or a heavy non-stick skillet – and while it's getting hot, fold the egg whites into the batter followed by the melted butter. Using a $^1/_4$ cup measuring cup for ease, dip the cup into the batter, fill it about three-quarters full and dollop this on to the hot griddle to make pancakes of about $3^1/_2$ inches in diameter – though size really doesn't matter here, so just however it comes…

It's important not to let the griddle get too hot, however, as you don't want the pancakes to burn on the outside before they cook through. Give them a good 3 minutes – over a low flame – on the first side and then flip them over and give about 1 minute or so on the other. You will just have to test as you go.

Eat with a good scoop of vanilla ice cream and a molten swathe of dark sticky toffee sauce.

KIDDIE FEAST

As someone who always looks with longing at what the children are being given to eat when there is split-generational catering going on, I don't expect these recipes to have age-limited application.

I am not quite sure I really buy into the idea of children's food anyway, in the sense that the more you restrict the sort of foods you give your children, the less adventurous they'll be about what they'll eat. Nevertheless, there is no point finessing recipes and spending hours slaving away on food they're just going to turn their noses up at. And I have noticed that the older children get, the pickier they become; peer pressure kicks in and they start loathing the foods they used to love.

I don't cook frenziedly for my children, and like many mothers, would be stricken at most suppertimes if there were no such thing as pasta, but on the weekends I cook for them for the simple reason that meals need to be cooked and children must be looked after and I can combine the two. Clearing up even the messiest kitchen is better, in my book, than hours spent running about in the park. Not all the recipes below are ones I'd expect them to help with – though "help" is generally a misnomer in this context anyway – but they can usually do some small thing, like peel a carrot or, with a pair of scissors, top and tail a bean or two. Otherwise, these are meals I make that they like and that I am happy to give them. Indeed, I did ask my children what ideal foods they would want included in their own feast-section and, broadly speaking, this is their list.

RITZY CHICKEN NUGGETS

These are not even remotely fancy: the "Ritzy" of the title refers to the crackers of the same famous name. I make crumbs out of them, and use them to coat small pieces of chicken that have been tenderized by being refrigerated in a freezer bag of buttermilk for a day or two.

Makes 12–16 nuggets to feed 3–4 children

2 chicken breasts (with the bone each weighing approx. 8oz; slightly less without)

1 cup buttermilk
1³/₄ cups Ritz cracker crumbs
¹/₂ cup vegetable oil

Cut out the chicken bone if there is one, and put the chicken breasts one at a time into a freezer bag so that they lie flat. Bash with a rolling pin until the chicken is quite thin, and then take it out and slice into about six to eight slices. Repeat with the other chicken breast. Scissors make this easy for children, too, and as long as you make them wash their hands well before and after, of course, you may hand a pair straight to a nearby child.

Put the slices into a freezer bag with the buttermilk and leave in the fridge to marinate for up to 2 days.

When you are ready to cook them, heat the oil in a large frying pan. Put the Ritz crackers into a bag, seal the end, then bash them as above and, once they have broken down a little, roll them with a rolling pin still inside the bag.

Tip the crumbs into a wide shallow bowl, and then shake off the excess buttermilk from the nuggets and dip them in the crumbs. Coat them well before laying gently in the hot oil, and cooking for about 2 or 3 minutes a side until they are golden brown. Transfer to some paper towel on a plate to blot the excess oil.

CAPERY SALAD TO TURN RITZY CHICKEN NUGGETS INTO A GROWN-UP MEAL

Most grown-ups, too, would be ecstatic to be given this for supper or lunch. When I eat them, this is the salad I make to go with.

4 little butter lettuces
2 large gherkins. to give approx.
  7 tablespoons diced

1–2 tablespoons capers
2–3 tablespoons chopped parsley

Serves 4–6
and eat 2 nuggets each or
make more

FOR THE DRESSING
2 teaspoons gherkin brine
2 tablespoons olive oil

$^1/_2$ teaspoon Dijon mustard

Slice the lettuce into $^1/_2$ inch slices across the lettuce and put into a bowl. Dice the gherkins and add to the lettuce with the capers.

    Combine the dressing ingredients, whisking together, and then pour over the salad, tossing it to mix. Arrange on a couple of plates and sprinkle over the parsley. And then just bring on the nuggets.

CHICKEN NOODLE SOUP

This is another real favorite in my house, and something you can cook when you're utterly exhausted. I buy vacuum-sealed packages of fresh – or rather soft ready-cooked – udon noodles from the supermarket and stash them in the cupboard with the pasta so that I know I've always got them on hand. It's a rare week when my children don't ask for this at least once.

Serves 2

note

I think if you're making this a grown-up meal, you do need to add some finely sliced hot red chilli and minced ginger to the broth, squeeze with lime and sprinkle with fresh cilantro as you serve.

2 cups chicken stock (good-quality instant or canned is fine)
1 boneless chicken breast, about 5oz, cut into strips
1 tablespoon soy sauce
$1/_4$ cup (about 4 or 5) baby corn, cut into 1 inch pieces

8oz fresh or ready-cooked udon noodles
$1/_2$ cup sugar-snap peas
$1/_2$ cup slender green beans

Heat the chicken stock in a saucepan. In a frying pan, cook the strips of chicken without any oil until they have lost their rawness, giving them a stir frequently, and then add the soy sauce to the hot pan of chicken, letting it boil gently a little before tipping the contents of the skillet into the saucepan of hot stock.

Bring the pan to the boil and add the baby corn, noodles, sugar-snaps and fine beans cut in half.

Let the pan come back up to boiling point and cook for a minute or so, so that the noodles are warmed through and the vegetables tender but still crisp.

CHICKEN POT PIES

I don't really think of these as chicken pot pies, but rather chicken pies – or, chicken and ham pies – but this is what my children call them, and who am I to argue? Sometimes I feel I've dropped down the gap between two eras: when I was a child I lived in a totalitarian state ruled by parents; now I live in a totalitarian state ruled by children. It's never been my turn, but perhaps that's just as well.

I know these are quite a lot of trouble, but they are a real treat, and even such instinctive ingrates as children will truly appreciate it.

Serves 4

FOR THE DOUGH
3 cups all-purpose flour
2 sticks cold unsalted butter

3 eggs

FOR THE FILLING

4 tablespoons butter

$^1/_3$ cup all-purpose flour

1 chicken stock cube or 1$^1/_2$ tablespoons concentrated chicken bouillon

2$^1/_2$ cups whole milk

1 cup frozen peas

2 cups cold cooked chicken, diced

1 cup cold cooked ham, diced (or 3 cups chicken alone if not using ham)

note

You can replace the peas with drained, canned sweet corn, or use half and half. The corn won't need the hot-water treatment.

Put the flour into a bowl – a shallow tray of some kind might be best – and add the butter diced into cubes. Give a shake, gently, then put into the freezer for 10 minutes. It's this that makes the dough so pliable as you roll it and so melting as you eat it, so don't miss out this stage. At the same time, beat 2 of the eggs with a tablespoon of iced water and stick in the fridge.

Tip the chilled flour and butter into a food processor, and then pulse the mixture until it resembles fine, dry rubble. Feed the chilled beaten eggs down the shoot of the processor while it is running, adding a little at a time until it begins to form a ball. You want to stop just as the ball is beginning to cohere and the dough clumps around the blades; don't carry on beyond that point, but be prepared to add some iced water down the chute if you need more liquid to bring this about. When making the dough, a freestanding mixer fitted with the flat paddle will do the job just as well, only slightly more slowly. And I find you need less liquid when using the processer rather than the mixer.

Tip out on to the work surface and form into four discs, making two slightly bigger than the remaining two. (These will make the base and top of the pies.) Wrap each dough disc in plastic wrap and let rest in the fridge while you make the pie filling.

So: melt the butter in a thick-bottomed saucepan over a low heat, then whisk in the flour and crumbled bouillon cube; if you're using the liquid bouillon concentrate you can add it after the milk. Off the heat, add the milk a little at a time, whisking to a smooth paste as you go. When all the milk is incorporated, put back on the heat, turn up to medium to high – but don't let it actually boil fiercely – and stir or whisk constantly for a few minutes to get rid of the starch in the flour and to make a really thick sauce. Do not stop stirring at any time. You may want to turn the heat down, though. Pour the thick white sauce into a bowl and cover with dampened parchment paper or press on plastic wrap to stop a skin forming, if you aren't proceeding to assemble the pies straightaway.

When you're about ready to get baking, slip a baking sheet in the oven and preheat it to 400°F. Put the peas into a sieve, and pour a kettleful of freshly boiled water over them, shaking off the excess water. Or you can sit the peas in warm water while you make the sauce: it all depends on your timetable.

Dice or shred the chicken or chicken and ham and mix the thawed peas (corn if using), chicken and ham into the cooled white sauce. I always make the sauce, like the dough, in advance which is why it's always cooled for me, but if you want to go straight through in one run, the sauce will still be warm, obviously.

It's easiest to do two pies at a time. Roll out one of the bigger discs of dough on a floured surface to a size big enough to line the bases and sides of two oval pie dishes (capacity about $1^1/_4$ cups, $5^1/_2$ inches at their longest point, $^1/_2$ inch deep). Leave a generous lip of dough hanging over the edge of each one.

Spoon half the filling into each of the two dough-lined pie dishes, and roll out one of the smaller discs of dough for the two lids. Dampen the dough edges of the pies with some water and lay the lids on top. Trim the excess dough from around the sides with a knife, and seal the edges with the prongs of a fork. Decorate with leftover dough.

Cut out any shapes you like for the top: I most often use little letter cutters either to spell out my children's names or to let them write what they want, within reason. Just dampen the underside of each letter or cut-out and sit it, pressing firmly but gently, on the top of the pie. Beat the remaining egg for the glaze, and paint each pie with a dough brush, and finally – to let out air – cut a tiny cross with the point of a knife in the middle of each one, or make little diagonal slashes with the point of a small, sharp knife.

Put the little pies on to the heated baking sheet already in the oven and cook for 15–20 minutes till golden and inviting. When the pies are ready, deftly turn them upside down using an oven mitt and slip them out of their pans. It's much easier than it sounds: don't let that "deftly" put you off.

CREAMED CHICKEN

I made this because my son came back from a sleepover once saying, "No offense, Mum, but they made this chicken thing that's much nicer than anything you've ever cooked." That's what I call a challenge. Luckily, it panned out. Of course, since then he's moved on, but that's children for you.

When I make it for myself, I add a slug of Noilly Prat vermouth along with the cream and chicken stock.

1 tablespoon unsalted butter
1 tablespoon garlic oil
³/₄lb chicken breast

¹/₃ cup chicken stock (I use hot water
from the kettle and some chicken
bouillon concentrate)
¹/₃ cup heavy cream

Enough for 3 children,
depending on age or course.

In a small frying pan with a lid, heat the butter and oil. Cut the chicken into bite-sized pieces and brown the chicken in the pan with a stir-frying action.

Stir in the chicken stock and heavy cream and clamp on the lid. Turn the heat down and let the pan boil gently for 3 minutes (or until the chicken is cooked through).

Serve with plain rice (and see note).

note
I couldn't cook for my children and keep my sanity without a rice cooker. Actually, I wouldn't be without one in any case. It's not just that it cooks rice so well – as indeed why wouldn't it? It has nothing else to do – but that you can stick the rice in, plug the machine on any time you want, and know that the rice will stay good for 12 hours. Or it does with my model – a Zojirushi, for the record.

The good thing about this is that you can leave the house in the morning, spend a day out with the kids, and know you've got the basis of supper cooked when you get home. A bit of sweet corn and some soy sauce stirred through and they're happy. And for grown-up catering, it does make dinner parties very much easier. But I often stick the rice cooker on just for the two of us in the evening, knowing that all I have to do is forage about in the fridge for some protein and cook it quickly, and supper is – fairly effortlessly – made.

SUNDAY NIGHT PASTA

This is the simplified version of the creamed chicken above, and as its title suggests, it is indeed what I cook every Sunday night, hovering about the table like a wheat-eating vulture, desperately anxious for their leftovers.

The amounts I specify below are not meant to be treated with too much reverence: you know what kind of an appetite your child has and how much pasta he or she will want to eat for supper. And to be honest, if I weren't writing a recipe for it, I wouldn't even start weighing out the pasta or measuring out the cream; it's not that kind of a dish.

Serves 2 (small) children

6oz pasta
a pat of butter
$^1/_2$ teaspoon garlic oil

2 teaspoons chicken stock concentrate or $^1/_2$ chicken stock cube
$^1/_4$ cup heavy cream

Put on some water to boil in a pan and when it starts bubbling, salt it and cook the pasta. Remove a $^1/_4$ cup of pasta water just before you drain it, though.

While the pasta sits in the colander, put the butter and garlic oil in the pan it cooked in, back on the heat and, with a wooden spoon, stir in the crumbled chicken bouillon cube or concentrate. Stir in the cream and let it bubble for a moment or two. It should be the perfect consistency for coating the small amount of pasta that's just waiting to be turned in it. Add some of the pasta cooking liquid if you want further lubrication or feel that the sauce tastes too intense.

Put the drained pasta in the pan with the sauce and stir to mix. Let the pan sit off the heat, so the pasta absorbs a little more of the sauce, for a minute or two and then divide between two plates.

PASTA WITH HAM, PEAS AND CREAM

I seem to remember that when I lived in Florence this pasta – with the cream, the peas, the ham – went under the name "alla Medici." After another long weekend with the little angels, the designation seems indecently appropriate.

If the thought is bad, the deed is good: for this is a really wonderful supper. I make it when I've got some ham left over in the fridge; the children seem to relish it particularly if it's left over from the ham in Cherry Coke (page 205).

7oz farfalle or other short pasta
²/₃ cup frozen petits pois
²/₃ cup heavy cream

1¹/₄ cups diced ham
2 tablespoons grated Parmesan

Serves 2–3 children

Cook the pasta according to package instructions in plenty of salted boiling water, and then after 5 minutes add the peas to the pasta water.

When the pasta is cooked, drain with the peas. Put the dry pan back on the heat with the cream, ham and Parmesan and warm it through. Add the pasta and peas back to the pan, tossing everything together well.

STIR-FRIED RICE

This is another excuse for using up leftovers. Don't regard the chicken or shrimp element as fixed: I sometimes use one; sometimes the other; sometimes both, as here. It really all depends on what I've got lurking about at home. And one of the things about having a rice cooker, is that there is nearly always some cooked rice left over. You can't let rice sit for long, but whatever is left makes the basis for a great supper the next day. So far as children are concerned – and who's to say they're wrong? – any meal is better if there's a serious carb content.

Serves approx. 3 small
children

1 1/2 cups cooked basmati rice
1 cup small cooked shrimp
3/4 cup chopped cooked chicken
1 cup corn niblets

1 tablespoon garlic oil
1 scallion, sliced
1 1/4 cups beansprouts
1 egg, beaten

Get out a large bowl and mix together the cold rice, the shrimps, the chicken, chopped or shredded as you prefer, and corn.

In a medium-sized skillet heat the garlic oil with the finely sliced scallion and cook, stirring, for a minute then stir in the beansprouts followed by the contents of the rice bowl. Stir well and briskly, until everything is hot, and then tip in the beaten egg and continue to stir-cook for another 1/2 minute.

SLOPPY JOES

You wouldn't want to be sitting opposite a small child eating these, but you can understand why they like them. This used to be their end-of-the-week Friday suppertime treat: burger buns (or better still, I think, as does my son, slightly sweet challah buns), split and oozing with this dripping mixture.

Serves 4–8

note
I often make this in advance:
with children, I think it's good
to separate the cooking from
the eating, so that your effort,

4 slices pancetta or 2 slices bacon
1 small or 1/2 medium onion
2 small–medium carrots
1 tablespoon parsley leaves,
   unchopped
1 teaspoon dried oregano
1 clove garlic, peeled

1 stick of celery, roughly chopped
2 tablespoons olive oil
1lb ground beef
1 14oz can Heinz tomato soup
2 teaspoons Worcestershire sauce
8 buns

Put the pancetta or bacon into a food processor and process until finely ground. Peel and quarter the onion, peel the carrots and cut them into chunks, and add both ingredients to the food processor. Add the parsley, oregano, garlic and celery and process until you have a finely chopped mush. You can do all this by hand, but it's the machinery that makes this so effortless.

Heat the oil in a heavy-based saucepan with a lid, and then fry the vegetable mixture until it has softened, about 10 minutes. Add the ground beef, turning it in the pan to brown and breaking up the lumps of meat with a fork so that it doesn't clump together. Finally stir in the soup and Worcestershire sauce. Cover with a lid and cook on the very lowest heat on the stovetop for 45 minutes.

Split the buns and slop on the meat sauce, then sandwich and apply to face.

however scant, is a distant memory once they're at the table. This lessens the sense of personal affront and hurt when they don't eat up every last mouthful.

If the idea of using canned tomato soup appeals, then simply use a can of chopped tomatoes, a teaspoon or two of sugar if you can bring yourself to, and a good slug of milk.

BABY BURGERS

Having made the burgers for myself following the Zuni Café method (see page 335), I tried out this modified version for the children. There's no reason why you shouldn't make them exactly the same way, cutting the rump and so on, but a kind of torpor can settle on me when I've spent long amounts of time with children, so this is what I more often end up doing. The meat should be – as for the recipe above, and indeed anywhere – top-quality, organic and not spookily reared beef.

8oz ground beef	1 tablespoon garlic oil	Serves 2
$1/4$ teaspoon salt	2 burger buns	
$1/4$ teaspoon superfine sugar	tomato ketchup to serve	

Mix the beef with the salt and sugar in a bowl with your hands, and cover the bowl with plastic wrap and leave for a couple of hours in the fridge or overnight or all day, if that's easier.

Let the beef come to room temperature and shape into two flattish patties about $3^1/2$ inches in diameter. Heat the oil in a skillet and sear the burgers over high heat, then turn it down a little and cook the burgers for 4 minutes a side. Wrap them each in a double layer of aluminum foil to make a parcel, and leave to rest for 4 minutes.

Split the burger buns and fry the cut sides in the meaty garlic oil left in the skillet for 1 minute, then arrange the burgers so that you have the bottom bun topped by a burger then tomato ketchup and then the top bun.

RICE AND MEATBALLS

Do not proceed with this recipe before reading my notes on the life-enhancing value of getting a rice cooker, (on page 243). Obviously, you can serve the meatballs with pasta, though, so don't make it a deal-breaker. It's simply that this is the combination my children particularly requested here.

Serves 8–10 children

FOR THE MEATBALLS

1lb ground beef

1 egg

2 tablespoons grated Parmesan

1 clove garlic, minced

2 tablespoons chopped parsley

3 tablespoons breadcrumbs or
  semolina

1 teaspoon salt

FOR THE TOMATO SAUCE

1 onion, halved

2 cloves garlic

1 tablespoon unsalted butter

1 tablespoon olive oil

$2^1/_2$ cups tomato pulp or thick puree

$^1/_2$ teaspoon superfine sugar

$^1/_2$ cup whole milk

Put all of the ingredients for the meatballs into a bowl, adding a good grind of black pepper. Either using your hands or a fork, mix thoroughly but lightly. The less you handle the mixture the better.

Shape teaspoonfuls of the mixture into balls, and place on a baking sheet lined with plastic wrap. Better still, get your children to do this: their smaller hands are much better suited to this work, and you do want these meatballs tiny. If they're small, you should easily get 50 out of this mixture.

Put the meatballs into the fridge while you get on with the sauce.

Put the onion and garlic into a processor and blitz to a pulp. Heat the butter and oil in a deep, wide pan, and then add the onion-garlic mixture to it. Cook over a low heat for about 10 minutes, stirring occasionally so that it doesn't burn. Add the tomato pulp and add half as much again of water to the pan, and season with the sugar, and some salt and pepper.

Let this bubble away for 10 minutes, and then stir in the milk and let the sauce come back to the boil.

Drop the little meatballs in one by one, but don't stir the pan until they have turned brown or they might break.

Cook the meatballs in the sauce for 20 minutes, partially covering with a lid so that the sauce thickens but not too much liquid evaporates. At the end of the cooking time check the seasoning.

In the normal run of things, I make a batch of this and then freeze bagfuls, so that I don't have to think of what to cook every night for the next few weeks, but if you're serving the whole lot, cook to go with it about 2$^1/_2$ cups of rice.

As you pass out each plate, mound with rice and top, as if an erupting volcano, with meatballs and tomato sauce.

CRÊPES-CANNELLONI

You can see the recipe for the crêpes on page 255, but I'll be honest with you: I nearly always make this with a package of bought crêpes. Once they've been in the oven soused with tomato sauce for half an hour, you really can't tell.

I made this as an easy alternative to lasagne once, and have never looked back.

6–8 large store-bought crêpes, or see page 255

FOR THE MEAT SAUCE

1 small onion	1 teaspoon salt
1 clove garlic	1 teaspoon superfine sugar
1 tablespoon olive oil	2 tablespoons tomato purée
$^1/_2$ teaspoon dried oregano	$^1/_2$ cup water
12oz ground beef	

FOR THE TOMATO SAUCE

2$^2/_3$ cups tomato pulp	1 tablespoon superfine sugar
1 tablespoon sea salt/$^1/_2$ tablespoon table salt	$^1/_3$ cup milk
	1 ball (about 4oz) mozzarella

Serves 4–6, depending on ages and appetite

note
You can always do away with the garlic but use garlic oil for frying instead; this to be borne in mind for a great many of the recipes here.

Preheat the oven to 400°F. Though ignore this right now if you're cooking the meat filling in advance, which is what I invariably do. I tend to like to stir a pan in the morning when I'm meant to be at my desk working. I congratulate myself on my maternal busy-ness but really it's just another instance of multishirking.

Chop the onion and garlic in a food processor until very fine. Heat the oil in a wide saucepan and cook the onion and garlic for about 5 minutes or until they are soft.

Add the oregano and the ground beef, and turn the meat in the hot pan until it browns. Add the salt and sugar, and then dissolve the tomato purée in the water and stir into the pan. Cook uncovered for 15 minutes, stirring occasionally and then set aside to cool (unless you're proceeding with the baking stage immediately).

To make the tomato sauce, put the tomato pulp in a measuring cup and stir in the salt, sugar and milk. Make sure the oven's on, and at the temperature above if not already preheated.

Fill the crêpes with the cooled meat filling; use approximately an espresso cupful in each one; I'm not sure I'd go to the guillotine on this, however, as I measure by eye only. The idea is simply to dollop the meat into each crêpe, and then make a bundle out of it. Either roll each one up, or turn the four curving edges in to make a small package. Lay the rolls or sit the packages snugly together in a dish 8 x 12 inches, or whatever you've got that seems suitable, and pour over the cup of tomato sauce to cover the crêpes.

Roughly chop the mozzarella, sprinkle over the top of the dish and put in the oven. Bake for 30 minutes, by which time the sauce should be bubbling and the cheese melting.

SOFT WHITE DINNER ROLLS

It may seem a crackpot idea to suggest you make fresh white bread rolls for your children's supper, but give me a moment. Please. Children absolutely adore making them, although the results often don't turn out to be bread rolls, but rather floury lumps and shapes covered in peanut butter, sprinkles and more flour (see below and facing page), as they, in turn, will be covered themselves.

Besides, if you do make them, you will find it astonishingly relaxing and gratifying, and your children will – unaccountably – thank you. Mine love them spread thickly with melting butter, and I can't say I blame them.

FOR THE DOUGH

$3^1/_2$–4 cups all-purpose flour

3 teaspoons (1 envelope) rapid rise, bread machine or other instant yeast

$^1/_2$ tablespoon salt

1 tablespoon superfine sugar

$1^1/_2$ cups milk

1 heaped tablespoon butter

FOR THE TOPPINGS

1 egg, beaten

1 tablespoon milk

pinch salt

1 teaspoon sesame seeds

1 teaspoon poppy seeds

Combine $3^1/_2$ cups of the flour with the instant yeast, salt and sugar in a large mixing bowl.

Put the milk and butter into a saucepan and heat until the milk is warm, and the butter is beginning to melt.

Pour into the bowl of dry ingredients and mix with a fork or a wooden spoon to make a rough dough, adding more of the remaining flour if the dough is too wet. Then either using your hands or the dough hook on an electric mixer, knead the dough until it is smooth and silky.

Put the ball of dough into a greased bowl and cover the top with plastic wrap, then leave in a warm place (I always sit a bowl of yeasted dough on a pile of newspapers) to rise for an hour by which time it should be double the size. Punch the air out of the dough with your fist and then turn it out on to a floured surface.

Pull pieces of dough the size of walnuts off the dough and form them into small round rolls, like ping pong balls, placing them as you go on to a greased or lined baking sheet. The balls of dough should be about $1/4$ inch apart so that once they have sat to rise they will be just about touching. I get 30 balls of dough, and I arrange them in six lines of five.

Cover them with a kitchen towel and leave to rise again in a warm place for about half an hour, preheating the oven to 425°F, while they sit. When the buns have puffed up, beat together the egg, milk and a pinch of salt and paint them with the glaze. Scatter alternate lines of buns with sesame and poppy seeds, leaving plain rows in between. (A teaspoon of seeds should decorate two rows.) That's to say, a row of poppy-topped, then a row of sesame-topped, then one row of plain and then repeat again.

Bake the buns for 15 minutes by which time they should be golden brown and joined together in a little batch. Remove them to a cooling rack or serve immediately. When I make these for adults I put them on the table and let people tear them off as they go. When I'm making them for a roomful of children, I wouldn't be as mad; the feeding frenzy is bad enough as it is, so just tear them off and hand a few round to them on a plate.

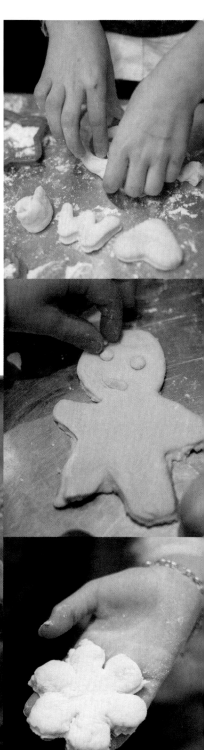

SWEET CORN FRITTERS

I don't know whether to suggest these to you in the first place for breakfast or for supper, such is my panicked hurry to convey to you the absolute necessity of cooking them at some time, regardless of hour or meal. They are wonderful with sausages or a fried egg or bacon, but pretty damn perfect by themselves. Children go mad for them, or at least mine do.

Makes 10

note

If you haven't got a smooth griddle or a good non-stick frying pan, then you should add some oil to the pan you have got, and fry them instead.

2 eggs, separated
scant $^1/_2$ teaspoon salt

3 tablespoons all-purpose flour
1 cup drained canned corn

Whisk the egg whites with the salt until stiffish, not fretting over them unduly, then – in another bowl – whisk the egg yolks for 2–3 minutes. Fold in the flour and sweet corn and then the whites. I just tip the bowl of whites into the yellow ingredients and fold, though not gently, with a rubber spatula until everything's combined.

Meanwhile, heat a smooth griddle or heavy non-stick skillet and dollop out the fritters: I use a coffee scoop which is a 2-tablespoon measure. Cook for up to 2 minutes per side. You end up with golden pancakes about $2^1/_2$ inches in diameter.

GRANDMA'S BEAN AND BARLEY SOUP

This recipe was given to me by my mother-in-law, Carrie Diamond, by special request of my children, who drool over this soup. And it's not often you find children willingly eating vegetables, let alone begging and pleading for them. The starchiness of the soup certainly helps make it sweetly alluring. I thought about halving the quantities here, but it's so good, it seems a waste of time just to make enough for one meal.

Get the children to pop the soaked lima beans out of their indigestible shells or do it mindlessly yourself. You'd be surprised how relaxing it is do something that occupies you entirely without challenging you at all. The contemporary ethos of relaxing by doing nothing, just chilling out, has a lot to answer for. Relaxing is the least relaxing thing you can do. As the old saying goes, "time on your hands, yourself on your mind."

Makes approx. 11$^1/_2$ cups

1$^1/_3$ cups dried lima beans
$^2/_3$ cup barley
$^1/_2$lb (1–2) parsnips
$^1/_2$lb (2–3) carrots
1 large onion

$^3/_4$ cup parsley
1lb potatoes
5 cups chicken stock
1 tablespoon superfine sugar

Soak the beans and barley overnight. Skin the beans. (If you forget to soak overnight, pour boiling water over beans and barley and leave for a couple of hours.) The skins are pretty tough, but a bit of pressure should loosen the two halves of the bean inside to pop out, like two little kidneys carved out of ivory. You may need to tear the outer casing a little with your fingers if they're resistant.

Chop and then process all the (peeled) fresh vegetables except for the potatoes; and I include the parsley here. Or just chop finely by hand. Add them to the stock in a large saucepan with the beans and barley. Now peel the potatoes and add them, diced small. Stir in the sugar and bring to the boil, then turn down the heat and let simmer for 2 hours. Add more stock or water if the soup gets too thick. Season to taste.

note
You can freeze portions of this, but don't freeze too much: it's so addictive that if you eat it for one meal, you nearly always want to eat it for the next, or maybe it's just me who's made like that.

CHEESY FEET

I have mentioned my cookie-cutter collection elsewhere (and see page 264) and knowing of children's predilection for the grosser things in life, how could I resist – when given a set of foot-shaped cutters by a friend back from New York – making some suitably cheese-tasting cookies with them. Naturally, they went down a storm. I've been tempted to serve them with drinks for grown-ups (as, actually, they taste fabulous) but am worried that the mixture between yukky and cute might not play so well there. I wouldn't want to embarrass myself, you do see.

1¹/₂ cups Cheddar cheese, grated
1¹/₂ tablespoons soft butter

¹/₃ cup all-purpose flour
¹/₄ teaspoon baking powder

Makes 16, or thereabouts

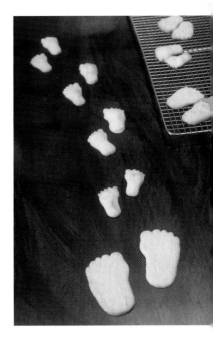

Preheat the oven to 400°F.

Put all of the ingredients into a food processor and blitz until the dough comes together. Just be patient: it will happen, I promise you. Form into a fat disc, wrap in plastic wrap and let it rest in the fridge for 15 minutes.

Roll out the dough on a floury surface to roughly ¹/₈ inch in thickness, and cut out your feet with your cutters. You can keep re-rolling this dough and cutting out feet until it is all used up.

Put them on to a lined baking sheet and cook in the oven for 10 minutes for the smaller feet, and 12 minutes for the bigger feet (see the photograph).

The biscuits will continue to crisp up as they cool on a rack, so take them out when they're still a little soft in the middle.

I am something of a tartar in one respect: I don't go in for desserts much at home. My children mostly get given a piece of fruit, or ice cream if I'm feeling remarkably indulgent. But every now and again I let them make or have something sweet as a special treat.

SCOTCH PANCAKES

When I was a child, we often had Scotch pancakes (out of a package) when we got home from school. And the thing – for those of you who don't know – about Scotch pancakes is that they are not eaten like pancakes – hot with syrup and a knife and fork – but like toast, spread with butter and jam. I always remember them being on the cold side of lukewarm, but I think warm, though not so hot as to burn your fingers, is what you're aiming for.

Makes 20 pancakes, approx. 3 inches each

note

Because of the 1 egg in the ingredients, it is pretty impossible, not to say pointless, to halve this, but it's worth knowing that you can leave them in the fridge and eat them as they are or microwaved back to comforting warmness at breakfast or tea next day.

$^1/_2$ teaspoon white wine vinegar
$^2/_3$ cup milk
$^3/_4$ cup all-purpose flour
$^1/_2$ teaspoon baking soda

1 egg
1 tablespoon vegetable oil
1 tablespoon dark corn syrup

Put the vinegar into the (preferably room temperature) milk and set aside while you measure out the other ingredients.

Put the flour into a wide-necked measuring cup or bowl and add the baking soda. In another glass measuring cup or bowl add the egg, oil, and then with the oily spoon measure the syrup in and whisk everything together. Add the vinegary milk, and then add the cup of wet ingredients to the dry, whisking to a batter.

Heat a flat griddle or heavy non-stick skillet with no oil. Add 1$^1/_2$ tablespoons of batter to make each Scotch pancake, and then when bubbles appear flip them over to make them golden brown on either side.

SHROVE TUESDAY PANCAKES

You do not have to be a devout Christian to observe Pancake Day. I couldn't let the date pass without making a batch of these: it would seem a sin against tradition, nature and greed, that other holy trinity.

They're not difficult to make – just your basic crêpes – and you can fill them however you like. I have to have mine as I always did as a child, that's to say, sprinkled with granulated sugar and squeezed with lemon juice. But we live in a more vulgar age now, and my children like theirs spread with chocolate and hazelnut spread.

2 tablespoons unsalted butter, melted, plus more for frying
1 cup all-purpose flour

1^1/$_3$ cups milk
1 egg

Makes 6 x 8 inch crêpes

The best thing to have to make proper pancakes is a copper crêpe pan, but it's hard to justify the expense since you're not likely to get much use out of it. Still, I love mine. Otherwise reckon on using a shallow pan, preferably one with sloping sides, of about 8 inches in diameter.

Melt the butter and let cool a little.

Put the flour, milk and egg into a blender and whiz to amalgamate. Pour into a glass measuring cup and stir in the melted butter. Otherwise, just pour the flour into a bowl, whisk in the egg and milk and finally, just before making the crêpes, the melted butter.

Heat a seasoned crêpe pan or the nearest equivalent (I like to melt some butter in one first, and then wipe it all off) and ladle 2–3 tablespoons of batter into the pan then quickly hold it up and swirl so that the batter forms a quick, thin pancake covering the base of the pan. This will cook in a minute so flip it and cook for 30 seconds to a minute on the other side, then remove the pale crêpe to a layer of parchment paper.

Continue with the rest of the batter. This is the work of moments, and crêpes, ready filled, or empty, reheat very well in a microwave.

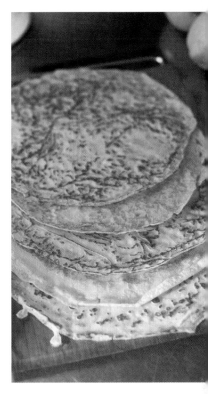

CHOCOHOTOPOTS

This is the richest, gooiest, most chocolatey pudding imaginable. These are a great favorite of my children, and named – by my son – with a concomitant respect for accuracy (and the ridiculous). They are chocolate, they are hot and they are cooked in little pots.

Makes 4

1 stick plus 1 tablespoon unsalted
   butter, plus extra for greasing
4oz semisweet chocolate (60%
   cocoa solids)
2 eggs

³/₄ cup superfine sugar
3 tablespoons all-purpose flour
¹/₂ cup white chocolate chips or
   morsels

Place a baking sheet in the oven and preheat to 400°F. Butter four ²/₃ cup ramekins. Either in a microwave or in a bowl suspended over a pan of simmering water, melt the butter and dark chocolate, then set aside to cool a little.

In another bowl, mix the eggs with the sugar and flour – I use my little hand whisk – and beat in the cooled butter and chocolate mixture. Fold the white chocolate chips or morsels into the cooled chocolate batter and divide this between the four buttered ramekins. Bake in the preheated oven for about 20 minutes by which time the tops will be cooked and cracked – like a macaroon – and the chocolate gungy and gooey underneath.

Place each ramekin on a small plate with a teaspoon and serve. Make sure to warn children that they will be HOT!

PEANUT BUTTER AND SNICKERS FUDGE SAUCE FOR ICE CREAM

I think the title says it all. Don't you?

Makes enough sauce for 6
children's bowls of ice cream

1 cup heavy cream
¹/₂ jar smooth peanut butter
   (approx. ¹/₃ cup)
3 tablespoons dark brown sugar

1 king-size Snickers bar (approx.
   3oz), broken into pieces
1 tablespoon dark corn syrup

Place all of the ingredients in a saucepan and heat gently. When everything has melted, raise to a simmer, stirring and scraping the pan for about 3 minutes.

CHOCOLATE CHOCOLATE-CHIP MUFFINS

Look, I'm not claiming this is the healthiest breakfast in the world, but I think you can let them try their hand at these once in a while at the weekend, don't you?

1³/₄ cups all-purpose flour
2 teaspoons baking powder
¹/₂ teaspoon baking soda
2 tablespoons best-quality
  unsweetened cocoa
1 large egg

³/₄ cup semisweet chocolate chips
  (plus more for sprinkling later)
1 cup milk
¹/₃ cup plus 2 teaspoons vegetable
  oil
³/₄ cup superfine sugar
1 teaspoon pure vanilla extract

Makes 12

Preheat the oven to 400°F and fill a muffin tin with paper cups.

    Measure out the dry ingredients into a large bowl. Pour all the liquid ingredients into a measuring cup. Mix both together, remembering that a lumpy batter makes the best muffins (although my children always over-mix as they argue over whose turn it is to stir next) then spoon into the waiting muffin cups. Sprinkle more chocolate chips on top then cook for 20 minutes or until the muffins are dark, risen and springy.

CHOCOLATE RICE PUDDING

I can see a definite tendency with the desserts here, but I don't suppose it's anything of a surprise, except to nutritionists and dieticians, that – duh – children like chocolate. For purists, the rice pudding below may seem an affront, but, once tasted, it proves itself the very opposite of unsettling.

a pat of butter
1 tablespoon unsweetened cocoa
1 tablespoon plus 1 teaspoon
  boiling water (ie 4 teaspoons)

1 cup milk
1 teaspoon pure vanilla extract
2 tablespoons arborio rice
2 tablespoons superfine sugar

Makes 2

Preheat the oven to 300°F, slipping in a baking sheet as you do so, and butter two small ³/₄ cup pudding dishes.

    Put the cocoa into a small measuring cup and dissolve with the boiling water then, stirring, pour in the milk. Add the vanilla extract and divide between the buttered dishes. Add 1 tablespoon of rice and the sugar to each dish, stir then put them on the hot sheet in the oven and cook for 30–40 minutes. Let stand for a while before eating.

TOBLERONE FONDUE

Buying the fondue set was my first mistake…

note

If you want to make this into a grown-up fondue, and believe me, there are takers, replace the milk with Amaretto.

1lb Toblerone candy bars
1 cup heavy cream

¹/₄ cup milk

FOR DIPPING INTO THE FONDUE
marshmallows
bananas

strawberries

Break up the Toblerone into pieces and melt the Toblerone, cream and milk together, using a no-doubt as yet unused fondue set – following the instructions that came with – or I suppose you could make do with a bowl over a pan of simmering water. Stir together and then if you want to minimize mess – though it's a losing battle – pour small amounts into warmed bowls for each child. Mine are resolute about having the flame – why wouldn't they be? It's potentially dangerous – and so I go along with it. It's a bit late to turn draconian.

SHIRLEY TEMPLE

This alcohol-free concoction was invented for Shirley Temple to drink at movie premieres, or so the story goes. Whatever, it is nectar to my children, the perfect kiddie-cocktail. I've put it here rather than list it under party food as, although I'm sure it would be a raving success, I wouldn't want to handle a roomful of children so stoked up on sugar and bubbles.

I'm not giving precise amounts, as you need a dash of Grenadine per glass, and only you know how many glasses you are making and therefore how many dashes of Grenadine, slices of orange and maraschino cherries you need. You can substitute Sprite for the ginger ale, if wished.

1 dash Grenadine
ginger ale (or Sprite)

slice of orange
maraschino cherry

Mix the dash of grenadine with the ginger ale in a highball glass packed with ice cubes. That's the accepted practice: obviously you don't have to go out and buy a highball glass; just use what's to hand.

Decorate with an orange slice and a maraschino cherry and serve with a straw.

BIRTHDAY CUSTARD SPONGE

I always used to make an elaborate cake for my children's birthdays but they've since got much more demanding – the car from *Grease*, James Bond, that sort of thing – so I now firmly order in from someone who can do this sort of thing better. Still, a very basic and heartlifting birthday cake is necessary in your repertoire: and this is beautiful and delicious and the one, incidentally, I make for adults who are less keen on sugarcraft.

Makes up to 12 slices, though small ones

note
This is the cake you want your children to bake you on your birthday, or for Mother's Day or whenever they want to show gratitude and appreciation for your presence. Ha! To order Bird's custard powder, see the sourcelist on page 260.

$1^1/_2$ cups all-purpose flour
3 tablespoons Bird's custard powder
2 teaspoons baking powder
$^1/_2$ teaspoon baking soda

4 eggs
2 sticks soft butter
1 cup superfine sugar
2-3 tablespoons milk

Make sure everything you need is at room temperature before you start. Preheat the oven to 350°F, and butter and line two 8 inch cake pans with parchment paper.

Put all of the above ingredients except the milk, into a food processor. Process to a smooth batter, and then add the milk a tablespoon at a time to make a soft dropping consistency. Divide between the two cake pans and bake for 20 minutes. The cakes will have risen and feel spookily puffy; this is because of the cornstarch in the custard powder.

Let the pans sit on a cooling rack for 5 minutes and then turn them out on to the rack, peeling away the paper.

FOR THE BUTTERCREAM FILLING

1 cup confectioners' sugar
4 teaspoons Bird's custard powder

$^3/_4$ stick soft unsalted butter
$1^1/_2$ teaspoons boiling water

Process the confectioners' sugar and custard powder to get rid of any lumps, and then add the butter, processing again to make the buttercream come together. Feed the boiling water down the funnel with the motor running to make the filling easier to spread. Then sandwich the cooled sponges together with the custardy buttercream.

FOR THE CHOCOLATE ICING

$^1/_4$ cup water
$^1/_4$ cup light corn syrup
$^2/_3$ cup superfine sugar (or use $^1/_4$
cup if using milk chocolate)

6oz semisweet chocolate
1 bottle multicolored sprinkles

Combine the water, syrup and sugar in a saucepan, stirring to dissolve over a low heat. Let it come to the boil and then take it off the heat.

Break up the chocolate into small pieces if you are not using chocolate buttons (as I do for cooking, but good quality not confectionary standard), and then add to the pan, swirling it around to cover in the hot liquid. Leave to melt for a few minutes, and then whisk the icing to make it smooth and shiny. Pour over the buttercream filled cake, letting it drip down the sides, and then scatter generously with the sprinkles before the icing sets.

Prong with candles, light them and sing.

CHOCOLATE CARAMEL CRISPY CAKES

No birthday party would be complete without these, and I think they're worth bearing in mind in place of more illustrious confectionary along with the coffee and tisanes after a grown-up dinner party, too.

I use Mars Bars, which give a chewy caramel bite; I have replaced the cornflakes with Rice Krispies from time to time, but the cornflake way is the right one, truly.

Makes approx. 40

2oz Milky Way bars
¹/₂ stick unsalted butter

2¹/₂ cups cornflakes

Break the Milky Ways into bits, and drop them into a saucepan, add the butter and melt, over a lowish heat, stirring frequently with a rubber spatula. When everything's melted (the nougat-like layer takes the longest to go), tip in the cornflakes and turn them, with your rubber spatula, in the chocolate mixture until they are all pretty well coated.

Fill mini-muffin tins with the mixture and put in the fridge, on a small sheet or tray, for at least an hour.

BIRTHDAY COOKIES

I've made these every year to mark the accretion of years for my children and it's part of our way of life now. The recipe for them is in its own special place of honor, on page 266, among my cookie cutters.

WHAT ELSE?

I've covered this ground before, and with each year and indeed, each book, I'm inclined to make less of a fuss. Anything you make to be healthy or to feed them properly goes ignored and you end up throwing paper-plate-fuls of food wastefully into the trash at the end. Children like cake – or rather, the icing – and they like potato chips, but I can't honestly say they want otherwise to eat at parties. They just want to open presents.

So, all I'd suggest you do is food that doesn't tax you at all: some little sausages (cooked in the oven, so no spitting fat from a pan) or bought mini-pizzas; now is not the time to put purist pressure on yourself. There is one crucial exception I make, and that is I always, always must provide some of my special patented Marmite sandwiches. Here's the trick: you whisk soft unsalted butter with some Marmite and then spread the peanut-butter-colored mix on to sliced white bread. For the record, I find 1 stick butter enough to sandwich the slices from one bought loaf. As I've said before, I can't be specific about the Marmite: it all depends on whether you want a mild-tasting, buff-colored cream or a salty-strong, sunbed-tan glaze.

And you do know, don't you, that you have to cut off the crusts?

Nor do I think you should save these up just for birthdays, or make them only for children. But then, that goes for all the food in this section anyway.

CUT-OUT
COOKIES

THIS FOR ME is the essential festive or celebratory recipe: there is scarcely an occasion for which you can't, or rather I can't, find a cookie to cut out, and the dough overleaf is a dream to work with. There's something so satisfying about cutting out the shapes and creating such dinky cuteness, and I say that as someone with a normally curtailed appreciation of either the dinky or the cute.

Obviously, you can find cutters you like and choose when and how you want to use them, but as a general guide you could think of snowflakes for Christmas, bells for weddings, shamrocks for St Patrick's Day, hearts for Valentine's Day, Dreidels for Hanukkah and eggs or chicks for Easter, numbers for birthdays (youthful ones) and so forth.

I have built up something of a collection of cookie-cutters; when anyone I know, however vaguely, goes away I ask them to bring me back a cutter and I'm always on the look out myself. I recently did an inventory of the cutters which I present – pathetically really – as after-dinner entertainment if I've drunk too much. I haven't drunk anything now, but I love my list too much not to present it to you.

COOKIE CUTTER LIST

Acorn	Daisy	Ice-cream cone	Pineapple
Alphabet	Diamond	Ivy leaf	Pumpkin
Anchor	Dog	Kangaroo	Rabbit
Angels	Duck	Koala	Rainbow trout
Apple	Easter chick	Leaf	Reindeer
Banana	Elephant	Lemon	Santa Claus
Bat	Feet	Lips	Shamrock
Bear	Fish	Lobster	Shooting stars
Bell	Flowers	Man – variety of poses	Snowflakes
Boat	Ghost	Map of Australia	Spades
Bones	Giraffe	Maple leaf	Spiky sun shape
Broomstick	Goblet	Mickey Mouse head	Squares
Bull's head	Hammer	Moon	Stars
Cactus	Hand	Moon with face	Statue of Liberty
Camel	Hearts – huge variety,	Moose – big and small	Strawberry
Candy stick	including broken, with	Mushroom	Teddy bear
Cars	arrows, double hearts,	Numbers	Ten-gallon hat
Cats	man with heart coming	Octagon	Train set (with signals etc.)
Christmas trees	out of chest.	Ovals	Trefoil
Circles	Hebrew alphabet	Owls	Tulip
Club	Hippo	Palm tree	Witch
Cow	Holly leaf	Pear	Wolf
Cowboy	Horse	Penguin	X (kiss)
Crocodile	Horseshoe	Pig	

CUT-OUT COOKIES

Makes 25–30

6 tablespoons soft unsalted butter
$^1/_2$ cup superfine sugar
1 large egg
$^1/_2$ teaspoon pure vanilla extract

1$^1/_2$ cups all-purpose flour
$^1/_2$ teaspoon baking powder
$^1/_2$ teaspoon fine salt

FOR THE FROSTING
1 cup confectioners' sugar, sifted
food coloring, preferably pastes

Preheat the oven to 350°F.

Cream the butter and sugar together until pale and moving towards lightness, then beat in the egg and vanilla. In another bowl, combine the flour, baking powder and salt. Add the dry ingredients to the butter and eggs, and mix gently but surely. If you think the finished mixture is too sticky to be rolled out, add more flour, but do so sparingly as too much will make the dough tough. Form into a ball, press down into a fat disc, wrap in plastic wrap and rest in the fridge for at least 1 hour.

Sprinkle a suitable surface with flour, place the disc of dough on it and sprinkle a little more flour on top of that. Then roll it out to a thickness of about $^1/_4$ inch. Cut into shapes, dipping the cutter into flour as you go, and place the biscuits a little apart on two – probably – lined baking sheets.

Bake for 8–12 minutes; obviously it depends on the shape you're using and whether they are on the upper or lower shelf though you can swap them around after about 5 minutes. When they're ready, expect them to be tinged a pronounced gold around the edges; they'll be softish still in the middle, but will set while they cool. So remove them, with a flat – preferably flexible – spatula to a wire rack. When they're all fully cooled, you can get on with the frosting. Put a couple of tablespoons of just-not-boiling water into a large bowl, add the sifted confectioners' sugar and mix together, adding more water as you need to form a thick paste. Color as desired. I think pastes are much better than liquid, not just because the range of colors is better but because they don't dilute the frosting as they tint. If you have trouble finding them locally, see the list of Stockists on page 461.

CHOCOLATE CAKE HALL OF FAME

I HAVE admitted before that I am surprisingly impervious to chocolate – which is honest, but only up to a point. Although I'm not someone who would wolf down any of the cakes that follow in their entirety, I seem to find them remarkably easy to eat by the generous slice and not just – as the saying goes – "in an emergency." And even if it's true that given a choice between a packet of potato chips or a bar of chocolate, I'd choose the salty over the sweet carb every time, chocolate cake is different. I hesitate to call chocolate cake the ultimate indulgence since by doing so I know I thereby disclose my Anglo-Saxon prejudices. In a 1999 research paper, a number of learned writers sought to describe and compare various attitudes to food. Subjects from France, Belgium, Japan and America were given several foodstuffs and required to give their immediate associations. To "chocolate cake" the Americans responded with "guilt"; the French countered with "celebration." (Just as to the word "cream," the Americans came out with "unhealthy" and the joyful French, "whipped.") In this context, I must declare myself firmly allied with the French. If chocolate cake is an indulgence, please don't consider it a sinful one: it is a confection to exult in, not to regret.

This isn't about gluttony or the wanton wallowing in excess. And, not least, I suspect more chocolate cake is consumed per capita in the United States than in la belle France. Attitudes towards food are not just signs of psychological difference, but have enormous bearing on physical health. Of all the countries represented in the study it was mainly Americans who suggested that food consumption was cause for worry and concern, whereas the French indicated that eating was primarily a source of pleasure. And it's the French who are considered the healthier of the two nations.

The lesson to be learned is that how we eat and not just what we eat has an impact on our health, ourselves, our lives. And that, too, is the essence of this book. A feast is not just a licence to eat, but an invitation to celebrate life, and what it is to be truly alive.

And there is something about chocolate cake, whether it is a proudly naked plain one or an elaborately constructed confection that issues this invitation most warmly. Whenever I have people for dinner and don't know quite what dessert to plonk on the table at the end, I plump for a chocolate cake and the eyes of even those who claim never to eat dessert light up. And while there is no absolute need – ever – to make or eat a chocolate cake, we are not talking need here, except perhaps in some psycho-social sense, however alarming that sounds. I sometimes make one on Saturday morning so that I know it's there, sitting welcomingly aloft on its platter over the weekend, turning the kitchen into the place of comfort and source of pleasure that we all, regardless of cooking ability or dietary models, need it to be.

note

Since there is the greatest agglomeration of cakes in this chapter, this is probably the place to reiterate that in baking what is most important is that all ingredients are at room temperature before you start.

If that's hard to arrange timewise, bear in mind that milk and butter can be warmed – go really slowly and gently – in a microwave, and fridge-cold eggs can be put in a bowl of warm water – just from the tap – for 10 minutes to take the chill off them.

If you bake more than once in a blue moon, it is probably worth cutting to fit discs of Silpat – the essential, non-stick, reusable parchment – and keeping them in your cake pans ready for action. (And see Stockists, page 461.)

OLD-FASHIONED CHOCOLATE CAKE

If you're going to get started, this is the cake you should begin with. Not just because it's simple, though it is – as are most of the cakes that follow – but because it is, for me, essence of chocolate cake: melting, luscious and mood-enhancingly good. A food technologist would explain this in terms of "mouthfeel" but I don't know quite how that makes me feel. I often describe this cake as a sort of idealized chocolate cake out of a box, which doesn't sound so very inviting either. But what I mean by this, is that the cake looks and tastes perfect and has that melting, smooth lightness – immensely chocolatey but far from rich. The fact that it is scarcely harder than making a cake mix (only worlds better) is an added joy. The recipe itself is an evolved version of a couple of cakes I've done before, and although the amounts and ingredients are slightly fiddled with, the real change, and an improvement in terms of ease, is that it can be made, all in one, in the food processor.

FOR THE CAKE

$1^1/_2$ cups all-purpose flour

1 cup superfine sugar

1 teaspoon baking powder

$^1/_2$ teaspoon baking soda

$^1/_3$ cup best-quality unsweetened cocoa

$1^1/_2$ sticks soft unsalted butter

2 large eggs

2 teaspoons pure vanilla extract

$^2/_3$ cup sour cream

FOR THE FROSTING

$^3/_4$ stick unsalted butter

6oz good quality semisweet
   chocolate, broken into small pieces

$2^1/_2$ cups confectioners' sugar

1 tablespoon light corn syrup

$^1/_2$ cup sour cream

1 teaspoon pure vanilla extract

sugar flowers, optional

Makes about 8 slices

note

I tend to keep my kitchen stocked with very good dark chocolate buttons (70 per cent cocoa solids) as this entirely dispenses with any need to chop chocolate before melting it (see page 461 for mail order stockists). Do not dream of using normal confectionary ones (except just to eat of course).

Take everything out of the fridge so that all the ingredients can come to room temperature. Preheat the oven to 350°F and line and butter two 8 inch layer pans with removable bases such as Silpat or parchment paper.

Now all you have to do is put all the cake ingredients – flour, sugar, baking powder and soda, cocoa, butter, eggs, vanilla and sour cream – into a food processor and process until you have a smooth, thick batter. If you want to go the long way around, just mix the flour, sugar and leavening agents in a large bowl and beat in the soft butter until you have a combined and creamy mixture. Now whisk together the cocoa, sour cream, vanilla and eggs and beat this into your bowl of mixture.

Divide this batter, using a rubber spatula to help you scrape and spread, into the prepared pans and bake until a cake tester, or a thin skewer, comes out clean, which should be about 35 minutes, but it is wise to start checking at 25. Also, it might make sense to switch the two cakes around in the oven halfway through cooking time.

Remove the cakes, in their pans, to a wire rack and let cool for 10 minutes

before turning out of their pans. Don't worry about any cracks as they will easily be covered by the frosting later.

To make this frosting, melt the butter and chocolate in a good-sized bowl either in the microwave or suspended over a pan of simmering water. Go slowly either way: you don't want any burning or seizing.

While the chocolate and butter are cooling a little, sift the confectioners' sugar into another bowl. Or, easier still, put the confectioners' sugar into the food processor and blitz. This is by far and away the least tedious way of removing lumps.

Add the corn syrup to the cooled chocolate mixture, followed by the sour cream and vanilla and then when all this is combined whisk in the sifted confectioners' sugar. Or just pour this mixture down the funnel of the food processor on to the confectioners' sugar, with the motor running.

When you've done, you may need to add a little boiling water – say a teaspoon or so – or indeed some more confectioners' sugar: it depends on whether you need the frosting to be runnier or thicker; or indeed it may be right as it is. It should be liquid enough to coat easily, but thick enough not to drip off.

Choose your cake stand or plate and cut out four strips of baking paper to form a square outline on it (this stops the frosting running on to the plate). Then sit one of the cakes, uppermost (ie slightly domed) side down.

Spoon about a third of the frosting on to the center of the cake half and spread with a knife or spatula until you cover the top of it evenly. Sit the other cake on top, normal way up, pressing gently to sandwich the two together.

Spoon another third of the frosting on to the top of the cake and spread it in a swirly, textured way (though you can go for a smooth finish if you prefer, and have the patience). Spread the sides of the cake with the remaining frosting and leave a few minutes till set, then carefully pull away the paper strips.

I love to dot the top of this with sugar pansies – and you must admit, they do look enchanting – but there really is no need to make a shopping expedition out of it. Anything, or indeed nothing, will do.

Opposite: old-fashioned chocolate cake

QUADRUPLE CHOCOLATE LOAF CAKE

This cake is not named for the bypass you might feel you'd need after eating it, but in honor of the four choc-factors that comprise its glory: cocoa to make the cake; chocolate chips or morsels to fold into it; a chocolate syrup to drench it once out of the oven; flakily sliced dark chocolate to top it before slicing.

    I love this for tea, even for weekend breakfast, or late at night when its melting squidginess tends to fall darkly onto my white sheets – and I don't care. It's always wonderful as a dessert: put it on the table, ready to slice, alongside a bowl of strawberries and another of crème fraîche.

    As with the old-fashioned chocolate cake, on page 269, this is a doddle to make.

Makes 10 generous slices, serves 10–12

note

Odd as it sounds, this loaf cake makes a very elegant birthday cake, and because it isn't too fragile, is worth bearing in mind if you want to take something into the office to have a little party for a colleague. The 10 slices I've stipulated are generous, and you could easily halve them to have enough cake – just to mark the occasion – for 20.

    But I should say here, anyway, that all these cakes, with the possible exception of the chocolate fruit cake, lend themselves perfectly to birthday celebrations.

    If you are making this by hand, cream butter and sugar, then beat in the eggs, fold in the dry ingredients followed by sour cream and vanilla.

FOR THE CAKE

1²/₃ cups all-purpose flour
¹/₂ teaspoon baking soda
¹/₂ cup unsweetened cocoa
1¹/₃ cups superfine sugar
1¹/₂ sticks soft unsalted butter
2 eggs

1 tablespoon pure vanilla extract
¹/₃ cup sour cream
¹/₂ cup boiling water
1 cup/6oz package semisweet chocolate chips (unless you'd prefer milk)

FOR THE SYRUP

1 teaspoon unsweetened cocoa
¹/₂ cup water
¹/₂ cup superfine sugar

1oz semisweet or bittersweet chocolate (from a thick bar if possible)

Take whatever you need out of the fridge so that all ingredients can come to room temperature.

    Preheat the oven to 325°F, putting in a baking sheet as you do so, and line a 2lb loaf pan (mine measures 9¹/₂ x 4¹/₂ inches and 3 inches deep and the cooking times are based on that) with plastic wrap. I use two overlapping pieces and leave a little overhang all around – and don't panic, it won't melt.

    Put the flour, soda, cocoa, sugar, butter, eggs, vanilla and sour cream into the processor and blitz till a smooth, satiny brown batter. Scrape down with a rubber spatula and process again while pouring the boiling water down the funnel. Switch it off then remove the lid and the well-scraped double-bladed knife and, still using your rubber spatula, stir in the chocolate chips or morsels.

    Scrape and pour this beautiful batter into the prepared loaf pan and slide into the oven, cooking for about 1 hour. When it's ready, the loaf will be risen and split down the middle and a cake-tester, or a fine skewer, will pretty well come out clean. But this is a damp cake so don't be alarmed at a bit of stickiness in evidence; rather, greet it.

    Not long before the cake is due out of the oven – say when it's had about 45–50 minutes – put the syrup ingredients of cocoa, water and sugar into a small saucepan and boil for 5 minutes. You may find it needs a little longer: what you want is a reduced liquid, that's to say a syrup, though I often take it a little further, so that the sugar caramelizes and the syrup has a really dark, smokey chocolate intensity.

Take the cake out of the oven and sit it on a cooling rack and, still in its pan, pierce here and there with a cake tester. Then pour the syrup as evenly as possible, which is not very, over the surface of the cake. It will run to the sides of the pan, but some will have been absorbed in the middle.

Let the cake become completely cold and then slip out of its pan, removing the plastic wrap as you do so. Sit on an oblong or other plate. Now take your bar of chocolate, wrapped in foil if you haven't got much of its wrapper left, and cut with a heavy sharp knife, so that it splinters and flakes and falls in slices of varying thickness and thinness. I've specified a weight, but really go by eye: when you think you've got enough to scatter over the top of the loaf, stop slicing. Sprinkle these chocolate splinters over the top of the sticky surface of the cake.

note
If you don't have a cake tester, use a piece of spaghetti, or, failing that, a fine skewer.

CHOCOLATE ORANGE CAKE

This has a very simple origin, which is just as it should be for a very simple cake. I think more people tell me they did my clementine cake in *How to Eat* than any other recipe, and when I was having some friends round for dinner one night, I thought I'd get ahead the evening before and try out a chocolate version. There's something about its citrussy wetness and yet the lightness you get from not using flour that makes this perfect to toy with over a cup of coffee at the end of an evening. And it's useful to bring out when you have to entertain the gluten-intolerant.

In fact, though, its somber plainness makes it really the antithesis of any dinner-party gâteau. If you want a cake to hang around the kitchen (it lasts for an almost spookily long time) to be sliced as mood and appetite dictate, then this is it.

Makes about 8 slices

note

You can leave out the baking powder and soda if dietary requirements make that desirable, but in that case, I'd use a 9 inch pan instead and expect it to need slightly less cooking time.

2 small or 1 large thin-skinned orange, approx. 14oz total weight
6 eggs
1 heaped teaspoon baking powder
$^1/_2$ teaspoon baking soda
2 cups ground almonds
$1^1/_4$ cups superfine sugar
$^1/_2$ cup unsweetened cocoa
orange peel for decoration if wished

Put the whole orange or oranges in a pan with some cold water, bring to the boil and cook for 2 hours or until soft. Drain and, when cool, cut the oranges in half and remove any big seeds. Then pulp everything – pith, peel and all – in a food processor, or see below if you're proceeding by hand.

Once the fruit is cold, or near cold (though actually I most often cook the oranges the day before I make the cake), preheat the oven to 350°F. Butter and line an 8 inch springform pan.

Add the eggs, baking powder, baking soda, almonds, sugar and cocoa to the orange in the food processor. Run the motor until you have a cohesive cake mixture, but still slightly knobbly with the flecks of puréed orange. Or you could chop the fruit finely by hand and then cream the butter and sugar with a wooden spoon and add the eggs one by one, alternating with spoons of mixed ground almonds and cocoa, then the oranges, though I have to say I've only ever made this the lazy way.

Pour and scrape into the cake pan and bake for an hour, by which time a cake tester should come out pretty well clean. Check after 45 minutes because you may have to cover with aluminum foil to prevent the cake burning before it is cooked through, or indeed it may need a little less than an hour; it all depends on your oven.

Leave the cake to get cool in the pan, on a cooling rack. When the cake is cold you can take it out of the pan. Decorate with strips of orange peel or coarsely grated zest if you so wish, but it is darkly beautiful in its plain, unadorned state.

HONEY CHOCOLATE CAKE

I was once in Dean & DeLuca in New York and saw a little chocolate cake decorated with sugar bees. Having gone through a Biedermeier period earlier on in my life, I have something of a weakness for bees, and have wondered for years how I could incorporate them in a cake of my own: this is it. It seemed only right, to make it a honey cake: beautiful, perfect, Napoleonic – though perhaps in a slightly Disneyfied way. You judge.

Makes about 10 slices

FOR THE CAKE

4oz semisweet or bittersweet chocolate, broken into pieces
1¹/₃ cups soft light brown sugar
2 sticks soft butter
¹/₂ cup honey

2 eggs
1¹/₂ cups all-purpose flour
1 teaspoon baking soda
1 tablespoon unsweetened cocoa
1 cup boiling water

FOR THE STICKY HONEY GLAZE

¹/₄ cup water
¹/₂ cup runny honey

6oz semisweet chocolate
¹/₂ cup plus 2 tablespoons confectioners' sugar

FOR THE BEES

1oz yellow marzipan

12 slivered almonds

Take whatever you need out of the fridge so that all the ingredients can come to room temperature. While that's happening, melt the chocolate from the cake part of the ingredients list in a good-sized bowl, either in the microwave or suspended over a pan of simmering water. Set aside to cool slightly.

Preheat the oven to 350°F, and butter and line a 9 inch springform cake pan.

Beat together the sugar and soft butter until airy and creamy, and then add the honey. Add one of the eggs, beating it in with a tablespoon of the flour, and then the other egg with another tablespoon of flour. Fold in the melted chocolate, and then the rest of the flour and the baking soda. Add the cocoa pushed through a sieve to ensure you have no lumps, and last of all, beat in the boiling water. (I don't suppose there's anything to stop you doing this all-in-one in the processor, blitzing everything except the boiling water, and then scraping down the batter and pouring the water down the funnel with the motor running.) Mix everything well to make a smooth batter and pour into the prepared pan. Cook for an hour, though check the cake after 45 minutes and if it is catching cover the top lightly with aluminum foil.

Let the cake cool completely in the pan on a rack.

To make the glaze, bring the water and honey to a boil in a smallish, though not tiny, saucepan, then turn off the heat and add the finely chopped chocolate (I use my mezzaluna or chocolate buttons made with 70 per cent cocoa solids), swirling it around to melt in the hot liquid. Leave it for a few minutes then whisk together. Sift in the confectioners' sugar and whisk again until smooth.

Choose your plate or stand and cut out four strips of parchment paper and form a square outline on the plate. This is so that when you sit the cake on and ice it, the frosting will not run out all over the plate. Remove the sides of the springform and sit the thoroughly cooled cake on the prepared plate. Pour the frosting over the cold honey chocolate cake and smooth it down the sides. I should warn you that the glaze stays tacky for ages (this is what gives it its lovely melting gooeyness) so ice in time for the glaze to harden a little, say at least an hour before you want to serve it. You can then very gently slide out the strips of baking paper to reveal a clean plate. Keep the pan of frosting, and don't wash it up, as you will need it to make the stripes on the bees.

Divide the marzipan into six even pieces and shape them into fat, sausage-like bees' bodies, slightly tapered at the ends.

Using a wooden skewer, paint stripes with the sticky honey glaze left in the pan. About three stripes look best, in my not enormously considered opinion, and then very carefully attach the flaked almonds at an angle to make the bees' wings, two on each one (unsurprisingly). They might snap as you dig them into the marzipan bodies, so have some spare. I have to admit that, I also like to give them eyes by dipping the point of the skewer in the glaze and thence on the bees: they look more loveable with an expression, but this is where the Disney effect comes in. If a more imperial dignity is required, forgo the dotting of the eyes and present this as your Napoleonic Chocolate Cake.

CHOCOLATE GINGERBREAD

I'd never come across a chocolate gingerbread, and after making this one for the first time, I wondered why not. There's something about the glottally thickening wodge of chocolate chip and cocoa that just intensifies the rich spices of gingerbread. The chocolate morsels add texture and nubbly treat within. This is very rich, very strong: not for children, but perfect for the rest of us.

Makes about 12 slabs

note
See stockists for suppliers of golden syrup, liquid amber in glorious culinary form that once you've tried, you're hooked on.

FOR THE CAKE

1 1/2 sticks unsalted butter
1 cup plus 2 tablespoons dark
   brown sugar
2 tablespoons superfine sugar
3/4 cup golden syrup or light corn syrup
3/4 cup black treacle or molasses
1/4 teaspoon ground cloves
1 teaspoon ground cinnamon
2 teaspoons ground ginger

1 1/4 teaspoons baking soda
2 tablespoons warm water
2 eggs
1 cup milk
2 cups all-purpose flour
1/3 cup unsweetened cocoa
6oz package or 1 cup semisweet
   chocolate chips

FOR THE FROSTING

2 cups confectioners' sugar
2 tablespoons unsalted butter

1 tablespoon unsweetened cocoa
1/4 cup ginger ale

Preheat the oven to 325°F and tear off a big piece of parchment paper to line the bottom and sides of a roasting pan of approximately 12 x 8 x 2 inches deep.

In a decent-sized saucepan, melt the butter along with the sugars, golden syrup, treacle or molasses, cloves, cinnamon and ground ginger. In a cup dissolve the baking soda in the water. Take the saucepan off the heat and beat in the eggs, milk and soda in its water. Stir in the flour and cocoa and beat with a wooden spoon to mix. Fold in the chocolate chips, pour into the lined pan and bake for about 45 minutes until risen and firm. It will be slightly damp underneath the set top and that's the way you want it.

Remove to a wire rack and let cool in the pan. Once cool, get on with the frosting.

Sift the confectioners' sugar. In a heavy-based saucepan heat the butter, cocoa and ginger ale. Once the butter's melted, whisk in the confectioners' sugar. Lift the chocolate gingerbread out of the pan and unwrap the paper. Pour over the frosting just to cover the top and cut into fat slabs when set.

CHOCOLATE FRUIT CAKE

I had a long and wittering conversation with myself about whether to put this here or into the Christmas section, but decided that its subtle chocolatiness is what truly defines it. Besides, this is the perfect cut-and-come-again cake for any time of the year. It lasts for ages, but has the squidgy fabulousness of something so much less serviceable-sounding.

I know there are a lot of ingredients listed, but you don't have to do much more than bung them in a pan and stir, and even then only lightly. The hardest thing you have to do for this recipe is wrap the pan with brown paper. And I'm not being disingenuous: it is the sort of task that makes a klutz like me hyperventilate, but I find there is nearly always someone around who can deal with that part with magnificent ease.

Makes about 10 slices

note

I don't tend to ice this cake, unless I'm making it for Christmas (in which case see page 97) but if you do want a chocolate frosting, all you need to do is pour $^1/_2$ cup heavy cream in a saucepan, along with a tablespoonful of Tia Maria and 4oz semisweet chocolate chopped into small pieces. Warm everything up and when the chocolate's melted whisk, till thick, glossy and smooth (which takes about half a minute or less with my little hand whisk) and pour over the cake. Bear in mind, though, that this frosting will not last anywhere near as long as the cake, so make it only if you plan to eat the cake over no more than three days.

12oz/2$^1/_4$ cups prunes (1$^3/_4$ cups when chopped)
8oz/1$^1/_2$ cups raisins
4oz/1 cup currants
2oz piece candied orange peel ($^1/_3$ cup when chopped)
1$^1/_2$ sticks soft unsalted butter
$^3/_4$ cup plus 2 tablespoons dark brown sugar
$^3/_4$ cup honey
$^1/_2$ cup Tia Maria or other coffee liqueur

juice and zest of 2–3 oranges (1$^3/_4$ cups juice)
1 teaspoon pumpkin pie spice
$^1/_4$ cup unsweetened cocoa
3 eggs, beaten
1 cup all-purpose flour
$^3/_4$ cup ground almonds
$^1/_2$ teaspoon baking powder
$^1/_2$ teaspoon baking soda

Preheat the oven to 300°F. Line the sides and bottom of an 8 inch, 3$^1/_2$ inch deep, round springform cake pan with a double layer of wax paper or parchment paper. Before proceeding any further, read the following which explains how to do it if you need the encouragement. The paper should come up higher than the sides of the pan; think of a lining that's twice as deep as the pan. Cut out two circles of paper, and two very long rectangles that will fit along the sides of the pan coming up from it like a top hat. Before you put the rectangular cut-out paper in, fold one long side in of both pieces, as if turning up a hem of about $^3/_4$ inch, and then take some scissors and snip into this hem, at intervals of about $^3/_4$ inch – as if you were making a rough frill. Grease the pan, lay one circle on the bottom and get one of your long pieces, then fit with the frilly edge along the bottom, which you press down to sit flat on the circle to hold it in place. Press the paper well into the sides, and repeat with the second piece. Now place the second circle of paper on the bottom of the pan, but on top of the two pressed-down frilly edges, which will also help to hold the pieces around the edge in place. Finally, wrap the pan with brown parcel paper, again making it higher than the sides, and tie it in place with kitchen twine.

Put the fruit, butter, sugar, honey, Tia Maria, orange juice and zests, spice and cocoa into a large wide saucepan and bring to the boil gently, stirring as the butter melts. Simmer for 10 minutes, and then take off the heat and leave to stand for 30 minutes.

After the 30 minutes are up, it will have cooled a little (though you could leave it for longer if you wanted). Add the beaten eggs, flour, ground almonds, baking powder and baking soda, and stir with a wooden spoon or spatula, however you like, to combine.

Pour the fruit cake mixture into the prepared cake tin. Place in the oven and bake for $1^3/_4$–2 hours, by which time the top of the cake should be firm but will have a shiny and sticky look. If you insert a cake tester into the center of the cake it will still be a little gooey in the middle.

Put the cake on a cooling rack. It will hold its heat and take a while to cool, but once it has, unmold it from the pan and, if you don't want to eat it immediately (and like any fruit cake it has a very long life), wrap it in parchment paper and then in aluminum foil and place in a tin.

CHOCOLATE MALTESER CAKE

This is one of those cakes that you make pretending it's for the children. And of course, they love it but not, I suspect, quite as much as the grown-ups. The maltiness is not overpowering, but subtly present and the Maltesers (Malted Milk Balls) look beautiful, making their ramshackle crown.

FOR THE CAKE

$^3/_4$ cup light brown sugar

$^1/_2$ cup superfine sugar

3 eggs

$^3/_4$ cup milk

1 tablespoon butter

2 tablespoons Horlicks malted milk powder

$1^1/_4$ cups all-purpose flour

$^1/_4$ cup unsweetened cocoa, sifted

1 teaspoon baking powder

$^1/_2$ teaspoon baking soda

FOR THE FROSTING AND DECORATION

2 cups confectioners' sugar

1 teaspoon unsweetened cocoa

$^1/_3$ cup Horlicks malted milk powder

1 stick plus 1 tablespoon soft unsalted butter

2 tablespoons boiling water

2oz Malted Milk Balls

Makes 8–10 slices

note

Do use malt balls in place of the slightly smaller Maltesers, if you want.

See stockists for suppliers of Horlicks malted milk powder.

Take whatever you need out of the fridge so that all the ingredients can come to room temperature (though it's not so crucial here, since you're heating the milk and butter and whisking the eggs).

Preheat the oven to 325°F. Butter and line two 8 inch cake pans with parchment paper.

Whisk together the sugars and eggs while you measure out the other ingredients; I use a standing mixer here which explains why I can do both things at once. Heat the milk, butter and Horlicks powder in a saucepan until the butter melts, and it is hot but not boiling. When the sugars and eggs are light and frothy, beat in the hot Horlicks mixture and then fold in the flour, cocoa, baking powder and baking soda. Divide the cake batter evenly between the two pans and bake in the oven for 25 minutes, by which time the cakes should have risen and will spring back when pressed gently. Let them cool on a rack for about 5–10 minutes and then turn out of their pans.

Once the cakes are cold, you can get on with the frosting. I use a food processor just because it makes life easier: you don't need to sift the confectioners' sugar. So: put the confectioners' sugar, cocoa and Horlicks in the processor and blitz to remove all lumps. Add the butter and process again. Stop, scrape down, and start again, pouring the boiling water down the funnel with the motor running until you have a smooth buttercream.

Sandwich the cold cake layers with half of the buttercream, and then ice the top with what is left, creating a swirly top rather than a smooth surface. Stud the outside edge, about $^1/_2$ inch, with a ring of Malted Milk Balls or use them to decorate the top in whichever way pleases you.

TROPICAL CHOCOLATE CAKE

Well, if I had a malted cake, I had to have a chocolate-coconut cake, and this is – along with just about every other cake in the book – my son's favorite, for all that I use Malibu (coconut flavored rum) in the batter. If you're worried about using alcohol in a cake that might – but doesn't have to – be destined for children, then just use two spoonfuls of the (usually apple) juice the pineapple was canned in. It also makes it less expensive to make if you don't keep Malibu in the house; frankly, though, I am never without it. But if I were you, I certainly wouldn't dream of going out and buying it especially.

This is a wonderful cake: amusing but no joke; the velvety cake is dark, moist and gently fragranced. Go easy on the extract in the frosting, though, or it will be just too Hawaiian Tropic.

Makes 8–10 slices

note

If the idea of making the soft meringue frosting doesn't appeal, for whatever reason, then just lose the chocolate-coconut connection and ice instead with a sweet-sharp cream cheese frosting. Follow the recipe for the topping for the chocolate Guinness cake on page 286, but spritz in a little lime juice and consider adding a drop or two of Malibu into the mixture as well. One thing, though: don't do the sides, too. Just sandwich the cakes with it, and swirl in a sprightly manner over the top and then dust with some desiccated or shredded coconut.

FOR THE CAKE
8oz/4 rings canned pineapple in juice
$^1/_3$ cup cream cheese
$1^1/_2$ cups all-purpose flour
$^1/_2$ cup plus 2 tablespoons superfine sugar
$^1/_3$ cup light brown sugar

1 teaspoon baking powder
$^1/_2$ teaspoon baking soda
$1^3/_4$ sticks butter
$^1/_3$ cup unsweetened cocoa, sifted
2 eggs
2 tablespoons Malibu (or use the juice from the canned fruit)

FOR THE FROSTING
2 egg whites
$^1/_2$ cup superfine sugar
$^1/_2$ cup light corn syrup
$^1/_4$ teaspoon salt

$^1/_4$ teaspoon cream of tartar
2 teaspoons coconut extract
$^1/_2$ cup desiccated or shredded coconut

Take whatever you need out of the fridge so that all the ingredients can come to room temperature. Preheat the oven to 350°F, and butter and line two loose-bottomed, 8 inch layer tins.

Process the drained pineapple (reserving the juice just in case) and cream cheese until smooth and amalgamated. Add all the other ingredients, and process again to make a smooth batter. Spoon the batter evenly into the two cake pans, and cook for 20–25 minutes. Once they're done, they should be beginning to come away at the edges of the pans and spring back when gently pressed. Let them sit for 5 minutes in their pans on a wire rack, and then turn them out to cool. They will look disappointingly flat, but don't panic in the slightest: they will redeem themselves once they are iced.

Once they're cold, you can get on with the gleaming white coconut frosting. Arrange a bowl that fits over a saucepan of barely simmering water to use as a double boiler, and put the whites, sugar, syrup, salt and cream of tartar into the bowl. Whisk with a hand-held electric mixer over the simmering saucepan until the frosting goes thick, white and glossy and is stiff enough to form peaks. This will take about 5 or so minutes.

I have never attempted this by hand, but obviously it would be possible with a balloon whisk, but it might also be agonizing.

Take the bowl off the saucepan away from the heat and whisk in the coconut extract.

Sandwich the cakes with just over a third of the frosting, and then ice the top and sides in a swirly, snowy fashion. Immediately throw over the desiccated coconut to coat the sides and top of the cake.

I don't bother with the paper square, though you could (see the old-fashioned chocolate cake on page 270, for example): I just brush off any stray bits of desiccated coconut from the edges of the plate, or just leave them where they've fallen.

This cake looks wonderful in its uncut fluffy bouffant whiteness, but I like it best once you've sliced in, so that the chocolate layers gleam out darkly, striped and edged in brilliant white.

CHOCOLATE GUINNESS CAKE

This cake is magnificent in its damp blackness. I can't say that you can absolutely taste the stout in it, but there is certainly a resonant, ferrous tang which I happen to love. The best way of describing it is to say that it's like gingerbread without the spices. There is enough sugar – a certain understatement here – to counter any potential bitterness of the Guinness, and although I've eaten versions of this made up like a chocolate layer cake, stuffed and slathered in a rich chocolate frosting, I think that can take away from its dark majesty. Besides, I wanted to make a cream cheese frosting to echo the pale head that sits on top of a glass of stout. It's unconventional to add cream but it makes it frothier and lighter which I regard as aesthetically and gastronomically desirable. But it is perfectly acceptable to leave the cake un-iced: in fact, it tastes gorgeous plain.

Makes about 12 slices

FOR THE CAKE

1 cup Guinness

1 stick plus 2 tablespoons
  unsalted butter

$3/4$ cup unsweetened cocoa

2 cups superfine sugar

$3/4$ cup sour cream

2 eggs

1 tablespoon pure vanilla extract

2 cups all-purpose flour

$2^1/2$ teaspoons baking soda

FOR THE TOPPING

8oz Philadelphia cream cheese

$1^1/4$ cups confectioners' sugar

$1/2$ cup heavy cream

Preheat the oven to 350°F, and butter and line a 9 inch springform pan.

Pour the Guinness into a large wide saucepan, add the butter – in spoons or slices – and heat until the butter's melted, at which time you should whisk in the cocoa and sugar. Beat the sour cream with the eggs and vanilla and then pour into the brown, buttery, beery pan and finally whisk in the flour and baking soda.

Pour the cake batter into the greased and lined pan and bake for 45 minutes to an hour. Leave to cool completely in the pan on a cooling rack, as it is quite a damp cake.

When the cake's cold, sit it on a flat platter or cake stand and get on with the frosting. Lightly whip the cream cheese until smooth, sift over the confectioners' sugar and then beat them both together. Or do this in a processor, putting the unsifted confectioners' sugar in first and blitz to remove lumps before adding the cheese.

Add the cream and beat again until it makes a spreadable consistency. Ice the top of the black cake so that it resembles the frothy top of the famous pint.

DINNER-PARTY CAKES

I don't go in for actual dinner parties, a table set with a panoply of glasses and groaning with silverware and artfully folded napkins, so what I mean here is that these cakes that follow are best suited for serving as dessert. It's not that I can't force a slender slice down in the middle of the day as I sit slumped by a mug of tea, but I just tend to make these when I have a particular event or occasion in mind. Any leftovers are a mood-enhancing bonus.

ROCOCOA CAKE

Forgive the whimsy of its naming, but every time I've tried to rename this cake, I veer back to this. I used to refer to it as Venetian chocolate cake, because its inspiration comes from a cake of that name in Nick Malgieri's luscious chocolate book but as my cake changed from his specifications, the title seemed misleading. Anyway, it's ended up like this simply because Caz, the designer, art director and adviser on my books ever since *How to Eat*, remarked on its baroque appearance (see page 290) as we were photographing it; from baroque to rococo to "rococoa" was an obvious stagger.

Don't be put off by the length of the recipe that follows. Some of my recipes appear long even if the methods are simplicity itself, because I cannot help but cover every eventuality and share my every thought process with you, but it's certainly true that there is a lot of actual practical process here, too. Still, time-consuming though it may be, the cake is not hard to make, and even easier if you ignore the instructions for making the cake itself, and instead buy a couple of ready-made (but good-quality) chocolate loaf cakes. I often do that myself, and even though I prefer the airy lightness of the homemade version, several people who've eaten both prefer it made with the store-bought cake. So there you go.

The point of the cake lies anyway in its layering: first the chocolate sponge, which you drench with syrup, smother with a kind of rum-infused zabaglione and mascarpone cream, cover again with cake, syrup, cream and cake and then leave in the fridge to set, removing the next day to top with a glossy chocolate frosting, which – and this is my particular baroque moment – you can adorn with a variety of golden sprinkles or baubles and, for their intense verdant beauty, a scattering of chopped pistachios.

Makes 10–12 slices

FOR THE CAKE

$^1/_3$ cup all-purpose flour	4 eggs, separated
$^1/_3$ cup cornstarch	$^3/_4$ cup superfine sugar
$^1/_3$ cup unsweetened cocoa	pinch of salt

or replace the above with 2 bought chocolate loaf cakes, each weighing approx. 12oz

FOR THE RUM-ESPRESSO SYRUP

$^1/_2$ cup superfine sugar

$^1/_4$ cup water

$^1/_4$ cup dark rum

$^1/_2$ cup strong coffee (or $^1/_2$ cup hot water with 2 teaspoons instant espresso powder)

FOR THE CREAMY FILLING

3 egg yolks

$^1/_3$ cup superfine sugar

$^1/_3$ cup dark rum

8oz mascarpone cheese

1 cup heavy cream

FOR THE FROSTING

$^1/_2$ cup superfine sugar

$^1/_4$ cup dark corn syrup

$^1/_4$ cup dark rum

1 teaspoon instant espresso powder

5oz bittersweet chocolate, chopped very small

gold sprinkles, chopped pistachios, wafer roses, sugar flowers or any decoration that pleases you

If you're going to make your own cake, proceed as follows. Preheat the oven to 350°F. Butter and line the bottom of a 9 inch springform pan.

Sift together the flour and cornstarch, and add the cocoa, pushing it through a sieve. Whisk the separated yolks with half of the sugar – you can judge this by eye – until the mixture becomes pale and moussey.

In a separate bowl, whisk the egg whites with a pinch of salt until firm, then whisk in the remaining sugar, one spoonful at a time, until you have gleaming white peaks. Gently fold the yolk mixture into the whites, and then add the flour, cornstarch and cocoa, folding gently again until combined. Pour this moussey liquid into the pan and bake for 30 minutes. The cake will be almost silicon-springy on top. Remove the sides of the pan and let the cake cool on a rack, right side up.

Meanwhile, to make the syrup, bring the sugar and water to a boil in a small saucepan and let it bubble for a scant minute before taking the pan off the heat and adding the coffee or espresso powder made up with water, and the rum. Stir – just with a fork or anything – pour the hot syrup into a glass measuring cup or bowl and let it cool.

To make the filling, put the yolks, sugar and rum into a bowl that will fit over a saucepan of barely simmering water. Whisk (I use a hand-held electric mixer for this) until the mixture has thickened airily and then lift the bowl off the pan and let it sit on a cold surface while you whisk for another few minutes to help it cool down. Don't agitate yourself too much about whether it's thick enough or not: as long as it has thickened, the marscarpone and cream will give it the right texture to fill the cake with later.

Make sure your rum-zabaglione mixture is pretty well cool before whisking in

the mascarpone. Softly whip the cream in a separate bowl and beat or fold that into the filling as well.

To assemble the rococoa cake, cut the cake you made into thin vertical slices, that's to say as if you were slicing a round loaf of bread rather than a cake. If using the bought loaf cakes, cut into slices along the length of the cakes, as thinly as you can. Don't worry about breakages: you are, after all, able to wodge everything together with the syrup in the pan. So: brush a 9 inch springform pan with some of the syrup and then layer a third of the sliced chocolate cake, laid horizontally, to line the bottom of the pan. Brush again with the syrup to dampen the cake and seal the joins.

Spread the layer of chocolate cake with half of the zabaglione using a rubber spatula and a light hand to coat evenly, and then add another layer of cake slices to cover. Dribble again or brush with the syrup until the cake is damp as before, and then spread over the final half of the filling.

Cover with the final third of chocolate cake slices and drip, pour or brush over the syrup to give the cake a smoothish layer, which can be iced later; if the cake is damp, there's no call to drench it. And if the top of the cake is quite wet, don't be tempted to use all of the syrup; the bought chocolate cake is often damper and denser (and needs less syrup) than the homemade cocoa-sponge.

Put the cake, covered with plastic wrap, in the fridge overnight to set. You can ice the cake ahead of your dinner party and put the cake back in the fridge again (though see the caveat in the final paragraph below), but do let it set overnight first.

To make the frosting, put the sugar, syrup, rum and espresso powder into a small saucepan and bring to the boil. Turn off the heat and add the chopped chocolate, swirling it around so that the chocolate melts in the hot liquid. Leave for a few minutes and then whisk everything together in the pan (just using a little hand whisk) to make a smooth shiny glaze. Moving quickly, spring open your pan, taking care with the sides as the cake will be damp and delicate; you might want to run a small spatula around the inside first. Sit the cake on a plate or stand (don't even think of trying to loosen it from the pan's base) and pour over the frosting, not worrying if it dribbles down the sides too much. You may need to ease it over the top of the cake while it is still malleable. It will set quite quickly – the fridge will have made the layer it sits on very cold – and you will ruin the finish if you try and spread the frosting after your initial pouring.

Scatter with gold sprinkles, chopped pistachios, wafer roses, sugar flowers or any other decorations of your choice. The glaze will dull a little if you put it back in the fridge, so on the whole it's best to ice the cake and decorate it about 20 minutes before you want to eat it, or just before you sit down to dinner.

Opposite: rococoa cake

CHOCOLATE ESPRESSO CAKE WITH CAFFE LATTE CREAM

The rococoa cake makes rich use of the blend of coffee and chocolate, but this one really exults in it. It's the perfect way to end dinner, and if there's any left over, a deeply pleasurable way of getting your caffeine fix in the morning.

A tub of crème fraîche would be lovely enough with the strong espresso cake, but I like to make a caffe latte or blonde mocha cream. Don't be put off if you don't like white chocolate: you don't taste it here; it just counters the sharpness of the instant espresso powder in a slightly caramelly way, which in turn is softened by the cream.

Makes 10–12 slices

FOR THE CAKE

5oz bittersweet or semisweet
  chocolate, chopped
1 stick plus 3 tablespoons butter
6 eggs
1$^1/_4$ cups superfine sugar

1 teaspoon pure vanilla extract
$^1/_2$ cup all-purpose flour
5 teaspoons instant espresso powder
$^1/_4$ cup/4 tablespoons Tia Maria or
  other coffee liqueur

FOR THE CAFFE LATTE CREAM

3oz white chocolate, broken into
  small pieces
1$^1/_2$ cups heavy cream

scant 2 teaspoons instant espresso
  powder

Take anything you need out of the fridge to bring to room temperature. The only truly important thing, however, is that the eggs aren't cold, so if they are, just put them into a bowl (I use the KitchenAid bowl I'm going to whisk them in later) and cover with warm water for 10 minutes.

Preheat the oven to 350°F. Butter and line a 9 inch springform pan.

Melt the chocolate and butter in a microwave or double boiler and set aside to cool slightly. Beat the eggs, sugar and vanilla together until thick, pale and moussey. They should have at least doubled in volume, even tripled. If you're using a standing mixer, as I do, this is effortless.

Gently fold in the flour and espresso powder, taking care not to lose the air you have created, and finally add the melted chocolate and butter, folding gently again. Pour into the prepared pan and cook for 35–40 minutes, by which time the top of the cake should be firm, and the underneath still a bit gooey. Immediately pour over the Tia Maria and then let the cake cool completely on a rack before releasing it from the pan.

For the cream, melt the white chocolate either in a microwave or double boiler, and let it cool. Fold in the cream and espresso powder, whipping the latte cream together to thicken it a little. For some reason the white chocolate seems to make the cream instantly thicker; if I whisk the cream first it can seize a little when it's stirred into the chocolate.

Sit the sprung cake on a plate and fill the middle sunken crater with the caffe latte cream and dust with a little cocoa, or just put the buff-colored cream in a bowl, with a spoon, to serve alongside the cake, dusting or not with cocoa or, indeed, instant espresso powder or a mixture of both, as you wish.

CHOCOLATE MERINGUE TRUFFLE CAKE

This is a dinner-party stalwart from a couple of decades back, and I like it no less than I did when I first tasted it, made by my sister Thomasina, about twenty years ago. But I have added something: I make a thin meringue base instead of crumbling biscuits into the pan. This is not hard, not even remotely, and you don't have to worry about anything since you don't want airy puffy meringue, but rather a contrastingly crackling base, with just a hint of chewy marshmallow.

Makes 10–12 slices

note

If you don't want to bother with the meringue fandango, you could crumble some bought meringue in a bowl, sprinkle with cocoa, mix well and then press this into the base of the cake tin (much as you do with graham cracker crumbs when making a cheesecake). Pour the chocolate truffle mixture on top and refrigerate.

Obviously, if you can get hold of almond oil, its delicacy and non-intrusive sweetness would work well for oiling the springform pan.

FOR THE BASE

1 egg white
$^{1}/_{4}$ cup superfine sugar

2 teaspoons unsweetened cocoa
drop of wine vinegar

FOR THE TRUFFLE FILLING

14oz bittersweet or semisweet chocolate
$^{1}/_{4}$ cup rum

$^{1}/_{4}$ cup light corn syrup
2 cups heavy cream
cocoa to decorate

Preheat the oven to 350°F. Line an 8 inch springform pan with parchment paper and oil the sides with some flavorless oil.

Whisk the egg white until foamy peaks form and then whisk in the sugar a little at a time to make a thick, glossy mixture. Sieve over the cocoa and sprinkle with the vinegar, and whisk again to combine everything. Spread as evenly as you can over the bottom of the prepared cake pan and then put in the oven to bake for 15–20 minutes. Leave to cool while you make the truffle filling.

Melt the chocolate with the rum and syrup in a bowl over a pan of barely simmering water. Remove the bowl from the saucepan and let it sit off the heat for 5 minutes or so.

Whisk the cream until it thickens slightly – it should be slightly aerated and have the consistency of thick pouring custard, no thicker. Pour into the chocolate mixture, beating gently until everything is amalgamated.

Pour into the meringue-bottomed pan and cover the springform with plastic wrap, and put in the fridge for a night or day, or for up to two days.

A short time before you are ready to serve the cake, take it out of the fridge and let it lose its chill. It will be easier to spring open if the chocolate truffle filling has become less fridge cold, although you don't want soft room temperature chocolate.

Remove the sides of the pan and transfer the cake to a plate without removing the base unless you think you can with ease (and have one of those big round spatulas). Smooth the sides with a spatula if you want a smarter look, and push the cocoa through a sieve to dust the top of the cake.

CHOCOLATE CHESTNUT CAKE

This is not very different from an earlier chocolate chestnut cake of mine – only, I suppose, fancier, and that is mainly because of the pan I cook it in. I use a braided bread ring mold of 4 cup capacity, but anything similar would do. Or you can just cook it in a regular 9 inch springform pan.

FOR THE CAKE

8oz bittersweet chocolate, broken into small pieces
6 eggs, separated
pinch salt
1 stick plus 1 tablespoon soft unsalted butter

2 cups unsweetened chestnut purée
2 tablespoons rum
$^1/_3$ cup superfine sugar

FOR THE DECORATION

whipping cream
marrons glacés

gold buttons

Makes about 16 slices – small ones, but this is rich

note
If you've made this in a spring-form pan, lightly whisk some cream and fill the slight crater of the top, then stud with a few pieces of marron glacé and dust with a little cocoa pushed through a tea strainer or small sieve.

Preheat the oven to 350°F. I use a very non-stick mold, but if you're not confident of yours, butter it.

Melt the chocolate in a bowl in the microwave or suspended over a pan of gently simmering water and then set aside to cool slightly.

Whisk the egg whites with a pinch of salt until firm but not stiff. In another bowl, beat the butter and chestnut purée and when they're combined, beat in the rum and then fold in the melted chocolate followed by the sugar. Stir in a fat dollop of whites, beat everything together vigorously to mix and then gently fold in the rest of the whites in three goes. Pour into the pan and bake for 40–50 minutes; you can pierce with a cake tester to make sure it's cooked through, but expect some gunge to stick to the tester. Cool in the pan on a wire rack before turning out on to a big plate.

I went into decorative overdrive, as you can see from the picture, and piped cream, studded it with gold buttons and dotted marrons glacés here and there. I think both cream and marrons glacés are needed, but the gold studs may be a touch too far.

CHOCOLATE CHEESECAKE

I was slightly anxious about including a cheesecake in this section as I'm not sure cheesecake counts as cake, but then a friend pointed out that I was unlikely to be taken to some International Court of Cakes. In any event, it would be such a pity to leave it out. In fact, I couldn't.

In the past, I've been apologetic about adulterating your basic cheesecake, but I've moved on. This is exceptional: exactly the right balance between satiny sweetness and smooth tang. Regard the glaze as optional: it makes it into more of a dinner party thang, but there is no call to get busy if you'd rather not. A few raspberries alongside would be heavenly, but again, no need to bother adding a single thing.

Makes 10–12 slices

FOR THE BASE
1 1/3 cups graham cracker crumbs   1 tablespoon unsweetened cocoa
1/2 stick butter

FOR THE FILLING
6oz bittersweet or semisweet   3 large eggs
   chocolate, chopped small   3 large egg yolks
2 1/2 cups Philadelphia cream   2/3 cup sour cream
   cheese   1/2 teaspoon unsweetened cocoa,
3/4 cup superfine sugar   dissolved in 1 tablespoon hot
1 tablespoon Bird's custard powder   water

FOR THE GLAZE (OPTIONAL)
3oz semisweet chocolate, finely   1/2 cup heavy cream
   chopped   1 teaspoon dark corn syrup

To make the base, process the graham crackers to make rough crumbs and then add the butter and cocoa. Process again until it makes damp, clumping crumbs and then tip them into a 9 inch springform pan. Press the crumbs into the bottom of the pan to make an even base and put into the freezer while you make the filling.

Preheat the oven to 350°F. Put a kettle on to boil. Melt the chocolate either in a microwave or double boiler, and set aside to cool slightly.

Beat the cream cheese to soften it, and then add the sugar and custard powder, beating again to combine. Beat in the whole eggs and then the yolks, and the sour cream. Finally add the cocoa dissolved in hot water and the melted chocolate, and mix to a smooth batter. Take the springform pan out of the freezer and line the outside of the pan with a good layer of plastic wrap, and then another layer of strong aluminum foil over that. This will protect it from the water bath. Sit the springform pan in a roasting pan and pour in the cheesecake filling. Fill the roasting pan with just-boiled water to come about halfway up the cake pan, and bake in the oven for 45 minutes to an hour. The top of the cheesecake should be set, but the underneath should still have a wobble to it.

Peel away the foil and plastic wrap and sit the cheesecake in its pan on a rack to cool. Put in the fridge once it's no longer hot, and leave to set, covered with plastic wrap, overnight. Let it lose its chill before unspringing the cheesecake to serve.

To make the chocolate glaze, very gently melt the chopped chocolate, cream and syrup. When the chocolate has nearly melted, take off the heat and whisk it to a smooth sauce. Let it cool a little, and then Jackson Pollock it over the chocolate cheesecake on its serving plate. Use the remaining glaze as an accompanying sauce.

A GEORGIAN FEAST

A FEW YEARS back, I was in St. Petersburg, Russia, waiting to discover the new, glorious, post-glasnost Russian cooking. Waiting and waiting, as it turned out, and walking an awfully long way down vast streets – the sort whose scope and architecture make one aware, in our puny mortality, and as only a post-Feudal, post-Soviet city can, of how immaterial we are in the grand scheme of things – to find yet another restaurant that served pancakes with floury chicken stuffing.

And so I asked a taxi driver. I don't know how I asked him, since I speak three words of Russian and he knew no English, but the language of food must be universal. He drove me to a Georgian restaurant – don't ask me what it's called or where it is – where I had one of the most wonderful dinners of my life up till then. That many hours of my life since have been spent pursuing the memory of that dinner, trying to rootle out the recipes and recreate those tastes, is, I do see, as much to do with a certain general obsessiveness on my part as with the specific transcendental miracle of the feast itself.

I don't say that in any ashamed or apologetic sense: I believe absolutely that the only way to live life is to throw yourself right at it; the price of excessive ardour may well be frequent disappointment, but that is surely better than feeling detached and disengaged, which must be the underlying, haunted state of the cautious and measured.

But it's a strange thing, a happy event to be so moved by the food of a people one knows so little about, of a country indeed never visited. All I know of the nation of Georgia is a large, dark room, split on two wood-floored levels, somewhere outside St. Petersburg. On the upper level were two tablefuls of what looked like gangsters straight out of central casting: businessmen, you understand, with three great hulks, each packing a piece, to watch their backs, and at the tables, the statutory posse of red Lycra'd Natashas, beautiful and fake.

We sat below, in a room decorated with those coppery brass and pewter knick-knacks – a few pots, maybe a blade or two – that restaurants in pretty well every European or Europeanish country seem to hang from the wall. The only thing I remember well was the table, a long skinny wood one, covered with plates of radishes and cucumbers and spring onions and trays of peppery herbs. I don't know if we ordered or if the food just came, but there it was, the sort of meal that you dream of every time you go on holiday.

Trays of scythe-slices of coral-orange melon were brought to the table, with them small bowls of chilli chopped with dill and cilantro, the chilled honeyed sweetness of the fruit soothing against the tongue-fuzzing heat of the relish. Then came two vast cheesebreads, that's to say something between a covered pizza and a huge disc of pita bread bulging saltily with melting white cheese. In fact, I'm not sure there was ever quite a marked "then," that's to say, there wasn't a stately procession of courses, but rather a dreamily chaotic hither and thither of dishes. Chickens were stuffed with nuts, rice and sweet-sour fruit; meat was pierced on long skewers and grilled; huge platters of vegetables kept coming, doused in yogurt and feathered with herbs, rolled and stuffed with cheese and nuts, puréed with garlic and what tasted like scented vinegar; the feast, what Georgians call the *supra*, would still be carrying on if we hadn't bowed out plaintively with bowls of nuts and fruit and dishes of dark, smoky honey.

A GEORGIAN FEAST FOR EIGHT

I can't pretend that this is an authentic Georgian Feast; certainly I'd cringe at the thought of presenting it as such to someone who came from Georgia. But it is a genuine attempt to recreate those Georgian tastes, that food which hovers somewhere between Middle Eastern and Mediterranean with touches of the Mughal-Indian empire.

MELON WITH HOT PEPPER RELISH

Overcome any prejudices you might have about eating sweet, juicy melon with garlicky, chilli-hot relish: it's an extraordinarily good way of waking up your tastebuds at the beginning of this feast. The melon slices must be cold, against the fiery dollop of relish, so leave the melons in the fridge until the last moment. Which melons you use depends on which are good in the markets when you are making this. I used charentais, those extraordinarily scented coral-fleshed globes, but cantaloupe would be fine, too. I've specified two melons, just because it isn't in the nature of this feast to hold back.

And you are going to end up with much more relish than you need, but I don't like to start faffing around with half a stick of celery and half a red pepper. Besides, it's good to keep a jar in the fridge to eat with grilled – or even cold – meats and to use as a quick, spiky sauce on pasta when I don't feel like proper cooking. The *adzhika*, to call the salsa-like relish by its Georgian name, needs to be made in advance, so that the flavors deepen and fuse into one another, but there's something rather wonderful about the slow process of building a feast that makes me like this rather than resent it.

As with many recipes in this chapter, what follows is enormously indebted to Darra Goldstein's *The Georgian Feast*: a rich source and surely the only cookbook with a puff-quote from Eduard Shevardnadze.

Makes about 2 cups

2 melons

FOR THE *ADZHIKA* **OR GEORGIAN SALSA**

8 cloves garlic, peeled
1 stick of celery, roughly chopped
4oz long red chillies, including
    seeds
1 red pepper, seeded

2 cups fresh dill
1¹/₂ cups fresh cilantro leaves
¹/₃ good-quality red wine vinegar
¹/₄ teaspoon salt

Put the peeled garlic into a food processor and pulse until chopped. Then add the celery, chillies and red pepper and process again until everything is coarsely minced, or chop them all and the herbs as finely as you can by hand.

Tip the dill, cilantro, red wine vinegar and salt, into the processor or a blender and pulse again before turning out the contents of the processor into a bowl.

Cover with plastic wrap and let the relish stand overnight. Decant into jars and keep in the fridge; it will mellow and taste better if left for about three days before eating.

When you want to eat, take the melons out of the fridge and cut them in half, spoon out any seeds, then cut each half into thin, curved slices. Cut away the skin and arrange this flotilla of slender melon-fleshed boats on a large plate or pair of smaller plates and send them to the table with a bowl or two of hot, leafy *adzhika*.

Opposite: melon – lazily unpeeled – with Georgian salsa or *adzhika*

NANA'S *HACHAPURI*

This cheesebread is the recipe that has really fixated me for the past few years. There's not a version I haven't cooked, and I think I must have bothered just about anyone who's come from or been to Georgia to try and help me with my mission.

It is the hardest thing to try and replicate a taste from memory, especially when few of the right ingredients are available back home. After all, I doubted I'd find on sale in London the soft, sour, sharp *imeruli* cheese I'd eaten oozing out of warm, almost puff-pastryish bread in my mysterious St. Petersburg restaurant – and I turned out to be right. Different sources gave varying substitutes: a mixture of Munster and cottage cheese, or feta and mozzarella were those most likely to make it off the bench. But chiefly the difficulty was in trying to make sure the *hachapuri* – or *khachapur* depending on which transliteration conventions you want to follow – I'd eaten, corresponded to the *hachapuri* other people had. It became evident that, as with all deeply traditional recipes, everyone had their own version of this cheesebread. And authentic as the recipes I was sent were, they weren't a true representation of the cheesebread I'd encountered. I won't make you live through my every cheesebread move, every hopeful kneading, every little setback and disappointment, but I certainly have many people to be grateful to, not least Bill Keller, the editor of the *New York Times*, who in turn put me on to Regina Maksutova, a Russian writer, translator and chef based in New York. And finally the real thanks go to Nana Eristavi whose *hachapuri* of divine memory I stumbled upon in an old pub turned into the Little Georgia Café –restaurant in Hackney in east London, and to Tiko Tuskadze who let me, a photographer and a small posse descend upon the place to see how the cheesebreads were made.

I had been near to giving up when I drove past the Little Georgia one Saturday lunchtime. I went in, ordered a cheesebread, and had a truly Proustian moment. Later on, when I called and explained my mission, asking for the recipe, I was told that Nana couldn't give me the recipe as she didn't follow one, but she could show me how she made the bread. That was it, really. If I hadn't been convinced already, this was enough to make me swear allegiance to her version, forsaking all the other nearly-rans, even recipes I'd have been happy to share. This is what I wanted: a cheesebread cooked by someone called Nana, who cooked from memory and the heart and not from a recipe book.

You can see she didn't disappoint. Everything I hoped she'd be, she was, and the same is true of her cheesebread recipe. I watched, played in my own kitchen and this is a formalized account of that, with weights and measures recorded as is only conventional in a cookery book.

My version of Nana's *hachapuri* is easier – I make one huge cheesebread rather than forming lots of little ones. In a restaurant it makes sense to make individual round breads, one per order; with friends, at home, the point is to break bread with people, which is exactly what you can do here.

Serves at least 8

FOR THE DOUGH

4¹/₂ cups all-purpose flour

2 cups plain yogurt

2 eggs

¹/₂ stick butter, softened

1 teaspoon salt

2 teaspoons of baking soda

FOR THE FILLING

1 cup ricotta cheese

3 cups feta cheese

2 balls (7oz) mozzarella

1 egg

note

Nana's method was to flour small 3 inch round pans and then tear off doughnut-sized pieces of dough working them into a rough circle. A generous spoonful of filling was placed in the middle and the sides of the dough were stretched up around it. The top was then twisted to form a knot and the excess dough torn off. (Such sleight-of-hand, she had; this was something in her blood and when I try it's much less flowing and efficient.) Nana then flattened out the sealed bread back into a smooth circle to fill the pans. Cook in a very hot oven as before, but only for about 10 minutes, and cut each pie into four as soon as it comes out of the oven.

Preheat the oven to 425°F, and put in a baking sheet to heat up.

Measure out the flour into a bowl. In a separate larger bowl tip the yogurt and break in the eggs. Using your hands or a fork, mulch the butter into the yogurt and eggs, and then add scoopfuls of flour, working it in to make a dough. You may not need all of the flour, but keep working the mixture with your hands until it comes away from the sides of the bowl to make a silky textured dough. This is gloriously satisfying. There's something so uncomplicated about this recipe in the first place that makes it gratifying, but I love all the handwork. I dare say you could put the flour in a mixer and add yogurt and so forth, kneading with a dough hook, but what a loss that would be.

Sprinkle in the salt and baking soda, a little at a time, working it in with your hands again. Tip the dough into a floured Tupperware container and cover with the lid. It will need to rest for about 20 minutes, but you can leave it in the fridge for up to three days. Or that's what Nana does.

To make the filling, crumble together the ricotta and feta, and drain and chop or grate the mozzarella, adding to the other cheeses. Add the egg and beat the cheese filling together.

Take your dough out of the Tupperware container and cut it in half. Roll one half of the dough on a generously floured surface into a circle to fit a 4 inch pizza pan. Spread over the cheese filling and leave a small border around the edge to help you seal it later. Roll out the other half of the dough in the same way to make another circle, and fit it over the top. Fold in the edges to seal the outside of the bread, curling them inwards to leave a roll of dough. Press the rolled outer edge with the prongs of a fork all the way around to seal it firmly, and then place it on the heated baking sheet in the oven.

You can decorate the cheesebread before you cook it with any scraps of dough, and since I'd been told by Regina Maksutova that grapes were traditional (Nana, eschewed any decorative touch though she conceded she might do a much more festive looking large round loaf if she were cooking for a party at home), I used a large icing nozzle to make some, arranging the small round cut-outs to form a bunch in the middle of the bread, fashioning a stalk out of a funny-shaped bit of dough left behind after cutting out the grapes.

Cook the cheesebread for 15–20 minutes; it should be golden brown, but still slightly doughy. Cut it into wedges while it is still hot.

There's a lot for eight but there's something about this bulging golden disc, oozing white cheese as it's cut, that turns a meal into a feast. And to bring in a prosaic note, any cold leftovers can be sliced the next day, shoved into the microwave and briefly nuked for a quick but perfect supper.

THE HERB PLATE

Along with the cheesebread put out a plate covered with some of the following:

scallions	**1 or 2 cucumbers, unpeeled, cut**
radishes	**into fat batons or sticks**
purslane, if you can find it,	**1 or 2 fat bunches flat-leaf parsley**
otherwise some peppery arugula	

Let people tear off some parsley as they want, and just tumble some arugula or radishes, the lot, on to their own plates, as they eat. The cold, crunchy raw vegetables and herbs are perfect with the palate-burning, out-of-the-oven heat of the melting cheesebread.

GEORGIAN STUFFED CHICKEN

I am never so innocently happy as when making roast chicken. This is a more work-intensive take on it, but the supreme dish for a feast: the bronze-breasted, crisp-skinned birds come to the table bursting with their sour-sweet rice stuffing. As I've said about turkey, in a very primitive way, the stuffing is meant to remind us of the fullness of life, which is what a feast essentially celebrates.

The rice stuffing takes on a deep savory meatiness as it absorbs more flavor than you ever thought a chicken could have, but the only problem is you don't get much more than a spoonful or two per person like this. You do lose some flavor, but it's worth cooking a batch of the rice mixture in a saucepan, too, in which case use chicken stock (mine is, as ever, concentrated-instant not freshly made, though fresh organic stock from a supermarket package would be a wonderful alternative) rather than water as you need to oomph up flavor. And when the rice in the pan is cooked, fork in a little butter as you add the parsley, sprinkling with more parsley and a few toasted pinenuts in the serving dish.

Please don't feel this Georgian stuffed chicken must be cooked only as a part of the full-on feast. I don't deny it's particularly good with the beets and beans on pages 313 and 315, neither of which could remotely be called quick everyday recipes, but without the cheesebread and melon beforehand, this makes a fabulous weekend lunch that wouldn't be ludicrously exhausting to make. Especially since the beets can be wrapped in foil and roasted the night before as you veg out in front of the TV, leaving you with a not too labor-intensive morning ahead and a lunch that's really worth inviting people to.

As part of a feast, though, no part of this meal requires defense or apology for the work involved. A feast demands concentrated effort and there is no point embarking on one unless you make a policy decision to enjoy the bustling preparations. This may not be possible very often, but when it is, try and go with it. If you choose to cook, it can, in the right frame of mind, feel like a devotional activity, a way to celebrate being alive; if you're forced into it, then it's drudgery.

Serves 8

note

Once the hot rice is spooned into the cold chickens they must go into the preheated oven IMMEDIATELY. But if you want, cook the rice in advance and either stuff the chickens immediately before cooking or, if both rice and chickens are cold, they can be left in the fridge for a bit before roasting. If they are fridge-cold, though, they will definitely need longer cooking, so add on another quarter of an hour before testing.

2 5lb chickens

FOR THE STUFFING
4 tablespoons butter (plus fat from inside the chicken cavity)
2 onions
2 cloves garlic
1 cup basmati rice

2 tablespoons soft butter

$^1/_2$ cup dried sour cherries, roughly chopped
2 cups water
$^1/_4$ cup chopped parsley

For the stuffing, melt butter along with any gobbets of fat from the chicken's cavity in a wide saucepan (one that has a lid). Process or finely chop the onion and garlic, and add to the pan with the butter, frying over a medium heat until the onion softens and begins to color.

Discard bits of the rendered chicken, add the rice and chopped cherries, and give everything a good stir so that the rice becomes slicked with the fat. Add the water and a sprinkling of salt and bring to the boil, then clamp on the lid and cook at the lowest heat possible for 15 minutes. While the rice is cooking, preheat your oven to 425°F. When the rice is ready, by which I mean all the water will be absorbed and the rice be more or less cooked, fork through the chopped parsley and season with salt and pepper.

Spoon the cherry-studded rice into the cavities of both chickens, and secure the openings with two or three cocktail sticks. The easiest way to do this is to pinch together the flaps of skin from each side of the cavity and make a stitch to hold them with a cocktail stick.

Rub the secured chickens with the butter and roast in the oven for $1^1/_2$–2 hours. The skin should be golden and crispy and the meat cooked through; test by piercing the bird between thigh and body and if juices run clear, the chicken's ready. The reason why the chickens take longer than you would normally give them is twofold: in the first instance, the rice stuffing impedes the flow of hot air; in the second, having two birds in the oven tends to make each take longer to brown.

Pull out the cocktail sticks and let the chickens rest before carving.

BEET PURÉE

The idea of beet purée, let alone a cold beet purée, may not be a particularly appealing one, but I love this and I'm someone who flinched at those flabby, putrid and jelly-fleshed beets at school. Many things redeem this beet purée: in the first instance, it is roasted – in aluminum foil – in a hot oven which gives it a wonderful rounded nuttiness; that nuttiness is enhanced by the fact that the beets, once cooled, are puréed with walnuts; herbs, garlic and some good red wine vinegar add zing.

You don't get an awful lot of puréed beets here, but it's quite intense in flavor and you wouldn't want to wolf down ladlesful. Besides, veg though it is, it's better thought of as a kind of relish, cold and strongly flavored.

1lb raw beets	$^1/_2$ cup fresh cilantro leaves	Serves 8
2–3 cloves garlic, peeled	$^1/_2$ cup flat-leaf parsley leaves	
$^1/_2$ cup shelled walnuts	$^1/_2$ teaspoon ground coriander	**note**
$^1/_2$ teaspoon salt	3 teaspoons red wine vinegar	I think it's crucial to use good red wine vinegar, but failing that use a not particularly special balsamic vinegar.

Preheat the oven to 425°F and wrap the beets in foil, making baggy parcels (so air can circulate) with tightly sealed edges (so steam builds up). Roast the beets like this for about 2 hours, though beets' cooking time – even before you take in size differential – can vary enormously, so unwrap one and pierce with a knife to see how cooked it is after an hour. But anyway you're best off cooking the beets in advance, so you've got plenty of time for it to cool before processing.

Put the garlic cloves into a food processor and blitz until finely minced; then add the walnuts, salt and pepper before processing again. Or chop everything finely by hand and squodge down with a masher.

Peel and roughly chop (wearing rubber gloves if you don't want your hands too spookily incarnadined) the cooled beets, adding the ruby pieces to the food processor along with the herbs and ground coriander and continue processing until you have a fine paste. Add the red wine vinegar and pulse again before tasting the purée; it may need more vinegar if the beets are very sweet.

Transfer the beet purée to a bowl and cover with plastic wrap before putting it to one side to steep and mellow for at least 2 hours.

GREEN BEANS IN HERBED YOGURT

This is one of those recipes you feel must be more trouble than it's worth – until you cook it. Obviously, there's nothing wrong with plain beans: cooked and drained and dripping with peppery butter, they are unquestionably wonderful; but these here are a different proposition entirely. It's taking an everyday ingredient beyond the usual that makes this dinner a feast.

2lbs slender green beans
2 onions
$^1/_2$ teaspoon ground cinnamon
pinch ground cloves
pepper
1 stick butter
$^1/_4$ cup cold water

1 cup Greek plain yogurt
$^1/_2$ teaspoon salt
1 small clove garlic
2 tablespoons each chopped
    cilantro, flat-leaf parsley and dill
1 tablespoon chopped mint

Serves 8

note
You can use regular plain yogurt here; it will just make a slightly runnier, less creamy sauce.

Top and tail the beans, and cut them in half or thirds depending on size. Par-boil them for about 5 minutes until still crisp and vibrantly green, then drain and run under cold water.

Peel and halve the onions, and put them into a food processor with the cinnamon, ground cloves and some pepper. Process until they are finely minced but not mushy. Or chop as finely as you can by hand, and add the spices in the pan.

Melt the butter in a large frying pan and cook the spiced onions in the pan until soft. Add the beans, cover the pan with a lid, and cook gently for about 10–15 minutes.

Pour the cold water into the yogurt in a wide necked glass measuring cup, add the salt, mince in the garlic and beat to mix.

When the beans and onions are soft, stir in all the chopped fresh herbs except the mint. Take the pan off the heat and turn the beans on to a large flattish plate. Pour over the garlicky yogurt and sprinkle over the tablespoonful of chopped mint.

Opposite: left, beet purée; right, green beans in herbed yogurt

WALNUT CRESCENTS

This recipe isn't at all Georgian, but since they use walnuts a lot in cooking in Georgia I thought I'd borrow from the local cupboard, as it were, to make a light, melting cookie to dip into some Greek yogurt (or ice cream if you want to go entirely but still pleasurably out of register) drizzled with honey. Otherwise, just make the cookies to eat with coffee, making sure the table is loaded down with luscious red grapes before you end the meal. Or, if you'd rather lighten your load, dispense with the walnut crescents and replace with some walnuts, to be cracked and eaten with the grapes.

Makes 24

note

As you will see, more so in the picture on page 303, they are not quite crescents, more like kinked semi-circles. This is because they were cooked here in an end-of-the-day oven, the heat of which (plus the fact that they hadn't been chilled before being formed) made them spread. But they taste just as good, so what's the point in worrying? That's life.

1 $^1/_2$ cups shelled walnuts
$^1/_4$ cup confectioners' sugar, plus more to decorate
1 stick plus 1 tablespoon soft butter

$^3/_4$ cup all-purpose flour
pinch salt

Preheat the oven to 325°F.

Toast the walnuts in a dry frying pan for a few minutes until they give off a nutty aroma. Pour into the bowl of a food processor and blitz until pulverized.

Take the nuts out for the moment, and add the sugar and blitz to remove any lumps. Now add the soft butter and process again, then add the flour and salt and process yet again. Open the lid of the processor, scrape down the sides, then add the nuts and pulse to mix, then tip out. The dough will be sticky but firm enough to mold with your hands; if it is too mushy put it, wrapped in plastic or in a plastic freezer bag, in the fridge for about 20 minutes.

To make the half moons, flour your hands and take scant tablespoons of the dough. Roll them into sausages about 2$^1/_2$ inches long, and then slightly flatten the sausage as you curl it round to form a crescent. Put them on to a parchment paper lined baking sheet and cook for about 25 minutes although start checking after 15 minutes, they will still be quite soft but the tops will be firm and beginning to go blondly brown. Let them sit on the baking sheet for a few minutes before you transfer them to a cooling rack. Be careful, as they will be very fragile.

Dredge them very thickly with confectioners' sugar pushed through a small sieve and leave to cool.

EID

THERE IS an organization in Chicago, whose advisory board I am lucky enough to sit on, called Common Threads. Broadly speaking, its raison d'être is to bring children and young people (though just using that term makes me feel so very old) together through food. People from different backgrounds and different cultures can often find, if not a link, then a point of interest, through the way they eat, how they eat, what they eat. Of course, no one can deny that food strictures and traditions are part of the way that we mark ourselves out, as a community, a family, a culture, but the fact that we all do this, unites us too.

At Common Threads, students can, for example, find a program on breadmaking that covers classic Southern cornbread, golden challah, naan, corn tortillas, Bahian kisses, Greek Easter spiral, Swedish rye and Ukrainian Christmas bread, learning about their respective cultures simply by baking.

The whole premise of Common Threads resonates with the implicit aims of *Feast*. I never think food is just food, although I love to eat. Nor am I an anthropologist who looks at food as the way "in" to a people, but it's a language I want to speak. And you know what a chatterbox I am.

I say this here, as the preface to a Muslim feast, since I am not a Muslim but am interested in the food, what it means, and of course, what it tastes like – above all what it tastes like. When I'm planning a holiday, I never read travel books, but instead investigate the cookery books of the region I want to go to. That's my approach to social and cultural history, too.

The festival of Eid is, like Easter, the feast that breaks a fast, in this case the fast of Ramadan. Indeed, literally Id-al Fitr, or Eid-ul-Fitr, means "the feast of fast-breaking." It is the moment of joyfulness at the end of a period of abstinence. As always, in order to celebrate the pleasure of being alive, you need food: the very symbol of life, and what sustains it.

Ramadan is the holy month that celebrates the revelation of the Qur'an by Allah to the Prophet Mohammed. And just as Mohammed fasted and prayed in the desert for 30 days, so his followers fast and pray. Thus it is also a purifying time, and the feast that follows is in some sense a rebirth. New clothes are worn, and people, friends and family come together again, giving thanks in the best way, united around a table full of food. And in common with other cultures, the food is often sweet – in Turkey, Eid is known as Sheker Bayram, meaning "sugar festival" – to denote the sweetness of life. It's a symbol of hopefulness and, consequently, faith. After a month of scarcity, there is abundance, the plentifulness that should mark any feast.

There are, I'm sure, as many versions of the great feast as there are families who celebrate it. These recipes, or the slant of them, were suggested to me by a British woman of Bangladeshi descent, Shahnaz Iqbal, and I want to thank her for her patience and generosity. Of course there are books, and there are websites, but in the end, I need to hear what someone cooks, and eats, in their own home. I wanted, though, only the frankest and baldest directive. The way her family celebrated Eid, she said, wasn't so much with traditionally specific dishes, but with food chosen for its luxurious richness: mild creamy curries, studded with nuts and dried fruit to indicate fullness and sweetness. As with other, culturally unrelated, feasts, this is a recurrent feature here and a necessary pattern in the history of how people use foodstuffs to convey meaning.

There were only three dishes – all of them desserts – that, she said, she'd be surprised to see missing from the Eid table; naturally I have included them. The curry banquet that precedes them is based on some of her suggestions and some of my own findings. I can't, of course, claim this as a rite of observance in my home, but I cook this feast often, to make what I think is one of the most welcoming, gorgeous dinners for a roomful of people you love.

A CURRY BANQUET

MUGHLAI CHICKEN
PHEASANT WITH GREEN CHILLIES
LAMB MAHARAJA
PILAF FOR A CURRY BANQUET
MUTTAR PANEER
ALOO GOBI
SWEET-SCENTED VERMICELLI
SWEET SAFFRON RICE
CARROT AND COCONUT HALWA

THE CURRIES

MUGHLAI CHICKEN

I've decided on a hybrid system of nomenclature as you can see. I did think of being purist and giving this sweet, mellow curry its proper name of Murgh Mughlai, but I wanted the kind of curry it was to be immediately apparent to readers, skimming through deciding what to cook. "Mogul Chicken" seemed to lack exoticism and romance, so I took the usual crass Colonial route, taking over what I wanted and discarding the rest.

Besides, what's in a name? The curry's the thing. This one in particular: for, much as I love all three curries here, I make this one the most often. Though I usually go for the most fiery and shockingly fierce of curries, there is an elegance and depth of flavor in this pale, mild, creamy braise that bowls me over every time.

I feel very strongly that you should use the moister brown meat, from the thigh, for this, but if you prefer breast meat, and it's a common preference, that's your choice. I can't pretend to understand it though.

There is a long list of ingredients below – and for all of these recipes – and I am not going to pretend this is the sort of food you can bang out in a moment. As with other examples of exuberant and traditional festive eating throughout the book, it has its roots in a culture in which, by tradition, women have gathered together for days, stuffing and rolling and grinding and stirring, to usher forth dishes; so, the cooking, the preparation, was part of the ritual. Some people might want to reject the food for the domestic imprisonment it engendered, but I am not one of those. I don't see where it gets you. I cook this gladly, and out of choice; obligation, I do see, would not make it a pleasure.

One ease-making factor to be borne in mind with all three curries: not only can they be made in advance, they *need* to be; only if you let them steep in their pan, overnight in the fridge, do they have the full depth and resonance of flavor.

Serves 8–10 as part of this feast

note
Should you have difficulties finding any spices for this chapter, turn to page 461 for mail order Stockists.

1 inch fresh ginger, peeled
4 cloves garlic, peeled
2 teaspoons ground cumin
1 teaspoon ground coriander
$1/2$ teaspoon dried chilli
4 tablespoons ground almonds
$1/2$ cup water
5 cardamom pods, bruised
1 cinnamon stick, broken in half
2 bay leaves
4 cloves
$1/4$ cup vegetable oil

3lbs boned, skinned chicken thighs, each cut in 2
2 onions
1 cup Greek yogurt
1 cup chicken stock
$1/2$ cup heavy cream
$1/2$ cup sultanas (golden raisins)
1 teaspoon garam masala
1 tablespoon superfine sugar
1 teaspoon salt
$3/4$ cup slivered almonds, toasted

Put the ginger, garlic, cumin, coriander and chilli into a food processor, and blend to a paste. Add the ground almonds and water, then blend again, and set aside. Traditionally, this would be done with a mortar and pestle, and there's nothing to stop you using those, or a little spice grinder.

Put the cardamom pods, cinnamon stick, bay leaves and cloves into a small bowl. (Obviously, you don't have to do this, but it saves flitting from cupboard to cupboard looking for the right spices while the oil's spluttering away later.)

Heat the oil in a large pan and add the chicken pieces – in batches so they fry rather than stew – and cook them just long enough to seal on both sides, then remove to a dish.

Tip in the bowlful of spices and turn them in the oil. Peel and finely chop the onions, add to the pan of spices, and cook until softened and lightly browned, but keep the heat gentle and stir frequently, to avoid them catching. Pour in the blended paste, and cook everything until it begins to color. Add the yogurt, $^1/_2$ at a time, stirring it in to make a sauce; then stir in the stock, cream and sultanas.

Put the browned chicken back into the pan, along with any juices that have collected under them, and sprinkle over the garam masala, sugar and salt. Cover and cook on a gentle heat for 20 minutes, testing to make sure the chicken meat is cooked through.

It's at this stage, that I like to take the pan off the heat and leave it to cool before refrigerating and then reheating the next day.

So, either now, or when you've reheated it, pour into a serving dish and scatter with the toasted slivered almonds.

note

Many recipes I came across indicated evaporated milk rather than cream, which makes sense if you're cooking in a hot climate. You could keep this in mind should you open a carton of cream and find it spoiled, but in that case don't bother with the spoonful of sugar.

I love the paleness of sultanas, their mellowness and how they merge into the curry later, but the usual brown raisins are just fine.

To toast nuts, simply shake them about in a hot dry pan until scorched in parts.

PHEASANT WITH GREEN CHILLIES

I had the most wonderful Indian meal a few months back at a small restaurant in London's Chelsea, called the Painted Heron, and this, or a smarter version of it, was the recipe I came back desperate to have; I'm incredibly grateful to Yogesh Datta for e-mailing it to me with such speed on my request, and for giving me a free hand with it. I find pheasant difficult to get excited about – except when I watch *Some Like It Hot*, when Marilyn is offered "cold pheasant and champagne" on the boat – that I couldn't believe it could be transformed like this. I've since come across another pheasant curry in a book I bought out of love for its title – *Kill It & Grill It* by Ted and Shemane Nugent – which convinces me this is definitely the way to go.

When I can't get pheasant, as for example when I wanted to make this to be photographed, I go for guinea fowl, which works just as well; in fact, I couldn't swear I don't prefer it. I know four breasts doesn't sound much, but there is a lot of other food around, and the flavor is intense. However, if I were making a simpler dinner for, say, just four of us with this and some plain basmati rice, I'd keep quantities as they are.

Serves 8–10 as part of this
feast

note
I prefer the thicker, creamier
Greek yogurt, but regular plain
yogurt will do just fine here.

4 pheasant or guinea fowl breasts,
   skinned
3 fat cloves garlic
1 inch fresh ginger
4 long green chillies, plus 1 to
   decorate
juice of 1 lime
1 tablespoon ground cumin
2 teaspoons garam masala

4 tablespoons mustard oil
2 cups baby spinach leaves
1 packed cup mint leaves
1 packed cup fresh cilantro leaves
1 cup Greek or plain yogurt
pinch salt
1 tablespoon vegetable oil or ghee
1 cup water

Put the garlic, ginger, chillies, lime juice, cumin, garam masala and 1 tablespoon of the mustard oil into a blender or processor and purée to a paste. I find a processor or mini grinder easier; you do have to do a lot of digging down and scraping in a blender canister, but it works all the same.

Slash the pheasant or guinea fowl across each breast on the diagonal about three times, not cutting all the way through, and lay them in a single layer in a shallow dish. Coat with the spicy paste on both sides, cover and marinate for a couple of hours, or preferably overnight in the fridge.

Process the spinach, mint and cilantro leaves. Add the yogurt – I always like Greek or whole-milk for body, but you can use any plain yogurt – the remaining mustard oil and the pinch of salt, and process to make a vibrant green sauce. Spread over the pheasant or guinea fowl breasts as before and leave again for an hour, or longer if you like.

Heat the oil in a frying pan, and then shake off the excess yogurty marinade from the pheasant or guinea fowl (reserving the marinade). Cook the breasts gently for about 5 minutes a side. Don't have the heat too high or the yogurt will stick and burn.

Add the cup water to the leftover marinade and stir into a cohesive sauce before tipping into the pan over the cooking poultry. Cook, gently as before, for another 5 minutes a side or until cooked through.

Take the breasts out of the pan to carve them on the diagonal into slices, put them on to a serving dish and pour over the sauce. Deseed the remaining chilli and cut into long, thin strips to strew over the top.

Opposite: top left, Mughlai chicken; top right, pheasant with green chillies; center left, lamb maharaja; center right, pilaf for a curry banquet; bottom left, muttar paneer; bottom right, aloo gobi

LAMB MAHARAJA

It seems fitting to end the meat section of the feast with this, the king of curries. This has a bit more heat than the chicken but nowhere near the fire of the pheasant. Anyway, the nuts bank everything down, infusing the curry with a rich sweetness, and making it look incredibly beautiful as you serve.

      I much prefer lamb shoulder, just because it is so tender, but obviously you don't want cubes ivoried with fat so get it relatively lean as you cut. And if the only lamb that's available is regular diced leg meat, that's fine, just make sure you don't let it bubble away too fiercely, as it can toughen it up a bit. Nevertheless, if you make this ahead, as I do, the meat will anyway tenderize as it sits, sousing, in the spiky, aromatic sauce. I promise you the nigella seeds are an authentic addition, not another exercise in culinary egomania. You may find them more easily under their Indian name, *kalonji*, or a variant thereof.

Serves 8–10 as part of this feast

note
My feelings about the yogurt component are as in the note alongside the pheasant recipe on page 322.

6 tablespoons butter or ghee
1¹/₂lbs onions
2 inches fresh ginger
6 cloves garlic
6 red birds-eye chillies or other small hot chillies (deseeded if you don't like it too hot)
2 teaspoons nigella seeds
6 teaspoons ground coriander
2 teaspoons garam masala
2 teaspoons turmeric
1 teaspoon ground black pepper
4¹/₂lbs lamb (from the shoulder), cut into 1 inch cubes

1¹/₄ cups Greek or natural plain yogurt
2 teaspoons salt
4 tablespoons white poppy seeds
4 tablespoons ground almonds
2 tablespoons lemon juice
4 tablespoons chopped cilantro
2 tablespoons chopped, splintered or slivered pistachios

Heat half the butter in a large pan, and process the peeled onions, peeled ginger, peeled garlic and chillies until finely chopped, then tip into the hot pan. Cook for about 5 minutes or until the mixture has softened, and then take out of the pan, put into a bowl and set aside.

      Measure the nigella seeds, coriander, garam masala, turmeric and black pepper into a small bowl. Heat the remaining butter over a low heat in the same pan, and add these spices, frying them for about a minute. Add the lamb, in batches, turning the heat up to brown the lamb in the oily spices. There is a lot of meat, so really the best you can expect is that it will be seared; I don't mean for you to cook it long enough to get really brown. Put all the meat back in the pan, lower the heat, cover and let the meat cook in its own juices for 5 minutes.

      Put the oniony mixture back into the pan of meat along with the yogurt and 1¹/₂ cups water. Stir in the salt, and bring the pan to the boil before covering it and simmering gently for an hour, or until the meat is tender. Remove the lid to stir the pan occasionally in this time, and if you think it's bubbling too fiercely, just put the lid partially on so the heat doesn't build up so much. You can cook the curry up to this point and then reheat the following day if that suits you better; as ever, I'd recommend this.

Grind the poppy seeds with the ground almonds in a spice or coffee grinder. Add this to the curry, and stir in the lemon juice. Decant into a serving bowl, or serve from the pot with the coriander and pistachios sprinkled over the magnificent maharaja.

PILAF FOR A CURRY BANQUET

I know this might not sound like a huge amount of rice, but it's all I ever do for the curries and dishes that surround it here. If you have a rice cooker, there's nothing to stop you (in that it won't add any work) making another bowl of plain, steamed rice to go on a platter alongside, as in an Indian restaurant. I adore this rice, its mellow fragrance and the beautiful speckled and spice-strewn appearance. And I think nothing of making it a good hour before, just leaving it to sit with its dishtowel and cover, on the switched-off stove until needed. It sits perfectly and patiently.

1 large onion, finely chopped	$^1/_2$ teaspoon cumin seeds	Serves 8–10 as part of this feast
2 tablespoons vegetable oil	$^1/_2$ teaspoon nigella seeds, optional	
2 cloves	$2^1/_2$ cups basmati rice	
3 cardamom pods, bruised	4 cups chicken stock (I use instant bouillon cubes)	
1 cinnamon stick, broken into 3	$^1/_2$ cup slivered almonds, toasted	

Cook the onion in the oil, in a deep saucepan – about $9^1/_2$ inches diameter – which has a lid that fits, with the cloves, cardamom pods, cinnamon stick, cumin seeds and nigella seeds (if using), until the onion is slightly browned and soft. Keep the heat medium to low and stir frequently; this should take about 10 minutes.

Add the rice and move it about in the oily spiced onion until it is slicked and glossy, then pour in the stock and bring the pan to the boil. Cover the pan with a lid and cook over the lowest heat possible – using a heat diffuser if you have one – for 20 minutes.

Turn off the heat, take the lid off, cover with a dishtowel and clamp the lid back on the saucepan. You can leave the rice to rest like this for at least 10 minutes, and up to about 1 hour. Fork the rice through when you are ready to serve it, scattering the toasted slivered almonds on top.

MUTTAR PANEER

You know how I can never resist a frozen pea, and I'm not sure they don't reach their apogee here. I could quite easily eat the whole lot myself in one go, but you'd be surprised at how little even greedy people (members of my family excluded) put on their plate when the table's full of food and the room full of chatter.

I found the paneer – a sort of Indian hard white cheese, rather like a mixture of tofu and haloumi – in my local supermarket; if you find it, buy a lot since it tends to have a long fridge life.

And it was something of a revelation making this. I always, always order it in Indian restaurants, but I never thought of it as something I would cook at home. How wrong I was: it's easy, and so much better this way. Now I can't stop.

Serves 8–10 as part of this feast

$^1/_2$ cup vegetable oil	1 teaspoon garam masala
1 x 8oz package paneer	1 teaspoon turmeric
1 onion	2 x 10oz packages frozen peas
2 cloves garlic	1 teaspoon tomato purée
1 inch fresh ginger	1 cup vegetable stock

Put the oil into a large skillet – one big enough to take all the ingredients later – and while it's heating up, cut the paneer into $^1/_2$ inch cubes. Tumble half of them into the hot oil, and fry until they are golden, removing to a double thickness of paper towel. Do the same with the remaining half. I have to warn you that the pan splutters a lot, so don't do this while wearing your best clothes.

Pour all but about 2 tablespoons of the oil out of the pan. Peel and halve the onion, peel the garlic cloves and ginger and slice them roughly. Put everything into a food processor and blitz to a coarse pulp. Fry gently in the oily pan for about 5 minutes with a sprinkling of salt. Stir in the garam masala and turmeric and cook for another 2 or so minutes before adding the still frozen peas.

Dissolve the tomato purée in the vegetable stock and pour over the contents of the pan. Stir again and turn the heat down to low, cover with aluminum foil – or a lid – and cook for 15 minutes, tasting to check that the peas are tender. You can cook muttar paneer up to this stage, then pause if you like, uncovering and reheating gently later with the diced, oil-crisped cheese, or proceed directly now.

In which case, take off the foil and add the golden paneer cubes, warm them through and revel in the glorious Bollywood brightness of the dish.

ALOO GOBI

I have spent more time than is reasonable wondering whether this recipe should actually be called aloo gobi or just cauliflower and potato curry. My hesitation is because I went so freeform here that I didn't know how much resemblance this would end up having to the original. Whatever, it's quite a sprightly version and I don't, on reflection, feel I should be apologizing for it.

You do need the potatoes, relatively waxy ones, to be ready cooked, so get on with that a day before if it helps. It wouldn't hurt to give the cauliflower florets 2 minutes in the boiling potato water too, but as a general rule, I just reheat the potatoes and make sure the florets are small enough to cook in the allotted time.

$1^1/_4$lbs potatoes, peeled, cooked, cooled and cut into $1^1/_2$ inch dice, to make 3 cups
4 scallions
1 large head cauliflower
4 tablespoons vegetable oil
1 teaspoon cumin seeds

1 teaspoon yellow mustard seeds
1 teaspoon ground coriander
$1/_4$ teaspoon turmeric
$1/_2$ teaspoon ground ginger
juice of $1/_2$ lemon
1 teaspoon salt
freshly ground black pepper

Serves 8–10 as part of this feast

Cook the potatoes whole and leave them to get cold, and then dice them into 3–4cm cubes when you come to cook the aloo gobi.

Slice the scallions into $1/_4$ inch rings. Cut or break the cauliflower into small florets, about $1^1/_2$ inches across the top of the floret.

Heat the oil in a large pan and cook the cumin and mustard seeds until they begin to pop. Add the scallions and cauliflower florets and cook over a medium to high heat until the cauliflower is scorched in places. Add $1/_2$ cup water, cover the pan either with a saucepan lid or aluminum foil and cook for 10 minutes, turning down the heat if there's too much fizz and splutter going on inside the pan.

Take off the lid, and add the other spices, along with the lemon juice, diced cooked potatoes, salt and a little pepper. Turn the pan and stir carefully to mix everything well and let it cook together for another 5–7 minutes or until the cauliflower is tender and the potatoes are heated through.

Season to taste and decant to a warmed dish.

THE ALL-IMPORTANT S

I have a confession to make. I've made no secret of the fact that I don't have a sweet tooth, but even those with a sweet tooth would, I think, get temple-achingly dizzy after too much of the dishes that follow. Taking a culinary-cultural relativist point of view, I didn't want to interfere with them, however.

I do recommend – though you will need a proper, Asian purveyor – some *pan masala mukhwas*, the perfumed mix of shredded betelnut and flavored seeds (like a sort of bag of aromatic nonpareils to sprinkle into bowls) so that people can take a pinch to clear out the curried fumes and aid digestion.

Apart from the halwa, the quantities you end up with are small, but at this stage in the game, no one will be wanting to tuck into a big bowl of anything: the foods here are to provide a perfumed sweet taste, and a generous symbolism, as well as offering a contrast to the fire of the curries.

SWEET-SCENTED VERMICELLI

Serves 8–10 as part of this feast

1 tablesoon butter or ghee
$1/_2$ cup cashew nuts
1 cup vermicelli
1 cup milk

2 cardamom pods
1 tablespoon rosewater
1 cup superfine sugar

Heat the butter or ghee in a saucepan, and fry the cashews until they are lightly colored, then take out and set aside.

Add the vermicelli to the pan and fry over a low flame until the little strands are golden brown. Add a cup water to the pan, cover with a lid and boil until the vermicelli is tender; this will take about 5 minutes.

In another pan – or in a glass measuring cup in the microwave – heat the milk with the cardamom and rosewater until it is nearly boiling, then stir in the sugar. Add to the tender vermicelli and simmer uncovered for about 5 minutes, then turn the heat off, clamp on the lid and let the noodles absorb the milk for about another 5–10 minutes.

Turn out the vermicelli in a tangled mound on a decorative dish, and sprinkle over the cashews.

Above: sweet-scented vermicelli. Opposite: top and left, carrot and coconut halwa, with, right, perfumed seeds

SWEET SAFFRON RICE

Serves 8–10 as part of this feast

1¹/₃ cups basmati rice
1 cup superfine sugar
1 pinch saffron strands
1¹/₄ cups water
2 cloves

4 cardamom pods
²/₃ cup sultanas (golden raisins)
1–2 tablespoons chopped or splintered
  pistachios to decorate

Cook the rice following the package instructions or your usual method; keep warm.

Put the sugar, saffron and water into a saucepan, stirring to dissolve over a low heat, then without stirring bring to the boil. Boil until the syrup reduces and thickens; add the cloves and cardamom pods and take off the heat to infuse for 15 minutes.

Stir the sultanas into the cooked rice, and then pour in the spiced syrup, turning it to coat all of the rice. Turn out into a serving dish, as before, and sprinkle with the ultra-green pistachio shards.

CARROT AND COCONUT HALWA

I don't know how best to describe this: imagine coconut ice and fudge, then try and think of something a hundred times sweeter. And maybe keep a good dentist's number on hand.

Serves 8–10 as part of this feast, and more besides

note
The easiest way to grate a coconut is to use the food processor, though the hardest thing is to break it open in the first place.

1 tablespoon butter or ghee
¹/₂ cup cashews
4 cups grated carrots
1¹/₂ cups freshly grated coconut,
  approx. ³/₄ of 1 coconut

3¹/₂ cups superfine sugar
¹/₂ cup sultanas (golden raisins)

Grease an 8 inch square pan thoroughly, and line the bottom with some Silpat or parchment paper as the halwa will be hellwa to get out later. Heat the butter or ghee in a wide saucepan, and fry the cashew nuts until they are golden brown, blot them on some paper towels and set aside.

Add the grated carrot and coconut to the pan and fry them together for about 5–10 minutes. Add the sugar, and the carrot and coconut will make their own liquid. Bring to the boil and keep stirring until the liquid evaporates; this will take about 10 minutes and a lot of effort. When the paste starts leaving the side of the pan, add the cashews and sultanas and tip the halwa into the prepared pan.

Leave it to cool and set. Once it has hardened, you can cut into very small squares – think petits-fours size as it is very sweet. Store it in an airtight container, and it will keep for about two weeks.

ULTIMATE
FEASTS

FOR ME, an ultimate feast, or the ultimate feasts that follow, merge two considerations: the last meal you might choose to eat on earth (let's not speculate here on heavenly delights to come); and my idea of the perfect supper, my favorite food: the ultimate choice.

There used to be a page on a website issued by the Texas Department of Corrections which listed the inmates' last-meal requests; it has now, deemed to be in bad taste, been deleted, although you can forage about for the sadly not updated text on the Net. I say sadly, as although of course it was in bad taste – in so many ways – it was also such compelling reading. Perhaps the saddest thing about it, though, was the asterisked line at the top which read "The final meal requested may not reflect the final meal served." Just when you thought your life couldn't get any worse.

Of course there has to be something incontrovertibly moving about reading a list of people's requests for the last meal. Luckily, there is a link to "offender information" so that you can click to find out what crime goes with what menu to counter too much compassion.

I felt it was in less execrable taste to give some of these requests if I withheld the names of the culprits. Whether you agree is entirely your affair: those who wish to may proceed to the recipes now; but I did want to give a little taste of what was wanted. Here, for pathos, low-rent amusement value and just plain old-fashioned interest, are my favorites.

Four pieces of fried chicken, mashed potatoes, two pints of ice cream, one bacon cheeseburger, and two vanilla Cokes.

Double meat cheeseburger (with jalapenos and trimmings on the side), vanilla malt, French fries, onion rings, ketchup, hot picante sauce, vanilla ice cream, two Cokes, two Dr Peppers, and a chicken fried steak sandwich with cheese, pickles, lettuce, tomatoes, and salad dressing.

One cup of hot tea (from tea bags) and six chocolate chip cookies.

Steak, baked potato, cherry cheesecake, salad, blue cheese dressing, rolls, Coke, coffee, strawberries, and oranges.

Liver and onions, two double meat hamburgers with bacon and mayonnaise, two orders of French fries, vanilla ice cream, two Dr Peppers, salad with ranch dressing, and M&Ms.

Thirty jumbo shrimp, cocktail sauce, baked potato, French fries, ketchup, butter, one t-bone steak, one chocolate malt, one gallon vanilla ice cream, and three cans of Big Red.

One whole fried chicken (extra crispy), salad with thousand island dressing, French toast, two diet Cokes, one apple pie, and French fries.

Not that I think you should wait until you're on Death Row before focussing on the importance of what you eat. Nor do I think you should fall into that contemporary trap of considering only meals eaten with company to be important. I hate the idea that cooking is for impressing others and not for pleasing yourself; and I know that if you don't make yourself something to eat in the normal run of things you will never learn to be at ease in a kitchen. And that's all that real cooking is.

I know quite how smugly idiotic it sounds to say that every meal should be a feast, but I certainly aim for that. "Much," as Byron wrote in *Don Juan*, "depends on dinner." What I eat myself or just the two of us eat nightly, when the children are in bed, has to be more important to the fabric of life than what I might choose to give a tableful of people once in a blue moon. So the recipes below are not just what I would choose for some hypothetical final-meal-on-earth – my desert-island dishes, if you like. Feeling fortunate that I don't have to cram everything into one last supper, I want to wallow in the ways I celebrate the comforting every-dayness of life. In this case actions do speak louder than words. There's a lot of food I could and would want to write about, but the recipes that follow are the ones I actually cook most often and never tire of.

LEMON ROAST CHICKEN WITH LAZY MASH

It's something of a family joke that, whenever any of my siblings asks what I'm cooking for supper, it's this. It's less a recipe than a blueprint for life. There are few things that can't be made better by a chicken roasting in the oven, and those that are impervious *are* beyond any intervention.

This is how my mother roasted her chickens, and I expect it's how my children will do theirs. The buttery lemony waft through the house is, for me, the smell of home. And there's something about that simple bird, that iconic form with its crispy skinned curves and kitchen-filling aroma that makes it *the* elemental and perfect, unbeatable feast.

I do everything in my power to get a proper, free-range and, more important, organically reared chicken, but this makes even something flaccid, pallid and fed spooky things throughout its tortured existence bearable to eat, from a gastronomic viewpoint at least. If you know that the bird you've got is the right real thing, then you should also check out the recipe for schmalzy chicken on page 146.

1 x 3lb 4oz chicken	**1 heaped tablespoon butter**	Serves 2–4
1 lemon	**dribble olive oil**	
1 tablespoon sea salt/$^1/_2$ tablespoon table salt		

note
When I'm feeling particularly summery, I turn this into the juicy roast chicken salad on page 231.

Preheat the oven to 425°F.

Make sure your chicken is at room temperature, and cut off any string or rubber bands. Sit the chicken in a roasting pan. Put $^1/_2$ the lemon into the chicken cavity, and sprinkle a little of the salt in there as well. Rub the butter over the skin and dribble with a little oil. Put into the oven and cook for 1$^1/_4$ hours. Let the chicken rest in the roasting pan for 15 minutes, sprinkling over the remaining salt and squeezing over the other half of lemon while it sits, then move to a carving board.

Deglaze the roasting pan with a little water, letting the juices and caramelized bits from the roast chicken make a small-volume but intensely-flavored gravy to spoon over the carved bird. Serve with lazy mash (see below).

This will serve up to four I suppose, but it's what I cook for two. That's part of the feast, but it's also the case that I live for the leftovers. When I'm making roast chicken for many I reckon on one bird per three eaters, give or take: so two chickens for six people, three for eight and if I'm feeding 10 then I move back down, exponentially speaking, by sticking to the three.

LAZY MASH

When it's the end of a working day, it is so much easier to make a supper that relies more or less entirely on oven-cooked stuff (I can manage to open a jar of French petits pois (peas) and heat them on the stove). Really, it's about having a proper dinner without having to be in the kitchen constantly to prepare it. Left to my own devices I am always happy in the kitchen, but the natural everyday havoc and exigencies of life don't always allow it. So I can make this regardless of bathtime or homework and whatever else brings the ceiling down lower in the evenings.

Serves 2

3 x 6–8oz baking potatoes
$^1/_2$ stick butter
freshly grated nutmeg, or a pinch
 of ground nutmeg

1 tablespoon sea salt
2 tablespoons heavy cream, optional

The oven needs to be at 425°F for the lemon roast chicken, so put the potatoes in, pricking them with a fork first, on a shelf with the chicken.

Cook the potatoes for $1^1/_2$ hours, which means that when the chicken comes out to rest, the potatoes will have another 15 or so minutes in the oven. If your oven is the sort that dips, heatwise, when it's full, then put the potatoes in the oven 20 minutes before the chicken goes in. Remember, they don't need to have crunchy skins, just to be fluffy within.

Once they're cooked, halve them gingerly and scoop out the flesh into a bowl to make the mash. Add the butter and grate over the nutmeg and some pepper, and add the salt, and cream if, delightfully, using. Beat everything together well – a fork is as good a tool as any – and serve with the lemon roast chicken and the gravy, and some peas if you feel like it.

BEST BURGERS

After roast chicken, a burger, more importantly a cheeseburger, is quite my favorite thing in the world to eat. I don't like any old burger though: I like real meat, hardly cooked, but tender beyond tender. That's the hardest bit: so often – and not just when out, I have often ruined them myself at home – the meat is dry and compacted and serves no more purpose than to give you indigestion instantly.

The difficulty is that so much guff is spoken on the subject. If I hear or read another person telling me that the best burgers are made with the cheapest cuts, I'll throw this book at them. How can that be true? It might work on a professional grill when the flames are fierce, and the outside seared instantly, but on a griddle at home you end up with a burger that even McDonald's would be ashamed to call their own.

I find that the only way of making sure of burgerheaven is to use a good cut (and see Stockists page 460); I choose sirloin. I was reassured about my choice – not that I doubted it exactly, but I was being made to feel ludicrously extravagant – when I asked Jeremy King of the Wolseley restaurant which serves, in my long experience, quite the best burger in London, which cut of meat they used: off-cuts from the sirloin was the answer.

I do another thing to aid the process along, and that's to cut the meat up in strips and leave it sprinkled with good salt and covered in plastic wrap in the fridge for a day before turning it into burgers, a tip I've picked up from the *Zuni Café Cookbook* (see also its corrupted version on page 247 for the baby burgers).

As for other requirements: I buy ready-sliced cheese (Swiss for preference) and cut out discs using a tumbler or cup; I don't want to taste one acrid bit of onion, but I do need a large slice of tomato and anything from a smear to a dollop of mustard, mayonnaise and steak sauce; and if we're talking last requests here, the clamshell of bread please to be a either a brioche bun or challah bun. There's something about the sweet dough with the intensely savory burger.

2 x sirloin steaks, approx. 8oz each	**scant teaspoon sea salt** **approx. 1 teaspoon olive oil**	Serves 2

Trim the fat off the steaks and cut them into 1 inch dice or strips. I think the ideal burger to make as well as to eat is about 6oz and you're likely to lose about 2oz in fat which is why I start off with such generous-sized steaks. If you're buying your meat from the butcher rather than the supermarket, you may as well buy the meat all in one slice.

Put the meat into a bowl with the salt and toss with your hands so that the steak is well coated. Cover the bowl with plastic wrap and leave in the fridge overnight or for a day.

Let the salted steak come to room temperature and then weigh out – or just go by feel and eye – half of the steak to chop or process at a time. Put a ridged griddle on to heat up while you make the burgers. Grind the steak in a food processor or meat grinder; if you've got a freestanding mixer, you can get a grinding attachment for it. This, or a proper old-fashioned meat grinder, makes the most beautiful burgers but I, in common with most people, tend to use the processor. What's important is never to process

note
To make Hamburger Holstein (no less good; fewer carbs) do without the bun and, in place of the cheese, top each juicy burger with a fried egg and a criss-cross of good anchovy fillets.

more than one burger's worth at a time, and go slowly so you don't turn the meat to mush.

Pulse the meat until it looks like ground meat, and then with your hands shape the burger gently into a fat patty about $^3/_4$ inch thick.

It's best to cook the burgers as soon as you've processed and shaped them, give or take normal kitchen kerfuffle. Brush with a little oil either side, or do what I do and pour a few drops – sparingly, as if applying expensive handcream – onto your palms and then pat the burgers to give them a light covering; re-oil between burgers. Griddle or fry the burgers for about 3–4 minutes a side. Let them rest, each wrapped in a double thickness aluminum foil – on a wooden not steel surface – for about 5 minutes (for rare).

If you want to make cheeseburgers, add a slice of cheese straight on to the cooking burger once it has cooked on one side. It will continue to melt as it sits within its aluminum foil tent.

T-BONE STEAK WITH POTATO WEDGES AND ONION RINGS

I used to think my dying wish would be for a steak Béarnaise. I don't know if in the post-Atkins era I'm just too egged and buttered out, but it doesn't seem such a treat any more. But this, on the other hand, a real steak-house steak, with a melting pat of Lea & Perrins Worcestershire sauce and parsley butter oozing over it and a bank of hot-spiced potato wedges nearby, plus as many light and crispy onion rings as I can muster: now *that's* what I call food to die for. Or, more importantly, it's food to live for.

2 x 14oz T-bone steaks

Serves 2

FOR THE WORCESTERSHIRE SAUCE-AND-PARSLEY BUTTER

$^1/_2$ **tablespoon very finely chopped parsley**	**1 teaspoon Worcestershire sauce** **1$^1/_2$ tablespoon soft unsalted butter**

note

Since the onion rings need to be soaked overnight you need to study the form there (see overleaf) before busying yourself with anything else.

Preheat a large griddle.

Stir the parsley and Worcestershire sauce into the soft butter and beat together. Shape the butter into a small fat, round pat, and wrap in plastic wrap. If you want a perfect-shaped little disc, then get a metal quarter-cup measure, line it with plastic wrap and squash in the butter and close up the wrap. Put this in the fridge to firm up while you cook the steak.

Fry or griddle the steaks. It's difficult to be helpful about timings as it so depends on how well done you like your meat and, of course, how thick the steaks are. You should aim to cook them till they are one definite notch more rare than you want to eat them though. This is because you wrap each one in aluminum foil – twice: so make one package then wrap the package again – and let it rest for 10 minutes, sitting on a wooden surface or a newspaper (a steel or granite one would chill it). Unwrap each double-wrapped package over the plate you are serving it on, to catch any drips. Halve the cold pat of butter through the middle, and put a disc on each steak and take meltingly to the table. Offer potato wedges and crispy onion rings (see overleaf) alongside.

POTATO WEDGES

I love the terracotta crispness of these, and the pale tender-fleshed interior.

Serves 2 (generously – which is how it should be)

1lb (2) medium all-purpose potatoes
2 tablespoons vegetable oil
$^1/_2$ teaspoon cayenne
1 teaspoon paprika

Preheat the oven to 425°F. Cut the potatoes in half lengthways, and then each half into two. Cut the quarters again into half lengthways: this should give you eight long, tapering wedges from each potato. Put the oil and spices into a roasting pan and add the cut potato wedges, turning them in the pan with your hands so that they get slicked with the spicy oil.

Cook the potato wedges for 20 minutes, then turn them over and cook for another 10 minutes and serve immediately so that they keep crispy.

CRISPY ONION RINGS

These are the onion-hater's onion rings. No burn, no acrid aftertaste, just buttery, melting sweetness. The secret is in their buttermilk bath, and I came across it after someone called Sue posted details on nigella.com. This recipe is – give or take – her "grandpa Bailey's onion rings" and I thank both of them wholeheartedly for it. As will you.

Makes approx. 12, or as many as are needed for 2

1 large Spanish onion, weighing approx. 8oz
1 cup buttermilk
1lb Crisco or other vegetable shortening
1 cup all-purpose flour
1 teaspoon baking powder
$^1/_2$ teaspoon baking soda
$^1/_2$ tablespoon paprika
$^1/_2$ teaspoon cayenne

In fact, you need only half the onion, or about 12 big rings, but since it's the inner large-diameter rings you need, that generally means starting with one huge onion and dispensing with the two ends. No need to throw them away: you can stash them in a freezer bag and chop them up next time you're making a stew.

So, peel the onion, chop off the two root ends mercilessly, and slice your big central piece into ringed circles about $^1/_2$ inch thick. Carefully separate the rings from the cut circles as you want to keep them perfect and unbroken. Choose the 12 you like best (unless you feel you can eat more than six a head, which would be easy). Put them into a bowl and turn the onion rings in the buttermilk, coating them all. Cover with plastic wrap and put in the fridge for 2–3 hours, but preferably overnight.

Melt the Crisco in a deep (for health and safety reasons) 10 inch pan over a medium heat. Combine the flour, baking powder, baking soda, paprika and cayenne in a shallow bowl. Take the marinated rings out of the fridge, shake off the excess buttermilk and dip them one at a time into the floury mixture before laying them to dry on a cooling rack. Once you have dipped all the rings in flour, go back to the first ones you coated and give them another layer of seasoned flour, coating them all again.

Cook the onion rings in the hot fat until darkly golden and crispy, flipping them over after a couple of minutes to cook on both sides. Drain them on a baking sheet lined with parchment paper and paper towels.

EGG AND CHIPS

Fish and chips, steak and chips, chicken and chips: all are desirable, but none comes close to the simple, harmonious perfection of egg and chips. At times, and that tends to be on a Saturday evening when I've cooked the ham in Cherry Coke (page 205) for dinner the night before, I will gladly stretch to ham, egg and chips.

The eggs need to be good, but I don't feel I need give direction as to how to fry them; the chips, real big fat Brit-chips, no namby-pamby French fries, I am happy to expatiate on. And I am a recent convert to home frying. I'd always thought chips were best ordered in restaurants, and for ease that's certainly true, but if there are only a few of you, and you have a deep-fat fryer, it's not that hard and what you produce will be superior to anything you're likely to buy.

The deep-fat fryer isn't really crucial, and I had started off thinking I'd set about this the unpretentious, old-fashioned way, with just a rickety old pot, a basket and a vat of oil. But since I know that the temperature of the oil is, indeed, crucial and since I also know that I am not someone who should be anywhere near a food thermometer, let alone be dipping it in boiling oil, I decided to keep the stabilizers on and get an electric fryer. My toy of choice is a fryer that you plug in but that doesn't come with a lid that snaps shut. You don't feel excluded; you are still part of the process.

The two rules for chips are simple: use good potatoes (preferably Maris Piper or russets) and cook them twice. You cook them first at a lower temperature in order to make sure they're cooked within; the second immersion at a higher temperature is to crisp them up. Apparently you can give them the first go and then leave them on paper towels for *hours*, just heating and crisping them up as you want to eat them. I haven't tried.

To specifics:

Serves 2

One decent sized potato (about 7oz, it wouldn't matter if it were more) per person should be about right.

Heat the oil to 325°F. And when I say oil, I mean a lot of oil. These babies swallow gallons at a time.

Peel the potatoes then slice them thickly, then cut these thick slices into thick chips (or the size you want them). Put a dishtowel out, plonk the chips in the middle and then wrap over the two ends, like a package, and give a gentle rub. Now your chips are ready for frying.

Put the chips into the basket and lower this into the hot fat and wait for it to rise, yellow and bubbling, up above the pale strips of potato. Unless the basket is really packed, 5 minutes is all you should need for this stage. Lift up the basket, give it a second or two to settle and for oil to drip off and then turn the chips out on to paper towels.

Turn the gauge up to 375°F and when it's reached that temperature, re-fry the chips. About 2–3 minutes should be plenty, but just do this by eye and ear: the chips should look golden and golden-brown in places (good to have some variety) and they should rustle when shaken in the basket and clatter when turned out on to a plate.

ROAST LAMB FOR ONE

I know that I am often regarded as somewhat odd for cooking entire meals just for myself, alone. I wouldn't think of apologizing. On the whole I am not someone either good with her own company or with a gift for solitude, but when it comes to eating, I am all for solitary pleasures. I like the quiet tinkering about in the kitchen; I like the reward later. At its most basic, perhaps, is the quiet satisfaction of knowing one is fending for oneself, the instrument of one's own survival. And, conversely, this is why sometimes it can be good to be cooked for, to feel protected and looked after. But of the two, I choose independence, and this is the perfect supper to celebrate it.

1 lamb shank
1 sprig rosemary
1 clove garlic, bruised
juice and zest of $^1/_2$ lemon
2 tablespoons red port

$^1/_2$ teaspoon olive oil
1 teaspoon sea salt or $^1/_2$ teaspoon table salt
$^1/_2$ teaspoon redcurrant jelly, optional

Serves 1

note
If you want potatoes, then forgo gravy later and cut up 1 largeish – 5oz–7oz – potato (scrubbed but not peeled) into 1 inch cubes and scatter them about the lamb as it roasts. Or just make the pea purée that goes with the cod (see page 344) but, add a $^1/_2$ teaspoon of dried mint to the water as the peas cook and maybe sprinkle with fresh mint after.

Put everything except the redcurrant jelly together into a plastic freezer bag, along with some pepper, tie securely and leave in the fridge to marinate overnight.

Preheat the oven to 400°F, and take the lamb out of the fridge to come to room temperature.

Put the lamb shank along with its marinade into a roasting pan and cook for 1–1$^1/_2$ hours, depending on the size of the shank. Supermarket lamb shanks are often smaller than the ones you can get from a butcher and, naturally, the time of year makes a difference too.

Turn the shank over halfway through cooking. By the time it's done, it should look bursting with bronzedness; let stand 5–10 minutes before eating, if you can. And while it's resting, you should put the roasting pan on the stove and stir in a little water and a $^1/_2$ teaspoon or so of redcurrant jelly to make a light gravy.

SAKÉ STEAK AND RICE

I cook this more often than I cook anything else, bar the roast chicken, in my repertoire.

Like all old favorites, this changes pretty well every time I cook it. Sometimes, I use the saké, both in the marinade and the fluid sauce later; sometimes I use Marsala or sherry. And there is no reason not to use wasabi paste for the English mustard, either. And chicken or duck breasts work in place of the steak, too.

What makes this such an easy supper for me is that, in the first instance, I have a rice cooker, so all I have to do is put rice, cardamom and water in this contraption, turn it on as soon as I think of it and I know the rice will be cooked and ready to be eaten whenever I need. The second thing that makes it low-stress, is that I cook the steaks only briefly, then I double-wrap them in aluminum foil and leave them somewhere not chilly for about 10 minutes by which time they are cooked perfectly, which for me is rare and rubied. And since you then cut them in very thin slices across, they are best like that: they're tender ribbons of meat, and it would be sad to overcook them.

Serves 2

note

The real thing to take from this, too, is the cooking method. This easily translates to bigger cuts as in my quick-cook long-rested fillet: when I've got people coming round and I'm not sure exactly when we'll be eating, I cook a large fillet of beef – about 5lbs for eight, or ten if you're a good carver. This is expensive but easy. Heat the oven to 500°F and sit the roast – no fat encasing it and no larding – on an aluminum foil-lined pan. Cook the meat for 25 minutes and then take it out, sprinkle with sea salt and grind over some pepper and wrap it in the aluminum foil it's sitting on to make a tightly-secured but baggy package. Now get another piece of foil out and enclose it again. Sit this in a warmish part of the

2 x 5oz fillet steaks
1 cup basmati rice
2 cardamom pods

1–2 tablespoons chopped fresh
cilantro to serve

FOR THE MARINADE
1 teaspoon English mustard
2 tablespoons Worcestershire sauce

1 tablespoon soy sauce
1 tablespoon garlic or chilli oil

FOR THE SAUCE
$^1/_4$ cup saké
1 tablespoon soy sauce
$^1/_2$ teaspoon fish sauce (nam pla) or
   brown rice vinegar

1 teaspoon Worcestershire sauce
1 teaspoon English mustard

In a plastic freezer bag, combine the marinade ingredients, and add the steaks. Leave to marinate for a few hours or leave in the fridge for up to two days. I nearly always have a bag of marinating meat on the go in my fridge.

Let the steaks come to room temperature before you start cooking, and you can put the rice on at the same time. Follow package instructions for the rice, or rice-cooker handbook or just put the rice in a pan, bruise the cardamom pods and chuck them in too, and put double the volume of water that you have rice. Bring to the boil, then turn down to the lowest you possibly can, clamp on a lid and leave till the rice has absorbed the water and is cooked, about 15 minutes. I never salt the rice here.

Heat a ridged griddle and then give the steaks, out of their marinade, 2 minutes a side or so, and remove the steaks, double-wrapping them in aluminum foil packages. Let them rest for 10 minutes on a wooden board or a pile of newspapers.

Bring the saké to a boil in a tiny little saucepan, like one you might melt butter in, to let the alcohol taste evaporate. Take the pan off the heat and add the other sauce ingredients. Unwrap the steaks, removing them to a wooden board for carving as you do so, and pour the red juices gathered in the foil packages into the pan of sauce.

Arrange some freshly boiled rice on two plates or one large one, and slice the fillet steaks into thin diagonal slices. Lay the carved steak on top of the rice and spoon over the sauce, letting it gloss the meat and drip here and there over the rice. Scatter the cilantro on top.

kitchen (ie not near an open window), either on a wooden board or on a pile of newspapers (these are insulating as cats and tramps know) for $1\frac{1}{2}$–2 hours.

TEMPURA-FRIED COD WITH AVOCADO AND ARUGULA AND A PEA PURÉE

I know that the notion of tempura can be frightening, but this takes the easy bits and dispenses with the high-stress elements. That's to say, this is fish in the lightest, dreamiest of batters – you just dip the fish in salted egg white and thence into a plate covered with rice flour – quickly turned in a skillet covered with a scant half inch of vegetable oil. Not tempura really, but perfection in its own way. If you want that authentic tempura puff, cut the cod into smaller pieces, whisk the whites till stiff and fold in 3–4 tablespoons of the rice flour, and deep-fry. That's work, but I make this pared-down version once a week, without fail, sometimes more. I have been known to make it for myself for lunch and dinner on the same day.

I have to have the pea purée, a version of the upmarket mushy peas of *How to Eat*, with this, and if I've got a small, ripe avocado around, I often add a tangle of peppery leaves and clay-cool green scooped segments (see picture on page 331).

Serves 2

note

Because I get my rice flour from a health-store, I always use organic brown rice flour, but it is super-light and not as hessian-weave as it sounds.

In place of the cod, I some-times cook a few, tender-bellied, soft, sweet scallops, about 6–8 for two depending on size. If the scallops are small, leave them whole, if large slice horizontally into two white discs. Dredge in a little cornstarch and fry in some butter with a drop of oil (or garlic infused oil) just till cooked through, about 2 min-utes a side, and serve with the pea purée.

1 clove garlic
sea salt
1 x 10oz package frozen peas
2–3 tablespoons crème fraîche
2–3 tablespoons grated Parmesan
   or pecorino cheese
vegetable oil for frying
1 egg white
$^1/_2$ cup rice flour

2 x 6–8oz skinless cod fillets
1$^1/_2$ cups arugula (or watercress)
1 small ripe avocado
good-quality white wine vinegar or
   lemon juice
dribble olive oil
sea salt
2 fat sweet-and-sour dill pickles to
   serve

Fill a saucepan with cold water and throw in the peeled clove of garlic. Bring to the boil and then add some salt and the peas. Cook until tender, drain and put into a food proces-sor, or blender, and add the crème fraîche and cheese. Purée the peas until knobbly and check the seasoning, adding salt if you need to. Tip the puréed peas into a bowl (or back in the pan is probably a better idea) and cover to keep them warm.

Heat $^1/_4$ inch oil in a frying pan. Whisk the egg white in a bowl until frothy, but no more, and put the rice flour into a shallow bowl or large plate. Dip the cod fillets first in the foamy egg white and then into the rice flour, patting them to get a good coating. Cook in the hot oil for about 3–5 minutes a side (depending on thickness) until golden in color. Remove to two double sheets of paper towel, and cover with another, single, layer.

Get out two plates, put a handful of rocket on each plate, and halve then slice the avocado over each pile of rocket, pour over a few drops of really good-quality white wine vinegar or, in the absence of that, lemon juice and a little oil. Sprinkle a small amount of sea salt on top.

Take the fish out of its paper towel swaddling and put on the plates and now spoon on the pea purée, add a gherkin and you're ready to go.

CRUNCHY PORK CHOPS WITH GARLICKY SPINACH AND TOMATO SALAD

The crispy breaded pork chops with baby spinach salad here is a kitchen act of *hommage* to one of my favorite New York restaurants, Balthazar. This shows how potent a force and motivator greed can be. I didn't even eat it myself, but was driven crazy with longing by a friend who went there for dinner and described every mouthful to me on her return. So this is appropriation by proxy and I have no way of telling how much it owes to the original. It takes a little time and effort but, boy, does it repay it. Besides, taking a rolling pin and bashing the living daylights out of the pork chops before you cook them is a great way of taking the office stresses out of your system before you sit down to dinner.

2 x 8oz pork chops
1 egg
$^1/_2$ teaspoon Dijon mustard
$^1/_4$ teaspoon dried oregano
1 cup breadcrumbs
1 tablespoon freshly grated Parmesan

1 cup peanut oil or similar for frying
3 medium tomatoes or 10oz in weight
$^1/_2$ clove garlic, minced
1 tablespoon olive oil
1 tablespoon lemon juice
4 cups baby spinach leaves

Serves 2

Trim the thick white fat off the pork chops, cutting carefully around the outside edge. Lay the chops between two pieces of plastic wrap and, using a mallet or a rolling pin, beat them until the meaty part of the chop is half as thick. You will need to beat around the bone, so turn them over once as you go.

Beat the egg in a shallow wide bowl with the mustard, oregano and salt and pepper. And, on a large plate or platter, combine the breadcrumbs with the Parmesan.

Press each of the chops into the egg mixture, coating both sides. Then dip the eggy chops into the breadcrumbs, covering them evenly. Let them lie on a wire rack to dry slightly while you heat the oil in a large frying pan. When a small cube of bread sizzles if dropped into the oil, you can get frying. You need to cook the chops until they're a deep golden color, about 5–7 minutes a side (depending on how thin you've managed to get them and how cold they were before going into the oil).

Meanwhile, quarter the tomatoes and take out the seeds, then cut them into strips and dice them. You can take off the skins, too, if you prefer, but because I didn't the first time, I haven't bothered since. If you plan to skin them, though, steep the tomatoes first in a bowl of just-boiled water for 3–5 minutes. Combine the diced tomato, minced garlic, oil and lemon juice in a bowl, and add salt and pepper.

When the chops are ready, toss the spinach in the tomato mixture and divide the salad between two large plates, putting each large, crisp, golden chop alongside.

SPAGHETTI ALLE VONGOLE

Long thin strands of semolina-sweet pasta with clams is one of the great suppers of all time. There is one proviso: the sauce must be "*in bianco,*" that's to say, unsullied with tomato. You do need to find those small Manila or littleneck clams, but that can mostly be done with relative ease. And like all treats, it doesn't have to be eaten often, but for me it has to feature high on any true compilation of desert island dishes.

Serves 1

2 cups small clams, such as
  Manila or littlenecks
5oz spaghetti
1 clove garlic
2 tablespoons olive oil

$^1/_2$ dried red chilli pepper flakes
$^1/_3$ cup white wine or vermouth
  (Noilly Prat for choice)
1–2 tablespoons chopped parsley

Put the clams to soak in a sinkful of cold water, while you heat the water for the pasta. When the water comes to the boil, add salt and then the spaghetti. Cook the spaghetti until nearly but not quite ready: you're going to give it a fractional amount more cooking with the clams and their winey juices so you need to leave room for absorption. Try and time this so that the pasta's ready at the time you want to plunge it into the clams. Otherwise drain and douse with a few drops of olive oil.

Mince, grate or finely slice the garlic and, in a pan with a lid into which you can fit the pasta later, fry it gently (it mustn't burn) in the olive oil and then crumble in the red chilli pepper flakes. Drain the clams, discarding those that remain open, and add the closed ones to the garlic pan. Pour over the wine or vermouth and cover. In 2 minutes, the clams should be open. Add the pasta, put the lid on again and swirl about. In another minute or so everything should have finished cooking and come together: the pasta will have cooked to the requisite tough tenderness and absorbed the salty, garlicky, winey clam juices, and be bound in a wonderful sea-syrup. But if the pasta needs more cooking, clamp on the lid and give it more time. Chuck out any clams that have failed to open.

Add half the parsley, shake the pan to distribute evenly, and turn into a plate or bowl and sprinkle over the rest of the parsley. Cheese is not grated over any pasta with fish in it in Italy (nor indeed where garlic is the predominant ingredient, either) and the rule holds good. You need add nothing. It's perfect as it is. If perfection can be improved upon, however, the thing that will do it is a glass of icy cold and flinty white wine or an almost-freezing beer to be drunk alongside.

INDIVIDUAL APPLE PIES

Any last supper I ever plan for myself is so heaped up with deliciousness before I make it to the final stage, that I never leave myself room for dessert. These individual apple pies are the only possible exception (save maybe for a couple of Bendicks Bittermints). This is the quintessential sweet treat: not fancy, but perfect in its simplicity; homey but not heavy. When I make a large apple pie or crumble, I would run to making custard to go with it (and see the recipe on page 42) but generally, when I make these small – but not so small – apple pies, the only accompaniment I want is some good heavy cream, or maybe a scoop of vanilla ice cream, to be scooped out and dolloped on top and left to melt milkily.

Don't be scared of making these: the pastry is a dream to roll out, so, far from being a demanding or stressful task, it is a deeply satisfying and pleasurable one.

FOR THE PASTRY   Serves 2

2 cups all-purpose flour $^1/_4$ cup cold cream cheese, cut into
pinch salt   small pieces
2$^1/_2$ tablespoons superfine sugar   1 egg
1$^1/_3$ sticks cold butter, diced   3 tablespoons sour cream

FOR THE FILLING

3 largeish eating apples,   1 teaspoon pure vanilla extract
   Braeburn or Cox's for choice   1 cinnamon stick
2 tablespoons butter   1 clove
2 teaspoons superfine sugar
squeeze of lemon, about 1 teaspoon

To make the pastry, process the flour, salt and sugar to combine. Add the cold and diced butter and cream cheese, and process again until you've got a mixture like damp sand. Beat the egg in a bowl, and take out about a third to glaze the pies later, then whisk the sour cream into the two-thirds amount of beaten egg.

Pour the egg and sour cream mixture down the funnel of the running processor, and keep the engine going until everything comes together in a silky dough. (It will seem like it's never going to make a dough, but leave it going and be patient and it will come together.) If you are doing this by hand, cut the fats into the flour and stir in the beaten egg and sour cream.

Turn the dough out on to a floured surface, and shape into two fat discs, one slightly bigger than the other. Put into freezer bags and leave in the fridge for an hour.

To make the pie filling, peel and core the apples. Roughly chop them and put into a pan with the butter, sugar, lemon juice, vanilla, cinnamon stick and clove. Put a lid on the pan and bring to a bubble over a medium heat, cooking the apple until soft but not puréed. Set aside to cool.

Preheat the oven to 375°F, and put a baking sheet into the oven to sit the pies on later. Roll out the bigger disc of dough, to give you – generously – enough pastry to cut and line the bottom of two individual pie plates or tartlet pans, allowing some over-hang. I use small round pie dishes of about 5 inches wide at the top point x 3 inches at the base (they fan out so have smaller bases than tops) x $1^1/_2$ inches high.

Roll out the smaller disc to make the tops of the pies; you'll have a lot of pas-try left over, but that's easier than having to wring every last inch out of it as you roll. Besides, you can use what's left over to cut out apples (should you run to such a cutter) or leaves or whatever pleases you, to decorate the tops of the little pies when their lids are on later.

Divide the apple filling between each dough-lined pie plate (you could make sure one person's pie has the clove, and the other's the cinnamon), and dampen the edges of the pastry with a little water, dibbling it on with your fingers. Cut out a lid for the top, again being generous in your sizes rather than exact; seal around the edges with your fingers by pressing the two layers of pastry together and then trim off the excess with a knife or scissors.

Use the prongs of a fork (turned upside down) to give a firm seal to the pie edges all the way around each pie plate. Cut out apples or whatever has taken your fancy to decorate your pies, and dab with a little bit of water to stick them down on top of the pastry.

Brush each pie with the remaining beaten egg, and put on to the baking sheet and cook in the oven for 20 minutes, by which time they should be golden and slightly puffed with heat. Let them sit for 5 minutes when they come out and then gingerly, and wearing oven mitts, ease them out of their pie plates! If you can, leave for at least 15 min-utes before eating: I think these are at their best warm rather than hot, but to be honest, there is no worst.

HALLOWE'EN

ALL AGES and all cultures create their own taboos. Ours used to be sex and money; now it's death. But perhaps it isn't so strange that the cult of Hallowe'en is growing. What might seem an initial inconsistency turns out to be perfectly understandable. Hallowe'en used to be an occasion to think about the dead: now it's some comedy parade, a cartoonification of death, which in turn is a kind of act of denial. In America, and increasingly in the United Kingdom, it's a carnival of spooksville and an excuse for fancy dress. You might think from my tone that I don't like dressing up, even though I admit to once broadcasting a Hallowe'en cooking segment on television done up as Morticia – well, it's not too big a leap.

But I don't want to sound too disapproving. Anything that keeps the children happy…. And although I despair at trying to remove all that face-paint at the end of the evening, quite as much as I dread the sugar-shock induced by all that trick-or-treating, I am perfectly happy to go along with it. It's only one night a year, after all.

Besides, ritual is an essential part of being human and I have grown to like my in-house year-in, year-out Hallowe'en menu which, you will be relieved to hear, involves the scantest of efforts. I don't think this an occasion that warrants great gastronomic feats. If there are adults along for the ride, then I invite you to turn to the black squid on page 352; although children love the jack o' lantern part, I've yet to meet one who wants to eat the grainy orange flesh that has been gouged out.

My children love the food that follows but relish most (as do I) the grossness of the recipe names. And to this grotesque list there are a few things I'd like to add in passing: the monster's eyeballs, from *How to Eat*, which are no more than the green flesh of a galia or ogen melon scooped out with a melon-baller; pesto sandwiches, for which I apologize to all Italians; and cookies cut out into Hallowe'en shapes – broomsticks, or witches on broomsticks, spooky cats, pumpkins, ghosts, bats and spiders are the usual ones (and see page 266 for the basic recipe).

SLIME SOUP

This is just the thing to set children up for a night of marauding through the chilly streets trick-or-treating, or to warm them up once they get home. I know the title sounds disgusting – it's meant to – but the soup itself, as any pea and cheese soup would be, is addictively wonderful and, as you can see, ludicrously easy to make.

Serves 4–6 children	4 cups or 2 x 10oz packages frozen peas	chicken or vegetable stock concentrate to taste or a stock cube
	1 scallion	3 cups boiling water from the kettle
		1 ball mozzarella

Cook the frozen peas and scallion in the boiling water with the stock concentrate or stock cube until tender and cooked through. Remove and discard the scallion once the peas are soft enough to be blitzed into soup.

Chop up the mozzarella roughly and put it into the blender – or a processor, but soup is always more velvety when processed in a blender – with the peas and their liquid. I do this in about three batches, pouring the vilely green and – it's true – slightly slimy soup back into the pan and heating gently to meld cheese and peas better together. Otherwise just set aside and reheat later.

Makes 4 cups, which is probably enough for four to six children, depending on how much sugar they've eaten.

BLOOD AND GUTS POTATOES

I think you could put ketchup in anything and children would eat it, but the blood-spatter effect here is particularly gratifying, obviously. A friend of mine says that children have the souls of serial killers and it's certainly true that, up to a certain age, they are a compassion-free zone, compelled towards rather than repelled by any sighting of damage, accident or catastrophe. Of course they do know that the blood and guts here are symbolic rather than real. As a general rule, children tend to be squeamish about the idea of eating actual innards or underdone meat, but the *evocation* of gore thrills them all the same.

Serves 4–8 children

note

If you're making these for a children's supper, it makes sense to put a tray of small sausages in the oven for about 30 minutes for them to eat alongside.

4 baking potatoes
3 balls mozzarella

2 tablespoons tomato ketchup, plus more to squiggle over when cooked

Preheat the oven to 450°F.

Prick the potatoes here and there with a fork and put them into the oven, straight on the wire rack, for 1–1 1/2 hours, depending on their size.

Take the potatoes out of the oven and let them cool down a little before you handle them unless you have hands of asbestos. Carefully slice each one in half and scoop out the fluffy potato flesh into a bowl, reserving the skins.

Drain and chop the mozzarella into small dice, put into the bowl of potato and add the 2 tablespoons of ketchup. Mix with a fork and then spoon the filling back into the potato skins.

Sit the loaded potato skins on a parchment paper lined baking sheet, and dribble over some more ketchup in a gory blood-dripping kind of way. Put back in the oven to cook for 15 minutes, by which time the cheese will have melted and the potatoes be warmed through.

Makes eight halves, so depending on the age of the children, enough for four to eight.

WITCHES' HAIR

I'm sure that children's rights activists will think it cruel and wrong to lie to children, but there is no way I would ever tell mine that black spaghetti is dyed with squid ink. In fact when my son asked me – annoyingly one of his friends' mothers had informed him of the fact – I acted out an Oscar-winning charade of scorn and bemusement. What a ridiculous thing for someone to tell him! The very idea!

I feel better about the deceit when I tell myself that it is highly likely the true culprit is good old-fashioned food coloring. Of course, that makes me feel worse about the health aspect, and I have to remind myself that I was lying anyway... A tangled web – and so appropriate to Hallowe'en.

1lb/1 package black spaghetti

3–4 tablespoons garlic butter or
2–3 tablespoons butter and
1 tablespoon garlic-infused oil

Serves 6 children, give or take

Cook the pasta in lots of salted, boiling water, according to package instructions, and drain and dress with the garlic butter. It's that simple.

note

My children have an inexplicable liking for store-bought garlic butter, but I just as often use ordinary butter and garlic oil. The only thing about using butter is that it does turn the spooky black a little grey (I tell myself that witches *should* have slightly greying hair), so if you want to keep the strands a glistening jet, just toss the spaghetti in a little garlic-infused, or indeed ordinary, oil.

BLOOD CLOTS

It's childish, but I think I am inordinately proud of this formulation (I can't call it a recipe): it's simple, therefore totally unstressful for parents, and children absolutely adore it. Yes, I know you're giving them pure sugar, but is this really the night to worry about it?

1 package each of strawberry Jell-o, raspberry Jell-o and blackcurrant
Jell-o

Makes about 10 blood-clot molds

Make up the Jell-o according to the package instructions, and leave to set in separate dishes approximately 10 inches x 8 inches, in the fridge. I just have a lot of these and like this the jelly takes less long to set, but any similar dish would do of course.

When the jellies have set, turn or mulch with your fingers and put them, squodged together on to plates or bowls in clumps like blood clots.

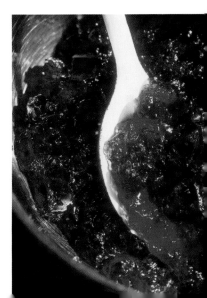

PUS

After the success of the blood clots, I felt confidently inspired to expand the theme by making up lime Jell-o with milk to create pus. It is hideously, fabulously realistic. I tend not to serve this on its own but rather dot the blood clots with it to evoke an attractive burst-boil appearance. But if you want some pus by itself, then maybe double the amounts below.

Makes enough to dot all the blood clots or to make up about 3-4 bowls of pus alone

1 package lime Jell-o

approx. 2 cups milk

Dissolve the lime Jell-o in a little boiling water as directed on the package. Then make up the quantity with milk rather than water. Put into a similar sized dish as above, and leave to set in the fridge. Once set, mulch with your fingers and drop small amounts here and there into the blood clots.

GHOUL-GRAVEYARD CAKE

OK, so this is my Meisterwerk. You can see how glorious it looks and you need to know now how easy it is to make. You just buy some Hallowe'en-themed lollipops (I use the jellied kind) which are scarcely hard to find at this time of year and stick them into a slightly babyfied version of a devil's food cake (what else?) made by bunging everything together in the food processor.

I use vinegar and milk as the liquid, but you could just as easily substitute buttermilk. And I've suggested an alternative of soft margarine for the butter which you would not normally find me doing, simply because if you're up against it and trying to make this in the middle of the week you are not likely to have time to let the butter soften, while the margarine is soft straight from the fridge. I'd also add here that children really are interested only in the icing and the lollipops, so if you wanted to make up a cake mix from a box, you won't find me giving you grief over it.

FOR THE CAKE

1 cup milk

1 teaspoon white wine vinegar

1¹/₂ cups plus 2 tablespoons
  all-purpose flour

¹/₂ cup unsweetened cocoa

2 teaspoons baking powder

¹/₂ teaspoon baking soda

1 cup superfine sugar

1 stick butter or soft margarine

2 eggs

1 teaspoon pure vanilla extract

Serves 12

FOR THE FROSTING

2¹/₂ cups confectioners' sugar

¹/₂ stick butter

2 tablespoons unsweetened cocoa

2 tablespoons dark corn syrup

¹/₄ cup milk

1 teaspoon pure vanilla extract

¹/₂ teaspoon black color paste

black sugar sprinkles

Hallowe'en-themed jellied lollipops,
  at least 1 per child

note

You'll probably need to go to a specialty shop to get the black food coloring paste (usually labelled licorice) and the black sugar sprinkles, so see Stockists on page 461 if you don't have a shop that sells them locally.

I also use the cake batter and frosting (though without the sugar sprinkles) to make Hallowe'en cupcakes; you should get 12 out of the mixture. I've used little orange bubblegums with pumpkin faces for decoration (see below) but you could stick in an individual ghoulish lollipop or indeed use anything suitable you can find or make.

Preheat the oven to 325°F. Grease and line a 9 inch springform pan. Mix the milk and vinegar together and set aside.

Make sure all your remaining ingredients are at room temperature if you can, but since no one's going to be overly worried about the cake, you shouldn't be either. If the ingredients are cold, the worst that can happen is that the cake will be heavy. But you do need soft butter (or the cake won't mix), so substitute marge if that's not a goer. Put everything for the cake, except the vinegary milk, into a food processor and blitz to mix. Remove the lid, scrape down with a rubber spatula and then put the lid back on and with the motor running, add the vinegary milk.

Scrape, spoon or pour the brown batter into the pan and spread to fill it evenly, baking it for 40–45 minutes until it is well risen and springy to the touch.

Remove the cooked cake, in its pan, to a rack and leave to cool for about ten minutes, then spring open the pan and let the cake get completely cold.

To make the frosting, first sift the confectioners' sugar. Boring, but it's got to be done. Melt the butter in a saucepan and when it's bubbling add the cocoa. Let it dissolve into the butter, stirring with a little hand whisk, then add the syrup, milk, vanilla and color paste. Stir or whisk well and let it bubble for a few minutes and then take the pan off the heat and whisk in the confectioners' sugar. Put the pan back on the heat and whisk again to help the sugar dissolve and the coloring disperse, then take it off the heat to let it thicken to the right consistency – thick enough to coat, but thin enough to trickle down to cover the sides too – as it cools slightly (but only slightly: it thickens fast).

Put the cake on torn-off pieces of parchment paper to form an outline of a square to catch the excess frosting. Place the cake just on top of the torn pieces of parchment paper so you can pull them away once the frosting has stopped dripping. Hold the pan of icing over the center of the cake and pour over it so that the top is covered and the frosting has dripped over and down the sides. You will not believe the incredible blackness of this. You'd have to pay me to eat it (good though it tastes) but my children, and all the children I've made it for, can't get enough. You can imagine what their mouths look like afterwards.

Working quickly, throw over the black sugar sprinkles to cover the top and sides of the cake before the icing dries.

Trim the lollipop sticks, so that you have a stem of about $1^1/_2$ inches to stick into the cake, and then plunge the sticks of the foreshortened lollies into the cake so that the ghoulish faces leer out from their black-frosted graveyard.

To be honest, this cake serves as many children as you can stick lollipops in for, if that makes sense. You could certainly find room for 12.

ROSH
HASHANAH

IT IS NOT a criticism to say that foods traditionally eaten by any religious group to mark important dates in the calendar tend towards a certain primitive symbolism. Rosh Hashanah is the Jewish New Year, and – as with so many cultures – the feast is chosen to denote the sort of year that is devoutly wished. Just as the Italians, in their New Year celebrations, cook lentils, which resemble tiny coins, to usher in a year of richness, plenty and prosperity, so the Jewish New Year is a time of sweet foods. At Rosh Hashanah, traditionally, the feast begins with an apple dipped in honey, and a blessing: "May it be Thy will to renew unto us a good and sweet year." Indeed, such is the feeling – a superstitious hope rather than a belief – that what is eaten at its beginning will color the year as a whole, that some Jewish cultures discourage dark, sour or bitter foods altogether at Rosh Hashanah.

This means green olives are eaten in preference to black; white pepper is used rather than black; chocolate and eggplant are out; mint tea is drunk at the end of the meal rather than coffee. Though these are largely the practices of the Sephardim, certainly some Ashkenazi Jews would consider it natural not to put pickles on the table: their sourness would strike a discordant note.

But of course, the Jewish New Year, falling as it does in fall, is not just a feast to celebrate the year ahead, but to give thanks for the richness of the harvest. The two dovetail: thus, the season that brings fruits, such as apples, pomegranates and quinces, also uses these same fruits to give meaning to the months to come.

Not only are the quinces sweet – as they should be at this time – but the pomegranates, with their multiplicity of seeds are supposed to encourage abundance and fecundity. In her history of Jewish food, Claudia Roden says that in Egypt, "we thought pomegranates would cause our family to bear many children." Joan Nathan, that other great chronicler of Jewish culinary practices, tells that, an apple having been dipped in honey the night before, on the second day of Rosh Hashanah a blessing would be said over another new fruit: "In the coming year may we be rich and replete with acts inspired by religion and piety, as this pomegranate is rich and replete with seeds."

But Judaism is a faith of interpretation, and for every act there are many possible explanations. (There is an old Jewish saying: four Jews, five opinions.) The important thing is that these foods, all the foods served, *mean* something, even if many of those eating them have no real interest in their meaning: the custom is what matters. Most families who eat the round sweet bread, the challah, at Rosh Hashanah, rather than the braided long loaf version, don't need to know that the roundness is to show the completion of the cycle, the new year that comes at the end of the old one; nor do they need to know that the roundness is to show a desire for a full and rounded life. The bread is there, it is broken; the feast is consecrated. This doesn't have to be about religion, but about life.

I've on the whole stuck resolutely to the required symbolism of the date, omitting only one significant part. Traditionally a sheep's or fish head would be served at the New Year. Partly, this must be to mark the "head" of the New Year itself, but it is also expressly indicated that this shows a desire to be a leader not a follower, and, more significantly, that the Jews will be able to hold their heads up high and not be trodden underfoot. In some parts of the world, the eating of the head has been superseded by the cooking of brains, in fritters for example, which makes perfect sense for a people who believe in the resonance of the life of the mind.

But perhaps that is taking symbolism a little too far. I haven't included a baked sheep's head or fish head here, and nor do I supply a recipe for brain fritters, much as I love eating them. Those who want to respect all parts of tradition, can turn to the roast sea bass recipe in the regular New Year section on page 112.

It's always difficult to stop piping up with other alternatives and suggestions – thoughts of food beget thoughts of food – but I will limit myself. To combine the two symbols, that's to say, food that is golden to bring forth happiness and prosperity, and food that is round to signify fullness, you could make double quantities of the yellow split pea soup on page 114, but instead of adding frankfurters at the end, you could add the aromatic lamb meatballs on page 441. After that, the lamb shanks would be wrong, so be utterly traditional instead with the roast sea bass, head and all.

ROSH HASHANAH FEAST FOR TEN

GEFILTE FISH
LAMB SHANKS WITH FIGS AND HONEY
SWEET POTATO MASH
GOLDEN CHICKPEAS
HONEY CAKE
POMEGRANATE JEWEL CAKE
RED-ROAST QUINCES WITH POMEGRANATE SEEDS
GOLDEN CAKE

GEFILTE FISH

Gefilte fish are perhaps the most traditionally Jewish food one can think of, the small fishballs or patties that are often eaten as part of Friday night supper. What I hadn't realized until researching this book is that the fried version is peculiarly British. Elsewhere, gefilte fish come poached, and are most often eaten cold in jelly. It's not that the poached variety isn't popular with British Jews (though not this one) but that the fried golden patties are particular to Anglo-Jewry. Indeed, it was the Portuguese Jews in the East End of London who, with their fried fish, gave rise to that great British – and non Jewish – classic, fish and chips.

Fried gefilte fish are meant to be patties, rather than balls, (despite the evidence of the accompanying picture here), and the plump little discs, resembling a fairy-tale stash of gold coins piled up on a plate, lend themselves well to the necessary symbolism of the New Year.

Use whatever mix of white fish you can get your hands on for these; I generally use pollack, cod and haddock.

There is one immutable law: gefilte fish must be eaten with *chrain*, the magenta sauce that is a mixture between beets and horseradish. Strictly speaking, you could argue that the bitterness of horseradish and the sourness of vinegar disqualify *chrain* from making a New Year appearance, but I offer the counter-argument of the sweetness of the beet.

I have only ever bought *chrain* from shops, and have never knowingly met anyone who made their own, but you could give it a try by grating each root, in ratios that please you, adding salt, pepper, sugar and vinegar to taste.

As for tips on pronunciation here: think "gefilter fish" and "hchrayn", if that helps.

Makes approx. 50

1 onion	**³/₄ cup matzoh meal**
2 eggs	**2lb 4oz white fish fillets, skinned**
2 teaspoons salt	**vegetable oil for frying**
3 tablespoons superfine sugar	

Process the onion, eggs, salt and sugar. Tip into a large bowl and stir in the matzoh meal.

Process the fish in two batches until very finely chopped; there may be other schools of thought – indeed there definitely are – but I don't mind a puréed mush here. Anyway, after each batch has been chopped, add it to the mixture in the bowl. Mix together well, cover with plastic wrap, and put into the fridge for 30 minutes (or more if that makes life easier).

Using your hands – and keep a big bowl of cold water and several paper towels nearby for dipping your hands in and wiping as you go – form into walnut-sized balls and then flatten into little discs.

In a pan filled about 2¹/₂ inches deep with clean, hot oil, fry – in batches – until golden brown. Remove to waiting pieces of paper towel and leave to cool. I know that, to the unitiated, cold fishcakes don't sound the most appetizing of dish, but believe me, these make converts (in a purely culinary sense) of everyone.

LAMB SHANKS WITH FIGS AND HONEY

There is something pleasingly biblical-sounding about the "with figs and honey." And it certainly makes the sweet, aromatic stew appropriate here. Though in either case, there is room for dispute (naturally). Since there is no mention of bee-keeping in the Bible, it is thought that the honey – as in land of milk and honey – was in fact a syrup made by boiling down dates. This is still used by Sephardi Jews, and indeed if you can get some from a Middle-Eastern store, there is no reason why you couldn't use it here for the honey, replacing, likewise, the dried figs with dried dates.

You do need a huge pot to braise the shanks (but at least it's getting easier and easier to buy the shanks in the first place). I always love clattering about with army-catering style pans, so this gives me pleasure rather than pause. And, although there is a certain fiddliness involved in the browning of the lamb shanks, this is easy for feeding large amounts of people because you do need to cook it the day before. Thus you're left with nothing more than a spot of reheating.

10 lamb shanks	1³/₄ cups/15oz can plain pumpkin purée	Serves 10
4 tablespoons olive oil (not extra virgin)	2²/₃ cups dried figs	
2lb onions	1 teaspoon ground allspice	
2 cloves garlic	2 cinnamon sticks, crumbled	
leaves from 2 sprigs fresh rosemary to yield about 2 tablespoons needles, or 3–4 stalks thyme	¹/₃ cup honey	
	1 750ml bottle red wine	
	2 cups water	

Heat the oil in a very large pan that will eventually accommodate the entire stew, and brown the lamb shanks in batches. Transfer the browned shanks to a bowl.

Using a food processor (or by hand), chop the peeled onions and garlic, rosemary needles (or thyme leaves) finely. Fry them in the oily pan until the onion is soft but not colored.

Add the pumpkin purée, dried figs, ground allspice, crumbled cinnamon sticks, honey, wine and water. Stir well and bring to the boil. Put the shanks back into the saucepan, turn down the heat and simmer for 1¹/₂ hours, partially covered.

It is best to cook up until this point before leaving the stew overnight, preferably near an open window or at least somewhere cold, as once it has cooled, a layer of fat will have formed on the surface of the stew, and you can remove this before reheating. I find the best way to do this is by putting on clean rubber gloves – or better still, those disposable latex ones that make you feel you're in "CSI" – and then use your hands, but you can also employ paper towels and a skimmer or fish slice.

Reheat the lamb shanks gently, and check seasoning before serving.

There is no reason on earth not to make the sweet mash below to go with this, but you could, if you wanted – and this is easiest if you own a rice cooker – make some golden rice, which is to say, plain rice tinted gold with turmeric. You could also make up a huge vat of polenta, just as suitably sunny and golden, though considerably harder work, unless you go for the instant kind, in which case use chicken stock, even out of a can, in place of the water that the package instructions say.

note

I don't like floury sauces, so I use canned pumpkin to help thicken the sauce, but you could just as easily throw in a couple of cupped handfuls of split red lentils.

It is entirely inauthentic, but I love this with the *haroset* from the Venetian Ghetto (page 176).

If you are not making this as part of the Rosh Hashanah feast, and therefore are not making either the pomegranate jewel cake or the quinces with pomegranates, then scatter some pomegranate seeds on the stew (and see also page 214–216 for the lamb meatballs and couscous, another contender here, now I come to think of it) once it is in its serving dish.

SWEET POTATO MASH

This, along with "Heaven and Earth" on page 39, has turned me around on the subject of messed-about-with mash. Until recently, I had thought that flavored mash was an abomination, dreamed up by bored restaurant chefs with not enough respect for the integrity of their ingredients. The whole point of mash is to be a starchy blanket, or perhaps more of a comforter, and the idea of adding garlic or mustard seems to miss the point. In this case (as with the "Heaven and Earth"), the essential properties are not interfered with, however. You want mash and you get mash: just sweeter, softer, more intense.

For some reason, I find this double-potato mash reheats better than the usual sort, so if you want to make it up ahead, then please do.

Serves 10

4lb 8oz sweet potatoes
4lb 8oz white all-purpose potatoes

$^1/_2$ cup olive oil
1 teaspoon ground mace

Preheat the oven to 425°F.

Loosely wrap the sweet potatoes individually in aluminum foil and cook in the oven for $1^1/_2$ hours or until cooked through. Leave to cool in their foil packages till handleable.

Meanwhile, peel and chop the white potatoes and cook them in salted water, drain and mash. Or, if you're using a potato ricer, dispense with the peeling part, as you can squelch the potatoes through the holes, and then pick out the skins that line the ricer.

Open the sweet potato packages carefully over the mashed white potatoes to catch all the sugary, syrupy juices that have leaked from them. Still holding each sweet potato over the other potatoes, peel the skin away – once they're cool, you can do this easily with your fingers without using even a knife – and scoop out the flesh, or just let it drop, into the mash.

Add the oil and mace and beat the potatoes together very well with a wooden spoon, adding salt and (white) pepper to taste. Don't use black pepper, as black food is not permitted at Rosh Hashanah, and would anyway mar the smooth, gleaming orangeness of this supple mash.

GOLDEN CHICKPEAS

The traditional Rosh Hashanah vegetable is carrot *tsimmes*, often just referred to as *tsimmes*, a dish of carrots sliced into coins and cooked with honey and apple juice, but I just can't do it. Please don't make me. Instead, I offer, for fecundity and golden happiness, this beautiful bowl of legumes.

Using canned garbanzos ensures this is a cinch to make and, actually, you don't need the dense weightiness of dried ones alongside the rich, dark stew. I know it's hard to find the golden sultanas, but I would be sorry to replace them with the dried-up brown raisins. This is an unfair prejudice, I know, but I can't seem to help it.

¹/₂ teaspoon saffron threads
¹/₂ cup sultanas (golden raisins)

1 tablespoon olive oil, plus some extra virgin olive oil for pouring over
6¹/₂ cups drained canned garbanzos

Serves 10

Put the saffron threads into a small bowl and soak in 1 tablespoon hot water from the kettle. Soak the sultanas in ¹/₂ cup hot water also from the kettle; leave both the saffron and sultanas to soak for 10 minutes.

Put the tablespoon of olive oil into a flameproof dish – I use a buff-colored, indeed garbanzo-colored, terracotta one that I can cook with and then bring straight to the table – and over a low to medium heat add the drained garbanzos, the saffron threads with their water and the sultanas with theirs. Swill the sultana water in the saffron bowl so no gold is squandered.

Stir the garbanzos well but gently – you want to get as many manilla-colored peas dyed by the saffrony liquid as possible. Cover the dish with some aluminum foil and let the garbanzos heat through and absorb the liquid.

Dribble the top with extra virgin olive oil and serve. Or decant to a serving dish if you've cooked these in a pan, top with a dash of oil and serve.

HONEY CAKE

This is *the* cake to make for Rosh Hashanah. Indeed, you couldn't proceed without it. Many people give these cakes as presents over the Jewish New Year and you are quite likely to end up with more than one of them if you've invited people over for dinner. And each one will be a little different from the last. This recipe comes from Michelle Guish, and is her mother's recipe, and hence is known as Mish-Gish's Mother's honey cake in my house. I have to say, I like a honey cake that doesn't have a drop of honey in it. See the stockists list on page 461 to buy the all-important golden syrup. What you end up with is a sticky, relatively pale gingerbread.

If you're having this as a dessert rather than an afternoon cake, consider draping it in a butterscotch sauce, which you make simply by heating 3 tablespoons of brown sugar, 2 of granulated sugar, $^1/_2$ stick of unsalted butter and $^1/_2$ cupful of golden syrup. After 5 minutes' bubbling away, add $^1/_2$ cupful of heavy cream. Stir well, and when all is smooth and combined, serve. You can just as easily make this in advance, leave it in the pan and reheat to warm when you want it. I want it always.

You do need to work out how *frum* anyone is first; the truly observant will, of course, not eat dairy with meat. Though it's also true that, if that were the case, you would have to be using kosher meat in the first place, a subject I haven't broached and don't feel qualified to.

Serves 10

note

See stockists for suppliers of golden syrup.

3$^1/_2$ cups all-purpose flour
3 teaspoons baking powder
1$^1/_2$ cups light brown sugar
3 teaspoons baking soda
1 teaspoon pumpkin pie spice

2 eggs
2 sticks butter
1$^1/_4$ cups or whole can of golden syrup or light corn syrup
1$^1/_4$ cups milk

Preheat the oven to 375°F.

Grease and line a 10 inch springform pan.

Put the flour, baking powder, sugar, baking soda and mixed spice into a bowl. In another smaller bowl beat the eggs. Melt the butter and golden syrup in a saucepan on a gentle heat, then add the milk and let it cool a little before adding to the flour mixture with the eggs. Whisk the mixture until smooth and then pour the batter into the greased and parchment paper lined pan, and cook for 1$^1/_4$–1$^1/_2$ hours. The cake will rise during cooking (but fall on cooling) though you want the middle to remain a bit sticky.

Let the cake cool in the pan completely before you take it out and serve.

POMEGRANATE JEWEL CAKE

It's strange how instinct, or maybe it's some deep, atavistic impulse, can lead one. That's to say, I wrote this recipe in the very early stages of making this book, before I even knew what the book might be exactly, and the following paragraph was what I wrote about it.

Many cultures use food that resembles money – lentils for coins, saffron for gold – in celebratory meals, to invoke a wish for prosperity and good fortune ahead, and this fragrant, light, flourless almond cake with its tumble of gleaming, rubied pomegranate seeds is my version: an open jewel-case of a cake.

Now, when I made this cake, wrote that paragraph, I was entirely ignorant of the relationship between pomegranates and Rosh Hashanah. Somehow, though, I feel it must be right if one can get there untutored.

FOR THE CAKE

8 eggs
pinch salt
1¹/₂ cups superfine sugar

zest of 1 lemon
zest of 1 orange
3 cups ground almonds

Serves 10

note
Because this is a flourless cake, it is worth considering for Passover, too; in which case, instead of the pomegranate seeds, scatter jarred or canned sour cherries and chopped or slivered almonds over the cake, using some juice from the can to wet the top of the cake first.

TO FINISH

2 pomegranates

Preheat the oven to 350°F. Grease and line a 9 inch springform pan.

Separate the eggs, putting the whites into a large grease-free bowl, and the yolks into a separate bowl. Whisk the egg whites with a pinch of salt until they are stiff but not dry and then whisk in ¹/₂ cup of sugar before putting them to one side.

Add the remaining cup sugar and zest to the yolks and beat until the mixture is light and airy (I use the flat paddle of the KitchenAid mixer for this), then beat in the ground almonds. This will be very thick and heavy, so lighten it with a good dollop of whisked egg whites before folding the rest of them into the mortar-thick, yellow almond mixture: I find it easiest to fold in the remaining egg whites in thirds. You need to work firmly, but gently, so everything is well combined without the mixture losing its air. Don't be too cautious, though: cooking, like children, picks up on lack of confidence.

Pour into the parchment paper lined and greased pan and bake for about 40 minutes, though check at 30 as you don't want this to scorch. If the cake is brown enough, while still gooey in the middle, loosely cover with a sheet of aluminum foil.

As soon as the cake comes out of the oven, juice one of the pomegranates and pour the juice over the cake while it is still hot and in its pan. Let the cake cool and absorb the pomegranate juice and leave until cold before removing the sides of the pan. Place the cake on a stand or plate, and then cut the other pomegranate in half and bash out the seeds over the cake.

RED-ROAST QUINCES WITH POMEGRANATE SEEDS

The red-roast quinces are from *Forever Summer* (via the Australian writer Maggie Beer), but since then I have seen something Claudia Roden wrote about scattering the seeds of a pomegranate over poached quinces in Egypt for Rosh Hashanah, and I have combined the two. Indeed, it was that which led me to the significance of the beaded, seeded fruit at this time of year.

In truth, the quinces, as biblical and beautiful as the pomegranates, are not roasted until red exactly, but scorched dark on the outside and a grainy, Elastoplast browny pink within. The seeds of the pomegranate shimmer redly on top, and their fragrant, sourly perfumed juices, perfectly offset the teeth-jolting sugariness of the quince.

Serves 10

5 cups superfine sugar
4 cups water

6 quinces
1–2 pomegranates

Preheat the oven to 400°F.

Put the sugar into a large, wide saucepan, cover with the water, swirl to help the sugar start dissolving and add one of the quinces, cut up roughly. This is about the hardest thing you'll be doing here: it's a very simple recipe, but quinces are pretty well as solid as rock. Use a heavy, sharp knife and proceed with caution.

Bring the quince, sugar and water to the boil and let boil away until you have a thick viscous syrup; this could take up to an hour, but don't be tempted to stray far as you need to keep checking after 30 minutes.

Cut each of the remaining quinces in half, much as you would halve an avocado and put each one, cut side down in a large roasting pan. Pour over the syrup and put the quinces into the oven for an hour. Turn the oven down to 325°F and cook for another 2 hours, basting and turning regularly so that they caramelize and color on both sides. Be prepared, however, to cook for longer if your oven tends to cook cool, or if you're using a gas oven. I know that gas and electric ovens should be at the same temperature if that's what the thermostat says, but in practice that isn't the case. My electric oven is "hotter" then my gas one, whatever anyone says. Now, this may not be temperature difference, but just that electric heat is more drying and therefore food scorches or caramelizes faster; in effect, though, it is the same as having a hotter oven.

Whatever, when they are ready, which is to say, caramelized on the outside and tender if you stick in a knife, remove from the oven and set aside, cut side up, so that the oven-scorched, red-glazed quinces stand in their sticky, ever-solidifying syrup as they cool. Set each half on a small plate or arrange all the halves on one large platter – more beautiful and welcoming really – and halve a pomegranate or two, bashing out the seeds to scatter on top, and squeezing a little juice from the emptied husks.

GOLDEN CAKE

I call this golden cake chiefly in honor of Rosh Hashanah but also to obscure its origins. Not that I'm ashamed of making a cake from canned peaches, especially when it turns out as gorgeous as this one. Indeed – think Portnoy – I feel this has a certain Jewish authenticity. And it makes it very easy. (Should dietary proscriptions not be a matter of concern, this too is very good with the butterscotch sauce on page 208.)

Serves 10

note
Although this cake is best warm, almost marzipanny in fact, it stays good for leftovers the next day, cold.

FOR THE BASE/TOP
4 cups peach slices in juice

FOR THE CAKE
1 cup instant polenta
2^1/$_2$ cups all-purpose flour
1^3/$_4$ cups superfine sugar
4 teaspoons baking powder

1^1/$_3$ cup canola oil
1^1/$_3$ cup juice from cans of peaches
   (*not* **syrup**)
4 large eggs

Preheat the oven to 350°F. Grease the sides and base of a 10 inch springform cake pan with a little bit of canola oil. Drain the peach slices and reserve the juice. Arrange the fruit in a pleasing fanlike display on the base.

Measure out the instant polenta, flour, sugar and baking powder in a bowl. In a glass measuring cup, measure out the oil and fruit juice and beat in the eggs, then beat this into the dry ingredients and pour into the prepared pan. Bake for about 1 hour or until a cake tester comes out clean and the cake is golden brown on top, springy to the touch and beginning to come away from the edges of the pan. You may need to cover the cake with aluminum foil after 45 minutes if it looks as if it's browning too much.

Put the cake on a cooling rack for about 5 minutes, and then carefully invert on to a serving plate. Remove the sides of the pan. Serve warm.

A VENETIAN FEAST

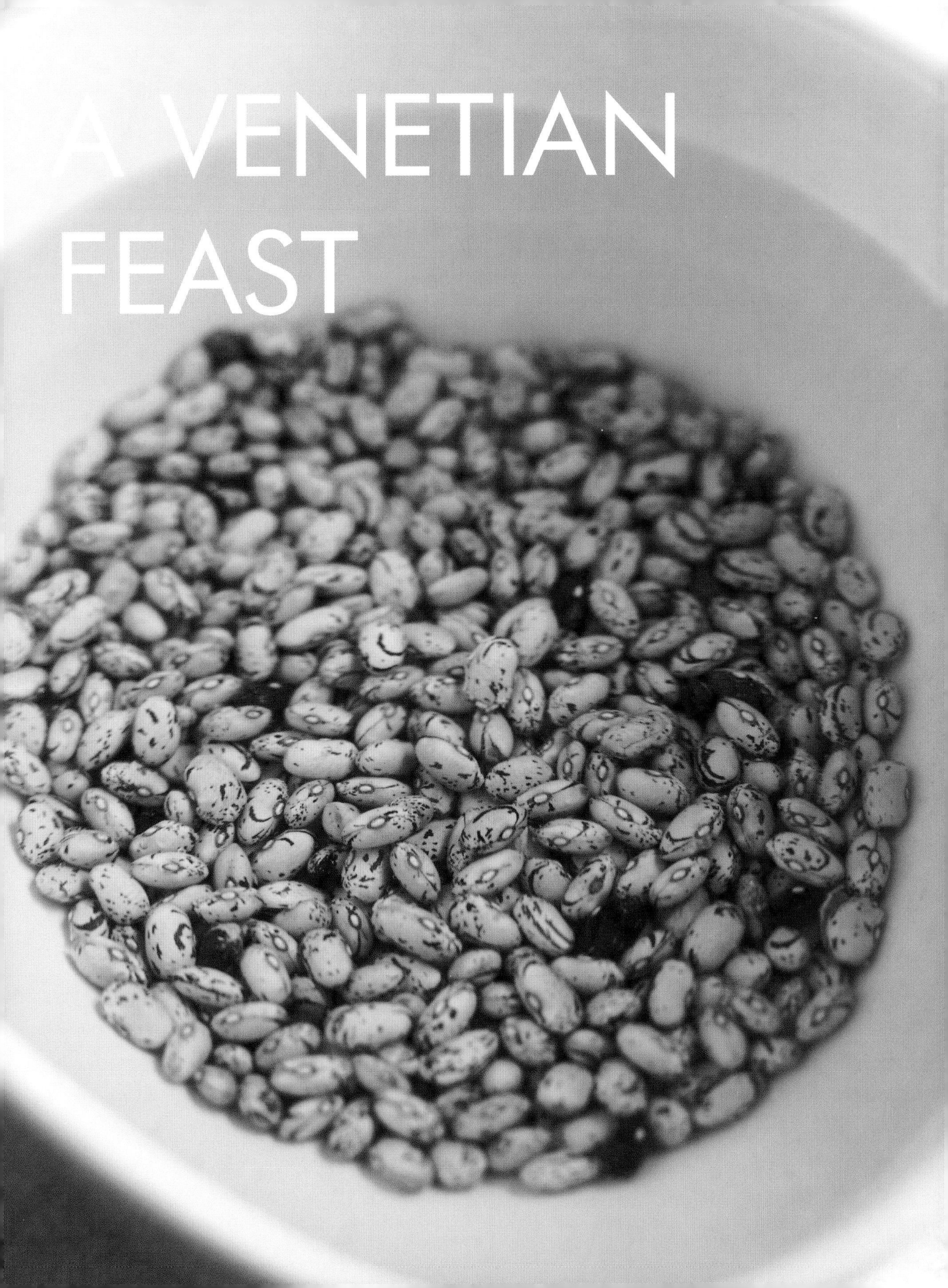

TELL ANYONE that you're going to Venice and they'll tell you how bad the food is. This is partly because the destination is such an obvious one that everyone is nervously keen to show their streetsmart bona fides: to be loftily disdainful of the food is to show you're no mere tourist; you know better. I concede, it is pitifully easy to eat badly in Venice. But the truth is, the food is wonderful, it's only the restaurants that seem to vie with one another to disappoint. If you stay in a hotel, you automatically make yourself victim of a severe, culinary deprivation exercise. There are good restaurants, or ones I certainly love going to, but Venetian food is about the market, the fish – so fresh you get no whiff of it even as you walk through the shimmering, mounded stalls – and the positively operatic displays of fruit and vegetables in the Rialto, as well as the puce pink prosciutto di San Daniele or fat-pearled local salami, *soppressato,* sliced for you in the dark corner *salumeria.*

About a decade ago, I used to rent an apartment for five days or a week from time to time in Venice, and found it liberating. I'd get in, dump the suitcase and head out, either on foot or by vaporetto to the Rialto. I'd buy a dimpled wedge of fresh ricotta, a pound of tomatoes, a couple of *etti* (an *etto* is $3^1/_2$ ounces) of prosciutto di San Daniele (which I'd always choose over Parma ham, and now, thankfully, it's fairly routinely available outside Italy), a head of radicchio di Castelfranco, which is the most glorious of lettuces – a loose bud of creamy yellow leaves, splattered with rusty red ("*Il fiore che si mangia*" said the handwritten sign over a mound of them at the market: the flower that you eat) – some bread, some olive oil, and a bottle of Prosecco, the light fizzy local wine that is, for me, instant good mood. (So much so, that on holiday with friends some years back, we renamed it Prozacco.)

Not all of that food is from the region, but it does remind you just how good and simple the food in Italy can be. It's a truism, I know, but nothing beats eating in context. That may be a provocative statement to head up a collection of recipes to be eaten miles away from Venice, but I don't pretend anything I cook in my kitchen will be the *same* as it would be if I were busying myself about in a *cucina veneziana.* Still, it should taste good, taste wonderful indeed, even far from the original source of inspiration. It's important to avoid looking as if you're trying to open a theme-park restaurant. I don't suggest you style napkins into gondolas, or "don" – and that would be the only word for such an exercise – a jewelled mask during dinner, but it is always possible to convey an honest savoring of foods eaten, tastes remembered or even dreamed of.

Not everything can be replicated: what is truly Venetian is the fish; this is no place for pisciphobes. In October or March, you can get *moleche,* the soft-shelled crabs that you throw, live, into the hot pan and eat a few, hot minutes later. I've heard of a supremely decadent Venetian practice of filling a bowl with beaten eggs and Parmesan and immersing the live *moleche* in it for a few hours. The *moleche* eat up the egg and cheese, and all you do is flour them, fry them in hot oil, and eat self-stuffed soft-shelled crab. At the risk of shocking those of you with tender sensibilities, I long to eat these. I love, too, the *gamberini,* tiny glassy grey shrimp – called *schie* locally – that scrabble about in their newspaper-wrapping like cellophane spiders: cook spaghetti and heat some olive oil in a pan with garlic and some hot red chilli pepper, toss in the live little shrimp and cook them till they're a vivid coral, throw in some white wine, and turn the roughly drained pasta in the pan. This is food that you just can't make for yourself over here.

For the same reason, when I'm in Venice, I buy *canestre* – like miniature scallops – which I fry for a bare couple of minutes, or *cicale di mare,* a sweet-fleshed, pale-carapaced local crustacean which needs a mere dressing of olive oil and lemon juice, squeezed and poured over as you eat. And the mussels, called *peoci* in Venetian rather than the Italian *cozze,* and clams are so much headier, more intense than the ones you're likely to find inland. At their simplest, all you need to do is toss them in a covered pan with some sautéed garlic and white wine – I use the Prosecco I'm drinking – and toss them into some cooked, drained and olive-oil-slicked spaghetti. Of course, round there, they do beg to be added to a risotto, but the point is you can do anything you want. It would be hard to make food this fresh taste bad.

Back home you just have to shop well and be happy conjuring up memories or fantasies of some Venetian feast, rather than worrying about not eating one in situ. These are the best souvenirs you can have. I'd much rather come back inspired to cook *bigoli con salsa*, the local speciality of wholewheat spaghetti in a syrupy sauce of slow-cooked onions and anchovies or a plate of juicy coral shrimp with beans which are the deep damask pink of a Venetian palazzo's walls, than return laden with Murano glass and malevolently feathered masks. And I'm not above recreating the touristic pleasures of Harry's Bar at home either: even without the aesthetic charge you get in its local setting, a jugful of Bellini (Venetian sparkling wine, Prosecco, thickened and perfumed with puréed white peaches), is the perfect, unimprovable cocktail.

A VENETIAN FEAST FOR EIGHT

The shrimp and bean salad – called "*i ricchi e i poveri*" (food for "the rich" being the shrimp, and for "the poor," the beans) – has many incarnations throughout Italy, but it is the cranberry beans, their pods so spectacularly cream and pink when fresh, as if they'd been tie-dyed, the beans a beautiful marbled rose when dried, which makes this (for all that they are sometimes known as Roman as well as cranberry beans in the States) seem so Venetian to me. That and the radicchio – *the* Venetian lettuce – that lines the plate the salad is mounded on. My version uses dried beans, soaked and then boiled with onion and bay leaves, but canned cranberry beans will help to make this a more quickly assembled dish. Indeed, you could use any beans here – I've made it with both cannellini and pinto beans in my time. Similarly, you could use ready-cooked shrimp instead of poaching the raw ones yourself. I can't pretend that the canned bean and cooked shrimp will be quite as good, but if you dress them well with good olive oil, lemon juice, some minced garlic and – if you can get hold of it – sea salt, you will still have something to be heartily proud of.

Bigoli con salsa is real Venetian cooking and you may as well cook it at home since these days you won't always find it on restaurant menus in Venice. To tell the truth, I've never been lucky in finding the bigoli themselves, which are the only authentically wholewheat pasta in Italy: thick buff-colored spaghetti-like pasta with a hole running through the middle of each strand, the better to trap the oozing sauce. I often, as here, use perciatellini (No. 14 in the fabulously good imported De Cecco range) or bucatini. At other times, I make this with linguine which is robust enough for the hearty dressing; though feel free to buy wholewheat spaghetti from the health store if you prefer. As to the sauce itself, I change this according to personnel at dinner. Twelve anchovy fillets are enough to make a sauce to coat a pound of pasta if you want to keep the saline fierceness at bay: you can taste the anchovy but it doesn't dominate. Add half as much again if you want to make this dish zing with anchoviness. Either way, two other factors keep the saltiness in check: you cook the onion long and slow, till it is a sweet, almost caramelized mush, so that the sauce is a balanced combination of sweet and salt; plus you add liquid in the form of milk. This too makes it soft and mellow.

And if when you've cooked it – which you can do well in advance, reheating the sauce and coating the pasta at the last minute if you like – you worry that there isn't enough sauce, bear in mind this is the way it's meant to be. This is not a sauce that lies in a pool on top of the pasta, but one that gently coats each strand, infusing the whole with flavor without too much saltiness. A small amount of pasta cooking water helps bind the sauce to the tangle of pasta in the bowl. And don't regard the parsley as optional garnish: true, you need the leafy greenness to relieve the otherwise dull brownness of the onion and anchovy mush, but its fresh herbal quality rounds out the musky mellowness of the sauce, too.

The *seppie al nero*, cuttlefish dyed black with its ink, is headily Venetian, especially when served with the white polenta that locals favor over the golden-yellow kind, and which is possible to find abroad. It's virtually impossible to find the cuttlefish with ink sacs intact, but I'm lazy anyway and buy the cuttlefish already cleaned and prepared along with a few sachets of cuttlefish ink. Some people might be alarmed at the prospect of eating something that looks as if it could star in a sci-fi film, but it only *looks* spooky: once you take the plunge, that mottled and bruise-black tangle of fish overwhelms any squeamishness. But if you want to leave it out of this feast, then do. These recipes are meant to be suggestions not dictatorial orders.

Talking of which, Arrigo Cipriani is very stern about his Bellini in the *Harry's Bar Cookbook*: he instructs us always to use white not yellow peaches and never to purée them in a blender, but to mash them with a fork or push through a food mill. So I must apologize to him, for although I adhere to his former admonition, I have ignored the latter. I used to pulp the fruit in my blender, and then stir it into a pitcher of waiting Prosecco; now I buy the white peach purée in large foil pouches (see Stockists on page 461) and pour that into the Prosecco instead, until I have a summer-scented pitcher of fizzy wine tinted a pearly, pale golden pink. The point is, it's so hard to find white peaches with actual flavor much of the time that you probably do better with the bought pulp. Whatever, stir, pour and drink instantly: Venice in a glass.

The dessert I offer here is only partly Venetian: *zabaglione* is traditionally made with Marsala, that wonderful smoky-amber fortified wine from Sicily, but the version which follows uses Prosecco. I feel that justifies it as the glorious culmination of a Venetian feast; its frothy lightness is anyway just what you need after the beans, the shrimp, the pasta and the cuttlefish. Besides, to dip into it I make some irrefutably Venetian cookies, the sultana-studded *zaletti* – *zaleti* in Venetian dialect – that you see displayed in every *pasticceria* you pass as you walk, climbing up and down all those arching bridges, through Venice.

I love this zabaglione, too, not poured into small glasses as here, but frothed over some pink-cheeked white peaches that have been fragrantly poached in a light Prosecco syrup: make up the Prosecco you have left from the zabaglione (maybe giving yourself a little glass to drink first) to 3 cups with water and make a syrup with an equal volume of sugar (and see the recipe for peach Melba on page 233.) Not Venetian at all in reality, but entirely Venetian in inspiration: for that, I hope I don't have to apologize.

BELLINI

I'd probably double this – maybe even triple it to be honest – if I were having dinner for eight people, but that may be because I have friends who drink a lot. Nevertheless, I just think it's more helpful to give the recipe like this, so you can see what the ratio of fruit to wine is at its most simple. Anyway, I don't think this sits well, so even if I were intending to double the amounts, I'd rather make a single batch up twice, than pour it and let it stand and separate in the pitcher.

As I said, I now order large pouches of white peach pulp, but if you're lucky and think you can get hold of white peaches that have managed to become everything they should be, then by all means do the right, real thing.

Makes approximately 4 cups, serves 4

note
Pour the Bellini immediately into your glasses before the mixture separates. If you find it easier, mix each glass separately: for one generous glass of Bellini you will need $1/4$ cup of peach purée and $3/4$ cup of Prosecco.

1 75ml bottle of Prosecco
1 cup white peach purée/pulp or 3–4 white peaches to yield approximately 1 cup of puree

confectioners' sugar, optional

Let's optimistically presume you're doing this, first off, with actual fruit. So, cut the peaches into quarters, and taking each quarter, in turn, hold over the mouth of the blender and peel off the skin (this is because you'll lose juice as you do it). Drop the skinned fruit into the blender canister and purée. If the purée is too tart, add confectioners' sugar to taste and purée again. (One of the virtues of the bought pulp, is that it isn't made with underripe fruit.) Leave this hamster-colored pulp in the fridge to chill.

Your only remaining job is to pour the bottle of also chilled Prosecco into a large pitcher, then pour in the white peach purée and stir together.

I RICCHI E I POVERI • SHRIMP AND BEAN SALAD

I first came across a version of this in Anna del Conte's *A Tavola*, one of my favorite books of all time. I feel I should start a petition to get it reprinted, as anyone who wants to cook Italian food, or just read about it, should have a copy of it, and indeed all her books.

I have specified raw peeled shrimp as that's the way they tend to come frozen and it does remove a fiddly step. If you're buying shrimp with their shells on, buy 2lbs. And I mean the medium-sized ones, as you can see from the picture, not the little teeny ones that generally come ready cooked.

If you want to eat this at its best, you really should start off with dried beans, though I do sometimes make it with canned. But surely, for a feast, it's worth pulling out all the stops.

Serves 8 as a starter

3 cups dried cranberry beans, or 2lbs fresh cranberry beans in the pod or 6 cups canned, drained cranberry beans

$1^1/_2$lbs medium raw shelled shrimp
1 teaspoon white wine vinegar
juice of $1/2$ lemon

1 onion

2 bay leaves

1 clove garlic, finely chopped or minced

$^2/_3$ cup extra virgin olive oil

1 teaspoon sea salt/$^1/_2$ teaspoon table salt

2 heads radicchio, or 1 head radicchio and 1 head radicchio di Castelfranco (if you can find it)

fresh flat-leaf parsley, optional

note

If you were making this to be eaten in the course of a normal supper, and not part of such a many-staged feast, then obviously it won't stretch to feed eight. Work on four to six, and this goes for the other recipes here too.

If using dried beans, put the cranberry beans in a large bowl and cover generously with cold water and leave overnight or longer.

Drain and put the beans in a large saucepan with the onion and bay leaves (no salt at this stage), pour in cold water to cover by about 5 inches and bring to the boil. Lower the heat, remove any scum that's come to the surface and cook at a gentle bubble for about 45 minutes or more (depending on how old the beans are for one thing) until tender. Fresh cranberry beans will need less time.

Drain them, remove the bay leaves and onion, then put the beans in a large bowl, mince or grate in the garlic, pour over half the oil and a generous sprinkling (about 2 teaspoons) of crushed-in-the-fingers sea salt. You can leave the beans like this now until you need them, though once they're a little cooler you should probably cover with plastic wrap to stop them getting a dry skin.

To cook the shrimp, put them in a saucepan, cover with cold water and add 1 teaspoon sea salt (or half, if using table salt) and the vinegar. Bring to the boil, turn down and let simmer gently, fishing one shrimp out after about 4 minutes to see whether it's cooked inside. You want gorgeously tender shrimp, but you want to make sure they're not still glassy within their coral skins. Drain, and set aside.

Combine the shrimp with the beans not too long before serving them, adding the remaining oil and lemon juice to taste. You may want to add more salt, too, but go gently. I love this salad best slightly warmer than room temperature, but often it's just easier to cook everything in advance and have it cold. The shrimp will toughen up if they go into the fridge for long, however, so don't cook them madly in advance.

Separate your beautiful red or speckled lettuces into leaves, and line a large serving plate with them. Heap over the shrimp and beans and sprinkle over some chopped parsley if you feel like it. Since there's parsley both on the pasta and in the cuttlefish, I often leave it out here unless I'm making this as a lunch dish in its own, solitary, right.

BIGOLI CON SALSA • PASTA WITH ANCHOVY SAUCE

I have a feeling that this is another recipe with a del Conte derivation, although I have cooked it so often over the years, I can't now remember what I've added to it and when. I know that people feel very strongly about anchovies, but just as with the cuttlefish, this is guaranteed – as much as one can guarantee anything – to overcome the most squealing of prejudices. Do not think of that salty dried-up thing that curls up and dies on top of cheap takeaway pizzas: the anchovies here are mellow and, with the soft-cooked onions, have a savory but honeyed intensity – not strong, just deep-toned and harmonious. To be on the safe side, you could just serve this as "pasta in Venetian sauce," failing to mention the anchovy element.

I know one package of pasta doesn't sound a lot for eight people, but this shouldn't be doled out in great big bowls; by this stage, you've already eaten one course and have two more to go. If, however, I'm making this for supper for two, I greedily just halve it.

Serves 8

note

Another Anna del Conte tip: if you're cooking pasta for a dinner party or any other occasion when you might be surrounded by people and forget to take the pasta off in time, you stand much less chance of overcooking it by following the Agnesi method. Bring your water to the boil, add salt, then tip in the pasta stirring well to make sure it's all in and not clumped together. Once the water's come back to the boil, let the pasta cook for 2 minutes then turn off the heat, cover the pan with a dishtowel (thin one, not the fat-waffled variety) and clamp with a tight-fitting lid. Let the pasta stand like that for as long as the package tells you to cook it by the normal method. At which time drain it, remembering to remove the $1/2$ cup of cooking water before doing so.

2 large onions
2 cloves garlic
$1/3$ cup olive oil
$1/2$ teaspoon brown sugar
12 anchovy fillets or 1 x 2oz can (total weight) in olive oil
1 tablespoon butter
tiniest pinch ground cloves

1 tablespoon water
$1/2$ cup whole milk
1lb package bigoli, bucatini, perciatelli or linguine or other long, robust pasta (see page 372)
1 cup freshly chopped flat-leaf parsley

Finely chop the onions and garlic. To be honest, I'd do this in the processor every time. It's not just that it's easier, but that it makes the onion meld into the sauce so well later.

Heat the oil in a heavy-based pan and cook the very finely chopped onion and garlic over a low heat until you have a soft, golden mush – about 10 minutes. Add the brown sugar (though white is fine too), stir it in and let the onion mixture cook for another minute or so.

Remove the anchovies from the can, and chop them very finely; I use my mezzaluna for this. Add them to the onion mush, stirring until they begin to "melt," then stir in the butter and the pinch of ground cloves, followed by a tablespoonful of water and when all is combined, gradually stir in the milk. When this has come together as a purée, take the pan off the heat.

Meanwhile, cook the pasta in abundant salted water according to the package instructions, removing $1/2$ cup of cooking liquid just before you drain it.

Tip the drained pasta into the anchovy and onion sauce and add the reserved cooking water to help lubricate the pasta. You may not need all of the water, so pour in gradually. Add some oil from the anchovy can if you need it too. And, of course, if the pan isn't big enough to take all the pasta, just put it back into the pan it was cooked in and pour the sauce over the top.

Sprinkle over most of the parsley, just roughly chopped, thoroughly turning the pasta in the pan to coat each strand in the anchovy sauce. Remove to a warm bowl, sprinkle over the remaining parsley and take to the table.

SEPPIE AL NERO • SQUID IN ITS OWN INK

If you can get baby squid, then you can make, to be precise, *seppioline al nero*; even if you can't, do make sure you're not sold tough and rubbery windsocks. It's not always the case in life, but here smaller is better.

This is not a pretty spectacle at the stove: at times it looks as if you're struggling with some primeval life force from the deep, which in a sense you are. Only it's not much of a struggle: a bit of chopping, a bit of stirring, no more. The real trouble lies in convincing people this is nothing to be afraid of. It makes sense to find out whether the idea of the *piatto* itself appeals before you plan the menu. I definitely think a lot of men, being faddier eaters than women on the whole, might be spooked by it.

Serves 8

2lbs squid, cleaned weight
1 small onion
2 cloves garlic
3 tablespoons olive oil
4 pouches squid ink

12oz (approx. 3) tomatoes ($^3/_4$ cup deseeded and diced)
$^1/_2$ cup white wine
$^1/_3$ cup/3–4 tablespoons parsley, finely chopped

Slice the cleaned squid into $^1/_4$ inch rings or strips. Finely chop the onion and mince or grate the garlic, and soften them in a wide pan with the oil over a gentle heat; this should take about 7 minutes.

Blanch the tomatoes in boiling water – just put them in a bowl, covering generously with boiling water and leave for 3–5 minutes – and then peel off their skins; make a small, shallow incision with the point of a sharp knife and the skins should then be able to be pulled off and stripped away easily. Discard the seedy pulp, and cut into small dice.

Add the squid and stir it around with the onion and garlic for a couple of minutes, then add the pouches of squid ink. Stir the pan again to get everything coated with blackness, though don't expect too much jet intensity at this stage, then add the wine, diced tomatoes, and finely chopped parsley to the pan and give it a good grinding of black pepper. I'd wait to salt them later.

Turn the heat down to low, and simmer the pan very gently for about 30 minutes, tasting for seasoning when ready. Serve with the white polenta, below.

POLENTA BIANCA • WHITE POLENTA

As a general rule, I think polenta tastes much better cooked in chicken stock (out of a can) but you don't need to add oomph here since you get plenty of that from the licorice lacing of the squid. If you can't find the white polenta from the Veneto, then blithely use the brighter, golden sort. And if you weren't going in for the pasta, you could simply turn this into a black risotto, or make a huge white risotto (follow the recipe for champagne risotto on page 116, but use Prosecco instead and double or triple the quantities depending on how much else you're cooking) and arrange it, Vesta-curry style on a large platter, with the black squid pooling in the middle.

9 cups water

3 cups white polenta

4 teaspoons sea salt/2 teaspoons table salt

Fill a large, deep saucepan with water, and when it comes to the boil add the salt. Take the pan off the heat for a moment, and add the polenta, letting it rain down in a steady though light stream from your clenched fist, while whisking with the other hand. Put the pan back on the heat and cook the polenta for at least 40 minutes – it depends on the dimensions and materials of your pan among other things – whisking, just with a hand whisk and not frenetically either, for the first 10 minutes, and then stirring with a wooden spoon every minute or so – sorry – as it cooks.

When it is ready, that's to say creamy and cohesive and with no grit of grain apparent as you taste, check for seasoning and serve straightaway with the black squid.

ZABAGLIONE AL PROSECCO

The quantities here may sound stingy for eight, but a little zabaglione goes a long way, especially after beans, shrimp, pasta, cuttlefish and polenta. For a simple two-courser, regard the ingredients below as enough for four. I made the *zaleti* slightly too large, so the Prosecco glasses look teeny-weeny in the photo overleaf. Speaking of which, these are the glasses that my maternal grandparents bought while on honeymoon in Venice and some have lasted all that time. I've used them for photos in earlier books, but never so aptly as right here.

8 egg yolks

³/₄ cup Prosecco

Serves 8

¹/₂ cup superfine sugar

note

Fit a bowl over a saucepan of barely simmering water, and put the egg yolks and sugar in it. Using a hand-held electric mixer, start whisking the yolks and sugar in their bowl over the simmering water. The mixture should become pale and thick like super-aerated heavy cream, and by the end it should have at least tripled in volume and be exuberantly frothy. This could take up to 15 minutes, but it's worth the wait. Sometimes I like a small excuse to get up from the table after dinner as well.

Continue whisking as you slowly pour in the Prosecco; you should then have a soft, billowing mass to spoon into waiting glasses.

Eat immediately – not that anyone should need encouragement – with the *zaleti* overleaf.

If it would make your life simpler, you could make a cold zabaglione (which means you don't have to do it at the last minute). Follow the recipe as usual, only once the zabaglione is ready remove the bowl from its pan of simmering water to a cold surface or stand it into a pan of cold water, and whisk until cool. Then whisk a cupful of heavy cream, fold the two together and pour into glasses.

ZALETI • POLENTA COOKIES

I've already confessed that I made these bigger than you'd actually find them in Venice. I also shaped them in a slightly more blocky fashion; there I seem to remember them more as irregularly tapering ovals. Whatever, I can't exactly apologize for them since they have been a raving success every time I've made them. They are particularly appreciated – I've noted – when dipped into a morning coffee. Now I come to think of it, you could dispense with a proper dessert and just serve these along with the after-dinner coffee. So as not to deplete the meal too much – you see I'm intent on having everyone stagger out at the end of the evening – I'd probably introduce a plate of cheese, and preferably some Venetian Asiago or Montasio at that, with some gorgeous red grapes.

Makes 16

note

I've specified sultanas here as I am wholly fixated with and on them, as I may have explained earlier, but I do know that they are hard to find. You could easily substitute dark raisins or whatever dried fruit you want. In fact, I think dried sour cherries or cranberries would look beautiful.

$^1/_3$ cup sultanas (golden raisins)
2 tablespoons dark rum
$^3/_4$ stick cold unsalted butter
1 cup fine cornmeal or polenta (one and the same thing really)
$^1/_2$ cup all-purpose flour
$^1/_4$ teaspoon salt
$^1/_4$ cup superfine sugar
1 egg
few drops pure vanilla extract
zest of $^1/_2$ lemon

Soak the sultanas in the rum for an hour or better still, if you can, overnight; this way the sultanas really plump up and juicily absorb the liquor.

Dice the butter into $^1/_2$ inch cubes. Mix the polenta, flour and salt and cut in the butter. You can do this in the processor or by hand or, as I do, using a standing mixer with the flat paddle attachment. When you have a sandy rubble, mix in the sugar and then the sultanas, reserving the residual rum.

Beat the egg with the vanilla and lemon zest and mix this into the as-yet unclumped dough. Keep mixing but if it still doesn't begin to form a ball, add the rum. Otherwise just drink it. Form the dough into a fat disc, wrap it in plastic wrap and put into the fridge for 15 or 20 minutes. As you put the dough in the fridge, preheat the oven to 375°F.

Flour your hands lightly and pinch off ping-pong-ball-sized pieces of dough, roll them into cigar shapes and then mold or press them into little oblongs, about 4 by 1 inch and about $^1/_4$ inch thick, placing them on a parchment paper lined baking sheet as you go.

Bake for 15–20 minutes until golden and firm, but not too hard. All cookies get harder as they cool, so bear that in mind as you test.

FESTIVAL OF LIGHTS

THE ONE important thing you need to know about this festival, properly named Hanukkah, is that it provides a divine ordination to eat deep-fried foods. That's the kind of religion Judaism is; and surely even those who are not the Chosen, have to respect that, admire that, love it. I can't think of any other faith that would lead one so directly to the deep-fat fryer, but then few religions express themselves so emphatically with food.

Here's what it's all about. In 165BC Judas Maccabeus led a Jewish uprising against the oppressive reign of King Antiochus Epiphanes and the Syrian Hellenists. On returning victorious to Jerusalem they found the temple had been desecrated. All but one of the oil vessels had been polluted with substances regarded as impure by the Jews, and there was only enough olive oil to burn for a day. But when, the story goes, the Jews poured it into the lamp – the *menorah* – it miraculously burned for eight days, giving them time to clean up and reconsecrate the temple. In commemoration, Hanukkah is known as the Festival of Lights and is celebrated over eight days. And the way it is celebrated is by frying.

Actually, up till fairly recently, certainly the Middle Ages, which counts as recent for such an ancient faith, Hanukkah was a very modest affair. That's to say, it was a religious occasion quietly marked at temple rather than a festival celebrated at home, as it then became, and officially declared a time when mourning or sadness was forbidden and singing and rejoicing were to be desired. A game that involved spinning a *dreidel*, a kind of top, came into play after the lighting of the eight-candled *menorah*, one candle each day. And so it remains. But it wasn't really until the late twentieth century that Hanukkah became a really big deal. Because Hanukkah tends to fall in December (the 25th of Kislet in the Jewish Calender), observant Jews who feel that their children are losing out to all the celebrations of Christmas, began raising its profile: presents are given, even an alternative to the Christmas tree, in the form of a Hanukkah bush, is put up.

But so far as I can see, the real deal about Hanukkah is that it's latke time.

LATKES

Just as "blini" is the Russian word for pancake, "latke" is the Yiddish one. In other words, you could make any sort of pancake, fry it and serve it up as a Hanukkah special. But that wouldn't be quite how it is. For Ashkenazi Jews – those of Central and Eastern European origin, which is about 80 per cent of world Jewry – a latke is a little potato cake, rather like a cross between a miniature rösti and a hash brown. That's in their idealized state. On the whole, in real life, they are overwhelmingly stodgy, and that is one of their charms, but they don't have to be.

I've given recipes for latkes twice before and the ingredients remain the same – as how could they not? – but I've altered the method slightly, to produce cakes that are crunchy on the outside, melting inside: no full-on stodge, but plenty of the bolstering warmth that only a carbohydrate can provide.

approx $1^1/_2$lbs potatoes to make
   approx $3^1/_2$ cups when grated
1 small onion
1 egg

1 teaspoon sea salt/$^1/_2$ teaspoon
   table salt
2 tablespoons Matzoh meal
olive (or other) oil for frying

Makes approx. 14

note
You don't *have* to use olive oil to fry them – and I certainly don't mean the extra virgin stuff – but it seems right to do so to make the quintessential Hanukkah offering, it being the oil that was miraculously replenished in the sacked temple.

Peel your potatoes, cut them into chunks and push them down the funnel of the food processor with the grater-disk fitted. Obviously latkes have been around for far longer than food processors – since the seventeenth century, when the Jews in the Pale of Settlement started making a version of them – and so it is perfectly possible to grate the potato by hand, and many people, you can be sure, still insist on it.

Either way, once the potato is grated, remove the shreds to a sieve, pressing down to squish out excess liquid, and empty the bowl of the processor of starchy water, too. Put the bowl back in place on the motor, fit the double-bladed knife and finely chop the peeled and quartered small onion (or $^1/_2$ normal sized one) together with any of the end pieces of the potato that didn't get grated properly earlier. Or chop by hand.

Tip the drained grated potato into a bowl, add the chopped onion, crack in the egg, sprinkle in the salt and the Matzoh meal, and fold or stir everything together to mix.

Heat enough oil to come $^1/_2$ inch up a heavy-based skillet, and form your latkes. I find the best way to do this is to use my hands. I scoop out a small handful (I suppose about 2 tablespoons' worth) and squeeze out excess liquid back in the bowl. I then press down and pat round to make into a little uneven cake about $2^1/_2$ inches in diameter and fry it, and all the others that come after it, for a good 2 minutes a side.

When they're ready, you have lacy little cakelets, as if you had made creamy potato patties and dredged them in vermicelli before frying, as the strands of grated potato get crackly in the oil.

Eat straightaway, as if you needed the encouragement. I love these just with some extra sea salt sprinkled over them, but they are good as they are traditionally eaten, with a splodge of cinnamony apple purée, too. (But if that's where your interest lies, then see the apple latkes over the page.) Or you could go the cocktail party route and eat them with smoked salmon and crème fraîche.

APPLE LATKES

I had thought of writing a recipe, or at least directions in terms of quantity, for making an apple purée to go with the potato latkes, but then I took it into my head to make some apple latkes instead. My appetite was whetted by reading Joan Nathan's really wonderful *Jewish Holiday Kitchen*. Of course many people mix potato, onion and apple in the one latke, but these are most definitely sweet – gorgeous fritters to be eaten for breakfast, afternoon tea or dessert, or just any time, straight from the pan and drenched with maple syrup.

Makes about 20 x 2–2$^1/_2$ inch latkes

note

If you eschew maple or golden syrup – why? – then you can simply mix a small amount of ground cinnamon and confectioners' sugar together, and push through a small strainer, delicately dusting the puffy, crisp-coated apple latkes

1 egg
$^1/_3$ cup Greek plain yogurt plus $^1/_3$ cup low-fat milk; or $^2/_3$ cup natural plain yogurt
1 cup all-purpose flour
$^1/_2$ teaspoon baking powder
$^1/_4$ teaspoon baking soda

$^1/_2$ teaspoon ground cinnamon
2 tablespoons superfine sugar
2 apples/$^1/_2$lb in weight; to make 1 cup grated apples
vegetable oil for frying
maple syrup or confectioners' sugar and ground cinnamon for serving

Beat the egg with the yogurt and milk or just the yogurt if you're using the plain normal variety, and set aside. Combine the flour, baking powder, baking soda, cinnamon and sugar in a bowl. Peel, quarter and core the apples, then grate them; I use a food processor, but a coarse Microplane or other grater would work easily I'd imagine.

Pour the egg-yogurt mixture into the flour bowl, tip in the wet, grated apples and fold all together.

Pour enough oil to come about $^1/_4$ inch up in a skillet and put on the stove to heat. Dollop spoonfuls – I use a round soup spoon – of the apple batter into the sizzling oil; a rubber spatula – the one you used to fold the batter together – will help you scrape the batter off the spoon and press down on the little latkes in the pan. Don't worry about making perfect round pancakes; I like these a bit raggedy and skew-whiff. Fry for a minute or two, until the latkes are a golden brown on the underside; you can see from the top as they start firming up underneath. Flip them with two metal spatulas, and fry for another minute on the uncooked side.

Remove to a tray lined with paper towels, to blot excess oil, and continue cooking until you've used up all the batter.

RUGELACH

A name like this – the *ch* is rasping, as if in exasperation – doesn't conjure up a rare delicacy, but it should. A rugelach in the normal run of things is fine enough, a tender sour-cream dough turned into a cookie that is rolled around jam or nuts, or both, but this is a cut above. The dough is made with cream cheese, sour cream and butter, making it melting and light – and, incidentally, incredibly easy to work with, like Play-Doh – and its filling comprises dark brown chocolate and light brown sugar, both bitter and caramelly at the same time.

The recipe is a slight reworking of one of Marcy Goldman's, from the *Best of Betterbaking.com*, a book culled from her addictive website. But my original inspiration was a fabulous bakery near me called Baker & Spice, whose light and puffy chocolate rugelach have often lured me from my desk.

I am not sure why these cookies are made for Hanukkah but research showed they were and I didn't have a satisfactory counter-argument. Quite the contrary.

FOR THE DOUGH

3 cups all-purpose flour

$^1/_4$ teaspoon salt

$^1/_4$ cup superfine sugar

1 package (3 teaspoons) active dry
   or instant yeast, optional

2 sticks cold butter, diced

4 oz cream cheese, cut or spooned
   into pieces

1 egg

$^1/_4$ cup sour cream

Makes 36

Briefly process the flour, salt and sugar, and yeast if you're using it, just to combine them, and then add the diced butter and cream cheese pieces, and process again until the mixture resembles damp sand.

Beat the egg and sour cream together, and with the engine running, pour down the funnel of the processor. Continue running the motor until it comes together in a silky dough; it will seem like it won't make a dough, but leave the motor running and be patient.

Turn the dough out on to a lightly floured surface, and divide into three, forming each one into a fat disc. Put the discs into freezer bags and leave in the fridge to rest for an hour – though you can leave them there for longer – just taking them out about 10–15 minutes before you want to get rolling.

FOR THE FILLING

8oz semisweet or bittersweet
   chocolate

$^1/_4$ cup light brown sugar

$^1/_2$ stick butter

FOR THE EGG WASH

1 egg, beaten with a pinch of superfine sugar

FOR THE SUGAR GLAZE

3 tablespoons superfine sugar

3 tablespoons boiling water

Preheat the oven to 375°F. Process the chocolate until it's battered into rubble, and then put these dark brown crumbs into a bowl with the sugar, using your fingers to mix them together. Melt the butter separately and let it cool slightly.

Roll out one of the discs of dough on a lightly floured surface to a circle 10 inches in diameter. With a knife, divide the circle into 12 equal triangles, like you would divide a pizza, only don't pull apart the triangles yet.

Brush the circle of triangles with the melted butter, and then spread or sprinkle a third of the chocolate filling to cover the circle. Then very carefully pull away one triangle at a time, rolling each one up from the thick end to the narrow end to form a bulging curly-whirly crescent; think of a croissant. Follow this procedure with all of the dough discs and their filling.

Put the rugelach onto parchment paper lined baking sheets (if you've used yeast, let stand on the baking sheets as they are for 20 minutes) and brush each one with the egg wash, and bake in the preheated oven for 20 minutes.

When they come out of the oven, browned and puffy, mix the sugar and water together for the glaze, and brush the rugelach with this to make them shiny. Let them cool on a rack. My daughter *begs* for these at any time of year, as well she might.

MINI JAM DOUGHNUTS

These are a doll's house-sized version of the *soufganiot*, which have come, strangely, via the Austro-Hungarian servant-class of the French court of Marie-Antoinette, to become *the* Israeli Hanukkah delicacy. I've made the doughnuts small, chiefly because it is much easier to fry them like this. When they're normal size – and we all know what normal size is for a doughnut, one of the most heavenly creations to have been put on this earth – I find it hard to get the center cooked before the outside burns.

Many people have very clever methods or tools for inserting the jelly into a doughnut, but I think they are all asking for trouble. I find that wrapping the doughnut up and over a little dollop of jelly doesn't make for any bursting or spillage, but I don't want to tempt providence.

Makes 25

$^1/_2$ cup milk
1 tablespoon unsalted butter
$^3/_4$ cup bread flour
$^1/_2$ package ($1^1/_2$ teaspoons) active dry or instant yeast
$^1/_4$ teaspoon salt
2 tablespoons superfine sugar

1 egg
$^1/_4$ cup strawberry jam
vegetable oil for deep-frying (more than I can bear to think: at least 2 big bottles)
1 cup sugar for rolling doughnuts in

Warm the milk and butter together in a saucepan, taking it off the heat when the butter is melting. Put the flour, yeast, salt and the 2 tablespoons of superfine sugar in a bowl. Beat the egg into the warmed milk and butter and pour this into your bowl of dry ingredients, mixing with a wooden spoon. Either using your hands, or the dough-hook of a free-standing mixer, knead the dough until it is smooth and silky. If you're doing this by hand, it'll probably take about 10 minutes, but it's beautiful to do, the feeling so glorious as the dough comes alive under your hands.

Pat the satiny dough into a round ball and put into a buttered bowl, cover in plastic wrap and leave to rise somewhere warm; it should double in size, and this could take 1–2 hours.

Punch the dough down, and knead again to make the dough smooth. On a lightly floured surface, roll the dough out to a $^3/_4$ inch thickness, and cut out circles with a $1^1/_2$ inch round cutter. You can re-roll the dough to make more circles.

Make the dough circles into flatter rounds in your hands and then put an $^1/_8$ teaspoon jam in the center and fold in half, like a pasty or an agnolotto, pinching the edges before rolling it in your hands to turn it back into a round doughnut. Sit the doughnuts on a baking sheet as you make them, flattening them down slightly, so that you have stout little bulging discs in front of you.

Meanwhile, heat the oil to 375°F in a deep-fat fryer, and then cook the mini doughnuts roughly six at a time for about 5 minutes in total, flipping them over halfway through cooking so that they brown evenly on all sides. If you're not using a deep-fat fryer but just a pan filled with hot oil, watch the oil doesn't overheat, as it'll make the little doughnuts darken too quickly.

Put the remaining sugar into a shallow bowl and as the doughnuts come out of the fryer, dredge them in the sugar, rolling them around to get an even coating.

note

You can play with this dough as you like: you don't need to make conventional doughnuts. I had a few rounds left over during the photo shoot, and divided each cut-out bit of dough into three, rolled each third into ribbons in my hands, as if I were rolling long lean straggly cigars, and then braided the three ropes together (something like remedial basket-weaving: I had really lost it, obviously). Deep fried and rolled with sugar they look like beautiful, speckled ears of puffy wheat.

ZALABIA

There's something curiously satisfying about ending a section with a recipe beginning with a "Z". But then, there's something gratifying about having a recipe beginning with "Z" in the first place.

If you are at all weak-willed or given to self-loathing and remorse, then I beg of you not even to think of making these. Once you've eaten a single crunchy, syrup-juicy twig of this stuff, you will be lost. But if you can allow yourself to take pleasure in it, a whole new world is open to you.

I can't pretend that I wasn't drawn towards this recipe, from Daisy Iny's *Best of Baghdad Cooking*, because of the fact that I am now married to a man who comes originally from the same place as the *zalabia* does. I think it's impossible to feel you know someone without having a feeling for the food they ate as a child or, at least, a curiosity about what they might have eaten.

To understand exactly what zalabia tastes like, you should try and imagine a thin tubing of crunchy batter, enclosing nothing but air, fried in squiggles and doused in fragrant syrup. It's that good.

It's easiest, I think, to make the squiggles by squeezing the batter out of a plastic ketchup dispenser – the sort that sometimes comes in the shape of a tomato – but you can just drip the batter off the tip of a spoon into the sizzling oil beneath instead, if you want.

1 cup all-purpose flour	1 package (3 teaspoons) active dry	Makes 15–18
1 cup lukewarm water	or instant yeast	
pinch salt	vegetable oil for frying	

FOR THE SYRUP

3 cups superfine sugar	1 tablespoon rosewater
1¹/₂ cups water	1 tablespoon orange-flower water
1¹/₂ tablespoons lemon juice	

To make the syrup, stir the sugar and water together, and then bring to the boil, never stirring again, and let it bubble and boil away for 5 minutes.

Add the lemon juice and let it boil for a further 2 minutes. Stir in the rosewater and orange-flower water, take off the heat and pour into a pitcher to cool (and thence to a fridge or a cold place, near the window, say). All these numbers are give or take: you want to end up with a syrup that's thick enough to coat, but runny enough to drip off the fritters, and remember it will thicken more as it cools.

Put the flour, water, salt and yeast into a blender, and blitz until smooth. Leave to stand in the blender canister for 30 minutes.

Fill a wide pan with enough oil, to come about 2 inches up, roughly, and over a medium flame, heat until hot. Take out a – clean – squeezy ketchup bottle, or you could use one of those water bottles with a built-in straw for the top – in either case, the aperture should be about the size of a lentil – and fill with the batter.

Squeeze ribbons of batter into the hot oil to make swirly encircling shapes like a pretzel. The conventional size of *zalabia* is 7 inches but you can make them any size or design you like. Don't worry if bits break off: they're the best part. And as I say, you can just drip some batter from the tip of a spoon, adding more water if the batter gets too thick to dribble off easily.

Fry until golden brown on each side, and then transfer to a shallow dish or ideally a baking sheet with small sides into which you have poured the syrup so that you can coat the *zalabia* as you go.

PARTYTIME

ONE DOESN'T really want to be quoting Goering, let alone misquoting him, but every time I hear people talk of Entertaining, I reach for my revolver.

I don't manage to stir myself to much more than trays upon trays of hot little sausages (cooked in the oven) and bowls of fabulously good potato chips for parties, but there are times when you need more of a spread. But what kind of food is really necessary is like asking how long is a piece of string. Drinks parties can turn into occasions where you need something more substantial so everyone doesn't decamp to go and get a proper dinner elsewhere, and sometimes you just need vast bowls of stuff on the table to soak up drink and keep the hard core happy at the end. In other words, you need to concern yourself with all the little twiddly bits and pieces, as well as the troughs for serious pigging out. It's all possible. It just needs planning.

UNHAPPY HOUR
Or Coping with Canapés

I can't pretend that cocktail party food wouldn't be a whole lot simpler if you got someone else to cook it for you. It's not easy making sure little light bites are warm and ready while letting everyone welcomingly through the door and keeping their drinks topped up.

I think the first thing you have to let go of is the anxiety about whether everything is being served at its point of perfection. It won't be. Some food will just cool down and even get a little leaden on the plate. But mostly, this doesn't matter. A few drinks in, and no one will mind. Otherwise, concentrate on food that either is OK at whatever temperature it's eaten, or that can be made in advance and kept warm in a low oven (generally 275°F is the setting you should switch the dial to) for a gradual, unstressful handing-out of foodstuffs for assembled friends. And try to remember they are your friends, not an army of roving restaurant or lifestyle critics, fierce judgements at the ready. If you can't quite feel that way about things, either change your friends or stop giving parties.

note

Since I don't know what size of party you're giving, or how many dishes you want to present, I've decided on quantities that are easy to double or fiddle with generally, rather than swamp you with huge amounts from the get-go.

PARMA HAM BUNDLES

This is the ideal recipe to start with as it's a model of good party food – simple to make and can be left to sit around happily. I'd make lots up in advance, though, leave them in the fridge, and then out in the kitchen, to be taken round to people later once the hot food has either dried up or got too cold.

Make sure the Parma ham, or other prosciutto crudo of your choice, is not too fatty nor cut too thin. Parma ham and figs is a time-honored combination and the soft sourness of the goat's cheese perfectly offsets the greater sweetness of the dried figs used here. I have made this, in late summer, with fresh figs, but actually I prefer it with the dried.

14oz sliced Parma ham (not sliced ultra-thinly)

$1^1/_2$ cups dried mission figs or other dried figs
$^1/_2$ cup mild soft goat's cheese

Makes 25

note
I use a French brand of soft goat's cheese called Chavroux, but any soft goat's curd cheese or creamy cheese would do.

Cut or tear each slice of Parma ham into two or three strips. Scissor each fig in half – if you're not using the little Californian mission figs, which I found in packages at the supermarket, you may need to quarter them – and spread a teaspoon of goat's cheese onto the cut half of the fig. Place the piece of fig cheese-side down on to the center of a strip of ham and then make it into a bundle. Sit each bulging pink parcel so that the darkness of the fig is hidden plate-side down.

RICOTTA AND SPINACH BACI

This is a savory mouthful based on the model of the *baci di ricotta*, those sweet airy ricotta kisses on page 126, and is warm and wonderful against the smooth chill of the Parma ham bundles. Plus, it is very important to make sure – and yes, it is me saying this – that you have enough food for non-meat-eaters.

Makes approx. 40

10oz frozen spinach, once thawed
  makes 1 packed cup
1 cup ricotta cheese
1/2 cup freshly grated
  Parmesan

freshly grated nutmeg
1/2 cup all-purpose flour
1 1/2 teaspoons baking powder
2 eggs, beaten
vegetable or corn oil for frying

Thaw the spinach and squeeze out any excess water; this is most easily done using a sieve, but really press down brutally. Mix the unwatery spinach in a bowl with the ricotta, and add the Parmesan, nutmeg and salt and pepper.

Stir in the flour, baking powder and beaten eggs and beat everything together to make a batter. Fill a wide, shallow pan with about 3/4 inch of oil. Heat the pan of oil until a tiny blob of batter sizzles when dropped into the hot fat. Drop rounded teaspoons of the ricotta batter into the pan, about 5 or 6 at a time; you will need to turn them over quite quickly so it's best to do only a few at once. As they turn a golden brown, visible despite the green, flip them over and leave for a minute or so on the other side. Put the cooked ricotta and spinach baci on some paper towels as they come out of the pan to remove any excess oil.

They are good eaten warm, rather than piping hot, which will work well for passing-around purposes.

MINI CRAB CAKES

There are a lot of crab cake recipes out there, that I don't deny, but there's a reason for this: people really love eating them. So why resist? Why hold back? These are simple to make, and I like them at any temperature – though as with most everything else here, they sit well under a loose covering of foil in a low oven – which is even better.

If you want to serve a sauce alongside, then make something along the lines of the wasabi-spiked mayonnaise for the crab cocktail on page 145, only a little stronger. Don't make it runny, though: you want more of an ointment than a sauce proper. So, more wasabi and more lime zest, but only a bit of juice, soy and Worcestershire sauce, and no sesame oil, and that's it.

Makes approx. 50

4 scallions
1 clove garlic
3 1/2 cups white crab meat

2 teaspoons Tamari or Japanese
  soy sauce

2 teaspoons Japanese wasabi paste
2 teaspoons rice vinegar

$^1/_3$ cup plus 1 tablespoon brown rice flour
vegetable oil for frying

note

I always buy organic brown rice flour at the health store, but if you can't find that, then use ordinary rice flour. Similarly, if you can't locate wasabi, use English mustard.

Trim the scallions and roughly chop them, peel the clove of garlic, and put both into a food processor and blitz until finely chopped. Add the other ingredients, apart from the oil, and process again until all has mixed together into a rough paste. Or you can chop finely by hand and mix in the other ingredients. In a large frying pan, heat $^1/_4$ inch of oil (vegetable or peanut). As soon as a little bit of mixture sizzles when it is dropped in, you're ready to fry.

Drop teaspoonfuls of crab mixture into the hot oil, and fry until golden brown and crispy all over. Cook about 10 at a time so that you can turn them quickly and the oil temperature doesn't drop too much. Drain the cooked crab cakes on paper towels and then transfer to a plate for serving. I'd kill for these at a party.

SALT AND PEPPER WINGS

2 tablespoons sea salt
4 cloves garlic
2 tablespoons pink or white peppercorns

$^1/_4$ cup olive oil
2 tablespoons lemon juice
2lb chicken wings

Makes approx. 28, depending on the size of the wings

Crush the salt and peeled garlic cloves in a pestle and mortar until it resembles a paste. Add the peppercorns and continue bashing until the pepper's slightly crushed, then add oil and lemon juice and pour the marinade into a plastic freezer bag. If you haven't got a pestle and mortar, pour the oil, salt and lemon juice into a plastic freezer bag and grate or mince in the garlic – or use garlic oil of course, an old favorite – and grind in a great deal of pepper. Add the chicken wings to the bag and squish them around in the marinade, then seal the bag and leave them in the fridge overnight or for up to two days.

Preheat the oven to 425°F. Let the marinated chicken come to room temperature. Line a shallow roasting pan with aluminum foil, then pour in the wings and their marinade, making sure everything's spread out. Roast for about 40 minutes, turning them halfway until they're cooked through and crisp, even slightly scorched in parts. Serve with napkins.

PORK NOODLE BALLS

Mad though it may sound to cook noodles and then stash them in a meatball mix before rolling into straggly rounds and frying them, you just have to trust me here. Make more than you think you need.

I find it easy to get into a real meatball thing for parties. As long as you keep a bowl of cold water nearby for dunking your hands in regularly, it's not so much bother. Indeed, I'd go further: this is just the sort of mindless repetitive activity that can calm and soothe.

Makes 25–30

note
These are good with chilli sauce to dip in alongside.
And turn to page 441 to see the recipe for aromatic lamb meatballs, as it's good to have a plate of those, too.

3oz or 1 sheet medium dried fine egg noodles (not tagliatelle)
8 oz ground pork
2 scallions, finely chopped
2 cloves garlic, minced
1 tablespoon minced ginger
1 tablespoon chilli sauce
1 tablespoon soy sauce
3 tablespoons semolina
1 egg
vegetable oil for frying

Cook the noodles according to the package instructions; generally you put the noodles into boiling water, stir gently and bring back to the boil. Turn off the heat and leave to stand for 2 minutes, then drain and rinse in cold water.

Cut the noodles with scissors into short pieces, and put them in a bowl with the ground pork, scallions, minced garlic and ginger, chilli sauce, soy sauce, semolina and egg, and then work everything together well with your fingers. Cover with plastic wrap and put into the fridge for an hour – or longer if that helps.

Have a bowl of cold water nearby, and with wet hands form the pork noodle mixture into just-smaller-than-walnut-sized balls. Line them up on a baking sheet lined with plastic wrap as you go.

Heat about 1 inch oil in a skillet and fry the balls in batches in the hot oil until darkly golden and the bits of noodle that show through or straggle out are crisp.

FONDUE BALLS

This is one of those love-'em-or-loathe-'em recipes. Half the people I've made them for can't get enough, the others are slightly spooked by the curious texture of soft cheese and ham sauce, melting into fondant in the middle. The title kind of lets you know what you're in for. And, obviously, I belong to the former category or I wouldn't have included them here.

$^1/_2$ stick butter

1 tablespoon olive oil

$^1/_2$ cup plus 1 tablespoon
   all-purpose flour

$^2/_3$ cup dry white wine

$^2/_3$ cup milk

dash of chicken stock concentrate
   or tiny crumble of chicken
   bouillon cube

$^1/_4$ teaspoon grated nutmeg

1 cup sliced, cooked lean ham,
   finely chopped

3 tablespoons chopped parsley

3 tablespoons grated Parmesan

1 cup breadcrumbs or matzoh meal

vegetable oil for frying

Makes approx. 45

note
The fondue balls can be frozen without their coating of breadcrumbs and then rolled in crumbs before cooking in the same way until golden brown, which will take a fraction longer from frozen. This is what I tend to do.

Melt the butter and oil in a saucepan and add the flour, stirring together to make a roux. Whisk in the wine and milk and part of a stock cube or some liquid stock concentrate and keep stirring over a medium heat until the white sauce comes to the boil and is really, really thick. Cook it, stirring, at boiling point for about 5 minutes. Take the pan off the heat and add the nutmeg, pepper to taste, ham, chopped parsley and grated Parmesan. Hold back on salt until you've tasted with the Parmesan in. Transfer the sauce to a shallow dish to cool and cover with some wet parchment paper (screw up a piece of parchment under a running tap and squeeze it out before using) or plastic wrap to stop the mixture getting a skin as it cools. The plastic wrap must actually cling: that's to say adhere like a skin to the sauce. When cool, put in the fridge to become completely cold and solid.

Roll teaspoonfuls of mixture with your hands into balls, and then roll in the breadcrumbs or matzoh meal in a shallow dish. Heat $^1/_2$ inch of oil in a frying pan and when hot cook the fondue balls until golden brown all over, about a minute or so on each side. Drain on some paper towels as you cook them in smallish batches.

The inside will be gooey, like fondue indeed, and taste quite winey. Very après-ski (though better without the actual exercise).

HOT BOCCONCINI otherwise known as Goldenballs

This isn't just to make sure vegetarians don't feel left out – I think it's the best possible use there could be for those undistinguished, marbly white baby eggs of mozzarella that are sold unconvincingly as if a delectable treasure.

It's hard to be precise about numbers, as it so depends on how many *bocconcini* – literally "little mouthfuls" – come in a tub. For reasons I can't absolutely fathom, I find 17 to be the most usual number, but that may just be particular to the brand I come across. If you can find Japanese Panko breadcrumbs – my supermarket has them – you will taste these at their best.

Makes approx. 17

5oz of *bocconcini*
$^1/_4$ cup cornstarch
1 egg, beaten with a little salt

$^1/_3$ cup Panko breadcrumbs
vegetable oil for frying

Drain the *bocconcini*. Put the cornstarch in a plastic freezer bag, and the salted egg in a shallow bowl with the Panko breadcrumbs in another shallow bowl.

Shake the *bocconcini* in the bag of cornstarch, and then dip them in the egg and then roll them around in the breadcrumbs. Use one hand for egg dipping and the other for breadcrumb rolling, this helps your fingers not to get glued up with the eggy breadcrumbs creating what Hettie, my assistant, and I wearily call goujon fingers.

Pour enough oil to come about 2 inches deep into a thick-bottomed pan and fry the *bocconcini* in two to three batches until they are golden brown and crisp. Test one – with caution, so that you don't burn yourself – to check that the middle is all stringy and melty, that familiar cheese-flavored chewing gum.

And I'll be frank: these are best eaten while still hot, fresh from the pan.

MAKE MINE A LARGE ONE

The food I like best at parties is the carb-rich stuff everyone falls for, having spent the evening virtuously turning down every mimsy little canapé. But then, that big-bowled end-of-party feeding frenzy is the best bit, when the few who are left are too nervous to leave, knowing that the minute they're out of the door, it's their turn to be given the full treatment.

This is the food you serve your friends, however, your best friends, who came early to lend support and who stay on because they need it.

CORNBREAD-TOPPED CHILLI CON CARNE

There are few more welcome sights than a big vat of chilli. The cornbread topping is a glorious golden touch, that everyone can crumble into the spiced meat as they eat, for ballast and crunchy contrast.

It makes your life easier and the chilli better if you make the meat up in advance, adding the topping and baking the lot just before you serve it.

FOR THE CHILLI CON CARNE

4 onions
2 cloves garlic
$1/4$ cup/4 tablespoons olive oil
2 teaspoons dried or crushed
chillies, or to taste
2 teaspoons ground coriander
2 teaspoons ground cumin
5 cardamom pods, bruised
2 red bell peppers

3lbs 4oz ground beef
7 cups canned chopped tomatoes
$1/2$ cup/8 tablespoons tomato
ketchup
$1/2$ cup/8 tablespoons tomato purée
1 cup water
2 tablespoons unsweetened cocoa
$3^1/2$ cups red kidney beans

FOR THE CORNBREAD

$1^1/2$ teaspoons salt
4 cups cornmeal
$1/4$ cup/4 tablespoons all-purpose
flour
6 teaspoons baking powder
2 teaspoons ground cinnamon

3 cups buttermilk
4 eggs
2 teaspoons honey
$1/4$ cup/4 tablespoons vegetable oil
2 cups Cheddar cheese, coarsely
grated

TO SERVE

4 ripe avocados
4 scallions
juice of 2 limes
$1/4$ cup chopped cilantro

2 cups sour cream
paprika to dust over
$3^3/4$ cups Cheddar cheese, grated

Serves up to 20

note
I don't know why, but this is
especially good cold the next
morning, too.

Peel and finely chop the onions; you might want to use the processor here, and if so, add the peeled garlic or mince it by hand. Heat the oil in a very large pan – it has to take everything later – and fry the onion and garlic until they begin to soften. Add the chilli, coriander, cumin and crushed cardamom pods and stir well.

Deseed and finely dice the red peppers, and tip into the spicy onion. Break up the ground beef into the pan and, using a fork, keep turning it to separate it as the meat browns. It's hard to brown quite so much meat, so just do the best you can.

Add the chopped tomatoes, kidney beans, ketchup, purée and water, stirring to make a rich red sauce. When the chilli starts to boil, sprinkle over the cocoa and stir it in. Simmer partially covered for $1^1/_2$ hours. At this point you can cool and freeze the chilli, or just keep it in the fridge – or a cool place – overnight.

Preheat the oven to 425°F. Tip the chilli into a large, wide dish or keep in the pan that is ovenproof.

Combine the salt, cornmeal, flour, baking powder and cinnamon in a bowl. Whisk together the buttermilk, eggs, honey and oil in a glass measuring cup, and then stir into the dry ingredients, mixing to make a vivid yellow batter.

Pour the cornmeal topping over the chilli con carne, or blob it over to cover the top as evenly as possible. Don't worry if some of the chilli seeps through as this won't matter one tiny bit.

Sprinkle the cheese over the top of the cornbread and then bake in the oven for 30 minutes or until the cornbread topping is risen and golden and the chilli underneath is bubbling. How long this precisely takes depends on how cold or hot the chilli was when it went into the oven. Since it's such a huge vat, you may find it simpler to reheat it on the stove in its pan, before it gets its topping, to start with.

Let the chilli stand for about 5 minutes once out of the oven before cutting the top into squares or slices to serve with a helping of chilli underneath.

And alongside this chilli, as with the vegetarian chilli overleaf, you should dollop out an un-chillied guacamole, some cool sour cream and a mounded pile of strong grated Cheddar. So, mash the ripe avocados with the finely chopped scallions and add the lime juice and some salt to taste. Stir in most of the chopped cilantro and turn into two bowls, sprinkling each with the remaining cilantro.

Divide the sour cream into another two bowls, and dust with a little paprika and, into yet another pair of bowls, grate the Cheddar so that people can take clumps and add the tangy cheese to their plates of guacamole and sour-cream splodged chilli.

VEGETARIAN CHILLI WITH CORNBREAD TOPPING

I know it must be irritating for vegetarians to have me commend this by saying it tastes wonderful to meat-eaters too, but that happens to be the case.

Serves approx. 10

2 tablespoons olive oil
2 medium onions, finely chopped
2 cloves garlic, minced
2 large red bell peppers, deseeded and finely diced, yields 3 cups
2 teaspoons dried chilli flakes, or to taste
1 teaspoon ground coriander
1 teaspoon ground cumin

3 cardamom pods, crushed
$1^1/_2$ cups red lentils
3 cups tomato pulp or thick puree
3 cups water
3 cups red kidney beans
$^1/_4$ cup tomato ketchup
$^1/_4$ cup tomato paste
1 tablespoon unsweetened cocoa

In a large pan – one that will take everything later and that has a lid – heat the oil and fry the onion, garlic and bell peppers until everything softens, about 10 minutes. Add the chilli, coriander, cumin and cardamom pods, stirring everything around in the spices. Tip in the lentils and stir again.

Stir in the canned chopped tomatoes, water, kidney beans, ketchup, tomato paste and cocoa and bring the mixture to the boil. Simmer, covered, for about 45 minutes stirring frequently. If the mixture is too liquid – check every now and again – uncover the pan slightly as it cooks.

The best way to approach this is as with the chilli con carne, so cook the above ahead of time and then transfer to an ovenproof dish – I use an old Pyrex one which is about 9 x 13 inches and about 3 inches deep – and keep, once cooled, in the fridge until you're ready to top with cornbread and bake.

The cornbread topping is exactly as for the chilli con carne, only you'll need half quantities; and I find in a dish of about these dimensions, the veggie-chilli needs about 25 minutes at 425°F.

The accompaniments of extra grated cheese, guacamole and sour cream are as for the chilli con carne, too.

RIGATONI AL FORNO

This started off life as an easy take on lasagne; now I'm beginning to think I prefer it. The difficulty with lasagne is that it is only truly good if you make the pasta yourself, which is not exactly difficult but, given that everyone is so used to lasagne as an ordinary, unspecial dish, the effort and labor tend to go unappreciated. This should not matter as much as I feel it does, I'm afraid. But anyway, it's not the pasta-making that's so hard; it's all the fiddly layering that can be tedious.

For this version you make up a meat sauce and a rather liquid béchamel, as for a lasagne, but then all you do is cook some short fat pasta tubes and toss all three components together before baking in the vast pan you have in front of you. Somehow this never feels like a big deal, but it looks so gloriously like a big deal: huge, welcoming, alcohol-absorbing.

3 1lb package rigatoni	1 cup Parmesan, freshly grated	Serves 16

FOR THE MEAT SAUCE

3 onions	3lbs 4oz ground beef
3 carrots	$1^{1}/_{2}$ cups tomato pulp or chopped
6oz bacon or pancetta	canned tomatoes
3 sticks of celery	4 tablespoons tomato purée
3 bay leaves	2 cups red wine
3 cloves garlic	$1^{3}/_{4}$ cups water, swilled in the
1 stick butter	tomato can
$^{1}/_{4}$ cup olive oil	

FOR THE BÉCHAMEL

$1^{1}/_{2}$ sticks butter	6 cups milk
$^{1}/_{2}$ cup plus 2 tablespoons	salt or stock granules to taste
all-purpose flour	freshly grated nutmeg

note
When I make this I often freeze the meat sauce, and then give it a slow overnight thaw in the fridge before using it. I make the béchamel a day ahead and leave it in the fridge overnight. You have to cook the pasta, I find, just before you put it in the oven. If, however, you're combining hot – rather than chilled – sauces with the pasta, you won't need to give the assembled dish as long in the oven.

Roughly chop the peeled onions, peeled carrots, the bacon or pancetta and the celery. Peel the garlic cloves and put them along with the chopped veg and bacon into a food processor and finely chop. Or chop them all finely by hand. Heat the butter and oil in a large pan and fry your bacony vegetable mush gently for 10 minutes or until soft.

Add the ground beef and fork it through until it browns in the pan as much as possible. Pour in the chopped tomatoes and purée, red wine, bay leaves and tomatoey water. Stir well, and bring to the boil, then turn down the heat, partially cover and let cook gently for 2 hours.

To make the white sauce, melt the butter in a saucepan, then add the flour and stir and cook together to make a roux. Take off the heat briefly, and whisk in the milk – just using a little hand whisk – then put back on the heat and, stirring all the time, let the

sauce come to the boil and bubble away for a few minutes to get rid of the floury taste. Season with salt and pepper (or you could use some crumbled stock cube or bouillon concentrate here), turn down the heat slightly and cook until slightly thickened, though bear in mind this needs to be liquid enough to coat the pasta easily. I find that once the flouriness has gone, it's fine, so just turn off the heat and stir in some freshly grated nutmeg. If you're making this in advance pour into a large batter bowl and press some plastic wrap on to the surface to stop it getting a skin as it cools.

Preheat the oven to 400°F and put the water on for the pasta. You need a gratifyingly large pan for this. When the water comes to the boil, add salt – bearing in mind that, as Anna del Conte says, the water for pasta should be as salty as the Mediterranean – and cook the pasta, making sure it's al dente; start tasting it 3 minutes before the time given on the package.

Drain the pasta and, while still a little wet, put it back into the big pan and pour over the white sauce, mixing well. Add the meat sauce, and mix again until the pasta is covered in both, though don't worry about combining the lot smoothly: I like to see the brown and white sauces slightly marbling the pasta, in some abstract version of Florentine swirls. Tip the sauced pasta into a large buttered roasting pan about $12^3/_4$ x $16^1/_2$ inches. Cover the top with the grated Parmesan and cook for 30–45 minutes or until the top is crispy and golden in places.

BIG PASTA WITH MUSHROOM, PARSLEY, GARLIC AND THYME

In some ways this is a non-meat-eater's version of the baked rigatoni above, and it's certainly true that for a big party I'd serve both together to please all-comers, but I don't see it as a consolation prize for the non-carnivorous. It's succulent perfection in its own right.

And as quintessentially Italian as the rigatoni al forne is, this just isn't: it's too garlicky somehow to be Italian, but that's fine. I don't make the point apologetically, I'm just keen to explain what's what. Besides, no false claims need to be made here: it argues its own case eloquently, aromatically enough.

Serves 16

3 1lb packages rigatoni or other big pasta of choice

FOR THE BÉCHAMEL
$1^1/_2$ sticks butter
1 cup all-purpose flour

8 cups milk
freshly grated nutmeg

FOR THE MUSHROOM MIXTURE

3oz dried porcini mushrooms,
  soaked in 2 cups boiling water

$^3/_4$ stick butter

1 tablespoon vegetable oil

$1^1/_2$ cups parsley, chopped, plus
  more for decoration

1 teaspoon dried thyme

3 fat cloves garlic, minced

1lb 8oz mixed mushrooms, about 12
  cups chopped

$^1/_2$ cup Amontillado sherry

2 cups Parmesan, freshly grated

fresh thyme for decoration

note

I use roughly 8oz each of button and chestnut mushrooms, roughly chopped, and 8oz shiitake mushrooms, stalks removed and caps sliced.

You can make the béchamel in advance, as for the rigatoni al forno above, as well as cooking the mushrooms, combining everything with the freshly cooked pasta just as it goes into the oven.

Soak the porcini in the boiling water in a small bowl. In a saucepan, melt the butter for the béchamel, and add the flour; cook gently to make a roux and then – off the heat – whisk in the milk. Turn the heat back on to medium, and stir the béchamel until it begins to thicken and come to the boil. Let it bubble for about 5 minutes to get rid of the floury taste. Take off the heat and season with salt, pepper and nutmeg.

Preheat the oven to 400°F. Heat a third of the butter and all of the oil for the mushrooms in a large wide pan. Drain the porcini, reserving the liquid, and chop before adding to the pan with half of the chopped parsley, the dried thyme and minced garlic. Stir for a couple of minutes then melt the remaining butter in the same pan and add the chopped mushrooms, stirring for about 5 minutes. The mushrooms will appear dry at first but will eventually start to give off some liquid.

Add the porcini soaking liquid, which the mushrooms will largely absorb, but keep stirring while adding the sherry and let it bubble away. Turn off the heat when you have a bronzed, syrupy stew. Stir the mushroom mixture into the béchamel and add half the Parmesan and the remaining half of the chopped parsley.

Put a big pan of water on for the pasta, and when it boils, salt it well. Cook the pasta until al dente, then drain and add to the mushroomy white sauce, stirring as best you can to get the pasta covered.

Turn into a large roasting pan, of approx. $12^3/_4$ x $16^1/_2$ inches. Sprinkle over the remaining Parmesan and bake for 30 minutes or until the top begins to turn golden in places.

When the pan comes out of the oven, sprinkle with some more chopped parsley and some sprigs of fresh thyme.

THE GRAND FINALE

You can always make a few desserts and cakes and dot them on the table after the vast bowls of chilli or pasta, or just make one magisterial great bowl of something so fabulous that no one will be looking around for alternatives. Surely this is the best option. Indeed, I know it is.

CHOCOLATE CHERRY TRIFLE

As impressive, gorgeous and generally unbeatable as this is, it's not actually difficult to make. The only thing you have to cook is the chocolate custard, and this is done well in advance. There isn't any point in making your own chocolate cakes to form the base, as once they're sandwiched with cherry jam and soused in cherry liqueur, you can't tell the difference. Having said that, I often freeze any leftover chocolate muffins I make (see page 257) or any chocolate cake I've made that hasn't risen properly, and use them here. Otherwise I buy two chocolate pound cakes and slice them up. It's not crucial, and you do whatever suits.

Serves 16

2 chocolate pound cakes (each approx. 12oz)
$^1/_2$ cup black cherry jam

$^1/_2$ cup cherry brandy
2 cups bottled or canned sour cherries, drained

FOR THE CUSTARD
4oz bittersweet chocolate, minimum 70% cocoa solids
$1^1/_3$ cups plus 1 tablespoon milk
$1^1/_3$ cups plus 1 tablespoon heavy cream

8 egg yolks
$^1/_2$ cup plus 1 tablespoon superfine sugar
$^1/_3$ cup unsweetened cocoa

FOR THE TOPPING
3 cups heavy cream

1oz bittersweet chocolate, as before

Slice the chocolate loaves or cake and make jam sandwiches with the cherry jam. Layer into the bottom of a large trifle bowl. Pour over the cherry brandy so that the cake soaks it up, and then tip in the drained cherries. Cover with plastic wrap and leave to macerate while you make the custard.

Chop up the chocolate and melt it; I do this on low to medium heat in the microwave, checking after 2 minutes, though it will probably need 4. Or you can stick the bowl over a pan of gently simmering water. Once the chocolate's melted, leave to one side while you get on with the custard proper.

Warm the milk and cream in a saucepan, and whisk the yolks, sugar and cocoa in a large bowl. Pour the warm milk and cream into the bowl, whisking it into the yolks and sugar mixture. Stir in the melted chocolate, scraping the sides well with a rubber spatula to get all of it in, and pour the custard back into the rinsed saucepan.

Cook over a medium heat until the custard thickens, stirring all the time. Make sure it doesn't boil, as it will split and curdle. Keep a sink full of cold water so that if you get scared you can plunge the custard pan into the cold water and whisk like mad, which will avert possible crisis.

The custard will get darker as it cooks and the flecks of chocolate will melt once the custard has thickened. And you do need this thick, so don't panic so much that you stop cooking while it's still runny. Admittedly, it carries on thickening as it cools and then when it's chilling in the fridge. Once it's ready, pour into a bowl to cool and cover the top of the custard with plastic wrap to stop it forming a skin.

When the custard is cold, pour and scrape it over the chocolate cake layer in the trifle bowl, and leave in the fridge to set, covered in plastic wrap, overnight.

When you are ready to decorate, whip the cream for the topping softly and spread it gently over the layer of custard. Grate the chocolate over the top. Let people fall upon it with greed and gratitude. They will go home happy.

MIDNIGHT FEAST

IT'S AN AWFUL thing to say, but I think I like coming up with recipes rather more than I like following them. Cooking is at its most enjoyable for me when I'm rummaging through the fridge hungry – not so hungry that I can't wait to cook the food before eating it, but hungry enough to pick what's there and go with it exuberantly. This is the sort of seat-of-your-pants, go-with-the-flow cooking that pares two essentials to their bare and most honest minimum: the ingredients on hand and your own taste.

In other words, this is intimate food, the sort you cook for yourself or two of you when it's late at night and you need something good to eat. By its nature, it's not fancy, it's just greedy opportunism. Relish it.

Of course the best sort of midnight feast needs no recipe. A bacon sandwich is never the wrong thing to eat late at night in front of the television, and all I'd say on this is that the perfect bacon sandwich is made by mushing the bread around in the oily pan in which the bacon has fried. You don't need butter, just this salty, greasy dripping that blackens the soft white bread slightly before being wodged around the crisp, bronzed crimson slices. I need English mustard here always, steak sauce sometimes.

A certain amount of judicious toying with leftovers is also integral, and here it's hardest to bark orders. I don't know what you've got in little plastic wrapped bowls in your fridge. I don't always know what's lingering about in mine. But if there's a small measuring cup of jellied chicken stock leftover from yesterday's roast lunch, consider boiling some pasta, draining it and dressing it in a little butter into which you have sprinkled some finely chopped rosemary and a drop of garlic-infused oil. Then, tip in the jellied stock and stir everything together until the pasta's glossy with amber juice. Eat as is, or flecked with just-chopped fresh parsley. See also the Sunday night pasta on page 244; you will see I sometimes don't even wait until I've got some stock leftover, but proceed blithely with concentrated chicken bouillon.

The ideal midnight feast doesn't have to be about using up leftovers, quietly satisfying though that is, but it can't depend on or have recourse to any major shopping expedition. I have a salty rather than a sweet tooth, and so my staples here are halloumi cheese and pancetta, both of which I must always have in the fridge, giving me the wherewithal for a quick supper at whatever time the mood strikes. Those whose midnight feasts are more likely to revolve around sugary items are, I've found, those who don't want anything cooked in the first place. You know who you are – and it's chocolate or ice cream you're after, not a quick batch of muffins or plate of syrup-doused pancakes. But it's always worth looking at the breakfast chapter for that sort of commodious late-night grazing. There's certainly nothing I'd eat first thing in the morning, that I wouldn't also love to take up to bed with me last thing at night.

Please don't ask me to be too strict about quantities here. Or rather, please regard any recipe in this chapter as guidance rather than pain-of-death order. I feel like that about recipes at the best of times, but late at night is no time to start treating your kitchen like some domestic science laboratory. The food that follows is nothing more than the happy accident of ingredients tumbled together in a pan and thence to your plate. Or rather, thence to my plate and thence, I'd urge, to yours.

THAT FIRST NIGHT...

SPAGHETTI ALLA CARBONARA

Well, I know there are those who feel that cooking sets a dangerous precedent, and I'm sure that up to a point they're right. I certainly wouldn't want to be going into hot *hausfrau* mode on a first date, setting dinner tables and the like; but a panful of hot pasta, to be taken back to bed and sharingly slurped is something else: I feel a first whole night together should be celebrated, even at three thirty in the morning.

I think spaghetti carbonara is what Meryl Streep cooks Jack Nicholson in the film version of one of my favorite books *Heartburn*, and it is so right for that chin-dripping, love-soaked primal feast, the first time someone actually stays through the night. Yes, I know a whole pack of spaghetti is far too much for two, but I want that whole panful lugged back to the bedroom. No namby-pamby mimsy little plated arrangement. So you'll have leftovers? Just work up an appetite for them later.

1lb package spaghetti
2 cups cubed pancetta or bacon
2 teaspoons olive oil
$^1/_4$ cup dry white wine or vermouth
4 eggs

$^1/_2$ cup Parmesan, freshly grated
black pepper
$^1/_4$ cup heavy cream
freshly grated nutmeg

Serves 2 (or 4 on less intimate occasions)

Put a large pan of salted water on to boil for the pasta. Cut the pancetta into $^1/_2$ x $^1/_4$ inch cubes. If the pancetta has its rind on, cut it off – and use a bigger piece of pancetta, as the amount I've specified is for the prepared cubes – and put the rind in a pan with a film of oil and cook it gently to render down.

Then in a large pan that will fit the pasta later, cook the pancetta cubes in the oil until crispy but not crunchy. Chuck over them the white wine or vermouth and let it bubble away so that, after a few minutes, you have a small amount of salty winey syrup left. Take the pan off the heat.

In a bowl, beat together the eggs, Parmesan, cream and some pepper. Cook the pasta more or less according to the package instructions, but since you want it kept al dente start checking it 2 minutes before the package says it's done. Lower in a cup and remove approximately $^1/_2$ cup of the pasta water before draining. Put the other pan, the one with the bacon cubes, on the heat and add the drained pasta, tossing well to coat with the syrupy pancetta. Add a little of the reserved pasta water to lubricate if necessary. Take the pan off the heat again and add the eggs and cheese mixture, swiftly tossing everything to mix. Grind over some more pepper and grate over the nutmeg, carry proudly aloft, and dive in.

Serves two hungry people, much too much in love to say goodnight (with apologies to Fats Waller).

SPAGHETTI FRITTATA

I am a great fan of a cold plate of spaghetti eaten while still leaning against the fridge's open door, but if there is one use for leftover pasta in any actual cooking sense, then this is it: an Italian omelette, thick with yesterday's pasta and still gooey in the middle. The frittata is especially good with leftover spaghetti carbonara: for choice, I'd always made a frittata with long pasta and I suppose, being an omelette, it lends itself more familiarly to pasta that's been in a bacony, cheesy sauce, but experiment by all means. See where it takes you. And if there's more than one of you, hope for more leftovers.

Serves 1

small pat butter
drop garlic-infused oil
1 cup leftover spaghetti
black pepper

3 eggs
1 scant tablespoon chopped
    parsley, optional

Preheat the broiler and melt the butter and oil in a heavy-bottomed or non-stick 8 inch skillet. Cut up the spaghetti into shorter lengths – I find scissors the best tool for this – and beat them with the eggs, adding a lot of freshly ground pepper. Pour this mixture into the hot pan and cook for a few minutes, swirling the pan about every now and again until the underside is cooked. Stick the pan under the broiler for a minute or so (taking care not to burn the pan's handle or yourself) until it's cooked on top and puffing goldenly.

    Stick your hands in some oven mitts – I can't tell you how many times I've burnt myself doing this – and take the pan out from under the grill, tilting it to slither the frittata out on to a waiting plate. Strew with freshly chopped parsley if you so wish.

GRILLED HALLOUMI WITH OOZING EGG AND MINT

I know I've enthused about halloumi cheese before, but can you blame me? This is chewy, salty and toothsome, and I love its rubbery texture – that softens on heating – and polystyrene rustle. And that's meant to be a commendation. If it helps, think of it as vegetarian bacon. Sometimes, indeed, I do just fry it in a dry pan and then plonk a poached or fried egg with it, but the following is my favorite, late-snacked supper or anytime hunger-appeaser. Use whatever salad you have to hand – arugula is good, baby spinach, those mixed leaves that come in a bag – and if you're fresh out of mint, then chop a chilli or a small gherkin, scatter with capers, or rootle out anything from fridge or cupboard that will give edge or bite.

Serves 1

4oz halloumi cheese
1 large egg

$1/2$ cup salad leaves
3 tablespoons mint leaves

Cut the halloumi into slices of about $^1/_2$ inch thick. I use about half a package of halloumi for this, which is about 5 slices. Fill a saucepan with water (for the egg) and if the egg's fridge-cold, stick it in and bring it to the boil, otherwise wait until the water is actually boiling before you lower in the egg.

Put a non-stick skillet on to heat up and when it's hot add the halloumi slices. They just need a scant minute or so before the dense whiteness begins to blister. So turn over and cook the other side. This is a very easy exercise in cooking, evidently, but the timing is crucial. You need to have the egg cooked about half a minute after you're satisfied the halloumi is done.

So, tumble the salad leaves over your plate, then lay the halloumi slices on top. After about $4^1/_2$ minutes' boiling time (that's half a minute more than I'd give an egg if I were eating it out of an egg cup), empty out the hot water from the egg pan into the sink and hold the pan under the cold tap for a while until you think you can bear to peel the egg. Peel it, not worrying if it starts to break as you do so; just hold it over the halloumi as you peel in case of disaster. Sit the peeled soft-boiled egg on the heat-scorched halloumi, then scatter with mint leaves, roughly torn in your hands.

BREAD AND MILK

This is another childhood-resonant plate of comfort food. Well, a bowl of it, actually. In general I do think that anything that can be eaten out of a bowl counts as comfort food but this goes beyond even that. It's almost embarrassing, as I suppose the aching desire for this is nothing more than an infantile yearning for mother's milk. (And, for me on more than one level, since it was my mother's favorite bed-borne supper.) But that craving is behind so much comfort or binge eating, you may as well cut to the chase. Think how many tubs of Häagen-Dazs you'll be saving yourself from.

So, for me, this is a midnight feast of the please-envelop-me-in-the-comforter kind; the sort of meal I pad downstairs for when the only nourishment I want is the sort that sidesteps chewing and has little to do with basic body requirements.

The bread can be slightly stale, but it cannot be of the ready-sliced variety.

2 fat slices good white bread
2 teaspoons superfine sugar or
  vanilla sugar

1 cup milk

Serves 1

Get out your favorite bowl. Tear the bread into rough chunks, and sprinkle with sugar. My mother always used ordinary sugar but if you have some already scented with vanilla, it's even better. Warm the milk and pour over the bread and sugar. This has to be eaten in a comfy chair or in bed, but never at the table.

MUSHROOMS ON TOAST

Mushrooms on toast – nothing fancy, just squeaky little button ones – with only the faintest breath of garlic and lots of butter and cream and nutmeg is like a high-fiber version of Heinz tomato soup: instantly comforting.

The bread must be white, and thick: a real doorstopper, and not toasted too much. I want a slightly crusty outside, but enough doughiness within to absorb the creamy mushroom juices. If you've got only plastic sliced white, then this is what I advise: toast two slices to a light gold and butter one of them, then put the buttered slice on the plate, and sit the unbuttered one on top ready for the mushrooms.

Serves 1

note

If you don't have any fresh nutmeg – though it makes such a difference to so many things, you really should consider getting some – stir in $1/4$ teaspoon grated nutmeg to the mushrooms just before you dollop them over the toast.

3 tablespoons butter
1 teaspoon garlic-infused oil
2 cups button mushrooms
1 teaspoon sea salt/$1/2$ teaspoon table salt
1 tablespoon Marsala, sherry or white wine (optional)
black pepper
$1/4$ cup sour cream
1 thick slice good white bread
lots of freshly grated nutmeg

Melt the butter with the garlic oil in a frying pan or wide shallow saucepan, and cut the mushrooms into quarters. I must be honest and say I don't go in for wiping, or cleaning of any kind, but understand if you want to.

Cook the mushrooms patiently over low to medium heat, sprinkling first with the salt and stirring frequently. At first, I know, it'll look as if the mushrooms need much more butter but if you carry on they will start giving off juices rather than just soaking them up. When that starts happening, add the Marsala, if you have it, and lots of freshly ground pepper and then stir and add the sour cream and let everything cook together for about 3 minutes, putting the bread into the toaster just after you've added the sour cream.

When the toast's ready, put the nice fat slice on a plate, pour over the mushrooms and give a good grating of fresh nutmeg.

BACK-FROM-THE-BAR SNACK

This is one of my favorite uses for leftover potatoes, although I just as often make it from scratch. I use pebbly new potatoes, halved, the better to absorb the cheesey, bacony, eggy sauce later, but I can't say I feel everything would fall to pieces if you did differently.

This is just what I want to eat when I've come back soured with cheap wine, but I have been known, often, to make this in perfect, uncorrupted health.

Its title is really just a gentle tease: this – a kind of Brit-style spud carbonara – provides heft, substance and comfort and allays the most implacable of midnight hunger pangs.

$^1/_2$ cup frozen peas

2 cups cooked all-purpose potatoes

2 slices bacon

1 teaspoon vegetable oil

2 eggs

$^1/_2$ cup Cheddar cheese, chopped

Serves 2

note
If you're cooking this from scratch, just add the peas to the potatoes when they're about five minutes from being cooked through.

Put some salted water on for the peas, and in a frying pan that will take the potatoes and everything later, cook the bacon – scissored into little strips – in the oil.

Cook the peas and at the last minute, tip in the potatoes just so they heat up. Drain and turn into the pan with the bacon and take off the heat. Whisk the eggs with the cheese (I can't be bothered to grate in the middle of the night so just chop it up roughly) and then pour this over the potatoes and peas in the pan. Mix well and pour straight into a bowl or two smallish plates.

BACON AND TOMATO HASH

I've made this a recipe for one which is mostly the way I cook it, but it doesn't take a degree in higher mathematics to double or even quadruple it. It's the best late-night homecoming supper I can think of that's actually cooked but so swiftly and with such ease you hardly notice. You have time to put the kettle on and make a cup of tea while it's cooking, which is the only drink I'd want with it anyway.

Serves 1

4 slices bacon
2 teaspoons garlic-infused oil
1 tomato, diced

2 teaspoons Worcestershire sauce
scattering of chopped parsley
      (about 2 tablespoons)
ground black pepper

Cut each slice into three or four pieces, and fry in the garlic oil until crispy (the bacon will also give up flavorsome fat of its own). Remove the bacon bits to a piece of paper towel.

Tip the chopped tomato, with all its seeded, gluey interior, into the hot oily pan, which will cause a great spitting and sizzling, and stir for a couple of minutes. Add the Worcestershire sauce and stir again, then put the bacon bits back into the pan, mixing it into the tomato before transferring to a plate.

Scatter with some parsley and lots of freshly ground pepper, and serve with bread to dip in the oily juices.

SOMERSET RABBIT

Somerset rabbit is not a new breed of foodstuff but, give or take, Welsh rarebit made with cider in place of ale. Plus, of course, the strong Cheddar – and I like real palate-burning stuff – comes from the West Country, too. However, I don't get too picky about what I use to make this when all I want is some gooey, strong, melted cheese on toast. Double Gloucester – geographically incorrect though it may be – works well here; and any leftover white wine that's hanging around in the fridge will do; in fact will do very well, giving it a bit of fondue mojo.

I like to smear the mustardy cheese sauce on top of some lightly toasted wholemeal muffins before blistering it under the grill. They make this more substantial somehow: the kind of midnight feast that makes up for having missed supper earlier, if anything ever could.

2 whole wheat English muffins (to make 4 pieces, when split in $^1/_2$)	**1 tablespoon all-purpose flour**	**Serves 2**
5oz strong Cheddar	**$^1/_2$ teaspoon English mustard**	
2 teaspoons soft unsalted butter	**1 tablespoon milk**	
	3 tablespoons cider	

Toast each half muffin lightly. Heat your broiler. Grate the cheese: it doesn't have to be finely grated, but it makes a difference if it's not freshly grated, so don't think of buying the ready shredded stuff.

Melt the butter in a small non-stick saucepan, and add the flour to make a roux. Off the heat, whisk in the English mustard, and the milk and cider. Put the pan back on the heat and keep whisking or stirring until you have a thick white sauce, though admittedly it will be tinged yellow by the mustard and cider, and don't expect to have much of it. This is a paste more than anything else.

Add the grated cheese, stirring until it melts and then take off the heat and divide the sauce between the four lightly toasted muffin halves, spreading each one to cover. Immediately place under the heated broiler until they blister on top and begin to brown in spots – which in my nuclear oven is less than a minute.

note
See page 63 for my Stilton and white port variant. I also like this with some Manchego cheese in with the Cheddar, and good sherry in place of the cider and a slab of *membrillo*, that rusty coral stickily solidified quince, to be eaten alongside. As ever, cooking is about what you do at the time, not about any particular recipe.

TOMATO COUSCOUS

This actually grew out of something I used to make my children for supper when they were very little, and still do sometimes, which is carrot couscous. I realized that if I chopped the carrot in the processor and cooked it in vegetable stock (instant) for 2 minutes, I could then tip in some couscous, put a lid on and leave it off the heat for 10 minutes by which time and with very little effort, I could end fractious whining.

No reason not to apply the same rules to myself. Actually, it's even simpler to make as there's no heavy machinery involved. And if it makes things easier than weighing stuff in the middle of the night, all you need to know is that I use as many little tomatoes as will fit comfortably into my cupped hands and as much couscous as will fill a teacup (ditto water later).

Serves 1

pat of butter
1 teaspoon garlic-infused oil
1 cup cherry tomatoes
$^1/_2$ teaspoon ground coriander

$^1/_2$ teaspoon ground cumin
1 teaspoon sea salt/$^1/_2$ teaspoon
table salt
generous $^1/_2$ cup couscous

In a saucepan, melt the butter with the oil and then halve the tomatoes and cook them for about 5 minutes. Stir in the coriander, cumin and salt and then the couscous. Pour over $^1/_2$ cup water and bring to the boil; this takes scarcely half a minute. Take off the heat, clamp on a lid and leave for 5 minutes. Tip out on to a plate, and using a fork, stir to mix and fluff up. If you want, add some freshly chopped cilantro or parsley or some unchopped whole, tender basil leaves.

FRENCH-CANADIAN TOAST

This is not so different from normal French toast, only I've used challah – brioche would also do – in place of the regular bread, and drenched it all in maple syrup, the food symbol of Canada.

I know, however, many people want this for breakfast. I don't: for an intimate snatched supper for two in the small hours it is perfect.

Serves 2

3 eggs
1 teaspoon superfine sugar
$^1/_2$ teaspoon ground cinnamon
3 pieces of bread cut from a round
staled challah loaf (or 4 slices
brioche)

5 slices bacon
1 teaspoon vegetable oil
good maple syrup

Beat the eggs with the sugar and ground cinnamon and pour into a dish which will fit the challah or brioche slices without squeezing them. I use a lasagne pan. Add the bread and leave it to soak for 10 minutes then turn and give another 10 minutes. If it's very fresh you'll probably find 5 minutes a side will do fine.

Cook the bacon in the oil until it's really crisp then remove to some paper towels, and wrap in foil while you cook the challah in the bacony juices in the pan. You need the eggy bread to have been scorched a deep brown in places and be slightly puffed up; each slice will be soft and squodgy inside, but that's desirable (or so I'm told).

Remove the golden challah to a plate and crumble the bacon in your fingers or break it up into shards and let them fall onto the plate. Pour over maple syrup in quantities that please you, leaving the bottle on hand so you can add as you eat.

ALCOHOLIC HOT CHOCOLATE

This is a nice, old-fashioned nightcap. What more is there to say? The ingredients speak for themselves.

Serves 2

2 cups milk
3¹/₂ oz best-quality bittersweet or semisweet chocolate, as preferred
1 cinnamon stick

2 teaspoons honey
1 teaspoon brown sugar
1 teaspoon pure vanilla extract
2 tablespoons dark rum or to taste

Put the milk into a saucepan. Break the chocolate into pieces and add to the milk along with the cinnamon, honey and sugar. Heat gently until the chocolate's melted. Add the vanilla and mix with a small hand whisk and, still whisking, add a spoonful of the rum first and taste to see if you want more (no point pouring in all at once as it's too late to do anything about it if it's too strong for you) and add more sugar if you want this sweeter, too. Take out the cinnamon stick and pour into two cappuccino cups or caffe latte mugs.

WEDDING
FEAST

I HAVE BEEN married twice, but have never had a wedding. Or not one with a menu. And were I to have one, I certainly wouldn't cater it myself. Getting married is stressful enough – and I say that as someone deeply wedded to the state of matrimony – that I wouldn't want to do anything to increase the chances of a total bust-up or break-down.

But a wedding doesn't have to be a big, fancy, clipboard-organized event to be worth celebrating. I'm not sure you even need guests. I don't say that because I'm antisocial – marriage is indeed a social contract – but because I know that the focus becomes the seating plan and the needs and wants of family and friends, with all their internal squabbles and old grievances, rather than the important thing that is actually happening. Though it's not as if a small wedding makes things easier (apart from at the culinary end) as then there's the great hovering weight of those who feel left out for not having been invited.

It is, however, entirely natural to want to make food to celebrate your marriage or, indeed, someone else's. Despite monumental social change, there seems to be something elemental in our nature that makes us want to celebrate the union of two people bound in hopeful trust to one another or, more cynically, as the journalist Sarah Sands epigrammed in her novel *Playing the Game*, "the point of marriage... investment in one's own decline."

But then, in human society, it's hard to think of any occasion that matters that isn't marked with food. So, although I give no recipes for an actual full-scale wedding breakfast, happy to abandon the more ceremonial aspects, I do think that the food you eat to celebrate a marriage should be vital and resonant.

THE PRENUPTIAL FEAST

Unless you are very elderly, the chances are that marriage brings you parents-in-law, and any early celebration of your intentions will include them. Better, then, that you're at the helm.

While it's highly unlikely that any initial post-engagement supper will be your first meeting with each other's parents, it might well be the first time both sets have sat down to a table together. And archaic as the practice might seem, the sentimental assembling of families – so much more panic-inducing and awkward in the post-divorce age of multi-marriage and step-parenthood – is, if friends are anything to go by, still a crucial step, and one very difficult not to stumble on. I feel blessed that not only have I never had a real wedding, I have never been engaged.

The food is likely to be the least of the stresses, but it still has to be broached. And there is an implicit difficulty, especially if you're the woman cooking rather than the man, however sexist that sounds. That's to say, you may feel the need to impress your prospective mother-in-law, but not threaten her.

So the meal should not be too fancy. You need to let the food do what it does best – make people feel at ease.

DINNER WITH THE PROSPECTIVE IN-LAWS

This is a simple meal to organize, which is the first step to a stress-reducing evening.

I'm always happier if I have something in the fridge marinating in advance as I feel things are underway without a great deal of frenzied activity. And although the chicken, lying so sweetly in its marinade, would be a substantial enough supper, I think it gives a more structured focus to the evening if there is a play of courses.

Different occasions require different approaches: more often I'd abandon the three-course dinner; here I'd rely on it. Anyway, the first course involves very little actual labor and happens to be the only example I can summon to mind of a cold food that is comforting (barring ice cream, of course). This may well be because a shrimp cocktail is old-fashioned and reminds me of childhood. But I don't offer it here with a post-modern nod towards the retro. I mean it for real.

The apple charlotte is the only course that can give you any trouble, in that it does take time to make and is fiddly. But it's not *difficult*, and there is always something homey and welcoming about anything with apples in. Besides, this is unpretentious but still pays the courtesy of having made an effort to please. If you want to abandon it for something less last-minute, do, and you could do worse than consider the wedding pavlova on page 431. This would mean you cook the meringue base a day or even a few days in advance and poach the peaches, too, if it helps, and then all you need to do is whip some cream and arrange the fruit for dinner. It's easy to break down into stages, which is sometimes better than the merely simple. And this is supposed to be a celebration.

All recipes serve six.

SHRIMP COCKTAIL

I know there are fancier ways to make sauce Marie-Rose, or certainly fancier ingredients to make it from, but I don't think you can make it taste better. To me, this is just how it should be. And I say that as someone who doesn't eat bottled salad dressing or mayonnaise in the normal run of things – not out of snobbery, but just because I don't like it – but here it works perfectly, like a dream.

Serves 6

1lb small peeled shrimp (cooked)
3/4 cup mayonnaise or Miracle Whip
3 tablespoons tomato ketchup
1 tablespoon lemon juice

few drops Tabasco (or to taste)
3 heads Bibb or small Boston lettuce
1 tablespoon pink peppercorns,
    crushed, or 2 teaspoons paprika

Make sure the shrimp are drained well of their briny liquid. Mix the mayonnaise, ketchup, lemon juice and Tabasco in a bowl. Tip in the shrimp and mix to coat them in the Marie-Rose sauce.

Finely shred the lettuce, and arrange as a bed on six small plates or in shallow bowls. Divide the shrimp in their sauce on the center of each plate in a kind of pyramid, and then scatter with roughly crushed pink peppercorns or dust with paprika.

As long as the shrimp were properly thawed and drained before you started immersing them in their famous coral pink sauce, I don't think it matters if they sit for a good few hours in the fridge before being dolloped out on to their lettuce-lined dishes.

note

This mixture also makes *the* most wonderful sandwiches: useful if you were having a short ceremony and wanted a plate of something to hand round with a glass of champagne after. Add some shredded lettuce if you like, but reckon, with or without, that this amount is enough to fill about 20 slices of bread, in other words, to make 10 full sandwiches, which can then be sliced in half or quarters as you wish. On one thing, however, there is no leeway: please, crusts off. And see, too, the salmon sandwiches on page 435.

ST. TROPEZ CHICKEN

I have lost count of the number of times I've made this, but it really does become one of those fall-back reliable suppers or lunches that you know will always work and, let's be more positive here, give universal pleasure. Its name comes not only from the fact that it is marinated in the smells and flavors of that part of the South of France – the rosé wine, the honey and the lavender – but in honor of its superbronzed and crisped skin.

1 large chicken, cut into 10 pieces
juice of 1 lemon
$^1/_4$ cup olive oil
$^1/_4$ cup honey
$^1/_2$ cup rosé wine (though white is
  fine too)

2 cloves garlic, bruised
1 tablespoon mixed herbs with
  lavender

Serves 6

note
This herb mixture comes variously named, but look for a mixture that includes – give or take – thyme, marjoram, rosemary, savory, fennel seeds and lavender flowers, and see Stockists on page 461 if you have trouble finding it.

Put the chicken pieces into a large plastic freezer bag or shallow dish. Squeeze the lemon juice into a glass measuring cup, and stir in the oil, honey and wine to dissolve the honey. Pour this mixture into the bag or dish of chicken and chuck in the bruised garlic cloves and the herbs.

Seal the bag or cover the dish with plastic wrap and put in the fridge overnight or for up to two days.

Preheat the oven to 325°F. Put the chicken into a roasting pan with its marinade, skin side up, and cover with aluminum foil. Cook for 2 hours, and then remove the foil from the pan and turn up the oven to 425°F. Cook for another 15–25 minutes or until the skin of the chicken is bronzed. Keep an eye on it, though, as the honey in the marinade will make it catch quite quickly. The time differential for the bronzing cooking stage, is just because I find it varies, depending on whether I'm cooking this in a gas or electric oven (the electric one crisps it up much, much faster).

Remove the chicken to a warmed plate, and pour or spoon off excess fat from the cooking liquid. Put the pan on the stove top, add $^1/_2$ cup water and deglaze the pan juices to make your glossy, golden-brown sauce-cum-gravy.

note
If you want (though you sacrifice some flavor this way), substitute six unskinned chicken breast portions: use $^1/_2$ the lemon and $^1/_4$ cup wine, but keep everything else as is. And then just cook at 400°F for 40–50 minutes without any aluminum foil, or until skin is bronzed. Deglaze the pan juices with $^1/_4$ cup water and bubble to reduce the total amount in the pan to just under $^1/_2$ cup.

You can cook the chicken in advance at the lower oven temperature under foil, removing it from the oven after the first 2 hours, and chilling it once it's cooled down. The next day you just need to remove the aluminum foil and cook the chicken in a 425°F oven for about 30–40 minutes, or until cooked through and bronzed.

SMASHED POTATO GRATIN

This is a cross between mashed potatoes and pommes dauphinoise, and as gloriously comforting as that suggests. You can cook the potatoes in their seasoned milk in advance if you like, and then tip the fabulous sludge into a buttered pan to sit in the kitchen until it's time to go in the oven. You can put the potatoes in, under the chicken, as you turn the heat up, letting them continue to cook and blister as the chicken has been taken out and is resting on a warmed serving plate.

Serves 6

2lbs 10oz all-purpose potatoes
3 cups milk
1 tablespoon sea salt/
$^1/_2$ tablespoon table salt
$^1/_2$ stick of celery

4 scallions
black or white pepper
1 stick of butter
2 tablespoons semolina

Preheat the oven to 425°F. Butter a shallowish roasting pan, approximately 14 x 10 inches.

Peel and chop the potatoes, and cut into approx. $^1/_2$ x 1$^1/_4$ inch chunks. Put them into a saucepan with the milk, salt, celery, whole scallions, a good grinding of black pepper and about $^3/_4$ stick of butter. Bring to the boil and simmer for 20 minutes.

Fish out the celery and scallions, and then pour the milky, buttery cooked potatoes into the prepared roasting pan and mash them lightly with a fork. You can leave them made up to this point to sit for a while; I'd even go so far as to say that it actually makes them better.

When you are ready to put them in the oven, sprinkle over the semolina and dot with the remaining butter. Cook the smashed potato gratin for 30 minutes or until hot through and beginning to catch and scorch in parts on the top.

THE PEAS

You can make this as easy as you like. I'm never opposed to a jar or two of those French, grey-green peas, and those you just turn out into a pan, heat and season. Otherwise, follow the recipe for petits pois à la française on page 148, only tripling quantities.

A light, crisp, astringent green salad might be good after or alongside, but is not imperative.

APPLE CHARLOTTE

This is a dessert that has been eaten in Britain since the end of the 18th century, and I can see why. As ever, simplicity, when done so perfectly, compels. This is just a buttery apple purée, flavored with lemon and cinnamon, bound with egg yolk and baked in a cake pan, lined with thinly sliced bread. Nothing can rival an apple pie, and no one should attempt to, but an apple charlotte is somehow both more basic and more spectacular. I suppose this is what real cooking is about: the glorious, unpretentious transformation of simple, everyday ingredients.

I am always drawn to recipes that use up leftovers, and this one is the perfect resting place for old bread. Since I had a challah lying about one day, past its best, I used that instead and now wouldn't deviate from it, though stale brioche works as well. This version is a dinner party one, which is my excuse, too, for folding golden sultanas soaked in Calvados into the eggy, buttery apple.

If you're up to it, make the custard on page 42 to go with, but I think I like this just as much eaten with a sour splodge of crème fraîche.

$^1/_2$ cup sultanas (golden raisins)
  or brown raisins
3 tablespoons Calvados
about 8 Cox's or other firm, tart
  apples (approx. 3lbs total weight)
$1^3/_4$–2 sticks unsalted butter,
  (depending on staleness of bread)
$^1/_3$ cup superfine sugar

1 cinnamon stick
1 brioche or challah loaf, sliced as
  thinly as possible and left to
  become dry, but not hard
3 egg yolks (retain the white,
  separately, of one of them)
2–3 tablespoons brown sugar

Serves 6

note
If you want to keep apple-y but prefer a pudding you can make entirely in advance – though you could prepare the apples for the charlotte early, you can't do more than that – turn to the apple cheesecake (always a grade A winner) on pages 207–8.

Preheat the oven to 350°F and at the same time slip in a baking sheet to heat up – or wait to do this when the apples are cooling if you prefer. Put the sultanas and Calvados into a small saucepan and bring to the boil, then turn off the heat and leave the fruit to plump up in the liquid while you get on with the purée.

Peel and core the apples and cut each one in half, and then each half into six. You don't have to follow these instructions to the letter, but that's how I go about it, if I'm in methodical mood. Put the apples, however they're chopped, into a pan with 2 tablespoons of the butter, $^1/_4$ cup water, the superfine sugar and the cinnamon stick. Cook over a fairly high heat with the lid on for about 10 minutes or until the apples are soft, then give a good beating with a wooden fork or spoon and transfer the rough apple purée to a bowl to cool.

Melt the remaining butter and paint the bottom and sides of a 8 or 9 inch springform pan (you either have a smaller deeper cake, or a larger shallower one, but there's not an awful lot in it). Line the bottom and sides with the dry sliced bread, painting it with butter first to mold it into a neat jigsaw puzzle of pieces with no gaps. Save some slices for the top. Paint the seams with egg white to help them adhere well and stick together. At this point, I should own up and admit that I let my bread get too dry

which is why it doesn't look as neat in the picture as it should. If you avoid my mistake, you end up with a smooth bread casing.

Beat the egg yolks and plump sultanas into the cooled apples, and then fill the bread-lined cake pan with them. Layer the top with buttered bread slices and then butter the top again, before sprinkling over the brown sugar. Cook on the preheated baking sheet for 30–40 minutes until the top – and sides, though you can't see them at this stage – is crispy and brown.

Remove to a wire rack, and leave the apple charlotte to reach the warmer end of room temperature before removing the sides of the pan. It's probably a safer bet to transfer it, pan and all, once you've reached serving point, to a plate or stand and unclip it there. Not that I've ever had any subsidence problems with it.

This happens to be wonderful for breakfast the next day should you have anything left over: the tartness of the apple stops it from being too dessert-like.

THE CAKE

I wouldn't dare give instructions for erecting one of those multi-storeyed wedding cakes, and actually much prefer the idea of a tower of beauteous little white-rose-topped cupcakes. I know you miss the symbolism of sharing the cake with all your friends and family, sending a piece to those who didn't make it, but I'd have thought it would be lovely to receive one perfect cupcake in a small box in the post instead. In the States, the couple symbolically share a slice of cake in front of the cheering crowd of guests, but there is no reason why this immediate consummation couldn't take place with the joint devouring of a cupcake.

If it's a proper fruit cake you want, there is a recipe and a full table of ingredients and cooking times, depending on the size of cake, in the Christmas section. And if there is just a small group of you, and you don't mind being untraditional, you could always make the chocolate raspberry heart on page 139. If you want it to look more weddingy, follow the recipe for the cake part only, sandwich it with the Yule log frosting on page 88 (you'd probably only need half) and then buy a 2lb package of roll-outable marzipan and the same amount of white fondant icing – which you can buy in specialist baking shops in block form – paint the assembled cake with warmed, sieved raspberry jam, then drape with marzipan, then with white icing and instead of dotting the outline of the heart with raspberries, use white wafer roses.

note
Remember, that when you're rolling out marzipan or fondant you dust the surface first with confectioners' sugar just as you use flour to stop pastry from sticking as you roll.

WHITE ROSE WEDDING CUPCAKES

Ever since I put a picture of the simple white-rose-topped cupcake on the cover of *How to be a Domestic Goddess*, I've wanted to make these part of a wedding celebration, and recently I did. Just follow the recipe for the love buns on page 138 – and you could make a few batches of those, too, if you wanted – and ice white, dotting with one perfect rose as you go.

To make them durable, though I know that doesn't sound inviting in the context of food, follow the recipe for the jewelled cupcakes on page 94. I always use, whether going for a plain cake base or fruit one, royal icing to top them, since you get a fabulous depth of thick snowy whiteness; reckon on one 1lb package of instant royal icing to ice 24 cupcakes. However, you do need to roll out some marzipan – a 1lb block should suffice – and cut out small round discs, the circumference of the cupcakes they are going to top (first brush the cakes with warm, sieved jam) to stop the brown of the fruit cake mixture bleeding into the white icing.

If you can't find any instant royal icing, it's not hard to make: all you need to remember is that for 4 cups confectioners' sugar (sifted, always) you need 2 egg whites and 1 teaspoon each of lemon juice and glycerine.

The method is as follows: whisk the whites until frothy and slowly beat in about 1 cup sifted confectioners' sugar then gradually beat in the rest, sprinkling with lemon juice and glycerine as you go. Keep beating until you've got the texture you want to ice the cupcakes. I like the royal icing to have a bit of pourability, rather than having to be spread on with a knife: it gives a smoother finish.

Enough for 24 cupcakes

note

If you are happier using dried egg white to make the royal icing, you can. For 4 cups sifted confectioners' sugar, you need 2 tablespoons dried egg white powder, 1 teaspoon cream of tartar and 6 tablespoons cold water. Beat everything together with an electric whisk until you've got a good coating consistency.

WEDDING MERINGUES

I don't think there is any point doing food for a wedding, however small and elegant, and then fighting the age-old symbolism. White is the color of weddings, and that's all there is to it. I can see why "meringue" is used as a term of contemptuous abuse to describe a wedding dress, but I defy anyone not to respond to the absolute beauty of a pile of these softly peaking meringues, sprinkled with white petals (preferably from untreated roses) and arranged in a dazzling white tumble on a plate or, frankly, straight on the table.

Makes 20 large meringues

note
Nothing beats squidgy-centered meringues with cream and berries, so place bowls of firmly but not stiffly whipped cream on the table alongside, and whatever berries are ripe and in season.

12 egg whites
white rose petals for scattering

3¹/₂ cups superfine sugar

Preheat the oven to 275°F.

Twelve egg whites are a lot, but I like these meringues to be swellingly over-sized; if you want yours smaller, either halve the quantities or make twice as many. Because of the volume of mixture, the length of time this takes, and bearing in mind the oven space you'll need for them, it might be wise to make these in two batches. If you have a large standing mixer and a double oven, you can bang them out at once.

Whisk the whites until firm and beginning to hold peaks, then gradually whisk in the sugar 1 tablespoon at a time, patiently whipping and waiting until you have a stiff shiny meringue.

Line two or three baking sheets with parchment paper and blob 3–4 inch circles roughly. Use dessertspoons to do this: about 2 spoonfuls per meringue should be the right amount, and leave space around each because they puff up as they cook. Then rough up the meringue circles with your spoons so that they are textured and frilly. Cook for 45 minutes to an hour; when ready, the meringues should be dry on the outside and still feel a little marshmallowy underneath. Once out of the oven, let them cool completely on the baking sheet before you try and move them. They will be fragile and shatter easily, so treat them with care.

WEDDING PAVLOVA

I feel about a pavlova much as I do about a trifle: no book of mine would be complete without one.

This is fancier than I normally go in for, as the occasion dictates. It does make a difference if you peel the peaches or nectarines, and as long as you dunk them briefly in boiling water, the skins come off relatively easily. I've specified white peaches – or nectarines – because I love their pale-fleshed beauty, and because they just seemed right here, though regular yellow-fleshed are not to be scorned. And should you be wanting to make something for a Golden Wedding party, you should certainly go straight for the yellow peaches.

The slight sourness of the passionfruit brings out the sweetness of the peach. I've pushed the pulp through a sieve here, but I don't always. You get more of a look of a bulging white meringue dripping with gold when the blue-black seeds are removed, but actually I love the crunch they add, so choose what you want to go for.

Finally, because I found some shaved coconut, gorgeous ivory-edged white curls, I decided to flavor the meringue base correspondingly, but if you wish, use vanilla instead and scatter the top with white rose petals, or even pale pink ones.

FOR THE MERINGUE BASE

8 egg whites

pinch salt

2¹/₂ cups superfine sugar

4 teaspoons cornstarch

2 teaspoons white wine vinegar

1 teaspoon coconut extract

Serves 10–12

FOR THE TOPPING

6 passionfruit

3 white peaches or nectarines

juice of ¹/₂ lime

2¹/₂ cups heavy or whipping cream

1 cup shaved dried coconut

Preheat the oven to 350°F. Line a baking sheet with parchment paper and draw a rough 10 inch circle, using a springform of that size as a guide if you have one.

Whisk the egg whites and salt until satiny peaks form. Then beat in the sugar, tablespoonfuls at a time, until the meringue is stiff and shiny. Sprinkle over the cornstarch, vinegar and coconut extract, and fold in lightly. Mound on to the baking sheet within the circle, flatten the top and smooth the sides. Put in the oven and *immediately* reduce the heat to 300°F and cook for 1¹/₄–1¹/₂ hours. It will have risen and cracked on the top and a little around the sides. If it is not dry and crispy on the outside give it a little longer. Then turn off the oven, open the door and leave to cool completely.

When you are ready to assemble the pavlova, blanch the peaches or nectarines in boiling water and slip off their skins. Cut the fruit in half and take out the pits, lay them in a shallow dish and squeeze over the lime juice to keep their color or "bleach" them. Invert the pavlova on to a plate and peel off the parchment paper – at least, that's what I normally do, though I see from the picture I didn't bother this time. But if the meringue base hasn't crumbled too much, it is the best thing to do, as it means you swathe the marshmallowy top (ie the inverted bottom) with the cream, and the two seem to meld together. If all is too crumbly, don't bother.

Whip the cream until thickened but still soft, and pile on top of the meringue, spreading it to the edges in a rough, swirly fashion. Cut the passionfruit in half, and scoop everything out into a sieve placed over a glass measuring cup and press through, so only the seeds remain in the sieve. Pour most of the juice over the swirly cream. Or just halve the passionfruits and scoop pulp, seeds and all, over the cream. Slice the blanched halved fruit into thin segments and arrange them on top of the cream and passionfruit juice. Then do a final pouring over of the remaining juice. Or, if you haven't sieved the fruits, just give a little squeezing over of the empty shells.

Sprinkle the shaved coconut over the top of the pavlova, like wedding confetti.

CROQUE-EN-BOUCHE

I've managed to write happily for some years now without ever having to resort to the word "centerpiece": I hadn't even thought it was in my vocabulary; but I find myself reaching for it now. For this, frankly, is what the croque-en-bouche, that French wedding cake made out of a tower of profiteroles, is. My version is a little more ramshackle and low-rise than the ones you come across at French weddings. Still, it didn't collapse, so I can live with its slighty adrift center of gravity. The filling and topping are just the ones I normally make for my own profiteroles: a crème pâtissière made smoky with the addition of some caramelized sugar, and a toffee topping that glistens a deep amber-gold.

Makes 75–80 profiteroles

note
As long as you can find something airtight to stash the choux buns in, you can make them a few days in advance. And you can often order them from bakers and just fill and top them yourself.

FOR THE PROFITEROLES/CHOUX BUNS

2³/₄ cups plus 2 tablespoons all-purpose flour	2³/₄ sticks unsalted butter, diced
3 cups water	pinch of salt
	8 large eggs, beaten

Preheat the oven to 400°F.

Sift the flour. Put the water, butter and a pinch of salt in a large saucepan on the heat and heat until the butter's melted and the water's begun to boil. Take the pan immediately off the heat (you don't want the water to evaporate at all) and beat in the flour. Use a wooden spoon for this and don't worry about how lumpy or how unyielding it is, just keep beating until it comes smoothly together. Put the pan back on the heat for just long enough to finish this process off, about a minute or even less, until the dough begins to come away from the sides of the pan to form a smooth ball.

Now beat in the eggs: I do this in the food processor though if you're feeling very butch you could do it by hand. So, either turn the dough into a mixing bowl and add spoonfuls of egg as you continue to beat with your wooden spoon, or turn it into the bowl of a food processor fitted with the double blade and gradually pour the eggs through the funnel while blitzing until you have a smooth, gleaming dough, soft enough to pipe but still

stiff enough to hold its shape. You may not need all of the eggs, so go carefully.

Get out four baking sheets (well, this is a wedding) and line them, preferably with Silpat. Using a $1^3/_4$ inch plain tip, or just a spoon, pipe or dollop little rounds about the size of a small walnut (they puff up to a grown-up walnut on baking), and bake for about 15 minutes until golden and crisp. Remove to a cooling rack and pierce each profiterole with a pin, to let the steam out and prevent their going soggy.

note

You could use the leftover egg whites to make the wedding pavlova on page 431 or the meringues on page 430.

See stockists on page 461 for the golden syrup. It's well worth ordering.

FOR THE CARAMEL CRÈME PÂTISSIÈRE FILLING

2 cups milk	**$^1/_3$ cup plus 1 tablespoon**
2 cups heavy cream	**all-purpose flour**
12 large egg yolks	**2 teaspoons pure vanilla extract**
$1^1/_4$ cups superfine sugar	**4 teaspoons water**

Warm the milk and cream in a saucepan. While you're waiting, beat the yolks and 1 cup of the superfine sugar until creamy, and then whisk in the flour. Stir the heated milk and cream into the egg mixture and whisk until smooth. Pour back into the saucepan and stir or whisk gently over a low heat until the custard thickens. Add the vanilla and set aside. Then caramelize your sugar by putting the remaining $^1/_2$ cup sugar and the water in a little pan and turning the heat to high, letting the sugar and water turn to a dark brown caramel. Using a little hand whisk, beat the custard as you pour in the molten liquid. When it's combined, pour into a bowl and let cool, placing a piece of plastic wrap on the top to prevent a skin forming.

FOR THE TOFFEE SAUCE

$^1/_3$ cup light brown sugar	**1 stick unsalted butter**
$^1/_4$ cup superfine sugar	**1 cup golden syrup or light corn syrup**

Put all the ingredients for the toffee sauce into a saucepan, bring to a boil and let them bubble away for about 10 minutes or so. You want it to become thick enough to coat the tops of the profiteroles in a shiny glaze, without running off too much. This goo serves as fixative as well as glaze.

Fit a pastry bag with a small plain tip; you can rest this while you fiddle about with the choux buns, first by putting it into a tall glass, tip down, and this also is the best way to fill the empty bag with the crème pâtissière. Stuff the profiteroles by splitting them with a small knife, inserting the tip into each one and squeezing. You can also do this with a teaspoon if you are not adept with a pastry bag, but it's not hard and I rather enjoy the squeezing and injecting process. As you fill them, arrange in a pyramid on a large flat plate, spooning over some of the toffee caramel on the top of each bun as you put it in place so that your pile-up is glued together safely.

Once you have a good pyramid and the croque-en-bouche is formed, spoon over more of the toffee caramel to give the whole thing a shiny, glinting glaze.

SALMON SANDWICHES

In all this sea of sweetness, it is good to have something savory, and I don't think that for an English person a wedding is quite a wedding if there is no poached salmon.

 This is certainly not the orthodox route, but it's the best use of poached salmon I've ever come across. I have Konditor & Cook, where I first ate them, to thank: a fabulous bakery in Borough Market, one of the most beautiful places, though more of a food-happening really, in London.

 There are two things that *make* these: the first is the black bread, heady with rye and caraway; the second is the scant time the fish is cooked. The salmon is poached so gently that its coral flesh stays bright and tender, flaked and folded into its basil mayonnaise.

1lb organic farmed salmon fillets, skinned
$^3/_4$ cup water
1 tablespoon lemon juice, plus more to squeeze into mayonnaise
1 tablespoon sea salt/$^1/_2$ tablespoon table salt

1 tablespoon black peppercorns
few stalks basil
4–6 tablespoons mayonnaise
$^1/_4$ cup/4 tablespoons chopped basil
16 slices black bread: you'll probably need 2 loaves

makes 8 rounds

note
The black bread tends to come from Polish bakeries, though many supermarkets stock it. Failing that, use the best brown or rye bread you can find. And if you have any black bread left – you're likely to get more than the 16 slices out of the 2 loaves – you can make another favorite, my Hungarian sandwich. This is an excellent cook's treat while you're busy with your labors: smear a slice of black bread with cream cheese, top with the best black cherry jam you can find, top with another slice. Eat with the greatest pleasure.

Put the salmon fillets in a large skillet, cover with the water and add the lemon juice, salt, peppercorns and whatever basil stalks you have, having torn off the leaves to chop into the mayonnaise later. Bring just to boiling point, turn the fish over and switch off the heat. Leave for 3 minutes, then remove with a slotted spatula to a large piece of aluminum foil to cool.

 Flake the fish with a fork, transfer to a bowl, and add the mayonnaise, basil, a further squeeze of lemon and salt and pepper to taste.

 You need no butter to make the sandwiches, just share the filling out between eight slices of black bread, top with another eight slices and cut in half. You might put a few cornichons, those tiny gherkins, around the sandwiches on their platter.

A MEZZE FEAST FOR TEN
TO TWENTY

EGGPLANT, MINT AND YOGURT DIP
RED KIDNEY BEAN DIP
BASIL AND GOAT'S CHEESE DIP
CUCUMBER AND POMEGRANATE SALAD
HERBED BULGAR WHEAT AND NUT SALAD
AROMATIC LAMB MEATBALLS
DAISY SAATCHI'S POTATO AND MEAT PATTIES
GREEN FATOUSH
GOLDEN CARDAMOM CHICKEN
CRISPY-ONION SPICED RICE

Whatever else is on the menu for a wedding celebration, I would want the day itself, or an evening near it, to be marked with some sort of festive banquet. And this is just the one: a plethora of little dishes for people to hang around picking from and dipping in to. Were you to be planning a hen night at home, this would be the perfect, laid-back, menu for it. Or rather, it's laid back for the eater: it certainly needs a great deal of preparation from the cook. But I'd bring in everyone: have your friends around, and spend the time in the kitchen, rolling and dunking and stuffing and mixing. There is nothing like a bit of companionable hanging out in a kitchen, as you slowly, satisfyingly build your feast, to relax you – really – and give you a sense of significant celebration.

There's a huge disparity in the numbers being served because in order to give plenty of choice at dessert time, you end up with enough of the sweet stuff to feed far more than 20 of you. I wouldn't cut down quantities for 10, just reduce the choice. The dips and so forth can easily be doubled for 20, but I'd leave the chicken and rice as they are (though I'd maybe cut the chicken pieces into smaller bits). The more people there are, the more talk there is (and the more uncomfortable it is to sit down), the less people eat. And there's only so much frying you'll want to do.

EGGPLANT, MINT AND YOGURT DIP

This recipe, along with many of the dips and salads here, is a variation on a dish I read about in Najmieh Batmanglij's *New Food of Life: Ancient Persian and Modern Iranian Cooking and Ceremonies*. It's hard to ascribe the origins of a recipe, or explain how I came to make something the way I do, as so often the recipe that appears here may be merely suggested by another I've read somewhere, while diverging significantly from it. I find it impossible to cook without fiddling: which means all my recipes are refracted through the prism of my own tastes and prejudices. I expect you correspondingly, to do the same.

3 small eggplants (1–1^1/$_2$lbs total weight) to make about 1^1/$_4$ cups when roasted, pulped and strained

2 tablespoons olive oil (not extra virgin)

1 large onion

3 fat cloves garlic

1 cup Greek plain yogurt

^{1}/$_4$ teaspoon saffron threads, soaked in 2 tablespoons warm water

2 tablespoons chopped mint

2 tablespoons toasted pinenuts

dribble of extra virgin olive oil to decorate

note

For all the dips here, you need a really good pile of flat breads and breadsticks for people to break off and smear with the aromatic purées or sandwich curlingly around the salads.

Preheat the oven to 450°F. Prick the eggplants with a fork and put them on a baking sheet to cook for 45 minutes to an hour. The insides of the eggplants should be soft and they will feel squishy to touch. Let them cool before peeling and mashing them, then leave in a sieve to drain.

Heat the oil in a pan and peel and finely chop the onion, adding the pieces to the pan. Peel the garlic cloves and mince or grate into the onion. Or just put onion and garlic together in a processor first and blitz. Cook until golden and then add the drained eggplant mush, cooking it with the onion and garlic for a further 5 minutes or so over a gentle heat, stirring frequently. Take off the heat, turn into a bowl to cool and season with salt and pepper.

Add the yogurt to the cooled eggplant mixture together with the saffron in its now golden water, stirring together well, and then turn into a bowl and sprinkle over the mint, toasted pinenuts and a dribble of oil.

RED KIDNEY BEAN DIP

Think of this as a terracotta, sweet and grainy version of hummus.

1 large onion	1 tablespoon tomato paste
3 fat cloves garlic	$^1/_2$ teaspoon ground cumin
3 tablespoons olive oil (not extra virgin)	$^1/_2$ teaspoon ground coriander
	$^1/_4$ teaspoon ground cinnamon
$1^3/_4$ cups kidney beans, reserving the gluey liquid	juice and zest of 1 lime

Peel the onion and garlic and process them until finely chopped. Or chop by hand, mincing or grating the garlic. Heat the oil and cook them until soft and golden.

Add the kidney beans in their gloop and stir in the tomato paste and spices and cook for a few minutes.

Zest the lime and reserve in a bowl for later, then juice the lime adding it to the kidney bean mixture. Take the pan off the heat and, when it has cooled a little, process the mixture until it is a bumpy purée. When it is cool, arrange in small bowls and sprinkle over the reserved lime zest.

BASIL AND GOAT'S CHEESE DIP

I know it's not at all in the correct register, but I love this smeared thickly over split, toasted and slightly cooled bagels. You can use feta in place of the soft, sour and salty goat's cheese here to balance the smoky sweetness of the nuts and mellow scent of the basil if that's easier to find or you just want something a little more pungent and less creamy.

1 cup walnut pieces	1 packed cup soft goat's cheese
2 scallions, roughly chopped	3 tablespoons garlic-infused oil
$1^1/_2$ cups basil leaves	

Process the walnut pieces, scallions and basil leaves, then add the goat's cheese and oil and process again to make a grainy paste. Transfer to a bowl and top with a basil leaf or two if it pleases you.

Top row, left to right: eggplant, mint and yogurt dip, red kidney bean dip, basil and goat's cheese dip; middle row, left to right: cucumber and pomegranate salad, herbed bulgar wheat and nut salad, aromatic lamb meatballs; bottom row, left to right: Daisy Saatchi's stuffed potato patties, green fatoush, golden cardamom chicken with crispy-onion spiced rice

CUCUMBER AND POMEGRANATE SALAD

Obviously, this recipe is only do-able if you can lay your hands on a pomegranate, though I should tell you that, as the pomegranate season draws to an end, or as I begin to have trouble finding them in the shops, I de-seed some and keep the beautiful jewels in a bag in the freezer for out-of-season scattering.

Luckily, their availability seems to be longer than when I was a child – when you found them only at Christmas – so you have an ever wider window of opportunity to make this at its best.

note
There are so many other good uses to which this can be put: wonderful as a salad with cold turkey and just as good as a cooling, fragrant relish with curry.

$^1/_2$ **cup finely sliced scallions**
**1 heaped tablespoon finely
  chopped mint**
1 cucumber

1 pomegranate
2 teaspoons lime juice
sea salt

Finely slice the scallions, and put into a bowl with the chopped mint. Peel the cucumber and halve it lengthwise, quarter each half and slice off the seedy edge. Then cut each quarter into dice crossways. Geometry is not my strong point, so all I am trying to indicate is that you should end up with little glassy jade cubes.

Add the diced cucumber to the bowl of scallions and mint. Halve the pomegranate and then bash the seeds out of each half into the bowl. Dress with the lime juice and a sprinkle of sea salt, and toss everything together.

HERBED BULGUR WHEAT AND NUT SALAD

I know there are a lot of ingredients here, but one shopping expedition to a Middle-Eastern store, if you are lucky enough to live near one, should do it. Otherwise, you should find most of the stuff in well-stocked supermarkets or a healthstore. The only truly elusive ingredient is the fabulously sour barberry; you can leave these out altogether if you can't find them, or replace with dried sour cherries, chopped up a little, dispersing small red cherry-confetti throughout the salad as you mix it.

1 cup bulgur wheat
$^1/_4$ **cup dried barberries, optional**
3 cups boiling water
**1 tablespoon pomegranate
  molasses**
juice of $^1/_2$ lemon
3 tablespoons olive oil
$^1/_4$ **teaspoon ground allspice**

1 teaspoon cumin seeds
**1 teaspoon sea salt/$^1/_4$ teaspoon
  table salt**
$^1/_4$ **teaspoon ground cinnamon**
$^1/_3$ **cup shelled pistachios**
$^1/_3$ **cup natural (unblanched)
  almonds**
2 tablespoons chopped parsley

Put the bulgur wheat and barberries into a bowl and pour over the boiling water. Cover with plastic wrap and leave for 20 minutes, then drain in a sieve and squeeze out any excess water. Put the pomegranate molasses, lemon juice, olive oil, allspice, cumin seeds, salt and cinnamon into a bowl and whisk together to make a dressing. Roughly chop the pistachios and almonds – I use my mezzaluna for this – and add them to the drained bulgur wheat with the dressing and chopped parsley. Fork everything through to mix well and turn into a bowl, sprinkling with a little more chopped parsley if you'd like.

AROMATIC LAMB MEATBALLS

I find a tremendous amount of use for these: to pick at over drinks (and see the Party section, on page 396), much as they are here, lowered into a vat of sweet vegetable stew with couscous (pages 214–16), piled into warm pita with salad and hummus, or just piled over plain steamed rice and sprinkled with toasted pinenuts and freshly chopped cilantro.

1 lb ground lamb
$^1/_4$ cup finely sliced scallions
$^1/_2$ teaspoon ground cinnamon
1 teaspoon ground cumin
1 teaspoon ground allspice

1 teaspoon salt
3 tablespoons semolina
1 egg
vegetable oil for frying

Makes 75–78 meatballs

Put the ground lamb into a bowl, finely chop the scallions and add to the meat. Sprinkle over the spices, salt and semolina, and beat the egg, adding to the bowl. Work everything together thoroughly but lightly with your hands, then cover with plastic wrap and leave in the fridge for 30 minutes.

Line a baking sheet with plastic wrap and scoop out small amounts of mixture – imagine a heaped $^1/_2$ teaspoonful, or scant teaspoon – roll them in your hands and place on the plastic wrap-lined baking sheet. Concentrate, as it's easy to make them bigger and bigger as you form them and you do want these toytown small. Have a bowl of cold water beside you to dampen your hands; this helps them not get too sticky for rolling the meatballs.

You should make about 75 lamb meatballs in total. I often stretch to 78 but have yet to make it to 80. When you are ready to cook them, heat about $^1/_2$ inch of oil in a skillet. Line another baking sheet with paper towels, and when the oil is hot fry the meatballs in batches without overcrowding the pan. Cook them for about 1 minute a side, or until golden brown all over. Place the finished meatballs on the paper towels. Taste as you go to check they are cooked through: you've got enough.

DAISY SAATCHI'S STUFFED POTATO PATTIES

This is one of those recipes that is fantastically good, but very fiddly and time-consuming – a real labor of love, which is entirely appropriate given the occasion and their derivation: the recipe is from my husband's late mother.

note

I get 18 patties out of this amount, but just divide each half of potato dough into 10 balls, and be prepared to be even more patient if you are cooking for 20 people.

Eat warm or cold, however makes sense to you: either way is good for me.

4¹/₂lbs baking potatoes (makes 6
   cups mashed)
1 onion
vegetable oil
$^1/_4$ teaspoon ground cardamom
$^1/_2$ teaspoon ground cinnamon
$^1/_2$ teaspoon ground cumin
$^1/_2$ teaspoon ground coriander
small pinch ground cloves
1 teaspoon ground allspice

8oz ground beef
$^1/_4$ cup water
$^1/_4$ cup finely chopped parsley
2 eggs
1$^1/_2$ teaspoons salt
$^1/_2$ cup all-purpose flour
2 cups matzoh meal to coat, or more
   as needed

Preheat the oven to 400°F. Pierce the potatoes and bake for 1–1$^1/_2$ hours according to size, and leave to cool.

Peel and finely chop the onion, and heat 2 tablespoons of the oil in a wide, shallow pan. Cook the onion over a medium heat until soft and beginning to color, then add all the spices, stirring to coat the onion. Add the beef and, using a wooden fork, break up the ground meat as it cooks and begins to turn brown, then stir in the water. Once the beef has cooked through, take the pan off the heat and transfer the aromatic meat to a bowl to let it cool a little before stirring through the chopped parsley.

Halve the cooked and cooled potatoes, scoop out the filling into a bowl, add the eggs, salt and flour and mix to a smooth dough. I use the flat paddle of the KitchenAid mixer for this, but mixing and kneading by hand is not hard. Whatever you do, *don't* put it in the processor.

Halve the dough and divide each half into 9 or 10 balls, then flatten each ball in the palm of your hand into a rough circle or oval. Put 1 teaspoon of the ground beef filling into the center of the flattened potato ball and then fold over in half, sealing the edges with your fingers. Roll back into a ball between your hands, and then flatten again into a fat disc; no beef filling should be visible. Dredge in the matzoh meal to coat each side and proceed with the rest of the potato and meat patties. You can leave them, fully formed like this until you want to fry them.

Line a baking sheet with paper towels and sit it near the stove. Put some oil in a skillet to come about $^1/_2$ inch up and heat. Fry the patties in the hot oil – though don't let it get so hot it burns the outside before the middle is warmed through – until they're golden brown. Turn gently, but not fearfully, so both sides are fried equally. You'll need to cook the patties in small batches, so the pan doesn't get overcrowded, removing the cooked ones to the paper-towel-lined baking sheet as you go.

GREEN FATOUSH

I've put this here, rather than with the other salady dips above, just because I wanted to draw your attention to the fact that the patties and this, served together, do make the most wonderful supper. I claim no authenticity for this particular fatoush: I've certainly never come across an avocado in a Middle-Eastern recipe, but I love the soft bland clay against the sharpness of the chillies and lime and the crunch of the lettuce and shards of toasted pita.

$^1/_4$ cup finely sliced scallions	sea salt
2 long green chillies	2 pita breads
1 head of Romaine lettuce	1 ripe avocado
zest and juice of 1 lime	$^1/_4$ cup chopped cilantro
2 tablespoons extra virgin olive oil	$^1/_4$ cup chopped mint

Preheat the oven to 450°F.

Finely slice the scallions, deseed the chillies and cut into very fine rounds and put both into a bowl.

Discard the outer leaves of the lettuce and then tear it into pieces adding to the bowl. Whisk the lime and oil in a small bowl and add a sprinkling of salt.

Open the pita breads up lengthways so that you have four very thin halves, and lay them on a baking sheet. Toast them in the oven for about 5 minutes to give them a bit of crunch, they will also turn a golden brown color – but keep an eye on them, as they might burn. Take the pita breads out and leave them to cool.

Halve the avocado, remove the pit and then using a spoon, scoop pieces of avocado on to the bowl of lettuce. Dress the salad with the lime and oil dressing and add most of the chopped herbs before tossing with your hands to combine. Snip with scissors or break the crispy pita bread with your hands into rough triangles, add most of the pieces to the salad and toss again before decanting to a serving bowl or platter. Scatter with the remaining herbs and toasted pita.

GOLDEN CARDAMOM CHICKEN WITH CRISPY-ONION SPICED RICE

Strictly speaking, this does not count as mezze, but even after so many bits and pieces, I thought it would be good to have some central, splendid dish.

It might be strange to name this recipe after a spice that appears in such small quantities, but it permeates the dish with such intense musky perfume that, without being overpowering, it demands the respect.

FOR THE CHICKEN AND MARINADE

zest and juice of 1 lemon

1 onion

$^1/_2$ teaspoon ground allspice

$^1/_2$ teaspoon ground black pepper

$^1/_4$ teaspoon cardamom seeds
   (from about 5 pods)

2 fat cloves garlic

$^1/_2$ cup olive oil

$^1/_2$ tablespoon sea salt/1
   teaspoon table salt

3lbs boned and skinned chicken
   thighs

FOR THE COATING

4 eggs

$1^1/_3$ cups cornstarch

$^1/_2$ teaspoon ground allspice

$^1/_2$ teaspoon paprika

$^1/_2$ teaspoon fine salt

vegetable oil for frying

FOR THE RICE

1 onion

3 tablespoons olive oil

$2^1/_2$ cups basmati rice

3 cardamom pods, crushed

$^1/_2$ teaspoon ground allspice

$^1/_2$ teaspoon ground cinnamon

4 cups hot chicken stock

1 cup pinenuts

1–2 tablespoons chopped parsley

1–2 tablespoons chopped mint

1–2 tablespoons chopped cilantro

TO FINISH

1–2 tablespoons pomegranate seeds (about $^1/_2$ pomegranate),
   if available

To marinate the chicken, put the lemon juice, peeled and roughly chopped onion, allspice, pepper, cardamom seeds, peeled garlic, oil and salt into a processor and blitz to a pulp. (Or just roughly chop the onion and peel and bruise the garlic and add everything else to make the marinade). Either way, pour the marinade into a large freezer bag. Chop the chicken pieces in half across the thigh – or make them smaller if you'd like – add them to the marinade in the bag and leave in the fridge overnight or for up to two days.

Let the marinated chicken come to room temperature before you cook it, and while it's losing its chill, start with the rice. Peel the onion and slice into very thin half moons. Heat the oil in a wide saucepan (one which has a lid) and cook the sliced onions in the oil over a fairly high heat until the straggly pieces are darkly golden and very crispy. Remove to a plate and reserve for later.

Turn the heat down, add the rice and spices to the pan and turn in the oil until the rice is slicked and glossy. Add the stock and let the pan come to the boil, then clamp on the lid and turn the heat down to the lowest heat possible. Cook without peeking for 15 minutes, by which time all the water should have been absorbed. Take off the heat and put a dishtowel under the lid on top of the pan, put the lid back on and leave to rest for about 5 minutes or longer if you need it. If you want the rice to stand for a long time, remove the lid when it's ready, cover with a dishtowel, then clamp the lid on again and let it stand with the heat switched off.

Meanwhile, you can proceed with the chicken. For the coating, beat the eggs together in a shallow bowl, and combine the cornstarch, allspice, paprika and salt in another.

Pour enough oil into a large frying pan to come up to about $1/2$ inch and heat until sizzling. Then shake the excess marinade off the chicken pieces and dip in the floury mixture, coating well, then the beaten egg mixture and put carefully into hot oil. In other words, you're doing this like an inside-out batter. Cook the meat until golden and crispy, which should take about 10 minutes, though cut one piece to check it's cooked through. You will have to do this in batches, and don't crowd the pan or the temperature of the oil will drop too much and the chicken will get greasy. Place the chicken pieces on a baking sheet lined with paper towels as you go.

When you are ready to serve, toast the pinenuts in a dry pan until singed with gold and work them through the rice with about half the crispy onion, using a fork. Add most of the chopped herbs, forking through the rice again and then tip out on to a platter.

Arrange the golden cardamom chicken on top of the rice and sprinkle over the final bits of crispy onion, and the herbs. Halve the pomegranate and bash some seeds out over the finished plate of rice and chicken.

By all means lighten your load by reducing the choice if you want (and see page 436 for portion guidance), but the figs can be done days in advance and kept in a sealed jar (and will only improve) and both the baklava and sticky semolina cake can be made a day early. The point is that a feast needs opulence, abundance and heady profusion. This is certainly what you get here.

BAGHDAD BAKLAVA

There are so many versions of this syrup-drenched filo-pastry and nut slice, but this one, with its cardamom and almond filling, has an Iraqi provenance that you don't have to follow all the way. Feel free to change the nuts. An earlier version of mine used chopped pistachios, but I've also made this with 3$^1/_2$ cups of walnut pieces, chopped small. Use packages of fresh, not frozen, filo only.

Makes 24

note
I know it's more expensive, but I have found – beyond doubt – that organic nuts from a good healthstore are so much better than supermarket packages, as to make the latter unusable.

FOR THE SYRUP
1$^1/_4$ cups water
2$^1/_2$ cups superfine sugar
juice of $^1/_2$ lemon

1 tablespoon rosewater
1 tablespoon orange-flower water

FOR THE PASTRY AND FILLING
1 stick plus one tablespoon unsalted butter, melted
14oz (2 packages) filo pastry

3 cups blanched almonds
$^1/_4$ teaspoon cardamom seeds

To make the syrup, bring the water, sugar and lemon juice to the boil, and keep at boiling point for 5 minutes. Add the rosewater and orange-flower water, then remove from the heat. Pour into a pitcher, let cool and then chill in the fridge.

Preheat the oven to 350°F.

I use a throwaway square aluminum foil pan, 9 x 9 x 1$^1/_2$ inches (available from a supermarket or kitchen shop) to make baklava, because I found this makes it easier to remove the pieces from the pan. Brush the pan with butter, and then brush each of the filo pastry sheets as you line the pan with them. Use one package for the bottom layer, placing them in the pan evenly so that the pastry goes up the sides with a little overhang. As the pan is square and the filo pastry is often a rectangular shape, you should try to arrange the sheets so that each side is covered in turn. When you have used one package, chop the almonds, with the cardamom seeds, in a processor or by hand until medium-fine and spread them evenly over the filo sheets. Then carry on with the rest of the pastry in the same way. The last sheet on top should also be buttered well, and then with a sharp knife trim around the top edge of the pan to give a neat finish.

Now cut across the baklava square in three lines, and then – regarding those three lines going from west to east (bear with me, as telephonists like to say), make five cuts diagonally down, north to south, give or take, so that you end up with 24 diamondy shapes. I hope the picture opposite will make this clear. Not that you have to follow my instructions: you can cut into diamonds/squares any way or size you like. Make sure you cut the baklava right through to the bottom, though (but without cutting through the tin foil).

Put in the oven and cook for 30 minutes, by which time the filo will have puffed up and become golden-brown. As soon as it comes out of the oven, pour over half the cold syrup. Leave it a few minutes to soak in and then pour over the rest.

HONEYED FIGS

I imagine that these figs would, in their place of origin, be eaten with buffalo-milk cream, but I am happy to make do with crème fraîche or Greek yogurt.

4 cups water
1 cup honey
3 bay leaves
2 cardamom pods, bruised

2 strips orange peel, about 4$^1/_2$ inches
$^1/_4$ cup fresh orange juice
3$^1/_2$ cups or 1lb organic dried figs

TO SERVE
1 tablespoon splintered or chopped pistachios

crème fraîche or Greek plain yogurt, optional

note
This recipe uses the "ugly" organic, real dried figs which are truly parched and need a lot of liquid to rehydrate. If using those squishy plump dried figs from a package, reduce cooking time and halve the water and honey.

Put the water in a pan and stir in the honey to dissolve over a low heat. Add the bay leaves, bruised cardamom pods, orange peel and juice, and bring to the boil. Let the syrup bubble for 10 minutes.

Add the figs and cook for 30 minutes, then turn off the heat and let the figs stand in the hot liquid for 10–15 minutes. Remove the figs to a container using a skimmer. Put the syrup back on the heat and bring back to the boil, letting it bubble away for 5 minutes. It should have reduced to about 1$^1/_2$ cups or just over a third of your original liquid. Put the figs back into the reduced syrup and let cool. Store in a jar until you want to eat them; I leave a jar of them in the kitchen so I've always got a good dessert at the ready.

To serve, put the figs in a bowl, pouring over a scant amount of syrup and scatter over the green, green pistachios. And pass round the crème fraîche or Greek yogurt.

STICKY SEMOLINA CAKE

I am an enormous fan of Tess Mallos's writing on Middle Eastern food, and this recipe – although I've certainly come across other versions – was inspired by a deeply pleasurable immersion in her brief but vibrant *Middle Eastern Home Cooking*. My version, apart from being adapted for a lazy person and therefore simpler, is more flowery, and since I'm going through my cardamom phase, more muskily aromatic. Change flavorings – say, by missing out the flower waters and substituting a drop of almond extract for the cardamom – if you like.

Makes 36

FOR THE SYRUP

2 cups superfine sugar

1 cup water

2 tablespoons lemon juice

1 teaspoon rosewater

1 teaspoon orange-flower water

FOR THE CAKE

2 cups semolina

$^3/_4$ cup superfine sugar

1 stick plus 1 tablespoon butter

1 teaspoon baking powder

$^1/_2$ teaspoon baking soda

zest of 1 lemon

2 eggs

$^1/_2$ cup Greek plain yogurt

$^1/_4$ teaspoon ground cardamom

36 whole blanched almonds, approx. $^1/_4$ cup

To make the syrup, dissolve the sugar in the water over a low heat then add the lemon juice. Turn up the heat and boil the syrup fiercely for 5 minutes. Take the pan off the heat, add the rosewater and orange-flower water, then pour the syrup into a pitcher to cool. Put the syrup in the fridge to chill down further.

Preheat the oven to 350°F, and butter a 9 inch square baking pan.

Put all of the cake ingredients except for the whole almonds into a food processor and process until you have a smooth batter. Tip into the cake pan and spread evenly. Dot the top with the almonds in 6 rows of 6, placed equally apart. Bake in the oven for 30 minutes, by which time the cake will have risen and become golden. Test it with a cake tester to check it's not doughy underneath.

Pour the cold syrup over the hot cake and leave to cool completely in the pan. Cut into 36 little squares, or however you like.

FUNERAL FEAST

It may seem odd to talk about what you eat at a funeral as a way of celebrating life, but at every level, that is exactly what it is. Nor do I mean a celebration in that cheery, if faintly maudlin sense of giving someone a good send-off, though that is a part of it. Any food is a vital reminder that life goes on, that living is important. That isn't brutal: it's the greatest respect you can pay to the dead.

I am not someone who believes that life is sacred, but I know it is very precious. To turn away from that, to act as if living is immaterial, that what you need to sustain life doesn't count, is to repudiate and diminish the tragedy of the loss of a life.

In many cultures the food that's eaten to commemorate the death, and thereby the life, of a person, marks the rift that has taken place: those who are living partake, the dead person is visibly cut off from the life-giving business of taking sustenance. At this early stage, as someone is being buried, the full understanding of their not being there any more is impossible, but this is the first important step.

It is hard to communicate the importance of the physical here. Too much emphasis, I think, can be placed on the spiritual aspect, and the urgent need to believe that the soul of a person lives on. That oft-quoted funereal platitude about the deceased not being gone but merely "in the next room" can feel like a painful denial of what a bereaved person is feeling. Memories are great, sure, but not yet. It takes time even to begin to accept someone's becoming part of a memory bank rather than a living, breathing person: the immediate loss is entirely, shockingly physical; their smell, the feel of them. They are not in the next room: they are gone.

And this is why many people find it difficult to eat when someone they love has died (not that that's ever happened to me). The act of eating can seem like the cruellest demonstration of the dreadful disparity that now exists, and is unbridgeable. Though you cannot bridge it by acting as if you, too, have died.

Not that anyone has a choice in how they react: some eat out of grief, some lose their appetite. But even those who, grieving, gorge may feel ashamed, as if the act is somehow obscene in the face of tragedy. M.F.K. Fisher tells the story in *An Alphabet for Gourmets* (included in *The Art of Eating*) of "the mysterious appetite that often surges in us when our hearts seem about to break and our lives seem too bleakly empty." Scornfully, she writes how "the prettifiers of human passion choose to think that a man who has just watched his true love die is lifted above such ugly things as food" when "the truth is most bereaved souls crave nourishment more tangible than prayers: they want a steak."

The story, within this entry ("S is for Sad"), is one in which she tells a friend that he is not to feel ashamed of having gone out and stuffed himself with food, meat and pies and French-fried potatoes, after he has watched his wife slowly die. He felt he was "gross, indelicate, unfeeling," and her explanation is crucial. The mind, she knows, cannot rest – grief is a constant torment – and so by overeating, by burdening the body with food, the system grows lethargic. What happens is a kind of necessary stupefaction, as sleepiness takes over from restlessness.

This is not in itself what lies behind the great funeral feasts of history. Family members often had to travel long distances to be at the graveside and they needed food after the journey. Moreover, the abundance of the feast showed the value of the deceased; it was a mark of respect, a way of honoring the life of that person. Particular foods, too, can be a living testament to the person it was who died. Recipes live on, and to eat foods that person either used to prepare or liked to eat can feel monumentally significant. In Thailand, I read in an article by Bee Wilson in the *Sunday Telegraph*, "mourners are often presented with a little cookbook...comprising the favorite recipes of the dead person. In this way the whole gastronomic person of the deceased is remembered." And I would say that the gastronomic personality is the persona. How you eat and what you eat is who you are.

There is another way food is important when someone has died: it marks a connection between the living. There is nothing you can say to someone who is bereaved that can make anything better and even the notion that you could make it better can feel offensive, even if the wish is declared out of kindness. But you can help, you can make food. And if you can't cook, or haven't got time, you can shop. The thing to remember in either case is never to burden the bereaved with a question: don't ask what they'd like you to get or what they might want to eat. Decisions are impossible: you have to do it, and do it without drawing attention to the act. I remember a friend of mine leaving some bags of shopping from the supermarket for me once. She hadn't told me she was going, she hadn't asked what I needed: she just left the bags outside the side door with a short note. It was one of the kindest things anyone could have done.

Important as the food is, it's not the cooking that matters and I have no plans to provide here some gastronomic reworking of the cakes and ale of the original funeral feast. But certainly, the recipes that follow may be used in the traditional way, to feed mourners and to provide ballast at a time of emotional fragility.

NURSERY FISH PIE

I start with this recipe for the simple reason that it was what I made on the evening following my mother's funeral. I don't think anyone wants to cook in the immediate shock of bereavement and in my experience you are anyway likely to need something like an overordered Chinese takeout, but a few days on cooking can be a calming act, and since the mind knows no rest and has no focus, the body may as well be busy. Or you may be making this for others in need.

3lbs all-purpose potatoes
1¹/₂ sticks butter
1¹/₂lbs haddock
2lbs 4oz smoked haddock
2 cups whole milk
3 bay leaves

1 tablespoon white peppercorns
1 cup frozen peas
¹/₂ cup all-purpose flour
1¹/₂ cups Cheddar cheese, grated
3 hard-boiled eggs

Serves 8

note
You can assemble the pie in advance and reheat when you want, but in that case it is important that the fish and sauce should be cold before they are combined, and put to one side. As long as the fish is fresh, you could do this a day in advance. I wouldn't spatch the potatoes on until I was putting it in the oven, even if I had cooked and mashed them in advance, too.

Peel the potatoes and cut them in half or quarters, depending on size, and put them in a pan of salted water to cook from cold. When they're tender, drain and then mash them with ³/₄ stick of the butter, seasoning to taste.

Put the fish into a large skillet with the milk, bay leaves and peppercorns. Bring the milk in the pan to a boil, then immediately turn down and simmer the fish until it is just cooked through. Remove the fish to a plate and pour the cooking liquid into a glass measuring cup, straining out the bay leaves and peppercorns.

Meanwhile, put the frozen peas in a bowl, pour over some boiling water and preheat the oven to 375°F, slipping in a baking sheet as you do so.

Melt the remaining ³/₄ stick butter in a saucepan and stir in the flour to make a

roux. Take this off the heat briefly, just while you gradually whisk in the fishy milk, then put back over a medium heat and keep stirring until the sauce comes to a boil and thickens. Let it bubble away for a couple of minutes and then take off the heat and stir in most of the cheese (leaving some to sprinkle over the top of the pie later) and the drained peas.

Flake the fish, making sure not to let it disintegrate too much, and use it to line a 12-cup ovenproof dish and pour the sauce over, using a rubber spatula to help you distribute it equally and meld it with the fish. Cut the hard-boiled eggs into slices and arrange the golden-centered discs over the top of the fish in sauce. Top with the mashed potato, using a spatula, again, to help you coax it right over the sides. With a fork, scrape lines up and down the length of the dish and then sprinkle with a little grated Cheddar cheese before putting it on the sheet in the oven for 20–40 minutes, depending on whether you're putting the pie in hot or cold.

SWEET LAMB TAGINE

A friend had told me of the Moroccan tagine, written about by Claudia Roden, which is made sweet with prunes and is as easy to make as it is comforting to eat. Prunes, I know are traditionally part of the funeral fare of many cultures – even though this is not part of any Moroccan mourning feast – since their black color is thought to be appropriate to the solemnity of the occasion. And so I appropriated this, not least because I felt it was one of those dishes that you could make at home and take round to someone's house for them to heat up and feed themselves and their family and so be taken care of by you.

I have fiddled a little, or quite a lot with this, reducing the amount of prunes that are often included, and making up the weight with some dense, grainy chestnuts.

Serves 8

3 red onions, total weight 1lb
2 fat cloves garlic
4 tablespoons peanut or light
   vegetable oil
3$^1/_2$lb shoulder of lamb, in 1$^1/_4$
   inch cubes
1 teaspoon ground ginger
1 teaspoon ground allspice
1 tablespoon sea salt/1$^1/_2$
   teaspoons table salt
1 teaspoon freshly ground black
   pepper

approx. 8 cups water
2 cinnamon sticks, broken into
   pieces (3 if small)
3 star anise
3 bay leaves
2 tablespoons honey
2 tablespoons black treacle or
   molasses
3 cups pitted prunes
1$^1/_3$ cups peeled cooked chestnuts
   (from a vacuum pack)

Peel the onions and garlic and chop finely in a food processor, or finely chop the onions by hand and mince the garlic. Heat the oil in a large pan that will take everything later, and fry the onion and garlic till soft, making sure they don't burn. Add the meat and brown lightly all over. Stir in the ground spices, salt and pepper. Cover with water, stir well, then add the cinnamon sticks, star anise, bay, honey and molasses. Stir again and let the stew come to the boil before turning down the heat to let it simmer for approx. 1 hour, or until the meat is tender, adding a little water if it becomes too dry. Add the prunes and chestnuts and simmer for 30 minutes longer.

This serves 8, generously, although it is very easy to boost or reduce quantities to suit.

LENTIL SOUP

Again, because of their dark color, lentils are considered fitting food for funerals, and, again, that is not the only reason for the inclusion of this soup here: it is both comforting and sustaining and, importantly, easy to transport and reheat.

4 carrots, approx. 1lb	$^1/_4$ cup garlic oil, or $^1/_4$ cup olive oil	Serves 10
3oz pancetta or bacon, chopped	with 1 clove garlic, minced	
6 scallions	$2^1/_2$ cups Puy or Beluga lentils	
$^1/_4$ cup chopped parsley	2 teaspoons wholegrain mustard	
leaves from 2 stalks fresh thyme,	$1^3/_4$ cups canned chopped tomatoes	
or $^1/_4$ teaspoon dried thyme	or pulp	
	8 cups water	

Peel and roughly chop the carrots, and put them into a processor with the pancetta or bacon, scallions, parsley and thyme leaves. Process to a mush, and then heat the oil in a saucepan and cook the processed vegetables over a medium heat until they are soft. (Mince the garlic clove in with the vegetables, if you are using it rather than the garlic oil.)

Stir in the lentils, letting them become slick and glossy. Then add the mustard, tomatoes and water. Bring the pan to the boil and simmer gently for 1 hour or thereabouts.

MEATLOAF

Meatloaf is always comfort food, and this is perfect for having sliced on a plate at a funeral tea or for sending round to someone's house. I like this better cold than hot in any event. It's somewhere between an Italian *polpettone* and an old-fashioned English veal and ham pie (without the pastry).

I tend to use brown bread, but it doesn't really matter: the only thing that's important is that you don't use pappy plastic white sliced.

There is something hopeful and cheering about the golden yolk of the egg showing through in each slice, and although I never think that one should attempt to jolly things up, I don't think it matters if the food does this of its own account. Besides, the egg – and see the hamine eggs below – is a recurring feature in funeral food, symbolizing as it does, the cycle of life, the end and the beginning in one.

Serves 10–12 (approx. 14 slices)

note

A cold slice of meatloaf makes the most wonderful sandwich; at times of stress, I think you often need your food conveyed directly, no knife or fork business.

3–4 slices (4oz) stale or slightly stale bread
$^1/_3$–$^1/_2$ cup milk
1 onion
1 clove garlic
$^1/_4$ cup chopped parsley
1$^1/_2$lbs veal, cut into cubes
$^1/_2$lb bacon, chopped

$^1/_2$ cup tablespoon grated pecorino or Parmesan
$^1/_4$ teaspoon cayenne
1 tablespoon sea salt/1 teaspoon table salt
black pepper
1 egg
4 hard-boiled eggs

Preheat the oven to 350°F. Soak the bread slices in the milk. Peel the onion and garlic, and put into a food processor with the parsley. Blitz until finely chopped and then add the veal and bacon, and process again until the meat is finely minced.

Turn the mixture out into a large bowl, and squeeze out the pulpy bread slices, adding them to the bowl and throwing away the milk. Sprinkle in the pecorino or Parmesan, cayenne, salt and some pepper, and mix very well with your hands. Break in the egg and mix again.

Line a 2lb loaf pan with plastic wrap, pressing into the corners and leaving some overhang at the top. Pack half the meat mixture into the lined pan; it's important to press in well, as it will affect the final shape of the loaf at the end.

Peel the hard-boiled eggs and press in a row down the middle of the pan, lodging them snugly. Pack in the final half of the meatloaf mixture, making sure you cover the eggs well as you press the meat around them. Smooth the top of the meatloaf with a spatula, wrap with whatever plastic wrap overhang you have (and yes, you can put plastic wrap in the oven), and put in the oven for 45–60 minutes.

Let the meatloaf cool in the pan on a rack: it will be fragile while warm and will hold its shape better once cold. And because of the plastic wrap lining you won't have any problems getting it out of the pan.

HEAVENLY POTATOES

This Utah dish, often more plainly named "funeral potatoes," is apparently the "mainstay" of post-funeral dinners for members of the Church of Jesus Christ of Latter-Day Saints – a Mormon post-mortem speciality. I thought they'd be perfect alongside the British traditional baked ham. (And for the ham you could follow the recipe on page 205, but if cooking ham in Cherry Coke seems insufficiently dignified for the occasion, replace with regular Coke and remind yourself that the dark color of the libation is fitting.)

1 cup sour cream	pepper	Serves 4–6
1 cup milk	5 cups potatoes in $^1/_2$–1 inch dice	
1 tablespoon sea salt/$^1/_2$ tablespoon table salt	1$^1/_2$ cups cornflakes	

Put the sour cream, milk, salt and some pepper in a pan. Peel the potatoes, and cut them in roughly $^1/_2$–1 inch cubes and drop them into the pan. Give a good stir to make sure they're immersed, then put on the heat, bring to the boil before turning the heat to low, partially covering with a lid, and simmering for about 30 minutes, or until tender.

While this is going on, put the cornflakes into a plastic freezer bag, making sure it's securely closed, and bash with a rolling pin so that you have a bagful of golden crumbs. This provides the crunchy topping for your melting, bubbling casserole of potatoes later. Preheat the oven to 425°F.

When the potatoes are ready, scrape them out of their pan to a dish – I use a circular slanted-side pie plate, approximately 10 inch in diameter – and cover with the crumbed cornflakes. Bake for 15 minutes in the hot oven. You can cook the potatoes in their pan in advance, pour them into the dish, and let get cold before covering with crumbs and reheating. In which case, I'd use a slightly cooler oven – 400°F – and give them about 30 minutes.

This serves 4–6, but obviously it's easy to boost numbers if you need to feed a multitude of mourners.

HAMINE EGGS

The traditional Jewish food of mourning is a hard-boiled egg, not as a symbol of regeneration, as the egg might suggest for Christians, but more as a symbol of perpetuation. Life ends, and life begins: life goes on, in fact. All foods that are round, too, have that significance – that the cycle of life and time continues – and as Martine Chiche-Yana explains in *La Table Juive*, they are described as being "sans bouche," without mouths to express sorrow and anguish. I find that appropriate: there is nothing to be said, or nothing that helps.

Hamine eggs are the Sephardi version, traditionally cooked in the dying embers of a fire. Here, they are cooked slowly on the stove top, with onion skins to tint the shells a rich woody brown; and although coffee grounds are often added, I emptied out the leaves of a used tea bag instead. After all, during World War II, women would use cold tea to dye their legs when stockings were not to be found.

onion skins from about 4 large onions	6 eggs	Serves 6
tea leaves from 1 used teabag	1 tablespoon vegetable oil	

Line a saucepan with onion skins, using about half your supply, and then add the tea leaves. Put in the eggs and cover with the rest of the onion skins (red onion skins will give a deeper, burgundy tinge). You don't want any onion, just the papery skin. Cover well with water, and pour over the oil to help prevent the water evaporating during the long cooking time.

Bring the pan to a boil and immediately transfer to a new, smaller burner with a heat diffuser on it and turn the flame to the lowest flame possible. Leave to cook very slowly for 7 or so hours, then turn off the heat and leave to cool before taking the eggs out of the murky water. I tend to cook the eggs in the daytime and leave them till the next morning before taking them out of the pan.

Hamine eggs are not exclusively eaten at funerals, though they are a feature of them, and these are beautiful on the outside, meltingly tender within and worth cooking not just in times of grief.

MARBLE CAKE

During the course of photographing this book, the mother of a very old friend of mine, Fiona Golfar, died, and this recipe is both a memorial to her mother, Joan, and a gift from her family. For this is the very cake (see photo opposite) made by Fiona's Auntie Ruth. She sent me the recipe, too, with the title Auntie Ruth's ("Shiver") marble cake. "Shiva" (the alternative spelling) is the traditional Jewish period of mourning, and she suggests that a marble cake is customary, perhaps because, as she said, "it looks so jolly in contrast to the bleakness." With respect, I'm not sure: to me it looks mournful, and I like that. I wondered, perhaps fancifully, whether originally marble cakes were thought appropriate in anticipation of the marble headstone that was to be erected. I make marble cake in a ring mold, as the circle is also significant. There is a cycle that continues but – after all, the cake is sliced and the circle broken – another that has ended.

I hope Auntie Ruth doesn't mind that I have fiddled a little with her recipe, and I thank her, and the shade of Joan Golfar, for allowing me to have her shiva cake for my book.

Makes approx. 20 slices

note
The espresso powder is really to enhance the requisite dark coloring, so if you do not want the coffee flavor, slight though it is, replace the teaspoonful of espresso powder with another tablespoon of unsweetened cocoa.

2 sticks soft, unsalted butter
1^1/$_4$ cups superfine sugar
1^3/$_4$ cups all-purpose flour
^{1}/$_2$ teaspoon baking soda
1^1/$_2$ teaspoons baking powder
4 eggs

zest of 1 orange, plus approx. 3 tablespoons juice
1 tablespoon unsweetened cocoa
1 teaspoon espresso powder
1 tablespoon milk

Preheat the oven to 350°F. Grease a ring mold 9^1/$_2$ inches in diameter, with 5 cup capacity.

Put the butter, sugar, flour, baking soda, baking powder, eggs and zest of orange into a processor and blitz to a batter. Pour the orange juice, with the motor running, down the funnel of the processor to make the cake mixture lighter and smoother.

Divide the batter between two bowls. Put the cocoa and espresso powder into a small bowl and whisk in the milk; fold this into one of the bowls of cake mixture to make it dark colored. Spoon a splodge of light-colored cake batter into the pan, and then a chocolate-colored spoonful working around the ring of the mold. Carry on with a second layer, but don't worry if it is haphazard and not terribly even as this is the whole point of the marbling. Once you have used up both the batters, give the contents of the ring mold a swirl with a spatula to create the marble effect, and bake in the oven for 35 minutes or until a cake tester comes out clean.

Let it sit on a cooling rack for about 10 minutes before turning out on to the rack to get completely cold.

FRUIT TEA LOAF

I think you need a fruit cake for a funeral: there's something both comforting and bolstering (and traditional) about it. This is an easy one to make, and wonderful sliced and spread with butter, eaten with a cup of tea, or plain with something stronger.

1 cup tea
$2^1/_4$ cups mixed dried fruit
$3/_4$ cup dark brown sugar
$1^3/_4$ cups all-purpose flour

1 teaspoon baking powder
$1/_2$ teaspoon baking soda
pinch cloves
1 egg

Makes approx. 10 slices

note
If you need more cake, boost quantities but use more pans of the same size, rather than moving up to a bigger loaf pan.

Make the cup of black tea (just using a tea bag), and pour it into a bowl with the dried fruit and sugar; stir well, then leave to macerate overnight.

Preheat the oven to 325°F. Line a 1lb loaf pan with a parchment paper or butter the pan and line the bottom with parchment paper.

Beat the flour, baking powder, baking soda and cloves into the tea-soaked fruit, and then beat in the egg. Spoon and scrape into the lined loaf pan, and bake for 1 hour – or until cooked – before letting the cake cool in its pan on a rack.

ROSEMARY REMEMBRANCE CAKE

I have given a recipe for a rosemary-scented cake before – though this is rather different – but felt it deserved its place here, for remembrance. Besides, my maternal grandmother, whom I loved inordinately, was called Rosemary, so I wanted it here, for her. Added to which, it is a beautiful cake, the rosemary sprig curving out over the top, down the length of the palely gold, dense loaf.

Makes approx. 10 slices

note
Again, make more of the same sized cake, not a big huge one, if you need more slices.

1 eating apple (approx. 6oz in weight)
1 small sprig and 1 long sprig rosemary

FOR THE CAKE BATTER
2 sticks butter
$^3/_4$ cup plus 1 tablespoon superfine sugar

1 teaspoon superfine sugar
juice and zest of $^1/_2$ lemon
1 teaspoon butter

3 eggs
2 cups all-purpose flour
2 teaspoons baking powder

Peel, core and roughly chop the apple and put into a saucepan with the small sprig of rosemary, the teaspoon of sugar, the lemon zest and juice, and butter. Cover the pan and cook on a low heat for 4–8 minutes until the apple is soft. How long this takes really depends on the variety of apple you're using. Coxes cook the fastest, and are good here. Leave to cool, and fish out the rosemary sprig when it is cold.

Preheat the oven to 325°F. Line a 1lb loaf pan with a loaf liner, or butter and line the bottom with parchment paper.

Put the cooled apple into a food processor and blitz to a pulp. Then add the butter, sugar, eggs, flour and baking powder and process to a smooth batter. Spoon and scrape into the loaf pan and smooth the top. Sprinkle the surface with the remaining tablespoon of sugar and then lay the long sprig of rosemary along the center of the cake. On baking, the rosemary sheds its oil to leave a scented path down the middle of the cake.

Bake the cake for 50 minutes or until a cake tester comes out clean, then leave to cool on a rack. Slip the paper-lined cake out of the pan once it is cool.

BIBLIOGRAPHY

Bareham, Lindsey, *In Praise of the Potato: Recipes from Around the World* (Penguin, London, 1991)

Batmanglij, Najmieh, *New Food of Life: Ancient Persian and Modern Iranian Cooking and Ceremonies* (Mage Publishers, Washington DC, 2003)

Bhogal, Vicky, *Cooking Like Mummyji: Real British Asian Cooking* (Simon & Schuster, London, 2003)

Chiche-Yana, Martine, *La table juive*; tome 1, *Recettes & traditions de fêtes*; tome 2, *Recettes & traditions du cycle de vie* (Edisud, Aix-en-Provence, 1992 and 1994)

Cipriani, Arrigo, *The Harry's Bar Cookbook* (Blake Publishing, London, 2003)

Clay, Xanthe (ed), *It's Raining Plums: Seasonal Recipes by Seasoned Cooks* (John Murray, London, 2002)

Ephron, Nora, *Heartburn* (Virago, London, 1996)

Finamore, Roy, with Molly Stevens, *One Potato, Two Potato* (Houghton Mifflin Co., Boston, 2001)

Fisher, M.F.K., *The Art of Eating* (Wiley, New York, 1990)

Goldman, Marcy and Yvan Luneault, *The Best of Better Baking.com: 175 Classic Recipes from the Beloved Baker's Website* (Random House Canada, 2002)

Goldstein, Darra, *The Georgian Feast: the Vibrant Culture and Savory Food of the Republic of Georgia* (University of California Press, Berkeley and Los Angeles, 1993)

Gray, Rose, and Ruth Rogers, *River Café Cookbook Two* (Ebury Press, London, 1997)

Iny, Daisy, *The Best of Baghdad Cooking With Treats from Teheran* (Saturday Review Press/E.P. Dutton & Co. Inc., New York, 1976)

The King Arthur Flour Company, *The King Arthur Flour Baker's Companion* (The Countryman Press, Woodstock, Vermont, 2003)

Mallos, Tess, *Middle Eastern Home Cooking* (Parkway, Sydney, 2003)

Malgieri, Nick, *Chocolate: from Simple Cookies to Extravagant Showstoppers* (HarperCollins Publishers Inc., New York, 1998)

Maresca, Tom, and Diane Darrow, *La Tavola Italiana* (Trafalgar Square, Vermont, 2000)

Nathan, Joan, *The Jewish Holiday Kitchen: 250 Recipes from Around the World to Make Your Celebration Special* (Schocken Books Inc., New York, 1988)

Norrington-Davies, Tom, *Just Like Mother Used To Make* (Cassell, London, 2003)

Nugent, Ted, and Shemane Nugent, *Kill It & Grill It: A Guide to Preparing and Cooking Wild Game and Fish* (Regnery Publishing, Inc., Washington DC, 2002)

Roden, Claudia, *The Book of Jewish Food* (Viking, London, 1997)

Rodgers, Judy, *The Zuni Café Cookbook: a Compendium of Recipes from San Francisco's Beloved Restaurant* (W.W. Norton & Co., New York and London, 2002)

Routhier, Nicole, *The Best of Nicole Routhier* (Stewart, Tabori & Chang, New York, 1996)

Rozin, P., Fischler, C., Imada, S., Sarubin, A., and Wrzesniewski, A., *Attitudes to Food and the Role of Food in Life in the USA, Japan, Flemish Belgium and France: Possible Implications for the Diet-Health Debate* (Appetite, 1999, 33, 163-180)

Sands, Sarah, *Playing the Game* (Macmillan, London, 2003)

Turner, Keith, and Jean Turner, *The Pudding Club Book: Luscious Recipes from the Pudding Club* (Headline, London, 1997)

Viestad, Andreas, *Kitchen of Light: New Scandinavian Cooking* (Artisan, New York, 2003)

STOCKISTS

I DO TRY, I promise I do, not to use ingredients that will be a nightmare for the non-obsessive food-shopper to find. I won't lie and say that I make sure that everything in the book can be found at a supermarket, but a great deal can and if I don't think any particular ingredient will be available down the street from you, then I've sourced a mail order or internet shopping site that will satisfy your needs and desires.

I have failed only in the small matter of golden sultanas (golden raisins). These can be found in middle-eastern shops and nowhere else insofar as I can find out, but since normal sultanas can be substituted, I think none of us should lose too much sleep over it: I just adore the pale golden beauty of the amber-yellow variety and have a slightly shuddery reaction to the brown, irrationally really; in short, it's an aesthetic rather than a culinary preference.

What follows is not the kind of comprehensive list that I compiled for *How to Eat* but a bare-bones guide to sourcing any particular ingredient or piece of equipment that it is either stipulated in or required for a recipe that you may not find easily on your own doorstep. All the companies below can send whatever necessary missing item you need.

MEAT AND FISH

It probably isn't altogether necessary to scrabble about for producers of organic meat now that supermarkets are more on the ball about stocking properly reared and treated meat themselves, but it can't hurt. I don't buy meat unless I know who I'm buying it from and they, in turn, know who is supplying it to them, and are sure that the animals are properly reared (including naturally fed), properly treated and can be surely sourced (that's to say the provenance of each creature can be checked).

You should always find out if there is a farm near you that you can build a relationship with and get your meat from direct, or if you live in the city, a faraway one you can build a telephonic relationship with (often the best kind) instead. The numbers below should help.

LASATER GRASSLANDS BEEF
Tel 1 866 454 2333
http://www.lgbeef.com
Beef steaks, roasts, ground beef & other cuts from cattle raised without antibiotics, pesticides, hormones, growth implants, animal by-products or steroids.

DIAMOND ORGANICS
Tel 1 888 674 2642
http://www.diamondorganics.com
Great selection of organic meats, poultry and fish, including beef, buffalo, pork, ham, chicken, turkey, organic hotdogs, wild salmon and tuna. Also smoked tuna, smoked black cod, smoked salmon and smoked oysters.

SCANPAN
1 201 818 2280
I use a ridged griddle for cooking meat a lot. Scanpan griddles have the virtue of being lighter than cast iron ones and much easier to wash up, too. For fish and pancakes you will need one of their smooth griddles too.
http://www.scanpan.com

Check the above site for a list of online retailers.

Not only does Citarella have geese, they have a very wide range of other poultry, seafood, meats and game meats and specialty foods. They have about half a dozen locations -- listed below is mail-order information and the location for the upper west side store. They do not have a toll-free phone number, but they have an excellent website.

CITARELLA
212.874.0383
http://www.citarella.com
Upper Westside location - 2135 Broadway (at 75th St)
New York, NY 10023

GOOSE
Sumptuous, succulent & welcome in its gamy taste, try roasting & serving these buttery, farm-fresh geese with a tart fruit sauce. Weight ranges from 10-16 pounds. Ordered in 2 pound increments.
Choose lbs. 10 12 14 16
Price: $3.99 per pound

HERBS AND SPICES

You may have noticed, and I have made no attempt to hide it, that I have gone all out for pink peppercorns in this book – indeed, in my life in general. Purists will sneeringly tell you that this is not proper pepper and just a whimsical fantasy. This may be so, but I like to use it and if you do you will need to find a good supplier, as you will for the mixed herbs with lavender that I use for the St Tropez chicken on p425 and many of the recipes in the Eid chapter.

ADRIANA'S CARAVAN
Not only does this company sell a huge selections of herbs and spices, they also supply various exotica and "world foods" that will be helpful for any far-flung ingredient needed.
Tel 1 800 316 0820
http://www.adrianascaravan.com

DRINK

THE PERFECT PUREE OF NAPA VALLEY
If you want to make the Bellini on p374, and don't have access to orchardsful of white peaches, you will need to buy top quality peach puree and this is the company that will make it easy for you.
Tel 1 800 556 3707
http://www.perfectpuree.com

BAKING & CAKE DECORATING

My weakness, I know, but if you don't have a specialist cake or baking shop near you, you really will need a good online or mail order supplier.

KING ARTHUR FLOUR BAKER'S CATALOGUE
Anything you need for baking, this company will send you. The range is huge and the catalogue is – for me at least – compulsive reading.
001 800 827 6836
http://www.kingarthurflour.com

SWEET CELEBRATIONS
http://www.maidofscandinavia.com

BROADWAY PANHANDLER
I couldn't live without reusable baking parchment, which is mentioned throughout the book: this store sells Silpat, Exopat and Fiberlux, and an enormous array of baking and other cooking items.
Tel 1 866 COOKWARE
http://www.broadwaypanhandler.com

SPECIALIST ENGLISH PRODUCE
MYERS OF KESWICK

If you require Marmite, golden syrup, Maltesers, Birds Custard powder, or various other items suggested in recipes in this book, then you're in luck.
http://myersofkeswick.com

For some reason, I couldn't find Horlicks (needed for the Chocolate Malteser cake on p283) at Myers of Keswick, but luckily you can get it from:

THE VERMONT COUNTRY STORE
You should know that Horlicks has less sugar and more malt flavor than American malted milk powder, so the distinction is important.
Tel: 1 802 362 8440
http://www.vermontcountrystore.com

ACKNOWLEDGEMENTS

THERE ARE many people who have helped, either by lending equipment or expertise, in the course of this book and to whom I owe thanks, most notably Tess Bartlett, Nicole Fabre French Antiques, Fiona Golfar, Guinevere Antiques, Julian Land (for exquisite pumpkin chiselling), Denise Landis, the Little Georgia café-restaurant, Nimmo & Spooner, Jane Sacchi Linens, Summerill and Bishop, and The Linen Shop.

I wouldn't like to show any less gratitude for the people with whom I am in daily communication, and who are endlessly helpful filling my admittedly extravagant orders, namely my butchers, Allen's and Lidgate's; my fishmonger, Chalmers & Gray; and greengrocers, Michanicou Brothers and Panzer's, who also keep me supplied, patiently and amiably, with anything else I could ever need in the kitchen.

Much of the help, however, is provided outside the kitchen. There couldn't be enough space to thank my literary agent, Ed Victor, but thank him I do, and deeply. I'd like to record my gratitude here, too, to my TV agent, Jacqui Drewe, who has calmly allowed me to stay off the television so that I could write this book, a book which wouldn't exist the way I wanted it without photographer-extraordinaire James Merrell, and Caz Hildebrand, my longterm – longsuffering – and much appreciated designer and art director, as well as Poppy Hampson, Mark Hutchinson, Gail Rebuck, Alison Samuel and Will Schwalbe.

I loathe sentimentality but I fear I risk it here. For starters, I must thank domestic goddesses Lisa and Francesca Grillo, whose work has enabled me to get on with my work. It's a truism that no one is indispensable, but I am not sure it is actually true: this book would not have been possible without Sharon Raeburn or the bolstering and affectionate efficiency and all-round support system provided by Zoe Wales and by Hettie Potter, who has cooked with me, cared for me, driven me mad and kept me sane.

And while I never need an excuse to eat, I haven't always felt like celebrating life. The fact that I do now I owe so much to my husband, Charles.

INDEX